The Harps that once . . .

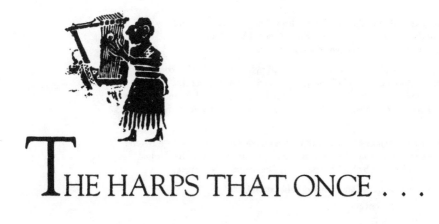

THE HARPS THAT ONCE . . .

Sumerian Poetry in Translation

THORKILD JACOBSEN

Yale University Press
New Haven and London

The preparation of the contents of this volume was made possible by a grant from the Translations Program of the National Endowment for the Humanities, an independent Federal agency.

Designed by Nancy Ovedovitz and set in Goudy Old Style type by Keystone Typesetting Company, Orwigsburg, Pennsylvania. Printed in the United States of America by Vail-Ballou Press, Binghamton, New York.

Library of Congress Cataloging-in-Publication Data

The Harps that once—.
   Bibliography: p.
   Includes index.
   1. Sumerian poetry—Translations into English.
2. English poetry—Translations from Sumerian.
I. Jacobsen, Thorkild, 1904–
PJ4083.H37   1987   499'.95   87-10559
ISBN 0-300-03906-9 (cloth: alk. paper)
ISBN 978-0-300-07278-5 (pbk.: alk. paper)

To Rigmor

CONTENTS

ACKNOWLEDGMENTS———————————

The author is deeply grateful to many friends and colleagues for help. I hope they will realize my very sincere appreciation of what each has done and accept my thanks to them without my specifying every contribution. Only two names should be singled out, that of Mrs. Susan Mango, without whose advice and support this book would not have been possible, and that of the editor, Charles Grench, whose constant encouragement has been of signal importance.

So, aware that perfection is not of this world, I send out for criticism and improvement my attempt to understand the ancients in their own terms, an aim very dear to my heart.

INTRODUCTION ————————————————————

Sumerian literature is one of the oldest known literatures in the world, perhaps *the* oldest, and stands out by the power, variety, and sheer mass of its content. Some of its works are exceedingly beautiful; others are perhaps less readily enjoyed by a modern reader, yet appeal as bearing witness to a strange, long-vanished world.

Writing was invented in southern Mesopotamia, Sumer, at some time around the middle of the fourth millennium B.C. It was at first a pure picture writing, but was soon supplemented by the use of signs for phonetic values without reference to meaning. By means of this bifurcate approach it became possible to reduce more and more complex texts to writing, whose domain had originally been limited to highly structured fields like accounting. The signs were at first scratched into the surface of tablets made of clay, but to avoid the ragged edges this produced, a technique of impressing the stylus rather than scratching with it evolved. The impressions, which tended to be wedgelike, gave the writing its special character and its name, *cuneiform*, that is, wedge-shaped. With time the original pictorial character disappeared, the pictures being abbreviated to the point of being unrecognizable. All that mattered was that a sign could be told apart from all the others.

Our oldest examples of written literary texts date from the third Early Dynastic Period at roughly the middle of the third millennium B.C. They were found at the sites of Fara, ancient Shuruppak, and Abu Salābikh. They are myths, hymns, and proverbs, and they make it clear that an extensive and varied oral literature must have existed, ready to become fixed by being written down. To what extent original composition in writing was practiced, without any oral stage to precede the written one, is a moot question. Mostly, one surmises, an original oral work will have been memorized, worked over, and put in written form by a learned scribe.

Most of the works of Sumerian literature are anonymous, but there are notable exceptions. Around 2350 B.C. a gifted poet, Enheduanna, daughter of king Sargon of Akkadê, wrote a cycle of hymns to all the major temples of Sumer—a last flowering of an old and established genre that appears to have fallen out of favor after her time. She also wrote an impassioned appeal to the goddess Inanna, asking to be reinstated in her office as high priestess (*en*) of the moon god Nanna in Ur and to have her foes, who had deposed her, vanquished.

A classical period was reached by the time of Gudea of Lagash (ca. 2125 B.C.), whose hymn celebrating the building of the temple of Ningirsu in Girsu, "Cylinders A and B," is outstanding in beauty and in the richness, clarity, and precision of its language.

The majority of works we possess seems to have come down to us in a form given them slightly later, during the period of the Third Dynasty of Ur, some of the rulers of which—notably Shulgi—were much concerned to preserve extant older literary works and to encourage the creation of new ones. The court background of these works is unmistakable. A great many compositions, such as the hymns to individual kings and the love lyrics to Shu-Suen, are directly inspired by the kings. Others, such as the epics celebrating rulers of the ancient First Dynasty of Uruk, were clearly governed in their choice of subject by the fact that the kings of Ur traced their lineage to that dynasty. In the presentation of the epic materials, current politics and the desire to please visiting dignitaries are often plain to see. The catastrophical end of the Third Dynasty of Ur, which in a very real sense was also the end of Sumerian civilization, gave rise to one last great masterwork, the wonderful "Lament for the Fall of Ur." After that, Sumerian essentially survived as a language of learning and culture in very much the role that Latin played in Europe in the Middle Ages.

The schools of the following period, that of Isin-Larsa, took over for their curricula as much literary remains from the court of Ur as they could lay hands on, royal correspondence from the chancellery side by side with literary works like love songs and hymns praising the kings. Much that cannot directly be linked to the court, traditional older works, wisdom literature, proverbs, etc. will most likely also have gone through the hands of Ur III scribes or scribal schools.

The schools created a coterie of literati living in a world of their own and gave rise, it would seem, to an "in-group" literature of partly satirical, partly moralistic compositions, known by modern scholars as Edubba texts, from the Sumerian term for school, *é-dubba*. Works continued to be written also in the established genres of hymn and lament. The flourishing of these schools and the enormous number of indestructible exercises and copies of literary works they produced is a main reason that we know as much about Sumerian literature today as we do. The discards from the schools were carted away by citizens who needed fill for their houses, so that now almost any excavation in private houses of the Old Babylonian and slightly earlier periods is likely to produce new such discards, supplementing and enhancing our knowledge.

Following the Old Babylonian period, the flood of Sumerian literary texts dwindled to a mere trickle. Some late laments for cities and temples, incantations, and epics dealing with creation and with the god Ningirsu/Ninurta were among the more notable survivors. Most of them had in Old Babylonian times been provided with remarkably precise Akkadian translations, which proved of fundamental importance for the decipherment of Sumerian in modern times. Of very considerable help here was also the survival of a large body of lexical texts translating Sumerian into Akkadian, and some valuable treatises on Sumerian grammar in lexical form.

The strictly literary Sumerian works can be defined generally as works of praise. The praise can be for something extant and enjoyed, a temple, a deity, or a human king. It can take narrative form as myth or epic, or descriptive form as hymn. The praise may also, however, be praise of something cherished and lost, a destroyed temple, a god who has died, or a dead human relative. These genres all seem to derive ultimately from incantations. The praise hymns appear to have their roots in spells meant to call up in, or lay into, the thing or person praised the innate and needed powers for proper effective functioning. The works of lament similarly will have developed from spells to bring back what was lost: the destroyed temple, or the dead god, through the magic power vested in fervent desire.

Very little is known about the occasions at which these various literary works were performed, so one must content oneself with conjecture. Epics and myths were rather clearly intended for performance by rhapsodes as entertainment at royal feasts; the royal love songs and works dealing with Dumuzi's wooing and wedding may well have served as amusement for the queen and her entourage. The laments for Dumuzi and gods identified with him will have been performed during mourning processions at the yearly celebrations of weeping for the dead god. The laments for temples served ritual purposes also, originally performed in the ruins to induce the gods to rebuild the destroyed structure. After the time of the Third Dynasty of Ur, perhaps at some time in the Isin-Larsa period, they came to be used generally for any rebuilding of a temple, and in the first millennium they became a standard feature of the daily service in major temples. The audience for which they were meant was thus not any human one, but rather the gods who held man's fate in their hands.

Also the praise hymns, lastly, would seem to have served cultic purposes. It seems likely that they retained some measure of the magic aspect to which their genre traced back and that they served to enhance and make manifest the powers inherent in the king or the temple praised. The royal hymns of the Ur III period appear to have been recited in connection with a new-year's festival at which the new year was named. On which occasions the praise hymns to temples were performed we do not know.

Myths and epics were probably recited by rhapsodes (*nar*) to the accompaniment of a lyre, *zag-mí*, the name of which became a term for "praise." Laments were the province of elegists (*gala*). Hymns and laments were usually meant to be performed as antiphons. A rubric "is the place of countering" (*ki-ru-gú-kam*) indicates in our texts the point where the antiphon sets in. The antiphon itself is designated by the rubric "is its antiphon" (*ĝiš-gi₄-ĝal-bi-im*). The various genres of texts had their own designations, but mostly it is difficult to see what distinguishes the texts of one such designation from similar texts otherwise labeled. One thing is clear, though: the designations are often names of the musical instruments to the accompaniment of which the text was intended to be performed. Thus the great laments for destroyed temples and cities usually divide into a part called *balag̃* "harp," which was to be sung to the strains of the harp, and a following *ershemma*, a lament to be accompanied by a tambourine-like drum called *shem*.

The genres that made up Sumerian literature as we have it are—if we may use modern, not ancient, distinctions, roughly the following: myths, epics, hymns to temples, gods, or kings, laments for temples, gods, or human beings, wisdom literature, including proverbs, fables, Edubba texts, and copies of then-ancient royal inscriptions. One should also mention, perhaps, practical genres like incantations, lexical and grammatical texts, mathematics and geometry texts, lists of year dates, and other.

Out of this plenitude only a very small part could be chosen for translation in the present volume if it is to be held to a reasonable size and if monotony is to be avoided. I have therefore concentrated on the Old Babylonian materials, and within these, on the poetry: myths, epics, hymns, and laments. Even within these narrow limits, though, selection had to be made, and here the choice has been subjective, perhaps arbitrary. The cylinders of Gudea and the lament for Ur were chosen for their beauty, the Dumuzi texts for their simple humanity, the text called "In the Desert by the Early Grass" for its eerie dreamlike quality. The epics selected show examples of different styles, heroic and romantic; the myths show myths still taken seriously along with others which had probably sunk down to function as mere entertainment. No attempt to render the selections truly representative has been made. Thus there are no examples of the prolific genres of royal hymns, Edubba texts, and the so-called debates. Reluctantly I have also omitted proverbs and wisdom literature. Proverbs are almost impossible to understand unless the situation in which they were used is known, and even then their subtleties of phrasing may defy adequate renderings in another language. Much that I would have liked to include, especially Gilgamesh materials, the story of the sorcerer from Aratta, and selections from proverbs and fables, must wait for a further volume, which I hope one day to write.

In translating I have used a high prose and short lines, resulting in a kind of free verse. The line division of the originals had been adhered to, so that when a line is broken down into shorter lines, the new lines formed are shown indented. Restorations are enclosed in square brackets, explanatory matter in parentheses. Ellipsis points fill in for a word or passage left untranslated because its reading or its sense is elusive; within square brackets, they indicate lost text not restored. I have added explanatory marginal glosses to indicate speakers and to clarify narrative structure. The division into stanzas has been made from inner criteria of meaning and has no overt expression in the texts. The Sumerian poets did not, as far as one can see, use rhyme. Meter and rhythm, which must be assumed to be a prominent feature since the poetry was sung, are not sufficiently recognizable from the texts to invite attempts at imitation. What is clear and can be readily appreciated in the poetry is its conceptual structure, its intricate—or simple—interweaving of meanings and, of course, its imagery.

The world in which the poetry moves is other than ours. It was governed by gods who met in assembly to make the decisions underlying events on earth, from the building of a temple to the destruction of a kingdom. The mountains of what is now Iran were the land to which men went after death, a netherworld. The living inhabitants of the mountains were perennial foes. The gods, originally numinous power experienced in phenomena of nature, assumed with time more human form and human nature, and were seen in a context of family and socio-political relations.

The most important gods were those of the cosmic triad: An, heaven, Enlil, the wind, and Ninhursaġa, the foothills. In the period of Isin and Larsa the place of Ninhursaġa was taken by Enki, the god of the fresh waters. Other important figures were the god of thunderstorms and flood, Ninġirsu or Ninurta, the goddesses Nanshe, goddess of fish and birds, and Gatumdug, perhaps a birth goddess.

The translations have been kept as literal, and held as close to the wording of the Sumerian original, as at all possible, and they are throughout consistent with Sumerian lexicon and grammar as we see them. The notes are intended for the general reader. Sumerologists will normally, I hope, have little difficulty in seeing how I arrived at the translations given. For cases where that is not obvious I hope to make available the relevant philological and text-critical notes in separate journal articles or otherwise. It should not be left unsaid, however, that knowledge of Sumerian is still in a rudimentary, experimental stage where scholars differ on essential points, so that translations, even by highly competent scholars, may diverge so much that one would never guess that they rendered the same text. The reasons for this uncertainty are numerous. The writing is in many respects vague and leaves a broad margin for variant interpretation; meanings of words have not yet been exhaustively defined; and —worst of all, perhaps—scholars have not yet been able to agree on basic grammar and its restraints.

The translations here presented can therefore be offered only as a subjective attempt, though one that I sincerely hope and trust is true in its essentials.

PART ONE
Dumuzi Texts

The worship of a young god representing seasonal abundance of one kind or another, who dies when the season and its bounties are over, seems to have been one of the oldest and most widespread cults in ancient Mesopotamia.

The god has different names and to some extent different character, depending upon which seasonal feature he is connected with. His best-known form is that of Dumuzi, or Tammuz, the shepherd, in which he was the power behind the successful lambing of the ewes and the related milking and dairy tasks of the shepherds in the spring. The cult celebrated his marriage with the goddess Inanna and lamented his early death. His mother was the goddess Turtur, a deification of the ewe or—originally perhaps in a herder context—the cow-goddess Ninsuna. His sister is Geshtinanna, the deified grapevine.

Other forms of the god were identified by the ancients with Dumuzi. One such was Ama-ushumgal-anna, a god of dates and the date palm. His cult had only the sacred marriage rite, not the lamenting of the dead god; perhaps because dates, eminently storable, remain with man the year around, so that there is not here any sense of loss. Conversely with another form, that of Damu, "the son", who represents the sap rising in the trees in spring. Here there is no celebration of the god's marriage. He is visualized as a young lad, who is greeted at his yearly arrival when the river rises, and whose death is lamented at the onset of the dry summer. The manner in which he dies is other than that of the death of Dumuzi the shepherd. In the ritual texts Dumuzi is killed with his servants and followers when his sheepfold in the desert is attacked by bandits from the mountains, a fate that must have overtaken many human shepherds too. The Damu mythology comes out of a different social milieu from that of the aristocratic shepherd. His world is the one of the army and labor forces of the king, serfs of the crown, due for labor or military service. Damu is a youngster, the only support of his mother and sister. He is taken away, or is captured trying to flee, by a detachment of recruiters, sometimes seen as nether-world police. This way of presenting the god's death was often taken over, particularly in purely narrative accounts, into texts dealing with Dumuzi the shepherd.

Besides the forms here mentioned there were a great many others, Ningishzida, god of tree roots and serpents, Ishtaran, Alla, etc. Even the kings who had incarnated the god in the ritual of the sacred marriage when alive were worshiped as forms of the god after their death.

Besides the differences due to particularities of the form of the god dealt with, the Dumuzi texts show differences of form and purpose. There are texts—especially lamentations—which seem to stem directly from a rit-ual; others are at some remove from ritual use, are myths told, it seems, mainly for entertainment; and others again are popular ditties dealing with Dumuzi's courtship of Inanna. In these the names Dumuzi and Inanna seem in fact to stand merely for those of two young lovers without any suggestion that deities are involved.

In the selection and ordering of the translations here presented no attempt has been made to group the texts according to the form of the god involved, or according to relation or non-relation to ritual. Rather, we have preferred to order them in terms of the underlying pattern of human life in which these powers of nature were understood and the human reactions to them expressed: courtship and wedding, death and mourning.

The New House

Dumuzi's and Inanna's parents have concluded arrangements for their children to marry,[1] and so Dumuzi has gone off with friends to build a house for himself and his wife-to-be near the house of her parents.

Inanna has not yet been told. Thus, when from the roof of her parents' house she becomes aware of a commotion in the street below, she thinks she and her girlfriends have been followed to the house by a brash youngster and is indignant at the intrusion.

Dumuzi is amused and keeps her in ignorance, so that he can tease her gently. Although she does not know it, he is no intruder but a member of the family, his father is now her father-in-law, and as such like her father; his mother, as her mother-in-law, is like her mother, and so on.[2]

Dumuzi has brought precious stones as a foundation deposit for his house, and they catch Inanna's eye. Full of curiosity she asks him for whom he is founding the house, and so at last he tells her the news. It pleases her well, she likes his tall stature and splendid beard.

INANNA

"Without leave of our mother
   he's come chasing after us
   into Aĝe-edinna Street![3]

"Without leave of our mother
   this young buck
   has come chasing after us
   into Aĝe-edinna Street!

1. It was customary for parents to arrange the marriage of their children. If the parents were dead, the oldest son would take their place.

2. Compare the story of "Dumuzi's Wedding" below and the instructions Inanna's mother there gives her. Her primary duty of obedience after her wedding is to her parents-in-law rather than to her parents.

3. The meaning of this street name is not known with certainty. It might indicate a street on the outskirts of town.

"Without leave of my mother, Ningal,
  he's come chasing after us
  into Aǧe-edinna Street!

"Without leave of Ningikuga[4]
  he's come chasing after us
  into Aǧe-edinna Street!

"Without leave of father Suen
  he's come chasing after us
  into Aǧe-edinna Street!

"Without leave of my brother Utu
  he's come chasing after us
  into Aǧe-edinna Street!"

DUMUZI   "Girl, please don't, as it were,
  start a quarrel,
Inanna, let us, as it were,
  talk it over.

"Inanna, please don't, as it were,
  .start a quarrel,
Ninegalla,[5] let us, as it were,   10
  wise you up.

"My father is as were he
  your father too,
Inanna, let us, as it were,
  talk it over.

"My mother is as were she
  your mother too,
Ninegalla, let us, as it were,
  wise you up.

"Geshtinanna is also
  as were she Ningikuga
Inanna, let us, as it were,
  talk it over.

"I am also
  as were I Utu,

4. Ningikuga, that is *nin-gi-kuga(k)*, "the lady of the pure reeds," was the mother of Ningal and wife of Enki. She is thus Inanna's grandmother.
5. The name or epithet *nin-egalla(k)* means "queen of the palace." In the rite of the sacred marriage Inanna is frequently so called, which suggests that it was the queen who represented the goddess in the rite.

Ninegalla, let us, as it were,
    wise you up.

"Enki[6] is also
    as were he Suen,
Inanna, let us, as it were,   20
    talk it over.

"Duttur is also
    as were she Ningal,
Ninegalla, let us, as it were,
    wise you up!"

NARRATORS   What they would be talking over
    was a matter for delight:
for delight of the
    would-be quarreler's heart.

The one with the gems,
    the one with the gems,
    intended founding (a house)
    on the gems!

Ama-ushumgal-anna,
    the one with the gems,
    intended founding (a house)
    on the gems!

The little gems of his gems,
    [O that they were for our] th[roats]!
[The big gems] of his gems,
    [O that they were for our p]ure breasts!

[The girl] leaning out from [the roof]
    was leaning out toward him
    from the roof,

[Inanna leaning out] from the wall   30
    was leaning out toward him
    from the wall

6. It seems at first glance odd that Enki, the god of fresh water, rivers, and ponds, should be the father of the shepherd-god Dumuzi. Actually, however, Enki is also god of the amniotic fluid, and the hymn to him called "Enki and the World Order" states that when he leaves a pregnant animal, ewe, cow, etc. a healthy young is born. Dumuzi is the power in the young of an animal—and perhaps human—to be born healthy. His name means "the one who makes the young one all right." The sequence in time of the breaking of the amniotic sac and the birth of a healthy young animal was seen, mythopoeically, as causal, one producing the other, that is to say, one engendering the other.

7. See below, n. 9.

—[. . .]8 called out
   to Ama-ushumgal-anna.

INANNA

"Founding (a house) on gems,
   for whom are you founding it?
Ama-ushumgal-anna,
   founding (a house) on gems,
   for whom are you founding it?"

NARRATORS

The little gems of his gems,
   O that they were for our throats!
The big gems of his gems,
   O that they were for our pure breasts!

Ama-ushumgal-anna
   answered the holy one:9

DUMUZI

"For none other than the holy one,
   for my spouse, the holy one,
   for her I am founding it!

"For holy Inanna,
   for the consecrated one,
   for her I am founding it!"

INANNA

"The one with his gems,
   intends founding (a house) on gems.

"Ama-ushumgal-anna   40
   the one with his gems,
   intends founding (a house) on gems,

"founding (a house) on gems—
   founding (a house) on gems—
   for whom is he founding it?
Ama-ushumgal-anna,
   founding (a house) on gems—
   for whom is he founding it?

"My one about to build for me,
   his beard is lapis-lazuli lustrous,

8. The broken passage here must have contained a term for Inanna.
9. The word translated "holy one" (*nu-gig* literally "sacred"/"taboo" person) designates a class of women the function and character of which is not clear. Inanna belonged to this class and typified the women belonging to it. The badge of these women was inlaid with the gems called *shuba*.

this tall poplar,
 my one about to build for me,
 his beard is lapis-lazuli lustrous,[10]
this lofty one,
 his beard is lapis-lazuli lustrous,
 his beard is lapis-lazuli lustrous!"

It is a KUN-GAR (-composition)[11] pertaining to Inanna
Written with a reed stylus.

10. The comparison is with the dark blue lapis lazuli which was often used as inlays in statues—e.g., for eyebrows—to represent black shiny hair.
11. It is not clear what the characteristics of this kind of composition were.

The Sister's Message

Geshtinanna has been invited in by Inanna so that Inanna can confide in her how utterly she has fallen in love with Geshtinanna's brother Dumuzi. Geshtinanna loses no time in relaying the exciting news to her brother, and Dumuzi—pretending to have official business in the palace—is quick to be off to reassure the suffering Inanna that he loves her too.

The ditty, rather amusingly, renders the teenage sense of drama. Geshtinanna's description of how Inanna suffers all the pains of love to the point of faintness is probably meant to be taken with a grain of salt. She is clearly not taken in by her brother's sudden official business at the palace, and her imitation of a pompous father at the end is very well done.

GESHTINANNA   "As I was strolling, as I was strolling
                [as I was strolling] by the house,
                    as I was strolling by the house,
                [my dear] In[anna s]aw me—
                B[rother, what did she tell me,]
                    [and what] more did she speak of to me?
                Brother, it was [of love], allure,
                    and utter blissful things,
                and accordingly my sweet Holy Inanna
                    disclosed something to me:
                she had met you, my beloved man,
                when I was addressing myself
                    to some errand,
                and fell in love with you,
                    and delighted in you!

                "Brother, she brought me into her house   10
                and had me lie down
                    on a honey of a bed

and when my sweet darling
    had lain down next to my heart,
we, chatting with one another,
    with one another
she, my good-looking brother,
    began moaning to me,
and there overcame her there
    like what overcomes
    one very weak,
and proneness to tremble
    from the ground up,
exceedingly much, befell her!
My dear brother,—
    smiting her hips (in agony)
does my sweet darling spend the day."

DUMUZI   "Let me go, sister!
    Let me go!
Please, my beloved sister,   20
    let me go to the palace!"

GESHTINANNA   "To my paternal eye
    you are verily still a small child,
—yonder Baba[1] may know you for a man.
I shall let you go to her!"

SUBSCRIPT   (It is a dialogue pertaining to Inanna.[2])

1. Baba is here used as a pet name for Inanna. It is possible, however, that the ditty originally had the goddess Baba rather than Inanna as the lovesick girl. Baba was the wife of the god Ningirsu.
2. The subscript is followed by two obscure lines.

The Wiles of Women

Inanna and Dumuzi have met the day before and have fallen in love. Inanna has whiled away the day, longing for it to become evening when, she hopes, he will show up after having finished the day's work.

He does so, and impetuously propositions her. This is not what Inanna wants, and yet she does not want to lose him by too severe a brush-off; so she pleads that she has to be home at a decent hour. He counters, offering to teach her excuses for being late she can tell her mother—his naiveté must have amused her—but when he comes out in the open with his proposal for lovemaking she tells him off. She is a decent girl, not a slut from the alleys. Eventually—the text has a lacuna here—she manages to steer him from propositioning her to properly proposing to her, and when the text resumes they are on their way to her mother to obtain her assent to their engagement. Inanna is sure that her mother will be happy to give it.

INANNA "I, having—being a lady![1]—
      whiled away the time since yesterday,
   I having—being Inanna—
      whiled away the time since yesterday,
   having whiled away the time, having danced,
   having sung ditties all day to evening,
   he met me! He met me!
   The lord, the peer of An met me.
   The lord took my hand in his,
   Ushumgal-anna put his arm around my shoulders.
   'Listen (you) wild bull![2] Let me go,
      that I may go home!

1. Inanna is stressing her upper-class status; work is beneath her, a matter for menials. Her day is spent in play and dance. There is a play on her name too, it contains the Sumerian word for "lady."

2. The Sumerian word for "wild bull," or "aurochs" is also used as a term for "shepherd." We have retained its basic meaning in the translation because Inanna clearly disapproves of his impetuosity. Undoubtedly, of course, the more neutral meaning "shepherd" also played in for the Sumerian listener.

10

Peer of Enlil, let me go, that I may go home!   10
What stories could I tell my mother?
What stories could I tell Ningal?' "

DUMUZI   "Let me teach you, let me teach you,
Inanna, let me teach you the stories women (tell):
'My girlfriend was strolling with me
    in the square,
to the playing of tambourine and recorder
    she danced with me,
our sad songs were sweet—she crooned to me—
the joyous ones were sweet—and time went by!'
With this as story confront your mother;
as for us—let us be dallying   20
    in the moonlight!
Let me spread for you the pure sweet couch of a prince,
    let me loosen your combs for you,
and let me pass a sweet time with you
    in joy and plenty!"

(is the "tightened strings" [section])[3]

INANNA   The [gi]rl I am [is] n[ot] of the alleyways.
If [I] am to em[brace] you,
[. . . .]. . . . .

(lacuna of some ten lines)
(The text when intact must have told how Inanna made Dumuzi change from
propositioning her to proposing to her.)

      35

INANNA   "He wants to stop at the gate of our mother,
I am fairly running for joy.
He wants to stop at the gate of Ningal,
I am fairly running for joy!
O that someone would tell my mother,   40
and she sprinkle cedar perfume on the floor,
O that someone would tell my mother Ningal,
and she sprinkle cedar perfume on the floor!
Her dwelling, its fragrance is sweet,
her words will all be joyful ones:
'My lord, you are indeed worthy
    of the pure embrace,

3. Instruction for the harp accompaniment.

Ama-ushumgal-anna, son-in-law of Suen,
Lord Dumuzi, you are indeed worthy
    of the pure embrace,
Ama-ushumgal-anna, son-in-law of Suen,
My lord, your riches are sweet,   50
your herbs in the desert
    are all of them sweet,
Ama-ushumgal-anna, your riches are sweet,
your herbs in the desert
    are all of them sweet!"

(is the "readjusted[?] strings" [section]).
(It is a composition for *tigi*-harp pertaining to Inanna.)

The Bridal Sheets

Inanna's brother Utu has made binding arrangements for her to marry Ama-ushumgal-anna. All that remains is for him to tell her. Not quite sure how his news will be received, he begins tactfully by suggesting that they need new sheets, not letting on that they are to be her bridal sheets. Inanna, however, at once guesses what it is all about and, nervous about whom her brother may have chosen for her, she tries to push the whole matter off. She is young and dainty and does not know how to spin, weave, etc.

Utu though, is not swayed from his purpose, he counters all of her objections, and at last the question has to come out in the open: "Who is he?"—Luckily he is the one she wants, the one on whom she has set her heart, Ama-ushumgal-anna.

NARRATOR   The brother had to tell his young sister,
            Utu had to tell his young sister:

UTU   "Young lady, the green flax is full of loveliness,
            Inanna, the green flax is full of loveliness,
            like barley in the furrow
                in loveliness and charm;
            sister, a grand length of linen
                does take one's fancy,
            Inanna, a grand length of linen
                does take one's fancy,
            let me grub it up for you, and give it to you green,
            young lady, let me bring you green flax!
            Inanna, let me bring you green flax!"   10

INANNA   "Brother, when you have brought me green flax,
            who will ret for me?
                Who will ret for me?
            Who will ret its fibers for me?"

UTU	"My sister, already retted let me bring it
	  to you!
	Inanna, already retted let me bring it
	  to you!"

INANNA	"Brother, when you have brought it to me
	  already retted,
	who will spin for me?
	  Who will spin for me?
	Who will spin its fibers for me?"

UTU	"My sister, already spun let me bring it
	  to you!
	Inanna, already spun let me bring it
	  to you!"

INANNA	"Brother, when you have brought it to me
	  already spun,
	who will double up for me?
	  Who will double up for me?
	Who will double up its threads for me?"

UTU	"My sister, already doubled up let me bring it
	  to you!
	Inanna, already doubled up let me bring it
	  to you!"

INANNA	"Brother, when you have brought it to me
	  already doubled up,
	who will dye for me?
	  Who will dye for me?
	Who will dye its threads for me?"

UTU	"My sister, already dyed let me bring it
	  to you!
	Inanna, already dyed let me bring it
	  to you!"

INANNA	"Brother, when you have brought it to me
	  already dyed,
	who will weave for me?
	  Who will weave for me?
	Who will weave its threads for me?"

UTU	"My sister, already woven let me bring it to you!

20

30

Inanna, already woven
  let me bring it to you!"

INANNA   "Brother, when you have brought it to me
      already woven,
  who will bleach for me?
    Who will bleach for me?
  Who will bleach its threads for me?"

UTU   "My sister, already bleached let me bring it
      to you!
  Inanna, already bleached let me bring it   40
      to you!"

INANNA   "Brother, when you have brought it to me
      already bleached,
  who will lie down thereon with me?
    Who will lie down thereon with me?"

UTU   "With you will lie down, will lie down,
  with you will lie down a bridegroom,
  with you will lie down Ama-ushumgal-anna,
  with you will lie down the peer of Enlil,
  with you will lie down the issue
    of a noble womb,
  with you will lie down one
    engendered on a throne dais!"

INANNA   "Is it true?—He is the man of my heart!
    He is the man of my heart!
  The man my heart told me!   50
  Not wielding a hoe,[1] heaping up piles of grain,
  getting the grain to the barn,
  a farmer whose grain is in hundreds of piles,
  a shepherd whose sheep are laden with wool!"

(It is a *balbal*-song pertaining to Inanna.)

---

1. The hoe would seem to symbolize the small farm cultivated by the owner or tenant himself as opposed to the large estates plowed by teams of oxen.

Let Him Come! Let Him Come!

Utu asks Inanna what she has been doing, and she answers that she has been bathing and dressing in all her finery—obviously with a view to receiving her bridegroom.

Utu realizes this and suggests that they send for him to celebrate the wedding.

Inanna agrees, and wishes to welcome him with wine. Utu will then escort her to the bridal chamber, where, he hopes, she may conceive a child as lovely as she is. The composition ends with a chorus of the bride's girlfriends who likewise escort her and rejoice in the occasion.

UTU, BROTHER OF BRIDE	"My sister, what did you do in the house? Little one, what did you do in the house?"

BRIDE,
INANNA
	"I showered in water,
	    rubbed myself with soap,
	showered in the water
	    of the bright copper ewer,
	rubbed myself with soap
	    of the shiny stone jar,
	anointed myself
	    with the stone jar's sweet oil,
	and dressed in the queenly robe,
	    the robe of the queenship of heaven.[1]

Thus (freshened up)
    I roamed around in the house.
I put kohl on my eyes,
the hair on the nape of my neck
    stood up—I straightened it.   10
I tied on my hipflask,
    was filling it with water,

---

1. As goddess of the morning and evening star Inanna was called "queen of heaven," and her name was interpreted to mean that.

I designated a weapon
  that will make the years of reign
  pleasant for him.[2]

(The hair of) my head
  was tangled.
  I straightened it.
The (tresses of) my crest
  had come loose,
  I combed them,
and let them fall
  on the shoulders
  and nape of the neck.
Rings of gold
  I put on my hands,
little stone-beads
  I hung around my neck,
straightened their counterbalance[3]
  on the nape of my neck."

UTU   "Sister, (in seeking a husband for you) I went leading the
way
  for your heart,
For your heart,   20
  the loving heart, I went.
Your tutelary goddess[4]
  has given you bloom (of health).
Sister, you are radiant, the honey
  of the mother who bore you!
My sister, worth any five to me,
My sister, worth any ten to me!
Since she[5] has perfected
  your shape for you
he will be wanting to come,
  O my most pleasing
  and radiant sister!"

---

2. This line, with its reference to Inanna's role as goddess of war, and as bride and protector of the ruling human king, fits rather oddly in the picture of her as a young girl about to be wed. It could well have been added out of deference to the king for performance in the palace.

3. Elaborate neck and chest ornaments would often be held in place by a long cord down the back ending in an ornamental weight to counterbalance them.

4. Even gods and goddesses had—like men—their tutelary deities. See "The Vain Appeal," l. 20, with n. 3.

5. I.e., the tutelary goddess.

INANNA

"Bring in my bridegroom
 from the palace!
May you send a man there
 about a wedding wassail.
Let me, to start with,
 pour wine for him,
thus may his heart rejoice,   30
thus may his heart be pleased.
Let him come! Let him come!
 by any means, yes, let him come!"

UTU

"My sister, let me escort you
 into the chamber,
may a lamb come, like unto the ewe,
 O may it come!
may a kid come, like unto the goat,
 O may it come!
May the lamb be as pleasing
 as the ewe,
may the kid be as pied
 as the goat!
My sister, let me escort you
 into the chamber."

GIRLFRIENDS
OF THE
BRIDE

"Now our breasts stand up!
Now our parts have grown hair!   40
Going to the bridegroom's loins, Baba,[6]
 let us be happy for them!
Dance! Dance!
Baba, let us be happy
 for our parts!
Dance! Dance!
Afterward they will please him,
 they will please him.

(A *babal*-song pertaining to Inanna.)

"Let him come! Let him come!
 By any means, yes, let him come!

       (is its antiphon.)

---

6. Baba is here used, as in "The Sister's Message," as a pet name for Inanna. It is properly the name of the wife of the god Ninĝirsu, and the song may have been taken over from her cult.

Dumuzi's Wedding

This idyllic little tale begins, rather incongruously, with an address to Inanna—presumably by her girlfriends—in which she is celebrated as goddess of war, devastating enemy countries.[1]

More in keeping with the rest of the tale is the accompanying praise of her for having such good providers serving as bridegroom and as attendants at her pending wedding. The praise apparently makes Inanna decide to set a date for the wedding, and so she sends messengers specifying what each is to bring as a wedding gift.

The groom, Dumuzi/Ama-ushumgal-anna, and the guests arrive, but are left waiting in the street until Inanna is ready. She has first to be instructed by her mother about her duties as wife and member of a new household, and she has to bathe and dress in all her finery. At long last she finally opens the door and lets in her bridegroom, who has been impatiently calling from the street. This opening of the door by the bride to the bridegroom counted as the formal act that concluded a Sumerian marriage.

At this point a serious gap interrupts the text. Probably it told of the consummation of the marriage and of the wedding banquet the following morning. When the text again resumes Inanna has said goodbye to her parents and left with Dumuzi to go to her new home, Dumuzi's house. He enters first alone, goes to the chapel of his family god, and prays that the god will give him a son. Dumuzi then invites Inanna in, but she is afraid and at a loss without her mother to tell her what to do.

Dumuzi then goes back to his family god for advice, but what the god said is lost in a new gap in the text. Presumably, he counseled gentleness and persuasion, for when the text resumes Dumuzi is reassuring Inanna: she will not have to do any work, and her position in the household will be an honored one. One assumes that his plea was successful, also that, doting on his young bride, he rather overstated

---

1. The incongruity arises from the fact that Inanna's standard epithets, which celebrate her as a ruthless goddess of war, or as a bright star in the sky, are applied to her also in stories in which, as here, she is depicted as a young and timid girl. Apparently the storytellers felt compelled to use them, however much they might be out of tune with the story. Similar usage is found in epic style elsewhere.

the leisure of the life that awaited her. How it all came out is unfortunately lost in a gap at the end of the text.

GIRLFRIENDS ["O you who like a . . . .]
[your bridallers are bountiful lords!²]
[you who like a . . . . . .] . . . . . .[. . . . . .]
[Lady,] your bridallers [are] bountiful lords!
O you who catch [enemy countries] like [bir]ds,
Ninegalla, your bridallers [are] bountiful lords!
O you, [cracking (enemy) countries] like one cracking eggs,
Inanna, your bridallers are bountiful lords!
[Ama-ush]um[gal] is in the first place,
the [fa]rmer in the inundation is second,   i.10'
none other than the [fo]wler is the third,
the [fi]sherman, the man in the midst of the canebrake,
    is the fourth of them."

INANNA "Let me, the lady, send a messenger³ to the shepherd:
may he treat me to prime butter and prime milk!
Let me send a messenger to the squire, the [far]mer,
may he treat me to [honey] and wine!
To the fowler, who has his net spread out,
let me, the lady, send a messenger:
may he treat me to choice [birds!]
And the fisherman, none other! To his reed hut   i.20'
let me, Inanna, send a messenger:
may he [tr]eat me to his precious carps!"

NARRATOR Her bridallers, taking the day off, came.
The fowler brought choice birds,
the fisherman brought precious carps,
filled them in a [. . . .] with Milady.
The shepherd carried (pails of) butter in his hands,
Dumuzi carried (pails of) milk hung over his shoulders,
butter and small cheeses he carried
    hung over his shoulder

---

2. The Sumerian term *en* which is generally translated "lord" denotes basically a productive manager, someone with magic gifts to make things thrive. The "bridallers" are the bridegroom and his friends who serve as honor guard. The bridegroom here, Ama-ushumgal-anna, is a shepherd, his friends are the farmer, the fowler, and the fisherman. They all are expected to bring gifts of their products for the wedding.

3. The messenger is to announce the wedding day and specify the wedding gifts.

whipped, herb-flavored, milk he carried   i.30'
    hung over his shoulder.
The shepherd called out unto the house,
Dumuzi thrust a hand against the door (crying:)

DUMUZI   "Make haste to open the house, Milady!
    Make haste to open the house!"

NARRATOR   . . . .
The pure one . . . .
The mother, hearing her, went
and was standing by the . . . . . (saying:)

NINGAL   "Verily, [you are] his [spo]use, he is your spouse
Verily you [. . . . .] for him
Verily he is . . . . . for you
Verily your father is (now) a stranger[4] only
Verily your mother is (now) a stranger only.
His mother you will respect as were she *your* mother!
His father you will respect as were he *your* father!"[5]   ii.10'

DUMUZI   "Make haste to open the house, Milady!
    Make haste to open the house!"

NARRATOR   Inanna at her mother's bidding
bathed in water, anointed herself with sweet oil,
decided to put on for outer garment
    the grand queenly robe;
she also took her man-beast amulets,
was straightening the lapis lazuli stones
    on her neck,
and held her cylinder seal in her hand.
The young lady stood waiting—
Dumuzi pushed (open) the door,
and like a moonbeam she came forth to him   ii.20
    out of the house.
He looked at her, rejoiced in her,
took her in his arms [and kissed her.]

(lacuna)

---

4. Literally "a Subarean" i.e., an inhabitant of a faraway region, the territory of the later Assyria, present-day northern Iraq and eastern Syria.

5. As a wife, her duty to obey will be to her husband and his parents, whose household she enters, no longer to her own parents.

NARRATOR
. . . .
Dumuzi [. . .]
the lord Dumuzi c[ame in to him (saying:)]

DUMUZI
"O my master, I [have come home,]
O my master, my bride [is accompanying me]
may she duly give [bi]rth to a little lad!
O my master, go in to her in the house!"[6]

NARRATOR
The shepherd Dumuzi said to his bride:

DUMUZI
"O my bride, ...
O Inanna, ... the chapel of my (personal) god. iii.10'
To the chapel of my (personal) god I have brought you.
You will sleep before my (personal) god,
and on the seat of honor of my (personal) god, my bride,
    you will sit!"

NARRATOR
Though he spoke thus to her,
she sat down beside the sill (saying:)

INANNA
["I need help!] I have always just obeyed [mother!]"

NARRATOR
To the (personal) god he wended (his) foot
spoke a greeting and prayer to him (as follows:)

DUMUZI
"O my master, ...

(lacuna)

. . . .

INANNA
. . . . "in your eyes
O my [Ama-]ushumgal, [I know not (how to use)] a loom."

NARRATOR
[The shepherd] put his arm around the young lady (saying:)

DUMUZI
"I have not carried you off into slavery,
your table will be a [splen]did table,
    will be a splendid table,
at the splendid table I eat!
Your table will be the splendid table,
    will be the splendid table,
you, you will eat at [the splendid table.]

6. The ancients believed that children were conceived only when the personal god and goddess of husband and wife, the family deities, entered the bodies of the couple in the act of procreation and made them fertile.

My mother eats at the beer vat,   iv. 10'
Duttur's brother eats not at it,
my sister Geshtinanna eats not at it,
(but) you, you will eat
    at the ⌜splendid⌝ [table!]
O my bride, cloth you shall not weave for me!
[O Inan]na, yarn you shall not spin for me!
O my bride, fleece you shall not ravel for me!
O Inanna, [warp] you shall not mount for me!"
            (4 lines too fragmentary for translation)
["Have no] fear . . . .   iv. 22'
bread you shall not knead [for me!]
O Nin-egalla,". . . . .
The shepherd Dumuzi she em[braced]
"I, who have pure splendor, [glow yellowish
    at] heaven's base,[7]
O my husband, [I] who have [pure] splendor, [glow
yellowish]   iv. 27'
    on heaven,
who [g]low yellowish" . . . .

(lacuna)

7. The reference is to Inanna as morning and evening Star.

Unfaithfulness

One of Inanna's slave girls has been sleeping with Dumuzi, and Inanna has found out. The girl's punishment is to be death. So Inanna sends her herald Ninshubur out to call people together for the execution of the condemned girl. They gather at the city wall, from the plinth of which Inanna throws the girl down to them to have them fall upon her with any weapon they have handy and kill her. Inanna has had her revenge, but the pain of having been betrayed by Dumuzi is not assuaged; memories of what the girl told her when she confessed torment her.

A large gap interrupts the text here. When it resumes Inanna has overcome her hurt, bathes, dresses, and returns from her state of grieving to normal existence. In the last section of the text which we have, she is getting ready to join Dumuzi in his sheepfold in the desert, perhaps to take revenge, perhaps only to learn that he has been killed out there.

The text as we have it makes an oddly disconnected impression. A line between lines 11 and 12 may indicate that part of the text is missing here, but also in many other places one has the impression that connecting links of the narrative are missing.

(beginning lost)

HERALD TO
PUBLISH
INDICTMENT

[Holy Inanna
    said to Ninshubur
"My ever loyal one,]
my handmaiden,
    of pleasing words,
my despatch rider,
    of true words,
[knowledgeable, of good j]udgment,
    mistress of the Akkil temple:

That [girl,]
    that slave woman,
    who did the forbidden thing,

1

that sl[ave woman,]
   source of the sin,
     who did the forbidden thing,
that [source] of the sin,
   that one of dire fate,
that one of dire fate,
   with face tear-blotched—

Having sat down
   on the sacred throne,
she then lay down
in the sacred bed,
came to know too   10
   the male member plied there,
learned too
   to suck the male member."

<table><tr><td>PEOPLE GATHER
FOR THE EXE-
CUTION</td><td>

"Come, let us go there,
   Let us go there!
Us, let us go there,
   to the city!
Let us go there,
   to the city,
   to the spectacle!
Let us go there, to the city,
   to Kullab![1]
Let us go there,
   to brick-built Uruk![1]
Let us go there,
   to brick-built Zabalam![1]
Let us go there,
   to Hursag-kalamma![1]
To the city! To the city!   20
   to brick-built Babylon![1]
At the word spoken by Inanna!"

</td></tr></table>

<table><tr><td>EXECUTION</td><td>

The girl, the source of the sin,
   had thrown herself down prostrate
   in the dust—
She (Inanna) looked at her,
   with that look of death,

</td></tr></table>

1. Kullab, Uruk, and Zabalam were important centers for the cult of Inanna in the south. Hursagkalamma and Babylon with the temple Eturkalamma were in Akkad. The mention of more than one locality suggests that the text belonged with a ritual drama performed in each of the cities and temples mentioned.

the mistress cried out,
  it was a cry
  ablaze with punishment.

By the forelock
  she seized her,
threw the girl,
  the source of the sin,
down from the plinth
  of the city wall:
"Let the shepherd kill her
  with his shepherd's crook,
let the elegist kill her
  with his timbrel,
let the potter kill her   30
  with his beer mug,
let the [guards]man kill her
  with his dagger and mace!"

REVENGE DOES   [She had told her]
NOT UNDO PAIN   everything,
AT BETRAYAL   amid tears and wailing.
O could but the princess's heart
  have held back the groans!
O the heart of Inanna!
  —Everything!

What there was and wasn't,
so that he showed her favor
  by day,
so that he spent the night
  with her.
[O could but] her heart
  [have held back the groans!]
[O could but her] ears
  [. . . . .]

(large lacuna)

RECOVERY   "I am the young lady [. . . . .]
OF PRIDE   [. . . .]
I am Inanna [. . . . .]
I shake the heavens, [make the earth quake]
  [that is my fame!"][2]

2. Self-praise was often used as a means of regaining composure and self-reliance after a severe shock.

MAKING HER-
SELF PRE-
SENTABLE

When she had sho[wered] in water,
   [rubbed herself with soap,³]
[When she had showered] in the water   50'
   of the bright copper ewer,
[had rubbed herself] with soap
   of the shiny stone jar,
[had anointed herself]
   with the stone jar's sweet oil,
she clothed herself in the queenly robe,
   [the robe of the queen]ship [of heaven,]
her turban cloth [she wound round her head]
[put] kohl on her eyes
[took] her bright scepter [in hand,
her kohl [. . . . .]

URGING TO
RECONCILIA-
TION

To where food is set out,
where bread from clean hands
   is served!
To the house to which a true lord   60'
   has invited!
[To the house] to which a sincere lord
   has invited!
To which a god, a lord,
   has invited!
Accept the entreaty!
   To the sheepfold
   at the shepherd's pleading!
To the pure sheepfold
   [at Dumuzi's] pleading!
To the pure sheepfold
   where lives [Dumuzi!]

(text breaks off)

3. During her grief Inanna would have disregarded dress and care of herself in the manner of persons in mourning.

Dumuzi's Dream

Forebodings of approaching death send Dumuzi lamenting out in the desert. Here he lies down to sleep but wakes up from a bad dream. His sister, Geshtinanna, who is fetched to interpret it, can only assert that it means he will die.

Dumuzi thus expects that Death, the netherworld and its powers, will send for him. Its ghostly emissaries are depicted in the myth under the image of army recruiters—in real life Death's messengers for many a young man—and he asks Geshtinanna to go up a nearby hill as lookout. Geshtinanna does so and sees a boat approaching. From the presence of captives in neck-stocks it is clear that it carries recruiters for the army. Dumuzi decides to flee and hide himself in the desert. He tells his sister and a comrade where he will be. When the recruiters appear, Dumuzi's sister stays loyal, but his comrade betrays him, lured by the gifts the recruiters tempt him with. Dumuzi then is surrounded and captured but appeals to the sun god, Utu, who as Inanna's brother is his brother-in-law. Utu changes him into a gazelle and enables him to escape. He is, however, again captured, escapes again, is recaptured, once more escapes, and comes to Geshtinanna's sheepfold. She is horrified to see him in his sorry state, but before she can do anything to ease him the recruiters invade the fold, destroying as they go along, and Dumuzi is killed.

FOREBODINGS
OF DEATH

Woe filled his heart,
 and he went out into the desert—
the lad, woe filled his heart,
 and he went out into the desert—
Dumuzi, woe filled his heart,
 and he went out into the desert,
rested the staff on his shoulder,
 walked along wailing!

Forthwith set up a wail!
Forthwith set up a wail!

O desert, forthwith set up a wail!
O Marsh, forthwith cry out!
O crayfish of the river,
    forthwith set up the keg of beer
    and a wail!
O frogs of the river,
    forthwith cry out![1]

And may my mother cry out!
May my mother Duttur cry out!
May my mother cry out: 10
    "He was worth any five!"
May my mother cry out:
    "He was worth any ten!"
If she know not my having died,
You, O Desert,
    can let my mother who bore me know!
May she, like my little sister,
    shed tears for me!

OMINOUS DREAM   He lay down to doze off,
    he lay down to doze off,
    the shepherd lay down
        to doze off,
    but instead of lying down
        to doze off,
    the shepherd was lying down
        to an ominous dream!

He started up,
    it had been an ominous dream,
    he shuddered,
        he had been in a trance,
    he rubbed his eyes
        they were full of drowsiness!

GESHTINANNA   "Fetch her!—Fetch her!
TO INTERPRET   Fetch my sister!
    Fetch my dear Geshtinanna!   20
        Fetch my sister!

---

1. Lament and wailing was considered a kindness and a boon to the dead. Beer was often served to the wailers.

"Fetch my scribe,
  who knows the writings,
    fetch my sister!
Fetch my chantress,
  who knows the chants,
    fetch my sister!

"Fetch my wise one,
  who knows the heart of matters,
    fetch my sister!
Fetch my wise woman, [2]
  who knows the meanings of dream omens,
    fetch my sister!
Let me expound
  my ominous dream
    to her!

CONTENT
OF THE DREAM

"In the ominous dream,
  my dear sister—
    in the ominous dream
    in the midst of my ominous dream,

"Rushes rose for me
  rushes grew up for me,
and a lone reed was shaking
  the head in grief [for me].
Of twin reeds
  one was taken away from me.
In the forest a tall tree   30
  was uprooted for me all by itself.
On my pure embers
  water was poured in my presence,
the owner's marks of my pure churns
  had been removed,
my pure cups that hang on pegs
  had been taken d[own]
    from the pegs,
and I had lost my staff.

"An owl had caught
  a lamb in the sheepcote,

2. Normally the mother would be the one to interpret dreams. Here, since Dumuzi's mother is not with him in the desert, his wise and knowledgeable little sister must take her place.

a falcon had caught a sparrow
    in the reeds of the fence.
My bucks and goats were dragging,
    to my (horror,)
      their lapis lazuli beards
    in the dust,
my rams, to my (horror,)
    were raking the ground
    with their big horns.

"The churns lay on their sides,
    poured out no milk,
the cups lay on their sides,   40
    Dumuzi lived there no more,
    the winds only swept the fold."

EVIL OF
DREAM NOT
TO BE
AVOIDED

Geshtinanna replied to it
    to Dumuzi:

"My dear brother, your dream bodes no good,
    nor may it be propitiated.
Dumuzi, your dream bodes no good
    nor may it be propitiated:
Rushes rose for you,
    rushes grew up for you:
Bandits will rise up
    from ambush at you.

"A lone reed
    was shaking the head
    in grief for you:
The mother who bore you
    will shake the head
    in grief for you.

"Of twin reeds
    one was removed for you:
they were I and you,
    one will be taken away from me.

"In the forest a tall tree   50
    was uprooted for you all by itself:
An evildoer will seize you
    within the walls.
On your pure embers
    water was poured in your presence:

The fold will quiet down for you
    into a silent house.
The owner's marks of your pure churns
    had been removed:
An evildoer will take them over
    into his hands.

"Your pure cups that hang on pegs
    had been taken down
    from the pegs:
You are about to fall
    from the knees
    of the mother who bore you.

"You had lost your staff:
A [little r]anger
    will throw it on the brazier.
An owl had caught
    a lamb in the sheepcote:
An evildoer will smite your cheek.

"A falcon had caught a sparrow
    in the reeds of the fence:
A big ranger will come down upon you
    from the reeds of the fence.

"The [ch]urns lay on their sides,
    [poured out no milk,]
    the cups lay on their sides,
    Dumuzi lived there no more,
    the winds only swept the fold:
A manacler will manacle your hands,
    a pinioner will pinion you.

"Your bucks and goats were dragging,
    to your (horror,)
    their lapis lazuli beards
    in the dust.
My (torn-out) hair
    will be flying around
    in the sky above you
    like (the cloud of) a flood-storm.[3]

60

---

3. Tearing out hair from one's head was part of mourning for the dead.

"Your rams, to your (horror,)
  were raking the ground
  with their big horns:
My fingers—like a comb(?) of boxwood—
  will be clawing my cheeks for you."[4]

GESHTINANNA
TO BE LOOKOUT

Hardly were those words   70
  out of her mouth when:
"Sister, go up on the hill!
  Sister, go up on the hill!
But, Sister, as you
  go up on the hill
may you not go up there
  like a human being.

"When you have [let]
  your hair down your back,
have [tucked] your dress
  up to your thighs,

"then, Sister,
  go up the hill,[5]
and, Sister,
  [when you] are up on the hill,
  look out from the hill!"

[They] bring pain,
  heartbreak for mankind.
The barges on the river   80
  [bring pain,
  heartbreak for mankind.]

They have the manacles
  [covered with] cloth,
have the neck-stocks
  veiled in linen.

RANGERS
SPOTTED

When mistress Geshtinanna
  was [on] the hill,
  she [looked out from there]—
Geshtinanna [espied]
  captives in neck-stocks!

---

4. Clawing the face was another expression of grief.
5. She is to camouflage herself. What she is supposed to look like from afar is difficult to say, perhaps an animal, perhaps a tree.

Her girlfriend Ansuddudu[6]
warn[ed her:]
"Seeing that you es[pied]
large [numbers of] captives
in neck-stocks,
[his (recruiting) rangers][7]
[are come] for him."

"It is the way
my girlfriend has warned,
I sa[w] up there
the captives in neck-stocks.

"My brother, your rangers
are come for you,
[duck the head
into the grass!]
["Dumu]zi, your rangers   90
are come for you,
[duck] the head
[into] the grass!"

DUMUZI TO   "My sister, let me duck the head
HIDE IN   into the grass,
DESERT   and may you not
reve[al] where I am!
Let me duck the head
into the little grass patches
and may you not
reveal where I am!

"Let me duck the head
into the large grass patches,
and may you not
reveal where I am!
Let me duck
into Arali's ditch,
and may you not
reveal where I am!"

6. The name of this goddess is not elsewhere attested. The name could mean: "The one who sets long ears (of grain)".
7. The netherworld rangers have come for Dumuzi, as in real life rangers would seek out anyone trying to avoid the military and labor service to which he was obligated. They operate like a press gang. The term means literally "retiarius," "fighter with a net," and it is logical to assume that in real life they were recruited from fishermen. As such they would be competent boatmen.

SISTER
PROMISES
SECRECY

"The day I be (tempted)
   to reveal where you are
      may your dogs devour me!
Your black dogs, the dogs of the shepherdship,
your noble dogs, the dogs of the lordship—
   may your dogs devour me!
Whatever instructions
   you have to give,
     give to one of your comrades,
a comrade, a friend.
How can they search   100
   [the wild desert?]
May they fail to [discover
   where you are,]
     and after they have searched,
may he let you know there!"

COMRADE
TOLD

"My comrade,
   let me duck the head
     into the grass
     and may you not
     reveal where I am!
Let me duck the head
   into the little grass patches,
   and may you not
   reveal where I am!

"Let me duck the head
   into the large grass patches,
   and may you not
   reveal where I am!
Let me duck
   into Arali's ditch,
   and may you not
   reveal where I am!"

COMRADE
PROMISES
SECRECY

"The day I be (tempted)
   to reveal where you are
     may your dogs devour me!
Your black dogs, the dogs of the shepherdship,
your noble dogs, the dogs of the lordship—
   may your dogs devour me!"

DEMONIC
CHARACTER
OF RANGERS

The men who went after him   110
   for the king
   were a motley crew,

they knew not food,
    knew not drink,
ate not flour
    strewn (as offering),
drank not water,
    libated (as offering),
accepted not
    pleasant greeting gifts,
filled not, as a sign of affection,
    a spouse's lap (with gifts),
kissed not
    that sweet thing,
    a child,
set not tooth
    into the pungent garlic;
they were men
    who ate no fish,
    men
    who ate not onions.

Two citizens of Adab
    went after him
    for the king,
a (stinking) camelthorn,   120
    urine of the corner,
    and a thorn bush
    in stinking waters,
his hand on the table
    his tongue in the palace.[8]

Two citizens of Akshak
    went after him
    for the king,
around their necks
    hung fly-shaped beads
    belonging to
    anointed priests.[9]

Two citizens of Uruk
    went after him
    for the king,

---

8. The comparison with camelthorn, urine of a corner used as a urinal, and a thorn in stinking
waters are generally vituperative epithets. That their hand is on the table, their tongue in the palace,
means that they reward hospitality by acting as informers to the authorities.
    9. I.e., they had robbed the priests.

weapons and severed heads
  tied to their hips.

Two citizens of Ur
  went after him
  for the king
  (. . . . .)[10]

Two citizens of Nippur
  went after him
  for the king
  (. . . . .)
  (. . . . .)[10]

GESHTINANNA   "Run, man against man!"[11]
LOYAL TO HER   and to the fold and pen
BROTHER   they went.
On the way to the fold and pen   130
  they seized Geshtinanna.

They were offering to give her
  the rivers in their (high) waters,
  but she accepted them [n]ot.
They were offering to give her
  the fields in grain
  but she accepted them [not]

The little ranger
  said to the big ranger:

"Wise ranger,
  ranger who lives,
Ranger who grandly lives
  in the middle section
  (of the barge)![12]

"According to
  what [no] wise one
  has forgotten,

10. The text is corrupt here. Apparently the section describing the rangers from Ur and Nippur was lost in the course of tradition. At one point a scribe tried to restore the Nippur lacuna with a standard epithet of that city, "clean clothes being on the quay," which has reference to the many sacred festivals in that city, all of which called for clean clothes. The quay was the traditional place for laundering clothes. It is obvious that the description does not fit the context but was added thoughtlessly. It also got into the lacuna after the line mentioning Ur rather than the one mentioning Nippur.

11. Seemingly originally a war cry for a frontal attack. Here it seems to serve merely as a shout of encouragement in setting out on a raid.

12. The captain and leader of the posse typically had his quarters in the middle section of the boat on which they traveled on their forays.

according to
  what is not withheld
  from [the perceptive one:]

"Since time of yore,
  who ever saw
a sister revealing
  the hiding place
  of her brother?"

THE COMRADE
BETRAYS
DUMUZI

"Come!   140
  Let us go to his comrade!"

Now to his comrade
they were. offering to give
    the rivers in their (high) waters,
    and he was accepting them,
they were offering to give him
    the fields in grain,
    and he was accepting them:
"My comrade
    may have ducked the head
    into the grass,
    but where he is
    I nowise know!"[13]

They were searching for
Dumuzi with the head in the grass,
    but they were not discovering him.

"He may have ducked the head
    into the little grass patches,
    but where he is
    I nowise know."
They were searching for
Dumuzi (with) the head in the
    little grass patches,
    (but they were not discovering him).

"He may have ducked the head
    into the large grass patches,
    but where he is
    I nowise know."

13. The comrade denies knowing where Dumuzi is hiding, yet he gives clear indications of where to search for him. He would thus be able to state that he had not given Dumuzi away.

They were searching for
    Dumuzi (with) the head in the large grass patches,
    [but they were not] discovering him.

"He may have ducked   150
    into Arali's ditch,
    but where he is
    I nowise know."

DUMUZI CAUGHT   In Arali's ditch
    they were catching Dumuzi.
Dumuzi puckered the brows,
    burst into tears:
"In town my sister kept me alive,
    my comrade has let me die!
If (my) sister may have
    to put out a child
    to stand in the street,
    may someone kiss it!
If (my) comrade may have
    to put out a child
    to stand in the street,
    may no one kiss it!"

The men surrounded (the ditch)
    opened up for the stagnant
    waters in it,[14]
were twining cords for him,
    knotting nets for him,
twining varicolored cords for him,
scoring cornel sticks for him.[15]

The man in front of him   160
    threw things at him,
the man in back of him
    was racing him
    to within a single ell,
was clapping manacles
    on his hands,

---

14. To be able to close in on Dumuzi.

15. Presumably the cords were attached to the nets, which were to be rotated in the air lasso-like to fall upon and cover the victim. What the cornel sticks of line 159 were for is not clear. The scoring suggests that cords were to be wound around them. Perhaps cords and nets were wound around them for convenience in carrying and to avoid tangling up.

was pinioning his arms
  in a shackle.

DUMUZI
APPEALS
TO UTU

The lad lifted his hands
  heavenward to Utu (the sun god):
Utu, you are my brother-in-law,
  I [am yo]ur sister's husband,
I [am] the one
  who carries firewood to Eanna,
I am the one
  who takes wedding gifts to Uruk,
[I am] the one
  kissed by the holy lips,
[I am] the one
  dallying 'twixt the holy knees,
  the knees of Inanna!

Once you have made my hands   170
  [like] unto the front hooves
  of a gazelle,
and have made my feet
  [like] unto the hind hooves
  of a gazelle,
let me slip away
  from [all] my rangers
and flee for my life
  to Durbidalla!"[16]

FIRST ESCAPE:
TO DURBIDALLA

Utu accepted his tearful plea,
and as a man of mercy
  he [showed him] mercy.
Once he had made his hands
  like unto the front hooves
  of a gazelle,
and had made his feet
  like unto the hind hooves
  of a gazelle,
he slipped away
  from all the rangers,
and ran for his life
  to Durbidalla.

16. This locality is not known. Presumably it was in the Arali desert between Uruk and Bad-Tibira. Very likely it had a Dumuzi sanctuary.

SECOND
CAPTURE

The rangers   180
   were [searching for him,
   but were not [discovering him.]

"Come! Let us go to Durbidalla!"

On the way to Durbidalla
   they were catching Dumuzi.

The men surrounded it
   opened up for the stagnant
   waters therein,
were twining cords for him,
   knotting nets for him,
twining varicolored cords for him
scoring cornel sticks for him

The man in front of him
   threw things at him,
the man in back of him
   was racing him
   to within a single ell,
was clapping manacles
   on his hands,
was pinioning his arms   190
   in a shackle.

SECOND ESCAPE:
TO BELILI'S
HOUSE

The lad lifted his hands
   heavenward to Utu:
Utu, you are my brother-in-law,
   I am your sister's husband,
I am the one
   who carries firewood to Eanna,
I am the one
   who takes wedding gifts to Uruk,
I am the one
   kissed by the holy lips,
I am the one
   dallying 'twixt the holy knees,
   the knees of Inanna.
Once you have made my hands
   like unto the front hooves
   of a gazelle,
and have made my feet
   like unto the hind hooves
   of a gazelle,

let me flee for my life
   to Mistress Belili's house!"[17]

Utu accepted his tearful plea,   200
and once he had made his hands
   like unto the front hooves
      of a gazelle,
had made his feet
   like unto the hind hooves
      of a gazelle,
he [slipped] away
   from [all the ranger]s
and fled for his life
   toward Mistress Belili's house.

IN   To Mistress Belili's house
BELILI'S   he drew near:
HOUSE   "Mistress! I am not just a man,
                I am the consort of a goddess.
             When you have libated water
                if I might drink
                   of the water?
             When you have strewn flour,
                if I might eat
                   of the flour?"
             When she had libated water
                when she had strewn flour
             he sat down amidst it.[18]

The mistress went out of the house   210
and the rangers,
   since they saw
the mistress going out of the house, (thought:)

"If today the mistress
   did not know
      where Dumuzi lives,
she should anxiously
   have been looking for him,

17. Belili's house was located in a town called after her and apparently situated in the Arali desert. Her relation to Dumuzi is not clear. She is hardly his sister, as the Akkadian myth of the "Descent of Ishtar" has her.

18. Libation of water and strewing of flour are usually offerings to the dead. One wonders whether Dumuzi at this point was already considered to be dead, and that it was his ghost that was caught and escaped. See n. 20, also "Inanna's Descent," n. 26.

should anxiously
    have been calling for him.
Come! Let us go
    to Mistress Belili's house."

THIRD
CAPTURE

On the way to Mistress Belili's house
    they were catching Dumuzi.
The men sur[rounded] it
    opened up for the stagnant
    waters (in the canals) there
were [twining] cords for him
    knotting [nets] for him
twining varicolored cords [for him]   220
scoring [cornel sticks] for him.

The man in front of h]im
    [threw] things [at him,]
the ma[n in back of him]
    was r[acing him]
    [to within a single ell,]
was clasping.[manacles,]
    [on his] hands
was [pinioning his] arms
    [in a shackle.]

THIRD ESCAPE
TO GESHTIN-
ANNA'S SHEEP-
FOLD

The lad lifted his hands
    heavenward to Utu:
Utu, you are my brother-in-law,
    I am your sister's husband.
I am the one
    [who carries firewood t]o Eanna,
I am the one
    who takes wedding [gifts] to Uruk,
I am the one   230
    kis[sed] by the holy lips,
I am the one
    dallying 'twixt the holy knees,
    the knees of Inanna.

[Once] you have made my hands[19]
    like unto the front hooves
    of a gazelle,
have made my feet[19]

19. The text has here mistakenly the third person singular suffix.

like unto the hind hooves
  of a gazelle,
let me flee for my life
  to the holy fold,
  the fold of my sister!"

Utu accepted his tearful plea,
and once he had made his hands
  like unto the front hooves
  of a gazelle,
made his feet like
  unto the hind hooves
  of a gazelle
[he slipped away   237a
  from all the rangers]
and fled for his life
  to the holy fold,
  the fold of his sister.

To the holy fold,
  the fold of his sister,
  he drew near.
Geshtinanna let screams   240
  draw near unto heaven,
  draw near unto
  the netherworld;
the sum of screams
  covered like a cloth
  the base of heaven,
  veiled it
  like a linen sheet.

She clawed (for grief)
  the eyes for the sake of him,
  clawed
  the mouth for the sake of him,
clawed,
  where she could be seen,
  the ears for the sake of him,
and clawed,
  where one goes with no man,
  her thighs for the sake of him.[20]

20. These are generally actions that are part of lamentations for persons who have died, to express excess of grief. Cf. preceding n. 18. From this point on the text is in bad shape. Essential passages are lost so that it is difficult to follow the exact course of events as originally told.

"Brother, crouch down in my waters
　　and when I have [. . . . .]
　　the stagnant water,

(ancient lacuna)

FINAL CAPTURE.　　　"If Geshtinanna did not know
DUMUZI KILLED　　　　　where Dumuzi lives,
　　she should anxiously
　　　　have been looking for him,
　　[should an]xiously
　　　　have been calling for him.

"Come! [Let us] go
　　to the fold and the pen!"

As the first ranger　　　　　　　　　　　　　　　250'
entered fold and pen,
he threw the pegs
　　of the rack for milk jugs
　　　　onto the brazier.
As the second one
　　entered fold and pen,
he threw the staff
　　onto the brazier.
As the third one
　　entered fold and pen,
he removed the owner's marks
　　of the pure churns.
As the fourth one
　　en[tered] fold and pen,
he poured water on the holy brazier
　　in his presence.
As the fifth one
　　entered fold and pen
[he took down] the cups
　　hanging on pegs
　　　　from the pegs.
As the sixth one
　　entered fold and pen
the churns lay on their sides,
　　poured out no milk.
As the seventh one
　　entered fold and pen

the cups lay on their sides,   260'
   Dumuzi lived there no more,
the winds only
   swept the fold.
Dumuzi was slain in (battle),
   the festival of young men.[21]

---

21. This phrase is a stereotype for recording the death of a young soldier. It is applied here mechanically, although it does not fit Dumuzi at all.

The Wild Bull Who Has Lain Down

The Sumerian shepherd, pasturing his flock in the desert in the spring, was always in danger of attack by marauding bandits from the mountains, and the death of Dumuzi was often visualized as due to such an attack.

The image gains deeper meaning from the fact that the Sumerians considered the mountains to be the realm of Death and the abode of the dead. In a sense, therefore, the attack is the powers of Death itself reaching out for Dumuzi.

In the lament here translated, Dumuzi's young wife, Inanna, has come to the desert to join him but finds him dead, "asleep," the fold raided, the sheep and goats killed.

She asks the hills of Death for Dumuzi and the servants he had with him to help him, and is told that the bison has taken them—that is, their shades—up into the mountains. The image is one of captives led off into slavery. The bison, since bisons roamed the foothills in antiquity, stands for the mountains, and so for Death. She pleads with it for mercy in its treatment of the young husband she loves.

> [The slain wild bull[1]
>   lives no more!]
>   The slain wild bull
>   lives no more!
> [Dumuzi, the slain wild bull,]
>   lives no more!
>   The slain wild bull
>   lives no more!
> [The herdsma]n, the master, the herdsman,
>   lives no more!
>   The slain wild bull
>   lives no more!

1. The term "wild bull," "aurochs" (*am*) was also a term for "shepherd". We have kept the meaning "wild bull" so as not to loose the contrast with the other bovine term of the lament, the "bison."

Mine, [the queen's] chosen husband
    lives no more,
my one and only [one]
    lives no more,
[the herdsm]an Ushumgal-anna
    lives no more.

The lord of Arali
    lives no more,
the lord of Bad-Tibira
    lives no more,
the shepherd, lord Dumuzi,
    lives no more,
the lord of the shepherd's hill[2]   10
    lives no more,
the chosen husband of Inanna
    lives no more,
the lord of Emush[3]
    lives no more,
the brother of mistress Geshtin[4]
    lives no more,
the one who makes the land look luxuriant
    lives no more,
the lord, anchor rope of the land,
    lives no more!

O you wild bull, how fast you sleep!
    How fast sleep ewe and lamb!
O you wild bull, how fast your sleep!
    How fast sleep goat and kid!

I will ask the hills and the valleys,
I will ask the hills of the bison:

"Where is the young man, my husband?"   20
    I will say:
"He whom I no longer serve food?"
    I will say:
"He whom I no longer give drink?"
    I will say:
"And my lovely [m]aids?"
    I will say:

2. "The shepherd's hill" was apparently a locality—town or temple—in the Arali desert.
3. Name of the main temple of Bad-Tibira.
4. A shortened form of Geshtinanna.

"And my lovely [young men?"]
   I will say!

"The bison has taken thy [husband away,]
   up into the mountains!
The bison has taken [thy young man] away,
   up into the mountains!"

[Bi]son of the mountains
   with the mottled eyes,
Bison of the mountains
   with the crushing teeth,
Bison! Having taken him up, away from me,
   having taken him up, away from me,
having taken him I no longer serve food   30
   up away from me,
having taken him I no longer give drink
   up away from me,
having taken my lovely maids
   up away from me,
having taken my lovely young men
   up away from me

The young man who perished from me
   (at the hands of) your men,
young Abu who perished from me
   (at the hands of) your men,
may you not make an end
   of his lovely look,
may you not have him open
   with quaver (of fear)
   his lovely mouth!

On his couch you have made
   the jackals lie down,
in my husband's fold
   you have made the raven dwell,
his reed-pipe—   40
   the wind will have to play it,
my husband's songs—
   the North Wind will have to sing them!

41 (lines). An *ershemma* (composition) pertaining to
Dumuzi.

Recognition

As work in the fold in spring became more and more demanding, the shepherds would send for their wives, mothers, and sisters to join them in the desert to help out.

Dumuzi has done that, but when the women arrive he is dead, killed by raiders from the mountains. The dirge here translated begins as a lament for his death by his wife, his mother, and his sister, but it quickly centers on the mother alone. It follows her as she walks up to her son's body and loses, as she recognizes it, any last hope she might have clung to.

The standard epithets given the three deities at the beginning of the lament appear, as so often, incongruous in the setting, but apparently they could not be avoided: the style insisted on them.

> A reed pipe of dirges—
>   my heart wants to play
>   a reed pipe of dirges
>   in the desert!
> I, mistress of Eanna,
>   who lays waste mountains,
> and I, Ninsuna,
>   the lord's mother,
> and I, Geshtinanna,
>   ward of the god of Heaven!
>
> My heart wants to play
>   a reed pipe of dirges
>   in the desert,
> play where the lad dwelt,
> play where Dumuzi dwelt,
> in Arali, on The Shepherd's Hill.
>
> My heart wants to play
>   a reed pipe of dirges
>   in the desert,

where the lad dwelt,   10
   he who is captive,
where Dumuzi dwelt,
   he who is bound,
where the ewe surrendered the lamb—
my heart wants to play
   a reed pipe of dirges
   in the desert—
where the goat surrendered the kid.

Treacherous are you,
   numen of that place,
where, though the lad said to me:
   "May my mother join me!"—
My heart wants to play
   a reed pipe of dirges
   in the desert—
he may not move toward me
   his prostrate hands,
he may not move toward me
   his prostrate feet.

She neared the desert,   20
   neared the desert,

—The mother who gave birth,
   what crushing blow
   awaits her in the desert?—

At the [l]ad's [territory,]
   his desert,
   she arrived,
at the [sh]epherd's [territory,]
   his desert,
   she arrived
to [Inan]na's husband's [territory,]

—The mother who gave birth,
   what crushing blow
   awaits her in the desert?—

She will be ab[le]
   to see her slain wild bull,
   will be able
   to see his face!—

The mother who gave birth,
  what crushing blow
  awaits her in the desert?
What shudder befell her?

. . . .

The lady drew near,
  for her to look closely.
Beside the son
  she stayed the foot.

—The mother who gave birth,   30
  what crushing blow
  awaits her in the desert?—

"It is you!" she says to him,
  "You have changed!"
  she says to him.

What crushing blow
  is waiting for her,
in woe for her house,
  in woe for being made to dwell
  away from her home!

Vain Appeal

Essentially a lament for Dumuzi the shepherd, this composition also incorporates passages that come originally from the Damu cycle. To it belongs the Damu litany, which lists Damu and the other local gods identified with him and Dumuzi. There belongs also the image of the dead god as a reed blown by the wind and pursued by his mother. See below, "In the Desert by the Early Grass" ll. 186ff.

The basic story deals with Dumuzi's little sister Geshtinanna who, coming out of the destroyed fold, follows a netherworld ranger down to her dead brother to urge him to come back with her to lament what has happened to his fold. She is depicted—a role given her also elsewhere—as a child too young to understand the meaning of death. The dead Dumuzi tells her that it would be of no use for him to follow her, and asks her instead to inform their mother, so that she can lament him and go to dress his body, which is lying untended in the desert, for proper burial.

OBV.   [The bitter cry for him! The bitter] cry [for him!]
[The bitter] cry for the captive D[umuzi!]
The bitter cry [for] the captive Ama-ushumgal-anna!
"Woe the lad, the lad my Damu!
Woe the lad, the child Ningishzida!
Woe the lad, Ishtaran of shining visage!
Woe the lad, Alla, owner of the net!
Woe the lad, the reeve Lugalshudi!
Woe the lad, my Lusiranna!

Raging winds chose to blow off with him   10
   to set him down
   in the grasping netherworld.[1]

---

1. The spirit, leaving the body in the last breath or—according to a slightly variant belief—having to be released as a wind from the body with a special formula said over it, was thought of as carried by winds and storms to the realm of the dead.

Like a reed he is swaying, is ru[shed] ahead,
the lad, woe his heart! Woe his body!
The shepherd Dumuzi—Woe his frailty!

His mother, weeping, is running to him,
is running to him weeping and lamenting,
she keeps going, is crying bitter tears!
She halts, puts a hand to the heart,
she weeps—those are tears of pain!
she wails—those are wails of pain!

As his sister was coming out of the fold,   20
as Geshtinanna, the lord's sister,
   was coming out of the fold,
a scout, a (netherworld) ranger,
   coming to meet her,
called out to Mistress Geshtin:
"Your brother is going to turn into a weeper
   over this!
Dumuzi is going to turn into a lamenter
   over this!"

She went with the ranger the road thither,
gritting (her) teeth
   and learning from him on the way.
To the manacled one
   she was hurrying with him,
to the pinioned one
   she was hurrying with him,
so that she would fall down with him,   30
   would rise up (again) with him,
in [. . . . . .] . . . they traveled toward him,
for [. . . . . . .] they were a match,
to [. . . . . . .] they were equal.

(The text is broken here. When intact it must have told that Geshtinanna found her brother in the netherworld and urged him to come with her to lament the ravaged fold. When the text resumes she says:)

REV.   [. . . . . .] they slew [. . . . . . .]
[O my brother,] they took your [ew]es from you,
   I can bewail them!
[O my brother, they slew your [lam]bs for you,
   I can bewail them!
[O my] brot[her], they were slaying your [goa]ts,
   I can bewail them!

[O my] brot[her], they were slaying your [ki]ds,
   I can bewail them!

[The lad, the sheph]erd Dumuzi,
   nowise took to heart
   the words his sister spoke
to [Mistress Gu]nura[2] he said:
["My sister,] leaving in [my state of . . . .]
   beating the breast for my ewes,
   where would I go with you?
[Gunura,] leaving in my state of . [. . .]
   beating the breast for my goats,
where would I go with you?   10

When you have sent [men] to my mother,
   let them tell my mother.
May she cry out my:
   'He was worth any five!"
May she cry out my:
   'He was worth any ten!'
May she bring [wo]ol to the de[sert,]
   so she may bind up the mouth
   with the small woof threads!

She will make you search for my corpse.
May she claw with you at the mouth (in grief)!
May she claw with you at the nose for me!
May she, where she can be seen,
   claw with you at the ears for me!
May she, where she goes with no man,
   claw at her [belly] with you!

May she [pray (?)] with you   20
   to her tutelary godd[ess][3] for me,
and may her name [rid] me, the lad,
   of the ranger!

2. Gunura is the name of Damu's sister, who is here, apparently, identified with Geshtinanna, as Damu is with Dumuzi.
   3. Gods and goddesses had—like men—their tutelary deities. See "Let Him Come," n. 4.

In the Desert by the Early Grass

The composition called, from its opening lines, "In the Desert by the Early Grass" is remarkably disjunct and diverse, having obviously been put together from many and various sources. Nor does it help attempts to understand it that lacunas of uncertain length keep snapping such thin thread of narrative as may once have existed, nor that we are forced, in seeking to restore the text of such gaps, to rely on later versions rather than on the Old Babylonian (OB) one, which forms the basis of our presentation here.

The sources on which the composition drew were, clearly, actual ritual laments used in the wailing for Dumuzi, or rather for a group of similar dying gods that were at home on the lower course of the ancient Euphrates and were early identified with him. This region was one of orchard-growers in towns along the river and of oxherds who grazed their herds on the green reeds in the nearby marshes. Prominent among their gods were Damu of Girsu-on-the-Euphrates—not the Girsu of the Lagash region—a god of the sap that rises in trees and plants in the spring, and Ningishzida of Gishbanda, also on the Euphrates, a god of tree roots and snakes.

The sequence of themes in the composition—one can hardly speak of any "story"—may be outlined as follows:

Introduction. After two lines from a lament for Dumuzi-the-shepherd spoken by his young wife who had come to join him in the fold only to find him slain, the text moves into a standard litany from the Damu cult, listing the various local figures identified with him. To its last lines references to Dumuzi and Inanna have been added to fit it in with the opening lines of the composition. However, the lament in dendral images which follows it suits the Damu context more readily than the Dumuzi one.

The Mother's Search. After a lacuna the text resumes in a repetition of the Damu litany, and about here begins what might be called "The Mother's Search," a series of laments by the dead god's mother as she vainly seeks to find him and bring him back. The first such lament bewails him as a young soldier who has not returned, whose slain body lies unburied on some battlefield, who will never reach fulfillment in a happy, normal life. Then after another one of the ubiquitous gaps follow two inserts with quite different views of how the god died. In one he is not a soldier but an anointed priest who is being captured and led away bound, in the other he dies a natural death from illness, after his sister, a physician, has kept vigil over him to the last. Both laments are put in the mouth, it seems, not of the sorrowing mother but of a narrator.

After these inserts we are back with the god as a young soldier. The mother recalls and curses the day he was conscripted, taken by unfeeling rangers from her arms and legs, in which she was frantically clasping him to hold onto him. She intends to go to the house of their commanding officer, the constable, and stand in his gate to lament and clamor until he gives her son back. At any rate, she thinks, when her son has finished his term of service, he will come back to her "out of the spring grass."

During all these laments of hers, the dead son continually cuts in, trying to dissuade her from her resolve to follow him. She cannot eat the food he, as an inhabitant of the grave, eats, nor will the netherworld authorities give her son back to her. The mother, who has not recognized her son's voice, continues her search oblivious to all else, like a cow searching for its calf—an image dear to the cowherders. The search takes her near the mountains, the realm of Death, but she presses on. She imagines she hears the sound of a hue and cry far away, as if from a crowd pursuing her son; and she imagines he has deserted and is fleeing to her. She dreams of how she will take care of him.

Here again her laments are punctuated by appeals from the dead son, who tries to dissuade her from following him. He has become a spirit, has left the body in his last breath, and is now being carried by the winds to the netherworld. She must not follow. This last warning comes, unlike the previous ones, not from the Damu, but from the Dumuzi body of laments.

The Spirits on the Road. After the laments belonging to "The Mother's Search" follows an episode with very different setting. The dead god meets a variety of persons on the road to the netherworld. He does not realize that he is dead and that these are ghosts, so he tries to send a message back to his mother with one of them to have her ransom him from the netherworld ranger who holds him captive. They answer that it would be of no use; they are ghosts and thus could convey no message the living could hear.

The dead god of this episode seems to identify the city to which he wants the ghosts to take his message as Tummal. Unfortunately the reading is not certain. If it is correct the god should be Ishtaran, who, the texts tell us, was at home in Etummala, "the dike of Tummal." I have tentatively accepted this interpretation.

The episode with the spirits on the road is followed by lines from a lament which apparently bewail the god's exhausted and disheveled state. These lines are set off in the text from what precedes by a double line, a sign probably that a section of text is omitted here, possibly due to a lacuna in the scribe's original.

The Reviving Beer. After a modern lacuna of indefinite length begins a part of the composition concerned with beer, which apparently was thought to have magic power to revive the god. When the texts comes in, it tells that his mother is nearing the "grange of the anointed ones," perhaps a structure near or in Enegi(r). She has prepared a meal for her son and has brewed beer. When the son has partaken of this he will come back to life and health. The god responds, hoping for life and referring to himself by the image of a cedar. The next lines tell that his sister is nearing the "chariot road" uttering lament. There follows an insert, some rather fine lines from a Dumuzi-the-shepherd lament in which the dead god sorrows at not being able to answer his mother or come back to her and grow up again as the desert grass in the spring.

Next the text moves into a remarkably long litany listing various local forms of the dying god by name, and telling where they lie buried. The litany, after it has exhausted the list of local gods, continues with the names of rulers of the Third Dynasty of Ur and of the dynasty of Isin, continuing, with gaps, to Cassite times. These rulers would have incarnated the god in the yearly ritual of the sacred marriage. After this litany, the text returns once more to the theme of the reviving beer. The beginning of a speech by the mother, in which she laments that her son's blood was spilt on the ground when he was killed, is lost in a lacuna. The son answers, asking her to dig it up—apparently it had turned into a red tuber of a kind used in beer making—and to chop it so that it can be used by his sister in brewing the beer that will warm him. He ends with a plaint that the killing of him was unjust, he was no enemy.

Dialogue with the Sister. The last of the themes dealt with by the composition is given the form of dialogues. It centers on the god's young sister and on her dependence on him. The form of the god from whose cult these songs came was apparently that of Ningishzida seen as a young soldier. The sequence begins with the sister wanting to find out from people in town what has happened to her brother. The actions of her mother in bewailing him has deeply disturbed her, even though she seems to have been too young to have understood their implications fully. The dead Ningishzida answers her and urges her to bear up under the blow fate has dealt her with his death. She replies that she must go to join him. He then asks whether she and her mother have anyone to take care of them now he is gone, and do they still have the house? She tells that the house, which was assigned to them by the authorities, has been reassigned to others, and that she and her mother suffer want. He exclaims at the destruction of his household. At this point the voice of the mother is heard. She states her resolve to join him in the netherworld to care for him, and he responds looking forward to her coming. As she walks through the desert to join him, she sees a physician standing at the roadside, a sign, of course, that someone is ill or has had an accident. She hopes it has nothing to do with her, but one surmises that the text now lost in the following lacuna will have told of her finding her daughter, Ningishzida's sister, dead. When the text resumes it repeats, much abbreviated, an earlier lament by the mother for her son who did not return from a military campaign; probably this is a later insert. The text then continues with the dead god, now Dumuzi-the-shepherd, greeting his sister as she joins him in the netherworld. She must, he wails, be both sister and mother to him, and she responds, accepting the double role readily. This ends our main OB version of the composition. A different version may have added a song, of which there remains a fragment, describing the dead god as he rests his pinioned arms in his sister's lap.

The forms of the dying god mentioned in the litanies of the composition, and the places where they were buried, should perhaps be listed with brief comments.

Ninazu is a netherworld god who seems to have been a god of the rains of spring which seep down into the earth. His city was Enegi(r) located on the old course of the Euphrates on the stretch between Larsa and Ur. Another city of his was Eshnunna (Tel Asmar) in the Diyala region. See also below, the introduction to "Enlil and Ninlil."

Damu seems to have been god of the sap that rises in trees and plants in the spring. The name Damu means "the son." His city was Girsu-on-the-Euphrates, not to be confused with the better known Girsu (Tello) in the Lagash region.

Ningishzida was a god of trees, particularly of the roots from which the tree grows up. His name means "the lord who makes the tree be right," and correspondingly the name of his wife Ninazimua means "the lady who makes the branches grow rightly." Since, mythopoeically, the ancients assumed tree roots and serpents to be identical and wrote the word for roots with a picture of crossed snakes, Ningishzida was also king of serpents. His city was Gishbanda, and in it was his tomb called "the mountain of lament."

Ishtaran appears elsewhere as a god of justice. The meaning of his name is not clear. Tentatively it may be interpreted as "the Turan hills" (with standard vowel assimilation of *Turan* to-*taran*). Turan is the Diyala river, and at the southeastern border of the Diyala region, in the foothills, lay Ishtaran's most important cult center, Dêr (older, perhaps Tur_x-an). The god may thus have been originally god of these foothills, the Turan hills, and his epithet "of bright visage" may refer to snow-capped mountain slopes. His tomb on the lower Euphrates was situated on the "dike of Tummal, the chariot road". This Tummal would have been a local southern one, not the better known Tummal of the goddess Ninlil in or near Nippur.

Allagula (the reading of the first syllable of the name is not certain) is otherwise unknown. His tomb is said to have been in Gamgamda, in the desert of Ku'ar. Ku'ar was a city near Eridu. Its chief god was the rain god Asarluhe.

Alla is known as a netherworld deity only. A late text identifies him with Ea, the Akkadian name of Enki. He may have been a river god and god of freshwater fishermen. His epithet "owner of the net" points in that direction. His tomb was in "the cupbearer's house among the little bronze cups."

Lugalshudi is mentioned in the great list of gods An: Anum as the name of a deified harp of Ningishzida's. The meaning of the name, "the king who hails," seems not unsuitable for a harp, which would accompany people seeking an audience with the god to whom it belonged, and whose mood it was meant to soften by a flattering address. Lugalshudi takes the military title "constable" (*nimgir*)—why is not clear—and has his tomb in "the street." It is called "the tomb of tears" and was, probably because of the god's connection with Ningishzida, situated on a street in Gishbanda.

Lusiranna, "the man condensing (the clouds) of the sky" was presumably a god of the spring rains. He is not known from elsewhere. He is said to be buried at "the road that makes an end of him who walks it," which can hardly have been the name of any actual locality.

Niminur's name is mentioned (Ur-Nanshe 24.iii.3–6) as designation of the human spouse of the goddess Nanshe, who presumably incarnated Niminur in the local sacred marriage rite. The name is, as others in the litany, given in dialectal (Emesal) form. The main dialect would have it as Niğin-ùr, which means "spider." He would thus be a deified spider, and so the laudatory epithet given him, "frisky bull," is not to be taken literally. His tomb was in some stepped dead-end street to the location of which we have no clue.

Lugalirra, "the king wept over," had his tomb in Shunagia (the name means "returned into his hands"), a village near Ur where there was a royal weaving establishment in Ur III times. The term "wild bull," "aurochs," can also denote a shepherd, so it is possible that this god was a shepherd god like Dumuzi.

Malaka, styled "king of warriors," and Kushab, where he was buried, are both unknown. He is followed in the litany by dead kings of the Third Dynasty of Ur and of the dynasty of Isin.

This litany constitutes, especially in its short form with only Ninazu, Damu, Ningishzida, Alla, Lugalshudi, and Ishtaran, the heart of the Damu cycle of gods and appears to be limited to local cults of the lower Euphrates region. Beside it, however, there is also a litany of rather wider geographical horizon. This latter litany is probably later in date and may reflect an adaptation of some or all of the Damu materials for use in the larger territories held by the kings of Isin. The goddesses listed in it are Ninnibru, Nab, Ninguenna, probably all from Nippur. Then comes the Isin pantheon of Ninniğinğarkuga(k), Ninurusağa, Nintinugga and Nininsina. Among them, probably through a scribal lapse, figures Ninsuna of Uruk and Kullab. Last comes Nanshe of Ninâ in the Lagash region. The goddesses, who are listed as mothers of dying deities, are followed by a list of their children. Most of these latter are only found here, and their relation to the mothers listed before them is not clear. They are: Ursağimina, Zurma and Zarimu, the great and the small twins, Buranesuga, Mesandu, Lulil, and the goddess Atu. Zurma and Zarimu were cloud goddesses, daughters of Ninğirsu and Baba in Girsu; Mesandu is mentioned in records from the Lagash region as recipient of offerings; Lulil we know to have been a dying god. His mother was Ninhursağa in Adab, and laments for him survive. Atu has the name of a class of priestesses in Ninhursağa's temple in Kesh, but that is about all that is known about her. The remainder of the names in the list are not known from elsewhere.

(INTRODUCTORY LAMENTS)[1]

NARRATOR

In the desert, by the early grass,
  she [holds not back]
  the flood of tears
  for her hus[band,]
  [in the desert,] by the ear[ly grass]
  [the mistress holds not back]
  [the flood of tears]
  [for her] husband!

INANNA LAMENTS
HER DEAD HUS-
BAND, DUMUZI,
NINAZU, DAMU,
ETC.

"Alas the lad, the warrior Ninazu!
Alas the lad, my lad, my Damu!
Alas the lad, the child Ningishzida!
Alas the lad, Alla, owner of the net!
Alas the lad, the constable Lugalshudi!
Alas the lad, Ishtaran of bright visage!
Alas the lad, my Lusiranna!
Alas the lad, Ama-ushumgal-anna!   10
Alas the lad, the brother of Geshtinanna!
The shepherd, lord Dumuzi,
  bridegroom of Inanna,
lord of Arali, lord of 'the shepherd's hill,'
my tamarisk, that drinks not water
  in the orchard bed,
the crown of which
  forms not leafage
  in the desert,[2]
my poplar, that has no joy
  of its watering pipe,[3]
my poplar
  pulled up by the roots,
my vine, that drinks no water
  in the garden bed,
[my vine
  that was torn] out!"

(lacuna of unknown length)

1. The following section, as far as the lacuna, is taken from the late version.
2. The "desert" stands here for the open country around the city, bordering on the city's orchards and gardens.
3. Trees in the orchards were watered by narrow ditches serving circular ditches around each tree. The water for an orchard's system of such ditches would come from a sluice with a pottery inlet pipe tapping a larger canal, so that the water going into the orchard could be regulated.

(SONGS OF THE MOTHER'S SEARCH)

(probable beginning of the older version)

["Alas, the lad, the warrior Ninazu!]   20'
[Alas, the lad, my lad, my Damu!]
[Alas, the lad, the child Ningishzida!]
[Alas, the lad, Alla, owner of the net!]
Alas, the lad, the constable Lugalshudi!]
[Alas, the lad, Ishtaran of the beaming visage!]
[Alas, the lad, my Lusiranna!]
[Alas, the lad, Ama-ushumgal-anna!]
[Alas, the lad, the brother of Geshtinanna!]
my one who was not [. . . .]
my [lad] who did not return   30'
    [to his barracks,]
my one [whose head
    earth] does not cover,
my one who will never grow old
    [in his house,]
my one [whose limbs]
    are scattered!

"My one who will never bring
    [betrothal gifts]
    [to a father-in-law's house,]
my one who [will never] carry
    [a wedding gift there,]
my one who [will never] make [love,]
    [to a young wife]
my one who [will never]
    beget [children,]
my one who [will never]
    raise [a child at his knee,]
my one who is slain
    [. . . .]
my one who [. . . . .]   40'
my one who [. . . . .]
my one who [. . . . .]
my one who [. . . . .]
my one who [. . . . .]
my [. . . . .]
my [. . . . .]

(lacuna of unknown length)
(late version)

NARRATOR	Woe! [. . . . .]
	lad, . . [. . . . .]
	on the road [they searched for him,]
	in the desert [they searched for him,] 50′
	they scanned [the desert, they saw him,]
	they cried out, [they seized him,]
	his girdle [they untied . . . . . .]
	the lad's thighs [they bared . . . .]
	he was blind[folded] and, bound [as he was],
	he was driven along, [allowed] no sleep.

"Alas, lad! Their hands have ca[ught you,]
lad, my Damu, the[ir] hands
    [have caught you,]
high-priest who no longer
    [will dwell] in the *gipāru*,[4]
its anointed one [who was stripped]
    of its wigs.[5]
Woe, lad,   60′
    their hands [have caught you!]
Lad, [my] Damu,
    [their hands have caught you!]
your hands [have been clapped
    in] manacles,
your arms [pinioned]
    [in] sha[ckles!"]

(lacuna of unknown length)[6]
(OB version)

NARRATOR TELLS	In Gamgamda in Ku'ar's desert,
HOW DAMU'S SIS-	on the dike of Tummal,
TER, A LEECH,	[on the chariot] ro[ad,]
ATTENDED HIM	[in] the cupbearers' house,
IN HIS VARIOUS	[among the little b]ronze cups,
INCARNATIONS	[in] the traces of the king[s,]
AND SANCTUARIES	[in] the grange
	of the anointed ones,

4. The *gipāru* was the traditional dwelling of an *en*, high-priest or priestess, often the title of a ruler or a manager with magic powers to make things thrive and to bring prosperity. Here the title serves to stress the dying god's role as a power for fertility and plenty.

5. It was customary for the priests to shave their heads to avoid infection with lice. For formal wear they would put on wigs. Here the wig symbolizes easy and luxurious living, which has suddenly and brutally come to an end. "Its" refers to gipāru.

6. The following section is from the OB version.

in the dininghall
  by the linen-clad ones,
was the leech,   70'
  who eats no fish,
  sitting by him,
  was the leech
  sitting by him;
was the leech,
  who eats no onions,
  sitting by him,
  was the leech
  sitting by him;
in a room in the gipāru,
  was his sister,
in a room in the gipāru
  since yesterday,
was Amashilamma, the sister
  of the dead anointed one,
the pure maiden
  of Azimua,[7]
Gunura, sister of Damu,
the holy older sister
  of the silvern,
  dried-up grain[8]—

(ancient gap of ten[?] lines)[9]

THE SISTER   My (dear) leech,
LEAVES TO   having gone out
SEARCH FOR   of the gipāru,
HIM   having gone out
                  of the gipāru,
                  is enquiring about him;
                  my (dear) only sister of Damu,   80'
                  my (dear) leech,
                  [is enquiring about D]amu.

(lacuna of unknown length)

. . . .

7. Amashilamma, a cow goddess, is Ningishzida's sister; Azimua is his wife.
8. A reference to Damu as the sap in the green grain. With his disappearing and death the fresh grain in which he manifested himself is become whitish and dry.
9. This seems indicated by the double line with the figure 10 which the text has at this point. Also, the verb appears to be missing.

(late version)

the rangers, full of fearsomeness
        hurtfully [. . . . .]

DAMU'S MOTHER
CURSES THE
DAY HE WAS
CONSCRIPTED.
MOURNERS
TAKE UP THE
CRY

"I am the mother who gave birth!
        Woe to that day, that day!
        Woe to that night!"
O Mother of the lad,
        Woe to that day, that day!
        Woe to that night!
"The day that dawned for my provider,
        that [dawned] for the lad,
        my Damu!
A day to be wiped out,
        that I would I could forget!
Yon night, [. . . .] that should [never]
        have let it go forth,
when my rangers, shamelessly, [10]
        made their way
        into my [presence.]
The lad—Woe! The day destroyed him,
        lost me a son!
The lad, my Damu [. . . .]
With the nails [most] burningly
        [I clawed my face . . . . . . "]

(lacuna of unknown length)

THE DEAD GOD
TRIES TO DETER
HIS MOTHER
FROM FOLLOW-
ING HIM

"Mother who gave birth,
        how [could you eat the food,]
        [how could you drink that water?)
Mother of the lad,   90'
        how could you eat the food,
        how [could you drink] that water?
That food,
        the surface of it has gone bad,
        how [could you eat] that food?
That water,
        the surface of it has gone bad,
        how [could you drink] that water?
The food I have eaten since yesterday
        my mother [should not eat,]

10. For men to intrude into the private chamber or a woman was an unheard-of breach of propriety.

the water I have poured for myself
my mother should no[t drink!"¹¹]

THE MOTHER
RECOGNIZES
NOT THE
VOICE

"I am the mother who gave birth,
but neither of heaven are you,
nor are you of earth!
I am the mother who gave birth,
but neither my husband [are you,]
[nor are you my son!]
I am the mother who gave birth,
[in my] burning with grief
[may you not(?) . . . .]

(OB version)

I am the mother who gave birth,
but neither of heaven are you,
nor are you of earth,
I am the mother who gave birth,
but neither my husband are you,
nor are you my son!"

THE SON CON-
TINUES TRYING
TO DETER HER,
THE AUTHORI-
TIES WILL NOT
GIVE THE SON
BACK

"Mother who gave birth,   100'
cow,¹² low not for the calf,
turn your face toward me!
Cow who will not make the calf answer,
turn your face toward me!
The constable will not
give you your son,
the lord (in charge) of the plowland
will not give him to you,
the lord, chief herdsman (?)¹³
will not give him to you!"

THE MOTHER
TELLS HOW THE
PITILESS RE-
CRUITERS NOW
TOOK BOTH

"The man, cause of dirges,¹⁴
the lord constable,
what sought he from me?
The constable, lord of the manor,
what sought he from me?

---

11. The dead son is speaking of the offerings of food and water that traditionally were placed in the grave with the body when it was interred.

12. The image of the mother as a cow is a complimentary one, particularly among herders. It stands for motherly love.

13. The reading "chief herdsman" presupposes an ancient scribal error. The military (constable) and civil officials (chiefs of plowing and herding, respectively) reflect the different uses of the conscripted men as army in war and as labor force in peace.

14. The following section until line 115' can be completely restored from the later version. From 115' on the later version differs.

HER SON
AND HER
HUSBAND

In Girsu on the bank of the Euphrates
He forced apart my thighs,
   robbed me of my husband,[15]
forced apart my knees,
   robbed me of my son!

SHE WILL
CLAIM HIM

"In the constable's gate   110'
   let me tread—
In the constable's gate
   let me tread my mournful measure,[16]
the 'Woe the lad!' that goes with it
   let me dolorously say,
'He was my good fortune!'
   dolorously let me say,
and my 'I, a mother who gave birth,
   driven like an ox!' burningly let me say!

SHE ASSURES
HERSELF THAT
HE IS IN FOR
A TERM ONLY

"After the term they have set
   for the lad, my Damu,
   he will come back,
   out of the spring grass!
After [the lad] passes the day set,
   he will come back,
   out of the spring grass!"
After [the days] are full [for my Damu,]
   he will come back,
   out of the spring grass!"

. . . .
. . . .

(lacuna of unknown length)

(late version)

The cow [seeks] the spot   120'
   where its calf is [lying,]
the cow lows and lows,
   [the cow lows and lows.]
Mother Ninnibru [seeks the spot]
   [where her son is lying,]
Nab, first-born child of An,
   [seeks the spot]
   [where her son is lying,]

15. She apparently clamped her arms and legs around her husband when earlier on he was taken for the army, and later around her son, hoping in each case to prevent their being taken away from her. The rangers thus had to use force to pry them loose from her frantic grasp.

16. A dance or traditional gestures expressive of grief.

Lady Ninguenna [seeks the spot]
  [where her son is lying]
Ninniğinğarkuga(k)
  [seeks the spot]
  [where her son is lying]
Ninurusağa [seeks the spot]
  [where her son is lying,]
the mother who gave birth,
  Ninsuna,
  [seeks the spot]
  [where her son is lying,]
Nintinugga [seeks] the sp[ot]
  [where her son is lying]
Nininsina [seeks] the sp[ot]
  [where her son is lying,]
the lady, Mother Nanshe,   130'
  [seeks] the sp[ot]
  [where her son is lying,]
where her son is lying,
where Ursağimina i[s lying,]
where Zurma and Zarimu [are lying,]
where the great and the little twins
  [are lying]
where Buranesuga [is lying,]
where Mesandu,
  overseer of the pressers of oil,
  [is lying,]
where Lulil, the god i[s lying,]
where Atu, the great lady
  i[s lying.]
The cow lows and lows,
  [the cow lows and lows,]
the cow, constantly calling   140'
  [. . . . .]
the mother who gave birth,
  the cow, constantly calling
  [. . . . .]

"I am the mother who gave birth,
  [what sought] the lord constable
  from me?
The constable, the lord (in charge) of the plowlands,
  what did he seek from me?

In Girsu on the bank of the Euphrates
he forced apart my thighs,
    [robbed me of my husband,]
[forced apart my knees,]
    [robbed me of my son."]

(lacuna of unknown length)

(OB version)	[. . . .] the cow to the calf
NARRATOR TELLS	. . [. . .] to [the calf]
HOW THE MOTHER	asked about.
IN HER SEARCH	From the cow its calf is gone,
IS GETTING	from the mother who gave birth
CLOSE TO THE	that which was her pleasure
MOUNTAINS, THE	is gone,
REALM OF DEATH	the waters have carried off 150'

    the precious one
    from her.[17]
To the mother who gave birth,
  enquiring, searching,
  the foothills
  were getting close,
like a ewe separated from the lamb
  she could not hold back.
like a goat separated from the kid
  she could not hold back.
The foothills were getting close.
  The mountain rises
  were getting close.

Before her rushes were rising high,
  halfa grass was rising high,
over the lad's mother
  the canebrake was rising high,
and on reed hummock after reed hummock
  the mother of the lord
  was letting tears fall.[18]

THE MOTHER	"He who will show me my provider
OFFERS	who will show me
REWARD	where my provider is

17. The image is that of a calf being lost in the onrush of floodwaters that carry it away.

18. The image is that of difficult walking in the southern marshes, familiar to singers and hearers on the lower Eugphrates. It seems less appropriate for nearing the mountains.

to that man let me give   160'
   things (numerous as)
   the stars of heaven!

"O lad, the things (numerous as)
   the stars of heaven,
   pertaining to you,
   things as of sounds of a hue and cry,
   come nearer and nearer,[19]
the things (numerous as)
   the stars of heaven,
   pertaining to you,
   that come to me,
keep frightening me,
   and I,
with hand stretched out,
   bless toward yonder.

"Where my calf is I know not,
I am wending my way,
search according to my own judgment,
noon has turned into evening for me,
   the things as of sounds of a hue and cry
   come nearer and nearer,
while it will come to me
   as were it illusion,
   it is true! It is true!
I am the mother who gave birth!
   I shall make Earth tremble
   like a cedar forest!"

THE DEAD SON   "Mother who gave birth,   170'
AGAIN TRIES   cow, low not for the calf!
TO DISSUADE   Turn your face toward me!
HER FROM   O you, cow who cannot
SEEKING HIM   make the calf answer,
the lord (in charge) of the plowlands
   is not giving it to you,
the lord (in charge) of . . . . .
   is not giving it to you!
Cow, from the riverbank
   turn your face toward me!

---

19. We tentatively assume that the mention of "things numerous" turns her thoughts to the constant sounds of many voices, a hue and cry far away, that seems to come to her. The term translated "hue and cry" refers to the sounds of a pursuing group. She is imagining she hears her son escaping and being pursued, and though it seems an illusion, she convinces herself that it is real.

Aurochs, from Arali and the high desert[20]
　　turn your face toward me!"[21]

(lacuna of unknown length)

(OB Version)

THE MOTHER DECIDES
TO FOLLOW HER
SON EVEN INTO THE
REALM OF DEATH

"If it be required, you lad,
　　let me walk with you
　　the road of no return.
Alas, the lad! The lad, my Damu!"

NARRATOR

She goes, she goes
　　toward the breast of the mountains,
the day waning, the day waning,　　　　　　180'
　　toward the mountains, still bright,
to him who lies in blood and water,[22]
　　the sleeping lord,
to him who knows no healing lustrations,
to the road making an end
　　of the one who walks it,
to the traces of the kings,[23]
to the grange of the anointed ones.[24]

The wind blew off a pure reed
　　from the gipāru,[25]
the wind blew off a pure reed, the lad,
　　from the gipāru.

THE DEAD DU-
MUZI'S DISEM-
BODIED SPIRIT
IS A WIND
BLOWING WITH
OTHER WINDS

"Since I am one lying in the south winds
　　lying in all the north winds,
since I am lying in the little ones
　　that sink the ships,
since I am lying in the big ones　　　　　　190'
　　that drown the crops,

20. The "high" desert is the part of the desert that does not flood in spring. This line with its mention of Arali looks like an insert from Dumuzi-the-shepherd materials.

21. The later version has further lines here but its text appears to be corrupt.

22. Reference is to the separation of the spilt blood into clot and serum.

23. The term translated "traces" denotes harness ropes by which a processional chariot was pulled. The place named from them may have been a depot for royal chariots, possibly to be connected with the "chariot road" where Ishtaran was buried. We tentatively consider it an actual place which very likely was a station of the way of a ritual lamentation procession.

24. Also perhaps a station on a processional road. A double line here suggests that a line was omitted anciently at this point.

25. The spirit, leaving the body with the last breath as a wind, was thought to be blown to the mountains, the realm of death, by the winds. Here the dead god's spirit, thus tossed about, is likened to a fragment of reed in a gale.

since I am lying in the lightnings
and in tornados,
she should not be
where (I,) the lad, am!
Why does she follow me?
She should not be
where (I,) Dumuzi, am!
Again, she who cries 'alas!' for me,
why does she follow me?"

THE MOTHER
IS SURE THE
SON WILL DE-
SERT AND IS
READY TO FLEE
WITH HIM

"For the [. . . .] who will come,
who will take refuge with me,
who in his fleeing before him
will take refuge with me,
my head (in readiness to leave)
is covered with a (head)cloth.
He will escape their capture,
and in his running
he will take refuge with me!

SHE IMAGINES
HOW SHE WILL
RECEIVE HIM

"Lie down! [I shall say,]
[as I] cover up the lad,
in his loins [I shall restore]   200'
the (power) to run,
the grip (?) on his pinioned arms
[I shall loosen.]
He may say: 'My hands!'
and the hands I shall [. . . . .]
He may say: 'My head!'
and I shall [bandage] it
with a piece of cloth.

SHE IS READY
FOR HADES

"Food that is not food
let me [eat] with him,
milk that is not milk
let me drink with him.
Alas! Woe! Be off! Be off![26]
Go out and away!
Never [. . . . . . .]
[Alas! Woe!] My Damu,
Be off! Be off!
[Go out and away!"]
[. . . .]

26. The son is to continue his flight after she has attended to him and bandaged him, for his pursuers are certain to look for him in her house.

(lacuna of unknown length)

(SONG OF THE SPIRITS ON THE ROAD)

(lacuna of unknown length)

(OB version)	["Let me instruct you about the] city
THE DEAD GOD	of my fat[her, who engendered me,]
MEETS OTHER	and may my compassionate [father]
GHOSTS AND	[make enquiries about me!]
WISHES TO	[Let me instruct you about] the city
SEND A MES-	of my mother, who conceived [me,]
SAGE HOME BY	[and may my compassionate mother
THEM, NOT	make enquiries about me!]
KNOWING THAT	[Let me instruct you] 210'
THEY AND HE	[about my tutelary god, who engendered [me,]
ARE GHOSTS	and may my compassionate tutelary god
ONLY	make enquiries about me!
	[Let me instruct you]
	about Ninsuna, who conceived [me,]
	[and may] my compassionate Ninsuna]
	make enq[uiries] about me!"
GHOSTS	"I am a girl, do not [instruct me!]
	I am a lad, [do not instruct me!"]
DEAD GOD	"Tummal [you could reach (?)] today!
	May my mother [make] enquiries about me,
	[you] lad, let me instruct you!"]
GHOST	"You lad, do not [give me any] instructions,
	at no instruction [you] might give [m]e,
	would your mother, lad, [come to you!]
	Nor, at your letting the call
	resound in the [dese]rt,
	will your mother, o you lad,
	come to you!"
NARRATOR	A songstress was walking along,
	a songstress was walking along,
	she knew how to wake up a sleeper,
	she stopped;
	amidst lament
	the songstress [stopped.]
GHOST MEN	"I am a man!"—"I am a lad!" 220'
GHOST WOMEN	"I am a girl!—"I am a woman!"

GHOST CHILD	"I am a little one in a street, somewhere I do not know!"

SONGSTRESS
GHOST
	"Little one, little one,
	    why come you to me?
	Setting up the wailing harp,
	    I shall stay with you.
	As for me, my setting up
	    a spirit harp in the wind,
	    what matters it?
	I am one versed in understanding spirits,
	    in dirges,
	    what matters (now)
	    my understanding?"

MALE GHOST	"I am a man,
	    I dance to the harp
	    the mournful measures;
	treading them all day
	    the day waned for me,
	    I was dancing the mournful measures."

DAMU	"May the spirits go
	    to the mother who bore me,
	may the spirits bring her tidings
	    about my one
	    who holds (my) spirit captive!
	Verily, I too am become
	    a lad to be ransomed,
	    may she order my
	    'Release him!'
	and may my ranger,
	    the one who was arresting me,
	lend her a hand in releasing,
	she is crying in the desert,
	    [letting the cry] resound!"[27]

NARRATOR	The hands dropped [. . . . .]
	    the belt [was untied,]
	    the lad was not light of heart,
	    not unclouded of [b]row.

230′

(lacuna of unknown length)

27. A double line here suggests that a line, or possibly a section, was omitted.

(SONGS OF THE REVIVING BEER)²⁸

RETURN TO THE
THEME OF SEARCH
THE MOTHER WILL
PREPARE A RE-
VIVING MEAL

[Your mother is approaching]
  [the gr]ange of the [anointed] ones,
for your mother's] approaching
  the grange of the anointed ones
your mother has laid out a meal,
  she is calling,
  your mother is calling,
your mother has brewed beer,   240′
  she is calling,
  your mother is calling!
When your mother who bore you
  has served
  her meal which she has laid out,
  may you eat of it!
When your mother who bore you
  has poured
  her beer which she has brewed,
  may you drink of it!
And may your mother,
  after she has come near,
  step with you
  (up) from the bank!²⁹
(In her stepping) toward
  the bank of the river
  may you still be a ghost.
(In her stepping) from
  the bank may you,
  eyes healthy, cheeks healthy,
  be a man!³⁰

DAMU

"May not the goats
  overturn my cedar crown,

---

28. These laments would seem to have their origin in the cult of an aspect of Dumuzi in which he was seen as the power in the grain and in the beer brewed from it. The feeling of bodily well-being induced by beer would attribute to it reviving power, so that by giving his "essence" back to the god he would be revived. In the second of the laments in this group the beer is directly identified with the god's vital fluid, his blood. The section following is from the OB version.

29. These lines are most easily understood if one envisages the mother as arriving by boat, the standard way of traveling on the river or in the marshes.

30. The meal and the beer will, it is hoped, instantly revive the god.

but may [my] roots
    stand firm [on the ground!]"[31]

NARRATOR

Your mother is calling: "Beer!"
When your sister has come near
    unto the chariot road
[she will cry (?)]:
    "O mother who gave birth,
    alas your son!
Alas your son!   250'
    Alas your captive son!"[27]

DAMU REALIZES
HE IS DEAD

"Woe! I am become a ghost!
    Woe, I am become a ghost,
I am not one who can answer
    my mother listening
    in Guedinna,[32]
my mother, who is calling to me
    in the desert,
who is letting the call for me
    resound in the desert.
She will not be answered
I am not the grass,
    will not grow up for her again,
I am not the waters,
    will not rise for her again,
I am not the grass
    sprouting in the desert,
I am not the new grass
    growing up in the desert!"[27]

THE NARRATOR
SINGS THE LIT-
ANY OF DUMUZI/
DAMU'S INCAR-
NATIONS AND
THEIR TOMBS

Since by flowing waters   260'
    of holy-water fonts,
    by waters
    poured out from
    holy-water fonts,
by flowing waters
    of holy-water fonts,

31. These lines may be intrusive and belong properly to songs dealing with Damu as the sap of trees. In that tradition of the god, Damu's mother is a sappy cedar, and he himself may have been seen as so embodied.

32. Gu-edinna "The borderlands of the desert" were fertile strips of land between Girsu, in the Lagash region, and Umma on the edge of the central grasslands. The reference to it and to the yearly sprouting of the grass in the desert suggests that this particular lament comes from Dumuzi-the-shepherd materials.

[amidst the water conduits]
  of the young [anointed ones,]
[in Enegi(r), the city]
  of the young (anointed ones,]
the war[rior Ninazu]
  is laid to rest—
Since in Arali,
  the desert of Bad-Tibira,
[Inanna's] husband
  is laid to rest—
[since in Girsu
  in ["the sheepshearing shed"]
the lad, my Damu
  is laid to rest—
since in Gishbanda
  in "the mountain of laments"
the child Ningishzida
  is laid to rest—
since on "the dike of Tummala,"
  the chariot road,
Ishtaran of bright visage
  is laid to rest—
Since in Gamgamda,
  in Ku'ar's desert,
my [Al]lagula is laid to rest—

Since in the cupbearers' house,
  among the little bronze cups,
Alla, lord of the net,
  is laid to rest—
Since in the street,
  in "the tomb of tears,"
  the constable Lugalshudi
  is laid to rest—
since in the stepped street
  of blind end
Niminur, the frisky bull,
  is laid to rest—
since in Shunagia[33]

270′

280′

33. The name of this village can be translated either as "returned into his hands" or as "returned unto her hand". This latter meaning is what the wailer accepts, and it leads in the next lines to a play between her bracelet, a "roaring aurochs" bracelet, and the epithet "aurochs" for a shepherd, here apparently the dead god. "Roaring aurochs bracelets," apparently bracelets shaped like, or decorated with, aurochses, are referred to also elsewhere in descriptions of feminine ornaments.

my roaring aurochs bracelet,
the great aurochs, Lugalirra,
    is laid to rest—
since in Kushab,
    the place of their leader,
Malaka, king of warriors,
    is laid to rest—

(lacuna of unknown length)

Since in Anshan,
    in its impenetrable highland,
lord Ibbi-Suen
    is laid to rest—
Since in Isin
    in . . . . (?)—
the warrior Ishbi-Erra
    is laid to rest—

(lacuna of unknown length)

Since in a tomb
    in the place of the kings
lord Iddin-Dagan
    is laid to rest—
Since in the orchard
    he himself planted
the shepherd Ishme-Dagan   290'
    is laid to rest—
since in the orchard
    he himself planted
the shepherd Lipit-Eshtar
    is laid to rest—
since at "the impresser of the seal,"
    his place of deliberating,
the shepherd Ur-Ninurta
    is laid to rest—
since on a comfortable bed
    in the kings' plot
the shepherd Bûr-Suen
    is laid to rest—
since in [. . . . .]
    the mountain of tears
[the . . . . Sams]uditana
    is laid to rest—

since in [. . . .]
the place of calming the heart
[. . . . .]-*shi-ilu*   300′
is laid to rest—
since in [. . . . . .]
a faraway place
[. . . . .]
is laid to rest—

(fifteen fragmentary lines before a lacuna of unknown length)

(OB version)

DAMU ASKS THAT
A KIND OF RED
TUBER, WHICH
IS HIS BLOOD
SPILT WHEN HE
WAS KILLED, BE
DUG UP AND
BEER BREWED
FROM IT SO
HE CAN DRINK
IT BACK

"(part) of what you must have handed
    to the earth,
of what you must have handed
    over,
O lad, of what you must have handed
    to the desert,
Alas lad! Lad, my Damu!
Alas lad! Child Ningishzida!
Alas lad! Ishtaran
    of bright visage!—
what you handed out there
    to the desert,
was your precious, precious blood!"[34]

THE SON

"O mother of my leech,   320′
    and mother of Gilgamesh,
dig it up for me,
    dig up my blood for me,
    the which you are to chop up;
mine, a (mere) lad's, blood
    you will take upon yourself
    to chop up,
    the blood(-tubers)
    you will take upon yourself
    to chop up.
May my breweress not chop it up
    with her hand for me
    on split reeds,

34. A certain unidentified tuber was apparently thought to represent the clotted blood of the god which was spilt on the ground when he was killed. It appears to have been used, chopped up, in the brewing of beer. Whether the beer thus brewed was of a special kind or a more general one is not clear. There was a kind of beer, undoubtedly a dark beer, that was called "blood"(*dāmu*).

> may she, like my mother, chop
>   on a mat for me
>   what is brought!
> As she would my father-in-law,
>   may the daughter-in-law
>   be disposed to heed me!
> Let me bring the blood(-tubers)
>   to my mother
>   and may she set up
>   the *itinbu* for me.[35]
> Let me bring them
>   to my little sister,
>   and may she brew
>   their beer for me!
> After I have drunk and drunk
>   that beer,
>   may its cheer
>   warm me.

HE COMPLAINS
OF THE UNDE-
SERVED KILL-
ING OF HIM
TO HIS MOTHER

> "The which—O my mother—
>   was not that
>   of an enemy
>   the which—O my mother—
>   was not that of an enemy,
> my neck when he had cut it,   330'
>   the which—O my mother—
>   was not that of an enemy.
> and my hands hurt,
>   and my feet hurt,
>   the which—O my mother—
>   were not those of an enemy,
> and my back hurts,
>   the which—O my mother—
>   was not that of an enemy."[27]

(DIALOGUE WITH THE SISTER)

THE MOTHER'S
ACTIONS TRYING
TO WARD OFF
EVIL FROM HER
SON MAKES HIS
SISTER APPRE-
HENSIVE

> "Let me run around in the city
>   (asking:) 'What, what has been done
>   unto the lad,
> my calf of sturdy horns, Ningishzida?
>   What has been done
>   unto the lad?'
> My mother is hailing him

35. It is not known what the *itinbu* was.

toward the foundations of heaven,
    toward the foundations of earth,
Woe! Toward the foundations of heaven!
    Woe! Toward the foundations of earth!
    She is hailing him!"[36]

NARRATOR
    The mother, keening in the desert,
        is purifying him there,
        is purifying him
        on the broad earth!

DIALOGUE BE-
TWEEN BROTHER
AND SISTER; WITH
HIS DEATH THE MILI-
TARY AUTHORI-
TIES REASSIGN
HIS HOUSE,
LEAVING HIS
MOTHER AND SIS-
TER HOMELESS
AND DESTITUTE
    "Under [the dire fate]
        that has been determined for you
        be firm, O my sister!
    It has been filled for you
        [into our hands.]
    Be firm, my sister!
    Be firm, my sister!
    Under that which has been filled   340'
        into our hands for you,
        be firm, my sister!"

SISTER
    "Let me set out!
        A sister always goes
        to be with the provider!
    O lad, let me set out!
        A sister always goes
        to be with the provider!"[37]

BROTHER
    "As for you,
        have you a provider still?
        have you a house still?
    Sister, I worry about you"

SISTER
    "As for the mother who bore you,
        and your dwelling,
        through (the rule) that
        dwellings must be relocated,
    your mother who bore you
        is waking up hungry[38]
        hunger makes *me* get up."

36. Not knowing where her son's spirit may be, she directs her blessing everywhere.
37. A double line here suggests a possible ancient omission of a portion of the text.
38. The houses and fields of the people of the army were not owned by them but were held as fiefs.
The owner was the crown, and when a soldier died his house and fields would be assigned to someone

BROTHER

"In my place the city
   has set up lament for me,
   my household (?)
   is destroyed,
my household,
   the evildoer, the ranger,
   let them not dwell with me,
the ones who weep for me
   in my city and chapel (?)—
   he lets them not dwell with me!"[37]

THE MOTHER
SPEAKS; SHE IS
DETERMINED TO
JOIN HER SON
IN HADES AND
CARE FOR HIM
THERE

"Alas lad! Lad about to enter prison,
   the pri[son (of) Ha]des,
. . . .   350'
of no sunset, of no sunrise,
with men who are to be replaced,
with such as cannot hold back
   tears in the heart,
Come! You for your part
   shall lie down
   in my motherly lap!"

NARRATOR

She goes,
   feels urged to go
   to the lad, their provider.

MOTHER

"Come! When I lay me down,
   let me lie down
   in your chamber!"

SON

"Come! I, a captive,
   shall for my part
   lie down in the lap
   of my mother who bore me!"

MOTHER

"On the doorstep of his door
   let me wake them
   to open up!"

SON

"Come! I, a captive,

---

else. Here, as also in "The Mother's Search," the mythology surrounding the god is sociomorph, reflecting the world of the half-free soldier and worker teams of the crown.

   The words translated "hungry" and "hunger" mean literally "thirsty" and "thirst". They convey the dire need of the Mother and Sister. We have translated "hungry" and "hunger" since in English these words, rather than "thirst," are used to symbolize general need.

shall for my part
lie down in the lap
of the mother who bore me!"

ON HER WAY "Standing by in the [deser]t,
THE MOTHER standing by in the desert,
SEES A LEECH O leech standing by
STANDING AT in the high desert,
THE ROAD- [leech, what concern of mine] are you?
SIDE IN THE What has happened
DESERT. SHE on the road
SUSPECTS AN of concern to you?
ACCIDENT [Leech standing by in the desert]
AND FEARS IT what concern of mine are you?
MAY BE SOME- [Leech standing by in the high desert,] 360'
ONE CLOSE TO [what has] happened
HER [on the road]
[of concern to you!"]

(long lacuna. The death of the sister could conceivably have been told here.)

. . . . [. . . . .³⁷]

END OF A LAMENT "Woe the slain one! Alas, the shepherd!
FOR DUMUZI BY Alas, the shepherd!
HIS MOTHER Alas, the lad, the lad, my Damu!
Alas, the lad, the child Ningishzida!
My son who was not
restored to his barracks,
my one . . . . ed into the envoys
by the chief herdsman."³⁷

DUMUZI GREETS "O my sister who for your part
HIS SISTER, WHO must also be a mother to me,
JOINS HIM IN Mother Geshtin, who for your part
HADES must also be a mother to me,
tears like a child I am weeping,
sobs like a child I sob to you!"

SISTER'S "O my brother 370'
LOVING REPLY of luxuriant face,
of lush face,³⁹
who is your sister?
I, I am your sister!

39. The reference would seem to be to the god's beard.

> Who is your mother?
>> I, I am your mother!
> The day that dawns for you,
>> will also dawn for me,
> the day you see, I shall also see."

(one unintelligible line)[37]

(perhaps part of a final song)

>> . . . .
>> . . . . [the lad on the chariot road] . . does . . . .
> Ishtaran of bright visage
>> on the chariot road (?)
>> does . . . .
> The lad rests his pinioned arms   380'
>> in the maiden's lap,
> Alla, owner of the net,
>> rests his pinioned arms
>> in the maiden's lap.
> The lad weeps
>> at the place of the foothills,
> the constable Lugalshudi
>> weeps at the place of the foothills,
> The lad at the place on the road
>> where they finished with him
>> [does . . . .]
> My Lusiranna,
>> at the place on the road
>> where they finished with him
>> [does . . . .]
>> . . . .

PART TWO
Royal Love Songs

A great body of courtly literature from the archives of the Third Dynasty of Ur made its way into the school curriculum of the Sumerian schools of the times of the dynasties of Isin and Larsa that succeeded it. Here belong royal hymns to the kings of Ur, highly polished administrative and political correspondence from the chancellery, and much more. Most surprising in this literary heritage is perhaps a collection of love songs—if one may take the words in their broader sense—most of which are directed to the fourth king of the dynasty, Shu-Suen. One guesses that this king, or perhaps more likely his queen, had in his entourage a woman poet who enjoyed singing about love and lovemaking, and whose works, since they were cast in the form of praise for the king's beauty and virile prowess, were favorably received and carefully preserved in writing.

The songs are sometimes reasonably realistic in their setting. For the song I call "The First Child," one can easily imagine King Shu-Suen, accompanied by a lord-in-waiting, sitting in a room next to one in which his queen Kubātum is giving birth with the assistance of Shu-Suen's mother, the dowager queen Abī-simtī; also his great relief at hearing his wife's happy hailing of the newborn child. This fits in with the opening address by Shu-Suen praising Kubātum—and with filial deference also his mother—for being now clear of obligation to produce offspring, having proved that she is fertile. She has started a family, which Shu-Suen likens to beginning weaving cloth by placing the warp on the loom; Abī-simtī, mother of a large family, he likens to the clothbeam with its finished cloth. Kubātum then thanks him for gifts he has given her—or perhaps promised—and ends her thanks with a traditional formula for hailing the king. She then, unexpectedly, recommends to him as drinking and bed companion her tapstress Il-ummiya—the name is partly erased—presumably for the period she herself will stay in confinement. The final lines are an address by a man praising Shu-Suen, probably a lord-in-waiting such as the one we imagined kept him company.

The unabashed recommendation of the tapstress and of her physical and intellectual attractions seems a rather uncommon feature in a composition such as this, and one is tempted to assume that it is the fashioner of the song who here takes the opportunity to feature herself. If that is so, Il-ummiya may be assumed to have authored also a great many, if not all, of the rather outspoken love songs to Shu-Suen.

One such song, which could well look like the work of a tapstress, is the bit of low life I have called "Tavern Sketch." The customer's beery propositioning of the tapstress in the song; her pretended anxiety that must be assuaged by the unknown customer swearing he is not an enemy; the archaic oath involving touching the genitals of the one to whom the oath is sworn—here obviously a mere erotic ploy—and her delight in seeing the ploy take effect, expressed in the well-worn metaphors of the apple tree and the pillar of alabaster, all suggests first-hand knowledge—and of the tavern more than of the palace. What role this song may have played at court and on what occasions one may assume it to have been performed is a moot question. Possibly it was seen as a bit of humor, amusing to a king more playboy than king.

Returning to the more realistic features of the love songs, one may point to the song "He Arrives" with its praise that is clearly praise of a king, since it mentions the acclaim of him for beauty in the assembly, his reign, and the work forces he can command to even the roads for him. In a more general way, the songs which presuppose that the beloved is traveling and is eagerly awaited may reflect the frequent travels of the kings of Ur to inspect and to participate in religious festivals in major cities of their kingdom.

The often passionate feelings of love and yearning for union with the beloved which characterizes almost all the songs may reasonably be seen as meant to reflect the love of the queen for her husband; they are hardly likely to celebrate other women's conquest of him. If so, however, poetic license will often have cast the queen in roles which, though well suited for the expression of love and desire, were not consonant with her status as wife and queen. While it is not impossible, of course, given a harem background, that even the frankly erotic "My 'Wool' Being Lettuce" and "Vigorously He Sprouted" may have been meant to express the queen's ardor in terms acceptable to her, one finds it rather more difficult to imagine the queen identifying readily with the girl who sits up waiting for "our son-in-law" to arrive. The term used, "our son-in-law," is a way of saying "my betrothed." It stresses that he has been accepted by her family. It also indicates that she is not yet married, since she would not refer to a husband as "our son-in-law," and her situation is thus quite different from that of the queen. The same difficulty of imagining the queen as speaker of the song meets one in "Love Song to Shu-Suen." Here the singer is a young unmarried girl living in her parents' house and burning to have her lover spend the night with her there. Probably one should take it that the two are thought of as engaged to be married, but even so the permissiveness the girl expects in her parents surprises. Since the girl is unmarried, she is not easily identified with the queen, and even if the song were intended to depict an imaginary scene from the time when Shu-Suen courted her, the suggested attitude of the parents would hardly be acceptable.

Most of the songs, it will be seen, have a rubric marking them as belonging to the cult of, or as dealing with, the goddess Inanna. This, at first glance, may seem odd, since they are thoroughly secular in all their features. If, however, as suggested above, they were meant for the queen, assigning them to Inanna would be fully understandable, for the queen *was* indeed Inanna, as she embodied her yearly in the rite of the sacred marriage.

Love Song to Shu-Suen

Man of my heart, my beloved one,
O! that to make your charms,
   which are sweetness, are honey,
   still more sweet—

Lad of my heart, my beloved one,
O! that to make your charms,
   which are sweetness, are honey,
   still more sweet,

you, my own lord and sergeant at arms
   would march against me!
Man, I would flee from you
   —into the bedroom.

O! that you, my own lord and sergeant at arms
   would march against me!
Lad, I would flee from you
   —into the bedroom.

O! that you would do,
   all the sweet things to me,
my sweet dear one   10
   you bring that which will be honey sweet!

In the bedroom's honey-sweet corner
 let us enjoy over and over
   your charms and sweetnesses!

Lad, o! that you would do
   all the sweet things to me,
my sweet dear one,
   you bring that which will be honey sweet

Man who has become attracted to me,
speak to my mother,
   she would let you!
she has worn down my father.

She knows where you would be happy;
to sleep, man, in our house till morning,
she knows where your heart would rejoice;   20
to sleep, lad, in our house till morning!

When you fell in love with me,
could you but have done, lad
   your sweet thing to me!

O! my lord and good genius,
   my lord and guardian angel,
my Shu-Suen, who does Enlil's
   heart good,

the place where, could you but do
   your sweet thing to me,
where, could you but
   —like honey—
   put in your sweetness!

O squeeze it in there for me!
   as (one would) flour into the
   measuring cup!

O pound and pound it in there for me!
   as (one would) flour into the
   old dry measuring cup!

A dialogue pertaining to Inanna.

As You Let Day Slip By

(gap)

O our son-in-law, as you let day slip by,
O our son-in-law, as you let night fall,
you (now) let the moonlight turn in,
the stars all wane!

O our son-in-law, as you let day slip by,
O our son-in-law, as you let night fall,
as you let the moonlight turn in,
the stars all wane,
I (now) unfasten for you bolt and pure lock
  from the door! Run! Come quickly!

(gap)

There is the (watch on its) round of the wall!   10'
  When the patrol has passed,
O our son-in-law, when the patrol has gone to rest,
seize the twilight by the hand, whatever such
  there (still) be,
they have unleashed daylight!
  Come to our house quickly!

(gap)

He Arrives

QUEEN

"O my one fair of locks!
   Oh my one fair of locks!
Sweet one, tree well grown!
   Oh my one fair of locks!
O my one fair of locks
   —like a date palm!
O my one fair of shaggy neck
   —like the date fibers!

"Man, who for your locks
   are acclaimed in the assembly,
my sweet one, who kisses
   our garment bosoms (in greeting),
lad, who for your locks
   are honored in the assembly,
my brother of handsome visage,
   who kisses our garment bosoms (in greeting)!

"O my lapis lazuli beard!
   O my roped locks!
My one with beard mottled   10
   like a slab of lapis lazuli,
my one with locks arranged ropewise!
You are my turban pin,
   my gold I wear,
my trinket fashioned by
   a cunning craftsman,
my trinket worked on
   by a cunning craftsman!"

SHU-SUEN

"My beloved bride makes my fame appear in all mouths!
As sweet as her words are her private parts,
   and as sweet as her private parts are her words."

(gap)

QUEEN   "Being a . . . .
       you are truly a sweet one to talk with!
      You are truly one producing
       a reign of pleasant days!
      You are truly one establishing   20'
       prime counsel and honest judgment!
      You are truly one establishing
       (in the cult) purity and clean hands!

      "Beloved of Enlil,
      may the heart of your personal god,
       should it become embittered,
       again relax!
      Come with the sun!
       Go with the sun!
      May your personal god
       light the way for you,
      have hod carriers and (pick)axe carriers
       even it for you!"

My "Wool" Being Lettuce

My "wool" being lettuce[1] he will water it,
it being box(-grown) lettuce he will water it
and touch the *dubdub* bird[2] in its hole!

My nurse has worked at me mightily,
has done my "wool" up in a "stag" (arrangement),[3]
has gently combed it,
and is straightening my "May He Come!" (breast-shields).

Let him come! Into my "wool," it being
    the most pleasing of lettuces,
I shall with arousing[4] glances
    induce the brother[5] to enter.
I shall make Shu-Suen—all ready—   10
    show himself a lusty man,
Shu-Suen, to whom my [allure] be without end!
[Shu-Suen, whose allure to me] will [never cha]nge!

(gap of some five lines)

You are truly our lord! You are truly our lord!
Silver wrought with lapis lazuli! You are truly our lord!
You are truly our farmer bringing in much grain!   20'

He being the apple of my eye, being the lure of my heart,
may days of life dawn for him! May Shu-Suen [live long
years!]

A dialogue pertaining to Inanna.

1. Wool and lettuce stand in these songs for pubic hair; watering the lettuce for sexual intercourse.
2. The *dubdub* bird is known, apart from this passage, only from lexical texts. It has not yet been identified. Here its name serves apparently as a sobriquet of the clitoris.
3. What precisely the stag arrangement was is not known.
4. Literally "invigorating," "vitalizing."
5. The terms "brother" and "sister" were used generally as terms of endearment among lovers without implication of actual kinship.

Vigorously He Sprouted

Vigorously he sprouted,
   vigorously he sprouted and sprouted,
   watered it—it being lettuce![1]
In his black garden of the desert bearing much yield
   did my darling of his mother,
my barley stalk full of allure in its furrow,
   water it—it being lettuce,
did my one—a very apple tree bearing fruit at the top—
   water it—it being a garden!

The honey-sweet man, the honey-sweet man,
   was doing sweet (things) to me!
My lord, the honey-sweet man, the godly one,
   my darling of his mother,
his hands honey sweet, his feet honeying,
   was doing sweet (things) to me!
His limbs being sweet, sweet honey,
   he was doing sweet (things) to me!

O my one who of a sudden was doing sweet (things)
   to the whole (insides up) to the navel,
   my darling of his mother,
my desert-honey loins, darling of his mother,   10
   you watered it—it being lettuce!

---

1. Lettuce stands for pubic hair here also. Barley stalk and apple tree are metaphors for the male member.

The First Child

SHU-SUEN
"She is clear: she has given birth![1] She is clear:
    she has given birth!
The queen is clear: she has given birth!
Abī-simtī[2] is clear: she has given birth!
The queen is clear: she has given birth!
My clothbeam which, as it aspired to, made
    a good job of the cloth, my Abī-simtī,
and my warpbeam which, as it aspired to, got
    warp on, my queen Kubātum!"

KUBĀTUM
"O my one (so) seemly of locks, my one
    on whom my eyes are riveted,
    my lord, Shu-Suen,
my one planned by Enlil,
    my Shulgi(r) son!
Because I hailed it, because I hailed it,
    the lord gave me things!
Because I hailed it   10
    with a cry of exultation
    the lord gave me things!
A gold pin and a cylinder seal of lapis lazuli!
    —The lord gave me things!
A gold ring and a ring silver inwrought!
    The lord gave me things!
O lord! Make your gifts full of allure,
    that you may lift your eyes to me!
Shu-Suen! Make your gifts full of allure,
    that you may lift your eyes to me!

1. That is, the queen is cleared of any suspicion that she could not produce offspring.
2. Mother of Shu-Suen, helping Kubātum give birth.

95

[. . . .] lord . . [. . . . .]
[l]or[d . . . .]
[. . . .] . . pleasing . . [. . . . .]
my [. . .] like a boxwood tree . . [. .]
May your city crablike raise its hands in greeting.
O lord Shu-Suen!
May it, like a lion cub
lie down at your feet (saying:)
"It is Shulgi(r)'s son!"

(2 blank lines)

The beer of my [. . .], Il-ummiya, the tapstress,
is sweet!
And her private parts   20
are sweet like her beer
—and her beer *is* sweet!
And her private parts
are sweet like her chatter
—and her beer *is* sweet!
Her bittersweet beer
and her (ordinary) beer are sweet!

LORD-IN   O Shu-Suen, my one with whom I am pleased,
WAITING   my one with whom I am pleased, my one
by whom I am made cheerful ever!
Shu-Suen, my one with whom I am pleased,
my Shu-Suen, beloved of Enlil,
my king, god[3] of his country!

A dialogue pertaining to Baba.

3. The kings of the Third Dynasty of Ur were deified.

Tavern Sketch

THE AMOROUS
TAVERN GUEST
"O my lushest one! My [lush]est one!
    My lushest one!
My most alluring one! [My m]ost alluring one!
    Mother's little honeybun![1]
My juicy chick-pea! My one who is father's "honey,"
    mother's little honeybun!
The glance from your eyes is sweet to me,
    quickly say yes, my beloved sister!
The chitchat of your mouth is sweet to me,
    mother's little honeybun!
The kiss on the chest of your greeting is sweet to me,
    —quickly say yes, my beloved sister!

"My lady! The beer from your grain does one good,
    mother's little honeybun,
the strength and glow from your wort does one good,
    —quickly say yes, my beloved sister!
In the house, desire for you so[on began to consume me,]
    mother's little honeybun,
My sister, desire for you [soon began to consume me,]   10
    [—quickly say yes,] my beloved [sister!]
Your house [is] an honest house, [may it pros]per,
    mother's little honeybun!
You [are] a (very) princess—quickly say yes,
    my beloved sister!"

TAPSTRESS
"You must swear to me that you live,
    that you live—

1. The translation given is rather free. Literally, the term means "my (one who is the) honeyed mouth of her mother who bore her" that is, whose childish chatter seems sweet as honey to her adoring mother. The term is clearly banal in the extreme, but is one the customer, in drunken sentimentality, might be likely to use.

Brother, you must swear to me,
       that it is just that you live in an outlying town.
You must swear to me that no enemy
       has put the hand in them,
you must swear to me that no enemy
       has brought the mouth [ne]ar to it!
My [letting down] for you
       the thin, exquisite gown,
O my beloved one, man [I am enraptured by,]
[will] set the (manner of) oath [for you,]
       o my brother (so) fair of face,
will set, my brother, the (manner of) oath for you,   20
       o my brother (so) fair of face!
Your right hand be placed
       in my private parts,
your left shall support my head,
and when you have neared
       your mouth to my mouth,
when you hold my lip in your teeth,
(then), thus you must swear me the oath![2]
Just so, o you, one (and only one) to (all) women,
my brother (so) fair of face!

"O my budding one, my budding one,
       sweet are your charms!
My budding garden of the apple tree,
       sweet are your charms!
My fruiting garden of the apple tree,
       sweet are your charms!
Dumuzi-Apsû himself,   30
       sweet are your charms!
O my pure pillar, my pure pillar
       sweet are your charms!
Pillar of alabaster set in lapis lazuli
       sweet are your charms!"

A dialogue pertaining to Inanna.

2. Swearing by touching the genitals of the one to whom the oath is sworn is mentioned also in Genesis 24:8–9 and 47:29.

PART THREE

Hymns to Gods

Hymn to Enlil

The hymn to Enlil here translated shows him—unlike the many addresses to him found in laments—predominantly as a benefactor of man and all life on earth.

The hymn begins with a description of his innate authority and power, which make the other gods recognize him as their lord and master. Next it tells how Enlil chose Nippur as his abode, and the sacred character of the city is stated, its quick and unrelenting retribution of all forms of evil or disrespect stressed. To ensure a firm basis for the authority structure in the family the citizens built the temple Ekur. Apparently, support of that structure was one of the magic powers that this temple was thought to exercise.[1] The cult and cult personnel of the temple is then dealt with. The latter includes the ruling king, who holds office as the "farmer" of the temple and its lands.

At this point the hymn briefly changes from description into a direct address to Enlil praising Ekur and its various parts and ending with a plea for victory for the king, with extension of his realm. After that comes a detailed description of Enlil himself and the superhuman intelligence with which he administers the world. His all-embracing powers are listed; without him nothing could take place. His orders are the very structure that upholds the cosmos.

In a last song Enlil's consort Ninlil is then hymned as a partner in his decisions, and with the standard line of praise for Enlil the hymn comes to an end.

ENLIL'S PRE-
EMINENCE
RECOGNIZED

Enlil—his orders august
    into the far yonder,
    his words holy,
his unalterable utterances
    decisive
    into the far future,
his lifting up the eyes
    taking in the mountains,

---

1. Cf. "The Cursing of Akkadê," n. 13.

his raising of eyebeams
   scanning the highland's heart—

Father Enlil—as he sat broad
   on a holy throne dais,
   an august throne dais,
as Nunamnir[2] was realizing
   lordliness
   and princeliness
   to perfection—
Heaven and Earth
   bowed of themselves
   down to him,
and all the gods of high descent
   humbled themselves before him,
loyally awaited for their part
   instructions.

HE CHOSE   The lord, great, outstanding,   10
NIPPUR   surpassing in heaven and earth,
AS SEAT   knowing counselor, wise,
of broad intelligence
   sat down in Duranki.[3]
In response, a building socle, Kiur,
   emanated of itself
   princeliness,
and in Nippur,
   heaven and earth's
   august leader-goat,[4]
he built an abode.

NIPPUR   The front of the city
A HOLY CITY   was dread nimbus and halo,
its sides the soaring,
   impenetrable heavens,
its interior the cutting edge
   of a pointed dagger.
It was a trap to rebel regions,
   a pitfall, a net wielded.[5]

2. An epithet of Enlil.
3. A name for the sacred district of Nippur around Ekur, or for part of it.
4. Goats were used to lead flocks of sheep owing to their greater intelligence.
5. The Sumerian fishermen—as Iraqi fishermen nowadays—whirled their nets horizontally in the air like a lasso and let the net fall from there down over the fish. The same technique was presumably

Not long was its blusterer living in it,
nor speaking aggressive words
    to start lawsuits.

None who dissembled,   20
    spoke not straight,
denied what he had said,
    was hostile, framed (people),
ensnared, was wicked,
    committed outrages;
(none) who looked (furtively) away,
    tricked, denounced,
acted high-handedly, bullied,
    was puffed up, or was lording it,
—abominations to the city—
    was walking in it.

Nippur's borders formed a great net,
inside it an eagle
    was spreading knees (to strike).[6]
Aggressors and evildoers
    escaped not its claws.
Justice was granted the city as a gift,
observance of truthfulness and righteousness,   30
    as ornament;
(holiday)-clean clothes
    were upon the quay.

IT BUILT
ENLIL A
TEMPLE

So that a younger brother
    honor the older brother,
    and *he* would act considerately,
that a father's word be heeded,
    and *he* make return
    for the reverence,
that a child humbly mind its mother,
    and she prolong
    (her) parental protection,
had the city, being Enlil's holy precinct,
had Nippur, being father Kurgal's[7]
    beloved temple close,

---

used by retiarii, warriors armed with nets, who were still remembered in literature and myth, even
though they may early have become outdated for actual warfare.

    6. An eagle strikes with both legs stretched forward, the knees apart, the talons open.

    7. The term means "great mountain." The origins and basic implications of this favored epithet of
Enlil are still to be clarified.

for its part raised up, out of loose soil,
   the dais of plenty,
   the lustrous house, Ekur,
and made it grow in a pure spot
   like a lofty mountain;
and its prince,
   the great mountain, father Enlil,
had sat down on the throne dais   40
   of the august manor,
   Ekur.

EKUR, ITS   The house's sacred offices
SACRED   were an unshatterable heaven,
OFFICES AND   its pure rites of handwashing
OFFICIANTS   unceasing like earth,
                 its sacred offices, offices of the Apsû[8]
                   for no man to see.
                 Its interior was the wide sea,
                   the unknown borders of heaven;[9]
                 amid the spreading reed uprights[10]
                   of the brick mantle,
                 the offering-table arrangements
                   and ancient sacred offices
                   were carried out to perfection.

Its incantations were blessings,
its spells words of prayer,
its words auspicious *kledon*-portents
   allotting (fortune) to (people) outside.[11]

Its cult was one involving precious things,   50
festivals laden with butter and cream,
   replete with plenty,
its schedule delight and joy of heart,
   its counsel (counsel) of great things,

8. The expanse of fresh water thought to underlie the earth. Because of the cleansing power of water, the rites of the Apsû stood for ritual purity in the highest degree.

9. The vast expanse of the temple makes it comparable to the sea with its far-off borders at the horizon, where heaven and earth meet.

10. The terrace formed by the upper edge of the brick mantle (*kisû*) was regularly lined with a fence of reed-bundle uprights, as shown by the Sumerian ideogram for it, which means "place where reed-bundle uprights are implanted."

11. A *kledon* portent is a word or statement accidentally overheard that is taken as an omen. People passing the temple will overhear words of good omen from inside it.

at evening festival,
  at morn great harvest.

The house of Enlil
  was a mountain of plenty,[12]
but he who stretched out the hand (greedily),
  was frowned upon,
  and he who stretched it out threatening
  was an abomination to it.
The *en*-priest[13] of the house
  was a diviner
its *lagar*-priest[14] truly perfect
  for blessing,
its font and the anointed ones
  fit for (administering)
  the handwashing rites,
its *nuesh*-priests[15] were perfect
  for the holy chalices,
its august farmer was
  the country's good shepherd.[16]
Born hale on an auspicious day,
the farmer was truly perfect
  for the broad acres,
and they for their part brought to him
  what pertains to great regular offerings,
but their plow teams he let not walk
  in the lustrous house, Ekur.

60

ENLIL
ADDRESSED

Enlil, to match that in your holy tract
  traced by you on the ground
you had built Nippur
  your own city,
you founded in Duranki
  in the center of the universe

12. A play on the name of the temple Ekur, i.e., "house (that is a) mountain."

13. Nippur seems to differ from other cult centers by having a male *en*-priest in a temple for a male god. Normally a god had a female *en*-priestess, an *entu*, while a goddess had a male *en*-priest. In the rite of the sacred marriage the *en* functioned as bride or bridegroom of the deity. Possibly in Nippur the *en* embodied Enlil, and the *en*'s wife, Ninlil, but that must remain purely conjectural.

14. The *lagar* ranks second in the hierarchy. The title is a variant of a word for servant (*labar*), and the *lagar* may originally have served the god generally in that capacity. In historical times, however, he seems to have functioned specifically as lamentation priest.

15. The duties of the office of the *nuesh* are not known. To judge from this passage, he could serve as divine cupbearer.

16. That is to say, the king.

Kiur, which graces
    your virgin mountain.

Its soil is the life's breath of the country,
    the life's breath of all lands.
Its brickwork—ruddy gold[17]   70
    on a foundation laid on lapis lazuli—
is tossing like an aurochs
    widely splayed horns in Sumer,
will lock horns with all lands.
At its great festivals
    the people are spending the day
    beside it amid plenty.

EKUR'S HOLY   Enlil, your holy secret premises
OF HOLIES   imbued with allure,
your font grandly fit
    for the holy throne dais,
your mountain top
    and sacred holy of holies,
    the place where you relax,
your Ekur, the pure house,
    the august abode,
    imbued with awesome nimbus—
its nimbus and halo
    bear against heaven,
its shadow for its part
    lies stretched over all lands,
its crest for its part   80
    recedes into the midst of heaven
—all lords, and all dwellers
    on throne daises,
send in to it straight
    the holy contributions,
are deferring to him
    in salutations and prayers.

THE KING   Enlil, unto the shepherd
    kindly regarded by you,
duly called and raised to office
    in the country by you,
lands to his hands, lands to his feet

---

17. The comparison is with the yellow clay of the bricks.

submit to him far and wide
   in the highlands.
In layers like snow,
   things from all the world,
greeting gifts, their heavy tribute,
he has arrive in the storehouse;   90
the regular offerings he sends straight
   to the main courtyard,
brings them in heaps (!?)
   into the lustrous house Ekur.

ENLIL
DESCRIBED
   Enlil, the good shepherd
   of (herds) multiplying
      one like the other,
the herdsman and leader
   of all in which is breath of life,
exercises his great princely office
   awe-inspiringly,
has the holy verdant crest-crown
   green.[18]
Having occupied the throne dais
   on (his stage tower) Imhursaǧ,
he (then), like the rainbow,
   for his part encircles heaven,
goes like a floating cloud
   in its awesome nimbus.[19]

He is the one prince of heaven,   100
   the monarch of earth,
august, tutelary god
   of the gods of high descent.
Accordingly he makes decisions
   by himself—
no god looks on.
His grand vizier, Nusku,
   leader of the assembly,

18. As god of "growing weather" and fecundity in nature, Enlil wore a crown into which a—presumably fresh and green—sprig of a tree or plant was set. See, e.g., the representation of him on the plaque in Hilprecht, *The Babylonian Expedition of the University of Pennsylvania,* Series A, 1/2, pl. *xvi,* no. 37. A similar crown—with a branch of a date palm (?)—was worn by the *en,* also as emblem of his powers for fertility. Cf. below "Enmerkar and the Lord of Aratta" n. 14, and note the headdress with palm fronds worn by the "figure aux plumes" from Tello.

19. The reference here is probably to Enlil as storm, the storm cloud encircling heaven, i.e., covering it from its base to its top.

can know and discuss with him
his commands and the matters
    that are in his heart—
most widely he will take
    directives for him,
salutes him (in parting)
    with a holy chalice in holy office.

ENLIL'S
COSMIC
POWERS

Without (warrant of) the great mountain, Enlil,
no city could be built,   110
    no population settled therein,
no byre built, its sheepfold not set up.
No king could be raised to office,
    no lord installed,
no high priest or high priestess
    designated by the (omen-)kid,[20]
no general or lieutenant
    could be had by the army.
The waters of the carp-flood[21] at its height
    could not dredge the canals,
the (flood arriving) after it,
    would tend to break out (from the bed),
    could not go straight,
    not extend (by scouring)
    the far reaches (of the canals).
The sea could not give birth
    to the heavy souther with its rain,
the freshwater fish could not spawn
    in the canebrake,
the birds of heaven not base their nests
    on the broad earth.

In the sky the rain-laden clouds   120
    could not open their mouths,
in the fields the tilth could not sprout
    the mottled barley;

---

20. "High priest" and "high priestess" here translate Sumerian *en*. The selection of a person to fill that high office was done by means of liver omina, the divine decision being indicated by the shape of the sacrificial kid's liver.

21. A term for the early flood, so called because carp in great numbers swam into and up the rivers at that time of year.

in the desert, its verdant spots
    could not let grass and herbs grow
in the orchards, the broad trees of the mountains
    could not bear fruit.
Without (warrant of) the great mountain, Enlil,
(the birth-goddess) Nintur
    could not let die (at birth), could not slay;
the cow could not lose
    its calf in the cattle pen,
the ewe not bring forth
    a premature lamb in its sheepfold.
The wildlife, grown numerous by itself,
could not lie down in their lairs
    or (settle on) their perches,
the (wild) goats and asses, the four-legged beasts,   130
    could not be fertile,
    could not (even) copulate.

Enlil, by your skillful planning
    in intricate designs—
their inner workings a blur of threads
    not to be unraveled,
thread entwined in thread,
    not to be traced by the eye—
you excel in your task of divine providence.
Your are your own counselor,
    adviser, and manager,
who (else) could comprehend what you do?
Your tasks are tasks that are not apparent,
your guise (that of) a god,
    invisible to the eye;
you are lord An and king Enlil (in one),
judge and decision maker   140
    for (both) heaven and earth,
you know no rescinder of your great decrees,
    they being as respected as is An,
to (hear) your words
    the gods of high descent
    undergo lustration.

ENLIL'S WORD   Your word is upward a stanchion,
CREATES FER-   downward a foundation terrace,
TILITY   upward a great stanchion
      bracing the heavens,

downward a foundation terrace
  not to be shattered.
When it has drawn near unto heaven
  it is abundance,
from heaven abundance rains down,
When it has drawn near unto earth
  it is verdant freshness:
from the earth verdure grows up.
Your word is vines, your word is grain.   150
Your word is the carp-flood,
  life's breath of all lands,
all things in which is breath of life,
  things that have come up out of the ground,
breathe in at it (fragrance of) grass and herbs,
  sweet breaths.
Enlil, you are the good shepherd,
  you know how to herd them,
they are having sweet, pleasant times
  under the speckled stars.

NINLIL   Ninlil, dreamt of, glowing bride,
imposing of countenance
  and radiant looks,
  whose stature and form
  are shapely to match,
is the fair woman
  whom you married at sight,
the allure of Ekur,
  the queen worthy of you.

In advising she finds the perfect word,   160
her word, her assuagement,
  is the heart's juniper perfume.
She, for her part too, dwells with you
  on a holy throne dais
  next to the pure throne dais,
advises with you, ponders with you,
makes with you the decisions
  at the (court held at the) place of sunrise.
Ninlil, queen of heaven and earth,
  queen of all lands,
honored in the praise hymns
  to "the great mountain,"

preeminent, making good
    her promises.
Her orders and aid (being) unalterable,
her utterance takes precedence,
her designs making the promise   170
    come true.

Great mountain Enlil,
    your praise is august!

Hymn to Inanna as Warrior, Star, and Bride

This hymn was apparently written under Iddin-Dagan, the third king of the dynasty of Isin, for he is mentioned by name in it. It may even be that it was meant for use at the yearly rite of the sacred marriage in which the king took on the identity of the god Ama-ushumgal-anna and as such married Inanna, who was almost certainly incarnated in the reigning queen, as shown by the epithet Nin-egala(k), "queen of the palace," by which she is called in connection with this rite.

The hymn opens with an address to the goddess as morning and evening star followed, in a second canto, by a statement of her powers of office in heaven, on earth, and in the Apsû. From these introductory matters the hymn then moves, with the third canto, into a description of a monthly ritual victory parade in her honor, celebrating her as warrior and goddess of war.

The parade is made up of cult personnel in her service and groups of guards, both of these groups representing warriors and acting out war games in which they cut themselves and each other with knives. In the parade march also young men in neck stocks representing captives, and young and old women who have curled their hair like harlots. They may represent camp followers or women whose providers have fallen in battle and who have had to turn harlots to survive. Beside the parade, or possibly as part of it, march solid citizens of the town, carrying harps and other implements designed to soothe and pacify the goddess.

The end of the sixth canto leads into a new section praising the goddess in her manifestation as the evening star; as such she marks the end of the workday and the quieting down and going to rest of all, men and animals alike. As they sleep, their dream souls appear before her with their requests, and Inanna discerns who is good, who evil.

With the ninth canto the hymn changes its image of the goddess from evening to morning star, and describes the morning offerings to her by people everywhere. Finally, with the tenth canto she is celebrated as the bride in the new year rite of the sacred marriage, in which the king—here Iddin-Dagan—incarnates the bridegroom, Ama-ushumgal-anna, and she, as mentioned, in all likelihood is embodied in the queen. The preparations for the wedding are described, the setting up and readying of the wedding bed, the bride's pre-nuptial bath, the consummation of the marriage, and the magnificent wedding banquet the next morning.

The hymn closes with an envoi with repeated praise of the goddess ending "Great she is, and august, in heroism surpassing."

PROEM: The one come forth on high,
STAR-RISE   the one come forth on high,
              I will hail!
          The [h]oly one,[1] come forth on high,
              I will hail!
          The great [queen] of heaven,
              Inanna,
              I will hail!
          The pure torch lit in the sky,
          the heavenly light, lighting like day,
          the great queen of heaven, Inanna,
              I will hail!
          The holy one,
              queen awe-laden
              of the Anunnaki,
          noblest one in heaven and earth,
              crowned with great horns,[2]
          oldest child of the Moon,[3]
              Inanna,
              I will hail!

          Of her grandeur, of her greatness,   10
              of her exceeding nobility,
          of her brilliant coming forth
              in the evening sky,
          of her lighting up in the sky,
              a pure torch,
          of her stepping up onto the sky
              like Moon and Sun,
          noted by all lands from south to north,
          of the greatness of the holy one of heaven,
          to the young lady I will sing!

1. The Sumerian term is *nu-gig*. See n. 9 to "The New House."
2. The horned crown was an emblem of divinity.
3. The text treats the moon as divine, as the moon god ᵈSuen. We translate "Moon" to retain the cosmic implications. Similarly we render ᵈ*Utu* as "Sun."

(FIRST PLACE OF COUNTERING)[4]

> "Her coming forth is (that of) a warrior"

(is its antiphon)

POWERS OF
OFFICE

She likes wandering in the sky,   20
    being truly Heaven's wild cow,
on earth she is noble, queen of all lands,
in the Deep,[5] in Eridu, she took office,
her father Enki conferred it on her,
laid to her hand lordship and kingship.
With An she has taken her seat
    on the great throne dais,
with Enlil she will be making
    the decisions for her country.
Monthly, at new moon,
    that the offices be carried out properly,
the country's gods gather unto her.
The great Anunnaki, having bowed to her,
are stepping up for prayer, petition, and plaint,   30
able to voice unto her
    the pleas of all lands,
and Milady decides the country's cases,
    settling them.
[Inanna] makes the decisions
    for the country,
    having them carried out.
The dark-headed people[6]
    are parading before her.

4. The cantos of the composition are—as usual with Sumerian antiphonal works—marked off by the rubric "place of countering," and the countering antiphon that follows has at the end the rubric "is its antiphon." In this composition antiphons are specifically indicated only after the first and the eighth cantos. Presumably that means that the first antiphon was to be repeated after each successive canto until, with the eighth canto, the second antiphon replaced it and served to the end.

5. The deep, Apsû, refers to the freshwater ocean which the ancients thought underlay the earth, thus forming a triad with the heaven and earth of the preceding lines. It was the domain of Enki, who resided in Eridu, and it came to the surface there in Enki's temple and the nearby marshes. A separate myth tells how Inanna received her offices from Enki in Eridu by taking advantage of his generosity when he was in his cups.

6. The Sumerians referred to themselves as "the dark-headed people." Why, and in contrast to whom, is not known.

(SECOND PLACE OF COUNTERING)

WARRIOR: MONTHLY
RITUAL TRIUM-
PHAL PARADE

Algar-instruments,[7] silver inwrought,
   they are beating for her,
—before holy Inanna, before her eyes,
   they are parading—
The great queen of heaven, Inanna,
   I will hail!
Holy tambourines and holy kettledrums
   they are beating for her,
—before holy Inanna, before her eyes,   40
   they are parading—
The great queen of heaven, Inanna,
   I will hail!
Holy harps and holy kettledrums
   they are smiting for her,
—before holy Inanna, before her eyes,
   they are parading—
The oldest child of the Moon,
   Inanna,
   I will hail!

(THIRD PLACE OF COUNTERING)

The guardsmen[8] have combed
   (their hair) for her,
—before holy Inanna, before her eyes
   they are parading—
they have made colorful for her
   the back hair with colored ribbons,
—before holy Inanna, before her eyes
   they are parading—
on their bodies are (sheep)skin (robes)   50
   (the dress) of divinities,[9]
—before holy Inanna, before her eyes,
   they are parading—

7. A musical instrument, most likely a small harp with the sides of the sound box covered with drumheads.

8. The term translated "guardsmen" is the Sumerian *saĝ-ursaĝ*, which denotes a class of cult personnel in the service of Inanna. Originally apparently a corps of warriors, they developed into actors in ritual performances such as the one here.

9. The precise meaning of this is not clear. Conceivably by the time the poem was written the old sheepskin mantles, were no longer in common use but were still shown on representations of gods.

Fine men, eminent ladies,
   the doyenne of the women sages,
—before holy Inanna, before her eyes
   they are parading—
who hold harps and calming instruments,
   march beside them.
—Before holy Inanna, before her eyes,
   they are parading

They (themselves) are girt
   with implements of battle,
—before holy Inanna, before her eyes,
   they are parading—
spears, the arms of battle,
   are in their hands,
—before holy Inanna, before her eyes,
   they are parading

(FOURTH PLACE OF COUNTERING)   60

Their right arms are clothed with cloth
   in male fashion,[10]
—before holy Inanna, before her eyes
   they are parading—
the great queen of heaven, Inanna,
   I will hail!
On their left arms they have pulled
   the cloth down and off
—before holy Inanna, before her eyes   63a
   they are parading—
the great queen of heaven, Inanna,   63b
   I will hail!
Playfully, with painted buttocks,
   they engage in single combat
—before holy Inanna, before her eyes,
   they are parading—
the oldest child of the Moon,
   Inanna,
   I will hail!

10. This is a reversal of normal usage. Both men and women covered the left shoulder; women also frequently kept both shoulders covered. Leaving the right arm and shoulder bare gave the right arm needed freedom. The significance of the reversal here described is not clear.

(FIFTH PLACE OF COUNTERING)

> (Captive) lads in neck stocks
>   bewail to her (their fate)
> —before holy Inanna, before her eyes,
>   they are parading—
> maidens and crones, curling the(ir) hair (as harlots)   70
> —before holy Inanna, before her eyes,
>   they are parading—
> daggers and clubs rage before her
> —before holy Inanna, before her eyes
>   they are parading—
> the *kurgarûs*[11] mounted (on chariots),
>   swing the clubs
> —before holy Inanna, before her eyes,
>   they are parading—
> gore is covering the daggers,
>   blood sprinkles,
> —before holy Inanna, before her eyes,
>   they are parading—
> in the courtyard, the (place of) assembly
>   of the temple administrators,[12]
>   they are shedding blood,
> (as) loudly resounds there
> (gay music of) *tigi*-harps, tambourines, and lyres.

INANNA AS
EVENING STAR

> The holy one has seen fit to step up   80
>   lone on the clear sky,
> and on all lands, teaming
>   like the nation's dark-headed people,
> from heaven's midst Milady
>   looks kindly down.
> August is the queen, the evening star, Inanna.
> Fitly (therefore) they praise the maiden Inanna.
> August is the queen, the evening star, Inanna,
>   unto the borders of heaven!

11. The *kurgarûs*, likewise cult personnel, also appear to have been warriors originally. The term may be abbreviated from *kurgugara* "the subjected lands" so that the *kurgarûs* symbolized warriors taken captive.

12. The Sumerian term means he gathering of *ens*". Since *en* basically denotes "productive manager" and since it forms part of the names for a great many professions of workers on an estate, farmer, head of the plowing teams, cook and baker, washermen, etc., we take "the gathering of *ens*" to mean specifically an assembly of administrators in which work plans and other matters relating to the successful functioning of an estate would be discussed and agreed on.

(SIXTH PLACE OF COUNTERING)

NIGHTFALL   The evening star, the brilliantly rising star,
                  shedding great light over holy heaven,
               the queen, the evening star, has seen fit
                  to come forth on high,
                  warrior-like in the sky,
               and in all lands the people
                  are lifting up their faces toward her,
               the man is cheering up, the woman is brightening,   90
               the ox in its yoke is turning the head (homewards),
               sheep and goats (?) (shuffling back)
                  make the dust settle (thick) in their folds.
               The numerous (wild) goats and asses of Shakan,[13]
                  the animals of the desert,
               the far-flung four-footed beasts,
               the orchard pits, the garden beds,
                  the green canebrake,
               the fish of the deep, the birds of heaven,
               Milady is making wend their way
                  to their lairs.
               (All) living beings, the numerous people,
                  are bending (their) knees to her.

               Called by Milady, the old women
               are providing plentifully   100
                  for great eating and drinking.
               (Then) Milady calms down
                  everything in her country,
               the playgrounds of the nation,
                  the holiday makers;
               and the young brave
                  holds converse with the wife
                  heart (to heart).[14]

               From heaven's midst Milady
                  looks kindly down,
               before holy Inanna, before her eyes,
                  they walk—
               August is the queen, the evening star in the sky,
               Inanna.
               Fitly (therefore) they praise the maiden Inanna.

13. God of goats, gazelles, and wild asses.
14. A literary stereotype. The quiet talking the day's events over by husband and wife takes place in bed after the day's work is over, for it is almost the only time they have to themselves.

August is the queen, the evening star in the sky
    unto the borders of heaven!

(SEVENTH PLACE OF COUNTERING)

Preeminent in the (rose-)tinted sky   110
    the alluring one, befitting broad heaven,
has risen like moonlight at night,
has risen like sunlight at high noon.
Having imposed sweet sleep
    on the nation's homes,
—while all lands, the dark-headed ones,
    the nation in its entirety,
sleep on roofs, sleep on city walls—
eloquent dream-soul afflati step up to her,
    bring her their cases.

Then she discerns the righteous one,
    discerns the wicked one.
The wicked one she will hand over
    to (serve) a wicked sentence,
    the evil one she will do evil to.
On the just one she looks truly,
    determines a good fate for him.
From heaven's midst Milady   120
    looks kindly down.
Before holy Inanna, before her eyes,
    they walk.
August is the queen
    hovering where heaven is founded,
    Inanna.
Fitly (therefore) they praise
    the maiden Inanna.
August is the queen
    going (down) where heaven is founded
    unto the borders of heaven!

(EIGHTH PLACE OF COUNTERING)

DAWN:INANNA   The queen preeminent, the alluring one of heaven,
AS MORNING   has seen fit to come out, warrior-like, on high,
STAR   lovely is she at An's[15] radiant side,

---

15. I.e., heaven's.

with An on his august couch
    she holds converse heart (to heart).[16]

"May she be found to be
    the young brave's and the warrior's only one!"

(is its antiphon)   130

She is mighty! She is noble! She is elevated to high rank!
    Great she is and august, surpassing in heroism!

(is what is sung at its middle)

The queen marveled at by the nation,
    the lone star, the morning star,
the queen hovering where heaven is founded,
    has seen fit
        to come forth warrior-like on high,
and all lands do tremble before her.

MORNING   The dark-headed people get up for her,
RITES   the young brave traveling the road
        sets his course by her,
the ox lifts up its head eagerly
    in its yoke.
While at the same time, in the nation's homes
    they provide everything aplenty,
hasten to holy Inanna,   140
and put it out in goodly fashion
    for Milady (up in) heaven's midst.

In the clean places, the clear places
    of the desert,
on the roofs, on the wall-tops,
    [of the dwellers on] wall-tops,
on mankind's smoothed-out spots (for offerings),
they bring her incense
    (fragrant) like a cedar forest.
Fine sheep, maned sheep, and grain-fed sheep
    they offer up.

---

16. The morning star appearing in the sky is seen as the goddess chatting in bed with the god of heaven before getting up. The line may reflect a momentary lapse into a variant theology which saw Inanna as the wife of An rather than of Dumuzi/Ama-ushumgal-anna. We assume that the term *ki-mah*, "high place," later used for sepulcher, originally denoted simply a dais on which one would place one's bedding and sleep. We translate it therefore as "couch."

For the holy one they clean up a place,
    set up handwashing (things) for her.[17]

Ghee, dates, cheese, seven kinds of fruits,
they fill, as breakfast,
    onto the country's table for her.
Dark beer they pour for her,   150
light beer [they pour] for her.
With dark beer and [emmer] beer. . . .
for Milady with (barley) beer and [emmer] beer
shaggubbe-pot[18] and the fermenting vat
    bubble, one as the other.
Of paste, liberally enriched with honey and ghee,
and of honey and dates, on cakes,
    they make loaves for her,
wine at dawn, finely ground flour,
    honeyed flour,
honey and wine at sunrise they libate for her.
The tutelary gods of the humans step, as their part,
    up to her with the food and drink,
and the holy one eats in the pure places,   160
    the clean places.

From heaven's midst Milady
    looks kindly down,
before holy Inanna, before her eyes,
    they wander.
August where heaven is founded,
    is the queen, Inanna.
Fitly (therefore) they praise
    the maiden Inanna.
August is the queen
    hovering where heaven is founded
        unto the borders of heaven!

(NINTH PLACE OF COUNTERING)

NEW YEAR'S SACRED   In the palace,
MARRIAGE: INANNA   the house that advises the country
AS BRIDE   and is a (restraining) yoke[19]
    on all foreign lands,

17. For washing her hands before eating the offerings.
18. Apparently a vessel used in brewing. Its precise character and use are still to be determined.
19. Literally a neck stock.

the house that is the river ordeal[20]
>of the dark-headed people,
>the nation in its entirety,
a dais has been founded for Ninegalla,
the king, being a god, will sojourn with her on it.   170

That she may take in charge
>the life of all lands,
has on New Year's Day,
>the day for rites
for reviewing loyal servants[21]
and performing correctly
>the rites of the last day of the month,
a bed been set up for Milady.
Halfa-straw they have been purifying
>with cedar perfume,
have been putting it on that bed for Milady.
Over it a bedspread has been pulled straight for her,
a bedspread of heart's delight
>to make the bed comfortable.

Milady bathes in water the holy loins,   180
for the loins of the king
>she bathes them in water.
For the loins of Iddin-Dagan
>she bathes them in water.
Holy Inanna rubs (herself) with soap,
sprinkles the floor with cedar perfume.

The king goes with (eagerly) lifted head
>to the holy loins,
goes with (eagerly) lifted head
>to the loins of Inanna.
Ama-ushumgal-anna goes to bed with her:

"O my holy loins! O my holy Inanna!"

After he on the bed, in the holy loins,
>has made the queen rejoice,

---

20. The river ordeal was used as a means to arrive at a divine decision in cases where there was, or could be, no decisive evidence. In metaphoric use, as here, it implies superhuman power to get at the truth and judge rightly.

21. New Year's Day was a day for reviewing the work of the staff of a temple or estate. See below, "The Nanshe Hymn" ll. 94ff.

after he on the bed, in the holy loins   190
    has made holy Inanna rejoice,
she in turn soothes the heart for him
    there on the bed:

"Iddin-Dagan, you are verily
    my beloved!"

WEDDING   To pure libations, lavers set up,
BANQUET   to gently wafted incense vapors,
    to lighted juniper incense,
to food portions standing ready,
    to jars standing ready
into his august palace
    she enters with him.
His loving consort has the arm
    around his shoulders,
holy Inanna has the arm around his shoulders,
shines forth on the arm-lean[22] throne
    like the dawn.
With her radiates there, on the long side of the table,   200
    sunlike the king.
Abundance, delicacies, plenty,
    they bring straight to her,
a banquet of sweet things
    they lay out,
the dark-headed people
    bring it straight to her.
The bard has the lute,
    that gives tongue from the podium,
the sweet-sounding *algar*-instruments,
and the lyre, which belongs
    where mankind is gay,
prove themselves
    in his song of joy of heart.

The king has reached out for food and drink,
Ama-ushumgal-anna has reached out   210
    for food and drink.
The palace is in festive mood,
    the king is joyous,

22. A chair with armrests was comfortable, and so suitable for a throne. Such chairs, used as divine or royal thrones, are often pictured on the monuments.

the nation spends the time amid plenty,
Ama-ushumgal-anna is come in joy,
long may he live on this pure throne!
On the royal throne dais she has
    (her) head on (his) shoulder.

ENVOI

O Milady, you are given praise
    to the borders
    of heaven and earth!
You being a holy one,
    engendered with heaven and earth,
holy passages, pure passages
    for a holy one
    are put in song!
O (you), chief ornament of the night,
befitting the assembly,
Inanna, oldest child of the Moon,
Queen, evening star, to praise you is sweet!   220

(TENTH PLACE OF COUNTERING)

From heaven's midst Milady looks kindly down—
before holy Inanna, before her eyes,
    they walk.
August is the queen, the evening star,
    unto the borders of Heaven!
Mighty she is, noble, elevated to high rank,
    great she is and august,
in heroism surpassing.

(is its antiphon)

A song of valor pertaining to Ninsianna.[23]

23. A name for Inanna as morning and evening Star, it means "heaven's radiant queen."

The Nanshe Hymn

The Nanshe Hymn is a difficult text, and much in it remains obscure, whether due to language difficulties or to our ignorance of life in an ancient temple with its particular set of values and of the common sins against them. The glimpse into that singular world it promises makes it, however, worth the attempt to understand as much of it as one can.[1]

The Hymn begins by telling how Nanshe, who was a native of Eridu, wanted to have a city of her own and how she chose Ninâ, the present Tel Zurghul, in the Lagash region. Ninâ at that time was just an ordinary city. Nanshe gave it cosmic significance by making it the seat of divine offices. She had her temple Siratr built there, and prosperity ensued for the city. Moreover, the weak in the society found a champion in her.

Next Nanshe installed as high priest the famous temple builder Gudea of Lagash, and he set about organizing the temple music, introducing combinations of instruments apparently new. The section about the music is followed by one describing the temple butler's competent handling of the serving of a large banquet, and that in turn is followed by an account of the installation of a woman majordomo who was to oversee the general running of the temple estate and to ensure honest dealing in the various economic activities in which the temple personnel was to engage.

Dispensing of justice is next on the list. It was in the hands of the god Hendursaĝa, who was helped by another, little-known god, Ningublaga, in dealing out punishment. Each new year there was a review of the personnel, undertaken by Nanshe's "secretary," the goddess of writing, Nidaba, and a roster of the servants commended by Nanshe was drawn up by the god of stores, Haya. Drunkards, slatterns, and other offenders were suspended.

A difficult section which now follows seems to deal with the taboo on officials who draw boundaries and with the selection of chants to accompany trial by river ordeal—possibly placed here because use of the ordeal may have figured promi-

---

1. A translation of the hymn much different from the one here attempted was given, with a careful edition of the text, by W. Heimpel in *Journal of Cuneiform Studies* 33/2 (1981). We have benefited from it in many details.

nently in boundary disputes. After that comes a long list of offenses of very varied character, which Nanshe will know about even if they are kept secret, and which, it may be presumed, she will punish. They range from cases of altering boundaries and cheating on weights to cases of mothers cursing their children and children being stubborn.

Hendursağa's rôle in maintaining fairness and justice is elaborated on in the last major section of the hymn. A shorter, following section tells how Nanshe, after she had arranged all of this, consulted the goddess of Lagash, Gatumdug, and was given good advice, how she seated herself on her throne in Siratr, gathering the gods around her, and how she there delegated the task of maintaining honest dealing in her realm to the god Ningishzida and—once more—to Hendursağa. A short envoi, praising her, forms the conclusion.

This résumé of the content of the hym leaves one question unanswered. Which time frame did the ancient author have in mind?

The beginning of the hymn, telling how Nanshe selected Ninâ and had her temple built there, suggests very early, half-mythical times when the gods settled in their cities. Certainly Ninâ and its temple Siratr with its cult of Nanshe go back to the early third millennium and probably much further, even to the first settlement of the country.

Such a dating of what is told in the hymn accords ill, however, with the appointment—as one of her first acts—of Gudea of Lagash as high priest. For Gudea belongs toward the end of the third millennium, and his inscriptions show that Nanshe and Siratr were well established in his days, as does, for times before him, the hymn to Ninâ and Nanshe written by the poetess Enheduanna around 2350 B.C.

The discrepancy is thus glaring, and there is probably only one possible explanation, namely that the author of the hymn wrote at some time after Gudea and, having only the vaguest of notions about when Gudea had lived, saw him already as a semimythical, timeless figure. When that may have been is of course hard to say. Most likely it was some time late in the period of the Third Dynasty of Ur.

ELECTION OF
NINÂ TO
COSMIC
OFFICE

Just a city it was, just a city it was,
    but she felt urged
    to begin envisaging
    its sacred offices.
Ninâ was just a city—
    but she felt urged
    to begin envisaging
    its sacred offices.
The holy city was just a city—
    but she felt urged

to begin envisaging
its sacred offices.
The mountain rising out of the waters[2]
was just a city—
but she felt urged
to begin envisaging
its sacred offices!

She felt urged to have the day
of a proper house
begin dawning,
felt urged to begin determining
its mode of being,
felt urged to have the appropriate brickwork[3]
make an appearance in the city,
felt urged to have the rites of mother Nanshe
begin being carried out right.
Its mistress, child born in Eridu,
Nanshe,
mistress of all the precious sacred offices,
was turning to a place of her (own).

ABUNDANCE
BROUGHT

A very herb mother,   10
a very tree-fruit mother,
Nanshe, a very mother
of all great things,
was able to cause pregnancy
in the country's wombs,[4]
was able to

. . . .
. . . . in the storehouses,
was able to set up jugs
not wanting for water;
and in the country's storehouses
bread baskets
were lined up for Nanshe,
as were they sediment
left by a river.

---

2. When one approaches Zurghul, the sight of the mound rising up over the intervening marshes and lagunas like a small mountain is quite striking.

3. Each temple had bricks of a size and shape proper to it. See n. 77 to Gudea Cylinder A.

4. Literally: "was able to have gravidity be in the country's wombs."

She was queen,
    checking the boundaries, (?)
    checking the fields,
giving advice that carried great weight.
Nanshe was queen,
    opening up irrigation ditches
    and giving irrigation ditches
    greater elevation.

SOCIAL   Waif and widow she delivered not up.   20
JUSTICE   She took note of men
    who used force against men,
    was mother to the waif,
Nanshe was the widow's guardian,
finding (justly) in cases in the millhouse.[5]
The queen carried fugitives on the hip[6]
searched the region for the helpless ones.
For the one pledging a basket to her
    she checked (things) out (?),
for the one pledging a flask of oil
    she obtained profit.
For the honest slave girl
    who had laid hold of her feet,
Nanshe was figuring up
    her warping and justly obtained wages,[7]
for the widow she had not helped to remarry   30
Nanshe was supporting,
    like a beam, a proper house.[8]

GUDEA   The queen had felt urged
INSTALLED   to make the appropriate brickwork appear.
Nanshe (thus) had been able
    to have Lagash spread the hands
    wide on the abundance[9]
She (now) felt urged

---

5. The millhouses in which flour was ground for the large establishments, palace and temple, were staffed with women slaves and their children, and served also as poorhouses for women without means of subsistence. It was inevitable that disputes and conflicts would arise there from time to time.

6. That is, took care of them. The image is that of a mother or nurse carrying a child riding on her hip.

7. That is, the amount of weaving the girl had done and the wage she should be paid for it.

8. The image may be that of a beam used as a pillar to support the roof.

9. The temple, as with temples elsewhere, seems to be credited with magic power to ensure fertility.

to envision in the holy heart
a high priest,[10]
she seated with her on the throne dais
Nanshe's lion,[11]
the beloved high priest of Lagash,
and granted august scepter to the shepherd.

GUDEA'S
MUSICAL
REFORMS

Gudea perfected for her
all her precious sacred offices.
Her shepherd, envisioned in the holy heart,
Gudea, ruler of Lagash.
stationed among the *tigi*[12] strings   40
the princely, sweet sounding, tambourines,
stationed with them holy harps,
and to the holy chants
and the antiphons
he had performed for her
lyres were giving praise unto the house,
whilst out from amid them
a chief musician
was sounding for her
the shofar horn.
Since she had deemed fit
to allot to the house
sacred rites from Apsû,[13]
he sang at its sacred princely rites
the latter's holy chants
in Siratr's courtyard.

SACRED
BANQUETS

A butler stepped up
to the libations for her,
took in hand for her
the sparkling silver goblet;

10. The term used is *shannu*; it denotes a high priest (*en*) in the service of Enki. Nanshe seems to have brought the term along from Eridu.

11. The Sumerian term here used, *ur*, can mean dog, or lion. Since ur-ᵈNanše is said by the ancients to mean "doorkeeper of the palace" we have preferred to translate "lion," since figures of lions were frequently placed at gates as guardians. Gudea of Lagash, to whom the title is here given, was, according to his own inscriptions, also *ur*, "lion," of the goddess Gatumdug.

12. The *tigi* was a musical instrument usually thought to have been a drum. We think it more likely that it was a kind of harp or lyre with the soundbox covered with drumheads and possibly provided with tinkling bells as well.

13. Apsû, the "deep." The freshwater ocean thought to underlie the earth was the domain of Enki, whose temple was in Eridu. It would be natural for her to institute the highly regarded sacred rituals of Eridu in her new city.

                    the butler [poured in]
                        the strong drink for her.
                    Hot dishes and cold dishes   50
                        he was directing up to her.
                    Dough (for) half a loaf
                        he had put in the . . . of the oven for her,
                    and at the first [loaf finished]
                        the chief peel[14] called loudly to him.
                    After what was butchered
                        had been brought in large bowls,
                    after cold water
                        had been brought from Siratr's river,
                    after delicacies
                        had been brought from Lagash
                    and wine[15] brought
                        from the countryside,
                    was—as he (the butler) was having
                        the great oven
                        keep up with the (needs of) the dining halls—
                    Nanshe's pantry
                        humming (right)
                        along with it.

MAJORDOMO   The lady, Enlil's matron,
INSTALLED   Nanshe, lady of abundance   60
FOR GOOD   living in the land,[16]
MANAGEMENT   calming (?) wrath, woman diviner,
                       Enki's daughter,
                   was on her part installing
                       an able woman
                       as majordomo[17]
                       for the properly run house.
                   After she had installed
                       an able woman
                       as majordomo
                       for the properly run house,
                   the daily revenues
                       were sent straightway
                       into the temple

---

14. A peel is a baker whose task it is to remove the baked loaves from the oven with a long shafted shovel.

15. The term used, *kurunnu*, was used also for a superior sort of dark beer ranking with wine.

16. That is, near, approachable, and with a personal interest in the country and its people.

17. The Sumerian term translated as "majordomo" is *lú*, which denotes a man (Akkadian *awīlum*) or woman (Akkadian *awīltum*) who heads a household, firm, or city.

from the *bursag*.[18]
Barley was not used as filler
    in the emmer-beer rations,
water was not poured as thinner
    into the (barley-)beer rations.
When its (the temple's) revenues
    had been brought in
    the majordomo
    was going to accept
    no more than was due.

BUREAUCRATIC   (Smug boasts such as)
CHISELING AND   "chiseled off [the food],"
MEANNESS STOPPED   "chiseled off the drink,"
    "revenue reserve,"
        "discontinued by the temple,"
    "discountable weighing adjustment exacted"   70
        on the fish of the fish-measure (?)
    "canebrake to be measured
        one *iku* from its beginning,"
    "Almond saplings taken
        (bundled)
        among the greens of a garden,"[19]
touched, after she had come along,
    no lips.[20]

PILFERING   Bread of the temple
STOPPED   was not carried into a city quarter
        for (private) food portions,
    the majordomo stood (guard)
        over the prime beer given out,
        (so) no hand was put to the cold water.[21]
    Its (the temple's) established libations
        she set to rights,
        that they cease not.

18. The *bursag* was the receiving point for deliveries to the temple of the various payments in kind due to it from dependent farms. From there the food received was distributed for use in offerings and as rations for the temple personnel.

19. These instances of wrongdoing seem to be those of overzealous temple officials thinking to save the temple expense by paying out less in food rations than due, accepting more in revenue paid in than due, designating the surplus thus exacted as "revenue reserve," discontinuing payments that should have been made, failing to make the adjustment in a fisherman's favor necessary to make up for his using a larger measure of volume than the standard one, and measuring work done in cutting reeds one *iku* short. An *iku* is approximately an acre. Finally comes stealing for the temple from private gardens.

20. Lit. "mouths."

21. That is, to thin the beer with it.

NEATNESS

Be it a butter-carrier
    who delivered butter for the temple,
be it a milk-carrier
    who delivered milk for the temple,
or a runner with fish[22]
of the men on daily wages
or a firewood-carrier of the desert,   80
    he was to take his load
    which he had passed
    into the temple of his mistress,
into its corners,
    was to take it in (along) its sides.[23]

DISPENSING OF
JUSTICE. HEN-
DURSAĞA AND
NINGUBLAGA

Affirming or denying
    what rolled off the tongues,
did the one who causes that outsiders
    enter Nanshe's house(hold),
    insiders leave it not,
Nanshe's temple's guardian,
    the son engendered by Utu,
lord Hendursaĝa,
    maintain order
    guided by their testimony.
The master recognized fair statements,
    recognized contentious ones.
Hendursaĝa recognized fair statements,
    recognized contentious ones.
[In the midst of] their testimony,
    which the contentious ones had twisted,
    he hewed them down for her like trees,
while Ningublaga,[24]   90
    son of the warrior, the gallant Suen,
in the midst of their making evil claims,
    was crushing them for Nanshe like reeds.

May all lands duly praise Nanshe,
    the lady of true words,
    whose sacred offices may not be scorned!

22. In the hot climate of southern Mesopotamia, fish had to be delivered quickly so they would not spoil. Therefore they were sent with runners.

23. Since three of the four types of carriers were men, we use "his" here, although the carriers mentioned last, the firewood carrier, were undoubtedly women. The Sumerian pronoun has no gender distinction. The point of the injunction was apparently to keep profane activities as unobtrusive as possible in the sacred precincts.

24. Very little is known about this god.

ADMINISTRA-
TIVE REVIEW
AT YEAR'S
END

At the new year, the day of assignments,[25]
did the lady shower
   the holy body,
on the day to review
   (performance for) food and fief,
did Nanshe hold
   review of the servants.
Her chief scribe, Nidaba,
put out of her own accord
   all valid tablets
   as they had been figured up,[26]
took the golden stylus in hand   100
and was lining up the servants
   for Nanshe in single file.
One (sheep)skin-clad one
   she would be letting
   enter to her from his skins[27]
one linen-clad one
   she would be letting
   pass on to her from his linen.[28]
An(other) (sheep)skin-clad one
   she would not be letting
   enter to her from his skins,
an(other) linen-clad one
   she would not be letting
   pass on to her from his linen.
With the men on the attendance lists
   ranged (side) by side,
she would be calling for
   eyewitnesses
   among them
   to a runaway of hers,
the witnesses to (one) of hers
   who had absconded from the temple,

25. That is, the day for reviewing the level of performance of the various offices and menial jobs in the temple.

26. That is, lists of attendance, work assignments, performance, etc., such as formed the temple's administrative records.

27. The skin-clad ones were that part of the temple personnel that worked outdoors in the fields, and who therefore wore sheepskin cloaks for protection in the sometimes inclement climate. To appear before the goddess they had to leave their clothes behind to confront her in ritual nakedness. Since they come from outside the house the verb used for them is "letting enter."

28. The linen-clad ones were the house servants, who worked indoors. They too had to appear in ritual nakedness, but since they already were in the house, the verb used for them is "letting pass on."

and shaking the head
    she would be discontinuing
    his position and box (of records).

NEW ROSTER   The master making inquiry   110
WITHOUT THE   about good servants,
UNDESIRABLES   Haya,
MADE UP BY   keeper of the seal,
HAYA   was listing on the roster
    the (names of) his mistress's
    good servants whom she mentioned;
a servant girl of his mistress
    whom she did not mention
    he left in reserve for the roster:
the ones mixing no water
    with their wine,
    who could not walk straight,
the ones not rinsing out the kneading trough,
carrying fire along
    in the house in the night time,
clamoring in the house
    during midday siesta,
the *shita*[29] priest of the temple close,
    who, while on *bala*[30] duty,
absented himself from his post,
the *shuzbu*[31] priest
    who laid claim to a fief-holder
    assigned to *bala*,
also the *sangu*[32] priest who,   120
    after he was through living in the temple,
did not divulge holy chants
    which he knew in his heart.
Had he taught what he knew
    to learned and unlearned
they could then with it have
    presented rites of Mother Nanshe's.

29. Conjecturally, a libation priest.
30. The *bala* duty involved annual service for a stated length of time in Enlil's temple in Nippur.
31. A purification priest.
32. The *sangu* was the chief temple administrator. The nature and extent of his priestly duties—if he had any—is not known.

AUTONOMY
OF THE SACRED
OFFICES

It (the temple) is not proliferating
    its spells unduly,
does not keep adding to its rites.
For its sacred offices
    —any sacred office—
no man can set bounds,
and thus, in order that
    bounds be not set
    for anything belonging to it,
no one setting bounds
    can enter Nanshe's temple;
the man must be passing by it
    by the white quay.[33]
In Nanshe's temple the river ordeal   130
    will clear a man.
Out of the holy chants,
    which divination will have elicited
    from the mouth of Apsû,
the selector of chants
    will recognize
    the (appropriate) chant,
and will invoke Enkum and Ninkum
    with it at handwashing.[34]

THE TEMPLE'S
COMMITMENT TO
FAIR DEALINGS

Words modestly spoken,
    but put in the mouth
    as if presumptuous,
are not added to what it (the temple)
    accepts as testimony,
and they who in bullying
    threaten with violence
    look not unto it.
He who, by laying hands on too much,
    receives grandly,
he who indulges in violence
    by nose pulling,
he who changes a foundation,
    alters a boundary,

33. Nanshe was specifically a goddess of boundaries and boundary markers. The taboo may express that she tolerates no others to set boundaries, e.g., the kings.
34. Enkum and Ninkum are shadowy figures. They seem to be servants or officials in the service of Enki. Their exact function is not known.

scowls at the place of oath,   140
he who taxes a (discountable) weight adjustment[35]
    on the 2-*ban*[36] measure loaves,
    who chisels on the 2-*ban* loaves,
he who picks a smaller stone weight
    out from among
    the large stone weights,[37]
he who picks a smaller *ban*-measure
    out from among
    the large *ban*-measures.
He who, after he has got a loaf,
    still demands the loaf,
he who, having already eaten,
    does not say the appropriate:
    "I have eaten!"
He who, having already had to drink
    does not say the appropriate:
    "I have drunk!"

DISAPPROVAL OF   The one inviting:
PRODIGALITY AND   "Let me set a bowl of soup for you!
AVARICIOUSNESS   Let me brew you beer!"
BOTH   After a servant girl has been lent to a god,
    to renege on the promise to the temple,
to scowl at menials
    after they have come
    to live in the temple,[38]
barring (the door)   150
    after one has begged:
    "Let me eat!"
barring (the door)
    after one has begged:
    "Let me have to drink!"

DISAPPROVAL   Nanshe will not have a man eat
OF VIOLENCE   shortening bread and plain eggs
    where there is brawling.

---

35. Weights and measures were not all standardized. Taxing—which was in kind—could obviously be done fairly only after differences due to the use of unstandardized measures had been adjusted.

36. A measure of volume holding about ten quarts.

37. That is: he who, pretending to pick up a heavy weight from the heavy weights, actually by sleight-of-hand picks a light one, thus weighing out less than he should. The same applies to the measures of capacity, *ban*, mentioned in the next lines.

38. Perhaps—to judge from the preceding line—slaves donated to the temple in moments of acute need for divine assistance.

The man who has eaten it
   during a brawl
     will not carry word thereof away,[39]
for the scowler, the grinder of teeth,
   and the one stamping the ground
he will be no match,
   will not be able
     to vie with them.
The one who by strength
   does . . . . to a man,
the strong one who grabs
   a girl in the street,
the married man whose wife
   came to him from out the widows,
and on a day when he was angry   160
   he ridiculed her,
or jeered at her
   in her days of infirmity,
thought she told not
   his gibing words to the lady,
(yet) the lady, guardian of all lands,
the damsel, Mother Nanshe,
   has looked into their hearts.

FURTHER CASES   Having misrepresented an orphan as a slave,
OF MISUSE OF   about to thwart the widow,
FORCE   to deliver up a homeless girl
                  to a powerful man,
or to deliver a powerless man
   to a powerful one;[40]
a mother having shouted
   threats at her child,
a child having spoken
   stubbornly to its mother;
a younger brother having opened   170
   the mouth (in a snarl)
   at his older brother,
     having answered back to the father,

39. This prohibition, so curiously specific, is probably connected with Nanshe's role as protectress of birds and goddess of grain. Things sacred to her must not be touched by strife and aggression.

40. We emend the text here to agree with the standard form of this stereotype. The text, for which we have a single witness only, has the strong man delivered up to the weak, which does not suit the context.

having had a sister lie down
　　for a man in the barn,
or conversely, got a man
　　into the barn for the sister,
Nanshe sees into the nation's hearts
　　as were it into a split reed,
sees its designs and its rulers' secrets.

HENDURSAĞA
AND HIS DIS-
PENSING OF
JUSTICE
Her constable, the lord Hendursaĝa
　　did the enlisting for military services
but her guardian angel
　　god of youngsters and oldsters
　　let them not go skirmishing.
Spirits
　　stationed at the mouths
　　were guarding the mouths

In her temple Siratr
　　having sprinkled water
in her chamber for the midday nap,
　　having swept it,
Nanshe [judged] with him[41]   180
　　their claims and their litigation.
The one who makes the scepter long-lasting,
　　[whose word is] prevailing
　　in the midst of the Apsû,
the lord of the *gigunu*[42] of Nanshe's temple,
　　a lord having no opponent,
the king, lord Hendursaĝa,   184
　　was ready and able to bring out
of Nanshe's temple its instructions;   183
like heavy smoke   185
　　they lay along the ground,
their words
　　hung under heaven
　　like drifting clouds.[43]
The bounded lands of married couples
　　were held jointly,
the king lord Hendursaĝa
　　split them off evenly.

41. That is, Hendursaĝa.
42. A hall on the temple terrace, often with trees planted around it.
43. The point of these similes is not clear.

A righteous one
    he stationed among righteous ones,
one who carried out evil   190
    he was delivering up to a place of evils.
The case of the waif
    he was having judged,
and the case of the widow
    he was letting follow,
even the case of the mother of a child
    he was setting straight.

CASES OF   Supposing a mother cursed out her child,
MOTHER AND   but ate with it,
CHILD   cursed it out,
    but drank with it,
and weeded out her cursings from her mouth,
(then) in their district
    the man in charge,
      who accepted their case for trial,
would not (need to) report to his mother
    the reconciliation of the brush-carrier in the desert,
and to the city's great mother
    who gave birth to her
he would not tell about it   200
    dry-eyed and in anger.[44]

Supposing a mother called her child
at the place of the (ensuing) quarrel,
and it pulled down the skeepskin coat
    of that mother,
and after it had drunk
    at her breast in which there was milk,
it sank with sharp teeth
    the teeth into that mother,
and she then and there
    abandoned the owner
    of the needle tooth;
(then) the king who loves fairness,
    Hendursaǧa,
would, after he had straightened out

---

44. The text takes a very serious view, it seems, of quarreling within the family, shown already above in lines 168–69. Even with the mother relenting, as here, the matter apparently had to be settled by the authorities, here the local person in charge.

the testimony about it,
and looked into that case,
impose the penalty for it
upon the mother of the child,
(so) that she would not   210
bear away from him
the wages of a heavy sin.
Still this human being
would not through prayers
obtain a personal god.[45]

Supposing a mother cursed out her child,
and would not eat with it,
cursed it out,
and would not drink with it,
and weeded not her cursing
out of her mouth,
and in their district
the man in charge,
who had not been able
to take up their case,
could not report to his mother
a reconciliation of the brush-carrier in the desert,
but told about it
to the city's great mother,
who gave birth to her,
dry-eyed and in anger,
(then) the king who hates violence,
Hendursaĝa,
would burst upon that human being   220
like flood waters in a catastrophe,
would reject her for that child
as is grain by salty soil,
and the words he spoke with the mother
who gave birth to her
he would be handing down
to people in charge,
as a firm bourne.[46]

---

45. Considering the harsh penalties meted out to a mother who quarreled with her child and would not be reconciled to it in lines 212–22, the penalty here for abandoning the child in the desert seems surprisingly mild. But the vicious behavior of the child here may have been considered an extenuating circumstance.

46. That is, his legal opinion in support of the penalty imposed. It is to be handed down to serve as a precedent for future similar cases.

ASSEMBLY OF
THE GODS OF
LAGASH

With her who makes the experts' words come right,
the lady and woman sage
   of settled Lagash,
Gatumdug, she ad[vised]:
and to Nanshe
   she spoke most fair words.
The lady, august,
   whose word, [proving true,
   takes precedence,]
the lady who makes decisions
   like Enlil,
[enthroned herself] on   230
   Siratr's throne dais.
She had looked into having
   her sacred offices immaculate,
and decided to assign
   sacred offices to the temple
   from Apsû.
The gods of Lagash gathered to her to Siratr.
To have honest stone weights weigh silver,
   honest (size) baskets carried,
to place certified *ban*-measures
   in the hands of all lands,
did she have the country's
   shepherd and guide,
   the leader of all lands,
a very Ishtaran[47]
   sitting in just judgment in the country,
the word[wise] Ningishzida,[48]
   be seated there.
[. . . .]
   she was setting to rights
[. . . . .]   240
   she was setting free (?)
To have [honest stone weights wei]gh [silver]
   honest (size) baskets carried,
to place [certified *ban*-measures]
   in the hands of all lands.
That [. . . . . . .] huge [. . . . . . .] of great tasks
[. . . .]

47. Ishtaran was a god of justice.
48. The sudden appearance of the god Ningishzida here seems puzzling. He has not been mentioned before. One possibility would seem to be that he represents Gudea, whose tutelary god he was.

that in the [well-stocked storehouses,]
and well-stocked treasuries
[. . . . . .] be not wanting in their [. . . . .]
and [. . . . . .] cease not in their coffers
that, when [. . . . .]
mistress of the treasury
had placed her exalted [. . . . . .] thereon,
profit from them be obtained.
Those [instructions] she gave
to [her constable] Hendursaga.

ENVOI   (O) M[ilady,] your sacred offices are august   250
sacred offices,
surpas[sing all (other) sacred offices!]
Nanshe, not any sacred office
can compare with your sacred offices!
King An is looking at you with happy eye,
with Enlil on the throne dais
you have sat down
to make decisions with him,
Father Enki has determined your mode of being.
O Nanshe, child born in Eridu,
to praise you is sweet!

PART FOUR

Myths

The Eridu Genesis

The fragment here translated was written at some time around 1600 B.C. It constitutes the lower third of a six-column tablet, the upper part of which, containing roughly some 36 lines per column, is lost. The content of the lost sections can be restored to some extent from other versions of the same tradition, most of which are of later date. By the time of the Assyrian Empire the tradition in somewhat shortened form had been included in the so-called Babylonian Chronicle, heading it.

The story, which has a structure much like that of the biblical stories in Genesis, dealt with the creation of men and animals, the antediluvian cities and their rulers, and finally the Deluge, paralleling in order the creation, the antediluvian patriarchs, and the story of the Deluge in the Bible. It may conceivably have served as model or inspiration for the biblical account.

(long lacuna)

MOTHER GODDESS
PITIES THE
NOMAD EXIS-
TENCE OF MAN

. . . .

[Nintur[1]] was paying [attention:]
"Let me bethink myself of my humankind,
    (all) forgotten as they are;
and mind[ful] of mine, Nintur's, creatures
    let me bring them back,
let me lead the people back from their trails.

"May they come and build cities and cult places,
    that I may cool myself in their shade;
may they lay the bricks for the cult cities
    in pure spots, and
may they found places for divination
    in pure spots!"

---

1. Goddess of birth and creatrix of man.

She gave directions for purification, and cries for clemency,
    the things that cool (divine) wrath,
perfected the divine service and the august offices,   10'
said to the (surrounding) regions: "Let me institute peace
    there!"
When An, Enlil, Enki, and Ninhursağa[2]
fashioned the dark-headed (people),[3]
they had made the small animals (that come up) from (out
    of) the earth
come from the earth in abundance
and had let there be, as befits (it), gazelles,
    (wild) donkeys, and four-footed beasts in the desert.

. . . .

(Lost account of first attempt at city-building failing for lack of leadership[?])

MOTHER GODDESS   [. . . .]

INSTITUTES   [" . . . . .] and let me have [*h*]*im* [a]dvise;

KINGSHIP   let me have *him* overse[e] their [la]bor,
and let *him* t[each] the nation to follow along
    unerringly like [cat]tle!"

When the royal [sce]pter was com[ing] down from heaven,
the august [cr]own and the royal [th]rone being already
    down from heaven,
he (the king) [regularly] performed to perfection
    the august divine services and offices,
laid [the bricks] of those cities [in pure spots.]
They were [n]amed by name and [al]lotted [ha]lf-bushel
    baskets.[4]
                                      40'

FIRST CITIES   The firstling of those cities, Eridu,
    she gave to the leader Nudimmud,[5]
the second, Bad-Tibira,[6] she gave to the prince and the
    sacred one[7]

2. The triad An, Enlil, and Ninhursağa constituted originally the highest deities. Ninhursağa, "mistress of the foothills," who was normally considered identical with Nintur, is here apparently seen as a different goddess.

3. A standing epithet for mankind, specifically for the Sumerians themselves.

4. Half-bushel baskets seem to have been used to pay workers the grain rations that constituted their wages. Apparently they serve here as symbols of the major centers of the economy. The word for them was also used to denote a standard measure used as a check.

5. A name for Enki.

6. The present mound Medinah.

7. "The prince" is presumably the god Dumuzi. "The sacred one" is an epithet of Inanna's.

the third, Larak, she gave to Pabilsaĝ,[8]
the fourth, Sippar, she gave to the gallant, Utu.[9]
the fifth, Shuruppak, she gave to Ansud.[10]

These cities, which had been named by names,
    and had been allotted half-bushel baskets,
dredged the canals, which were blocked with purplish
    (wind-borne) clay, and they carried water.
Their cleaning of the smaller canals
    established abundant growth.
[. . . .]

(Lost account of the antediluvian rulers,[11] and of how human noises vexed the chief god Enlil so much that he persuaded the divine assembly to vote the destruction of man by the deluge.)

    . . . .   80'

That day Nin[tur] wept over her creatures
and holy Inanna[12] [was full] of grief over their people;
but Enki to[ok] counsel with his own heart.
An, Enlil, Enki,[13] and Ninhursaĝa
had the gods of heaven and earth [swear[14]]
    by the names An and Enlil.

8. Larak has not yet been located. Its city god Pabilsaĝ is a god of trees.

9. Sippar is the present mound of Abu-Habba. Its city god, Utu—Akkadian Shamash—was god of the sun and of righteousness.

10. Shuruppak is the present mound Fara. Its city goddess Sud or Ansud "the lush ear of grain" was a grain goddess. As consort of Enlil she was known as Ninlil.

11. The list as found in parallel accounts differs on minor points. The form in which it appeared in the Babylonian Chronicle probably read "in Eridu Alulim reigned 36,000 years, Alalgar ruled 10,800 years. Two kings reigned 46,000 years, Eridu's term. Eridu's term was commuted. In Bad-Tibira Enmenluanna reigned 46,800 years, Enmengalanna reigned 64,800 years. Dumuzi, the shepherd, reigned 36,000 years. Three kings reigned 147,600 years, Bad-Tibira's term. Bad-Tibira's term was commuted. In Sippar Enmeduranki reigned 64,800 years. One king reigned 64,800 years, Sippar's term. Sippar's term was commuted. In Larak Ensipadzianna reigned 36,000 years. One king reigned 36,000 years, Larak's term. Larak's term was commuted. In Shuruppak Ubaratutu reigned 28,800 years. Ziusudra reigned 64,800 years. Two kings reigned 93,600 years, Shuruppak's term. Five individual cities, nine kings reigned 352,800 years, their terms. Enlil took a dislike to mankind, the clamor they made kept him sleepless."

The reigns were extraordinarily long. A similar feature is the long life of the biblical antediluvian patriarchs. For Mesopotamia, a document called "The Lagash King List" indicates that these early people were thought to have developed very slowly. The idea is also found in Greece, where the childhood of the people of Hesiod's silver age lasted a hundred years.

12. A many-sided deity, among other things goddess of love and war.

13. God of the waters in rivers and marshes and god of practical wisdom.

14. The oath was one of abiding by the decisions of the assembly.

ZIUSUDRA'S
VISION OF
THE GODS
ASSEMBLING
	At that time Ziusudra was king
	    and lustration priest.
	He fashioned, being a seer,
	    the god of giddiness[15]
	and [stood] in awe beside it, wording his
	    wishes humbly.

[As he] stood there regularly day after day
something that was not a dream was appearing:
    conversa[tion]   90′
a swearing (of) oaths by heaven and earth,
    [a touching of throats[16]]
and the gods [bringing their] thwar[ts] (up) to [K]iur.[17]

ENKI'S ADVICE   And as Ziusudra stood there beside it, he [went on he]aring:
"Step up to the wall to my left and listen!
Let me speak a word to you at the wall
    [and may you grasp] what [I] say,
May you he[ed] my advice!
By our hand a flood will sweep over
    (the cities of) the half-bushel bas[kets, and the country;]
[the decision,] that mankind is to be destroyed,
    has been made.
a verdict, a command of the assemb[ly
    cannot be revoked,]
an order of An and En[lil is not known   100′
    ever to have been countermanded,]
their kingship, their term, [has been uprooted
    they must bethink themselves of that]
Now [.   .   .   .]
What I ha[ve to say to you .   .   .   ."]
[.   .   .   .]

(Lost account of Enki's advice to build a boat and load it with pairs of living things and Ziusudra's complliance.)

---

15. Ecstasy was apparently induced—as in the modern dancing dervishes—by giddiness, which was why Ziusudra made a statue of the god inducing it. The ancient rulers combined administrative, military, and priestly functions. To the last mentioned belonged divination, because it was essential for a ruler to know the will of the gods and to act in conformity to it.

16. The touching of the throat symbolized a wish that it be cut if the person doing it broke his or her oath.

17. Kiur (Ki-ùr) was the forecout of Enlil's temple in Nippur. The divine assembly met in a corner of it called Ubshu'ukkinna. The gods would arrive by boat on a canal flowing close by.

THE DELUGE	. . . . 130'

        All the evil winds, all stormy winds gathered into one
and with them, then, the Flood was sweeping over (the
    cities of)
    the half-bushel baskets
for seven days and seven nights.
After the flood had swept over the country,
after the evil wind had tossed the big boat
    about on the great waters,
the sun came out spreading light
    over heaven and earth.

ZIUSUDRA'S   Ziusudra then drilled an opening in the big boat.
OFFERING AT   and the gallant Utu sent his light
END OF FLOOD   into the interior of the bit boat.

        Ziusudra, being the king,   140'
stepped up before Utu kissing the ground
    (before him).
The king was butchering oxen, was being lavish with the
    sheep
[barley cak]es, crescents together with [. . . . .]
[. . . . .] he was crumbling for him
[. . . .]
[juniper, the pure plant of the
    mountains] he filled [on the fire]
and with a [. . . . .] clasped to
    [the breast he . . . .]
[. . . .]

(Lost account of Enlil's wrath at finding survivors and his mollification by Enki.)

END OF ENKI'S   . . . .
SPEECH   "You here have sworn
    by the life's breath of heaven
    the life's breath of earth
    that he verily is allied with you yourself;
you there, An and Enlil,
    have sworn by the life's breath of heaven,
    the life's breath of earth,
    that he is allied with all of you.
He will disembark the small animals
    that come up from the earth!"

ZIUSUDRA   Ziusudra, being king,

REWARDED   stepped up before An and Enlil
                         kissing the ground,
                     And An and Enlil after hono[ring him]
                         were granting him life like a god's,
                         were making lasting breath of life, like a god's,   180'
                             descend into him.
                     That day they made Ziusudra,
                         preserver, as king, of the name of the small
                         animals and the seed of mankind,
                     live toward the east over the mountains
                         in Mount Dilmun.[18]
                         . . . . [. . . .]

18. Dilmun was the present Bahrein. Here in the tale it seems to have been considered a faraway, half-mythical place.

The Birth of Man

Two originally separate and independent stories are combined in this composition,[1] which celebrates Enki and mankind's debt to him. He was the one who thought up a way for man to be born, and he was the one who devised ways in which the physically handicapped could yet earn their livelihood as useful members of society.

The first of these stories tells how in the beginning the gods had to farm for their food themselves. The hard work of cleaning rivers and canals weighed heavily on them and put them in a rebellious mood, so that they blamed Enki and, in the periods of rest from work at noon and in the evening, wantonly destroyed what they had just accomplished.

Enki's mother, Namma, brought their distress to her son's notice and suggested that he devise a substitute for the gods who could take over their toil and so relieve them. Enki pondered the problem and was reminded of how he himself was engendered by "the fathering clay from the Apsû," that is to say the clay of the vast body of fresh water which the ancients thought underlay the earth, what we should call the water level. Accordingly he asked his mother to give birth to man from it, and she readily complied. After she had moistened the clay to its core, the ovary goddesses made the fetus grow big and solid, whereupon Namma put limbs on it and determined what it would be like. Finally she gave birth, attended by the goddess Ninmah as midwife and a group of minor goddesses as birth helpers. Thus, without any male being involved, man came into being and was born.

The second story deals with a contest between Ninmah and Enki, which Enki wins. It tells how Enki decided to celebrate the birth of man with a party. At this party the beer flowed freely, and both Ninmah and Enki felt its effect. Ninmah began to boast that it actually was she who controlled what man was to be like; at her whim she would make a good or a bad job of him. Her challenge was taken up by Enki, who ventured that he would be able to mitigate any harm she might wish to do. Ninmah then took a lump of the "fathering clay of the Apsû" and molded successively from it seven human beings, each with a different bodily defect. To

---

1. New materials have made me change my opinion from that expressed in my previous treatments of this myth on several points. This is particularly true of Ud-mu'ul.

each of them, however, Enki was able to assign a place in society, a trade, attendance at court before the king, etc., where the handicapped person would fit in and earn his or her living.

Eventually Ninmah gave up and angrily threw the clay on the ground. Enki picked it up and suggested that *he* now fashion a creature for her to cope with, as he had coped with the ones she made. He then, with intent to destroy her city, fashioned a creature from the clay and asked for a woman to give birth to it. Ninmah provided one, but the days for the creature to develop did not become full, as Enki intended them not to; it was aborted before its time. The creature, named Udmu'ul, "Premature," literally: "the day was far off" (*ud mu-ul*) suffers from all kinds of bodily ills, cannot eat or drink, cannot sit or lie down, cannot talk.

Ninmah does not know what to do with it, she is unable to support it. Enki taunts her, reeling off the list of her creatures which he took care of, and Ninmah, in despair, bursts into wailing: her city is destroyed, she herself a fugitive. Enki, however, consoles her. He tells her to put Udmu'ul down off her lap and points out that what is wrong with him is precisely that he lacked what only she could contribute. He will serve, thus, as a reminder of the need for her work during gestation whenever Enki's male member is praised. Enki concludes with calling on two divine figures to console her, and to praise her martial prowess. The composition ends with the comment that Ninmah did not prove the equal of Enki and a standard line of hymnic praise.

As will readily be seen, this second story does not fit in too well with the first one, but differs from it noticeably in both basic setting and outlook. As it is presented in the composition, it deals with events at a party given by Enki to celebrate the birth of man. That, however, can hardly have been its original setting, for throughout it human society is assumed as already in existence. Enki assigns Ninmah's creatures to positions at the courts of king and queen, one of the creatures was engendered by a Subarean, etc., all of which does not fit with man's just having been born and swathed in wool by Enki (l. 45).

A rather more significant difference is the very different roles the goddess Ninmah plays in the two stories. In the first she is a very secondary figure, mentioned only as the midwife when man is born; in the second she appears quite differently in her capacity of goddess of gestation and birth, the numinous power of the uterus to expand, shape, and mature the embryo, the power shaping any child anywhere. It is in that capacity that she can claim power over how man is to be, and in that capacity she produces the misshapen beings to prove her powers.

Another difference between the two stories is the significance they accord to the "fathering clay of the Apsû." In the first story it has fathered Enki in what was apparently a unique cosmic event, and is called upon to father man, also in a unique event. In both cases, it should be noted, it is considered different from, and replacing, male semen. The engendering of man was effected, it is stated, without benefit of a male. In the second story, in contrast, the "fathering clay of the Apsû" is a very obvious and transparent image for and is representative of male semen. When Enki forms a being from it, that being still has to be borne by a woman because "the semen the male member is emitting when discharged into a woman's womb is given birth by that woman." In fact, it may even be that the image of the clay and the forming of it as one would a figurine was imposed by the poet on a more direct original statement, due to the mention of that clay in the first story.

Last there is Ninmah's reaction to Udmu'ul, which again only makes sense if she is seen as the power in gestation generally, and Udmu'ul likewise as a general rather than a unique occurrence. As is clear from the text, Udmu'ul represents the phenomenon of abortion, the male seed—the ancients seem to have been ignorant of the role of the ovum—prematurely ejected. Enki has thus saddled Ninmah with what amounts to the complete nullification of her powers, for it is to be assumed that her acceptance of the wager he offered her bound her to abide with it. If she has to keep Udmu'ul with her, it will mean that gestation will have become intimately associated with abortion, so that with no completed pregnancies her city will become depleted and she herself frustrated in the very things she stands for. Apparently Enki's words telling her to put Udmu'ul down off her lap release her.

In the following part of Enki's speech he then assigns to Udmu'ul the role of "reminder" when Enki's male member is praised. What he is to remind of is, of course, the fact that the male germ of a child is not enough, gestation is just as essential, and the story ends on a note of the equality of the sexes' contributions to healthy propagation.

ORIGINALLY
THE GODS
HAD TO TOIL

In days of yore,
 the days
  when heaven and earth
  had been [fashioned,]
 in nights of yore,
  the nights
  when heaven and earth
  had been [fashioned,]
 in years of yore,
  the years
  when the modes of be[ing
  were determined,]
when the Anunnaki gods
 had been born,
when the goddess-[mothers]
 had been chosen
 for marriage,

when the goddess-mothers
  had been assigned
  to heaven or earth,
and when the goddess-mothers
  [had had intercourse,]
  had become pregnant,
  and had given birth,

did the gods
  for whom they baked
  their food portions[2]
  and set therewith
  their tables,
did the major gods
  oversee work,
  while the minor gods
  were shouldering the menial labor.
The gods were dredging the rivers,   10
  were piling up their silt
  on projecting bends—
and the gods lugging the clay
  began complaining
  about the corvée.[3]

APPEAL TO
ENKI

In those days
  lay he of the vast intelligence,
  the creator bringing
  the major gods into being,
Enki,
  In E-engur,[4] a well
  into which water seeped,
  a place the inside of which
  no god whatever
  was laying eyes on,
on his bed, sleeping,
  and was not getting up.
The gods were weeping
  and were saying:
  "He made the present misery!"

2. The food portions consisted of flour to be baked into bread.
3. The gods were thought of as engaged in irrigation agriculture with its strenuous yearly corvée work to clean rivers and canals of accumulated silt.
4. É-engur, "house watery deep" was the name of the temple of Enki in E.idu. The word *engur* is another term for the Apsû, the water table.

yet they (dared) not rouse
  the sleeper, him who lay at rest,
  from that bed!

Namma, the mother primordial,
  bearer of the major gods,[5]
took the tears of the gods to her son:
"Since, after you will have rested,
  since, after you will have sat up,
[you] of yourself [will] rise: 20
The gods are smashing
  at noon and at eventide
  what they have (just) made!
My son, rise from your bed,
  and when you
  with your ingenuity
  have searched out
  the (required) skill,
and you have fashioned
  a fill-in worker
  for the gods,
  may they get loose
  of their digging!"

ENKI THINKS   Enki,
OF A WAY   at his mother Namma's word,
                       rose from his bed,
                     in Halankug,
                       his room for pondering,
                       he smote the thigh,[6]
                     The ingenious and wise one,
                       skillful custodian

5. Namma, Enki's mother, was probably seen as the power in the riverbed which, empty or nearly empty in summer, gives birth to the fresh waters, to Enki, in the spring flood. This interpretation gains a measure of support from the fact that the cuneiform sign with which her name was written served also, if supplemented with the sign for "water," to write the word for "river."

Etymologically the name Namma goes back to Nin-imma (nin-imma>nan-amma>nanma>namma) "lady female genitals," a personification of the numinous power to shape, mature, and give birth to the child, and it is as birth goddess generally, rather than as goddess of the riverbed, that the text here characterizes her. That latter aspect she may conceivably have acquired because the mythopoeic imagination conceived of the great gash in the earth which the dry riverbed presents as the genitals of Mother Earth herself, and the prototype of all female parts everywhere. Namma's role as birth goddess generally and as the one who gave birth to man probably represents a local tradition, perhaps at home in Eridu. Elsewhere it is the goddess Nintur, or Ninmah as she is called in this composition, who is thus viewed.

6. A gesture expressive of decision, approximately: "Let us get on with it!"

of heaven and earth,
creator and constructor
of everything,
had Imma-en and Imma-shar[7]
come out.
Enki reached out
his arm toward them,
and a fetus
was getting big there,
and for Enki it was awakening
to consciousness in the heart
(thoughts of) his own
creator and constructor.
To his mother Namma
he called out:
"O mother mine, since the sire   30
(who was once)
provided with heir
by you
is still there,
have the god's birth-chair (?)[8]
put together!
When you have drenched
(even) the core
of the Apsû's
fathering clay[9]
Imma-en and Imma-shar
can make the fetus bigger,
and when you have
put limbs on it
may Ninmah act
as your (birth-)helper,
and may Ninimma, Shuzidanna
Ninmada, Ninshara, Ninbara
Ninmug, Dududuh and Ereshguna

7. These two are personifications of the ovaries. *Imma* denotes the female genitalia. The epithet *en* denotes "productrix," *shar* "The bountiful one."
8. The translation "birth-chair" is a guess from the context.
9. "The fathering clay of the Apsû" apparently refers to the clay of the water table through which water seeps to fill wells or ditches dug down into it. Enki, the waters of the river, was thus thought to have been engendered by the clay of the Apsû emitting its waters into the dry riverbed, Namma.

assist you
at your giving birth.[10]
O mother mine,
when you have determined
its mode of being[11]
may Ninmah put together
the birth-chair (?)
and when,
[without any m]ale,
you have built it up in it,
[may you give birth]
to manki[nd!"]

MAN IS
BORN

[Without] the sperm
of a ma[le]
she gave [birth]
to offspri[ng,]
to the [em]bryo
of mankind.

[When she had br]oadened   40
[its shoulders,]
she made [a hole] in the head
(for) the mouth
she [. . . . .]
and [enclosed] its body
in an amnion,

(two lines not understood)

Enki tied wool for swathing
around it
and its heart rejoiced.

10. Ninmah, "the exalted lady" is one of the many names for the birth goddess par excellence, Nintur. As for the other goddesses listed, no obvious reason for their selection presents itself. Possibly they were meant to represent merely a varied group of friends and neighbors such as would normally come to help at a birth in a Sumerian town. Three of the attendants were possibly meant to represent experts: the name Dududuh seems to denote "the one who opens the one giving birth"; Nin-imma—originally the same as Namma but here differentiated from her—and Ninmug are both deities of the female genitalia. Ninshara, Ninbara and Ereshguna are different forms of the goddess Inanna. The first represents her as spouse of the god of heaven, An (Akkadian Anu), and avatar of his traditional spouse An (Akkadian Antu), the second as she was worshipped under the Akkadian title *Têlîtu*. Lastly there are two goddesses connected with the household of the god Enlil in Nippur, his concubine Shuzidanna and his snake charmer Ninmada.

11. That is to say, what it is going to look like. The reference is to the power of the uterus to give form.

FEAST TO
CELEBRATE
MAN'S BIRTH

For his mother Namma
    and (for) Ninmah
    he thought he would make
    a feast.
To the gathering of Imma-en,
    Imma-shar,
    and princesses,
    (to) the makers of decisions
    and chief . . . . .
    he fed bread[12]
but for An and Enlil together
    the lord Nudimmud[13]
    roasted to a turn
    a ritually pure kid.
The major gods
    were offering up praise:
"Lord of vast intelligence,
    who could be imagining it!
O great lord Enki,
    who would be equal to
    the things you do!
You are like a father
    who has produced a son,
    you who are our
    decisionmaker
    for the country!"

50

NINMAH
SCOFFS

Enki and Ninmah
    were drinking beer
    and began to feel good
    inside.
Ninmah said to Enlil:
"(As for) the build of men,
    what makes it good
    or bad
    is mine (affair),

12. Imma-en, Imma-shar, and the princesses are apparently the female guests invited, while the decision makers, that is, gods who vote in the assembly of the gods, and the chief . . . represent the males. The meal served seems inordinately frugal for a feast: only An and Enlil are served meat. Perhaps the storyteller wishes to intimate that the gods lived on meager rations before they had man to support them.

13. This epithet of Enki means "the man-fashioner."

whichever way
   my turn of heart,
   I am making the decision
   about mode of being,
   good or bad."

Enki replied thereunto
   to Ninmah:
"In that decision about the mode of being
   desired by the heart
   let me mitigate
   the good or the bad."

NINMAH MAKES   Ninmah took
FREAKS FOR   the fathering Apsu clay
ENKI TO   and molded from it
COPE WITH   the "Man-unable-to-close-
                    the-shaking-hand-upon-an-arrow-shaft-
                    to-send-it-going,"[14]
                    a seeing man.

When Enki had looked   60
   the "Man unable to close
   the shaking hand upon an arrow shaft
   to send it going" over
he determined a way for it to be,
   had it stand at attention
   by the head of the king.

Next she molded from it
the "One-handing-back-
   the-lamp-
   to-the-men-who-can-see."[15]
[When] Enki had looked
   the "One-handing-back-
   the-lamp-
   to-the-men-who-can-see"
   he determined a way for it.to be,
   he allotted to it
   the musical arts

14. In Sumerian lú-šu-šú-šú-šú-di-di-dè-nu-gam.
15. In Sumerian ǧišnu-gi₄-gi₄-lú-u₆-e(k).

had it sit . . . on the long side
   in front of the king.[16]

Third [she molded from it]
   the "Hobbled-by-twisting-ankles."[17]

When En[ki] had lo[oked]
   the "Hobbled-by-twisting-ankles"
   over,
he [taught](?) it the work
   of metal casters and silversmiths,
   and . . . .

Fourth she molded from it   68a
   the "Moron,-the-engenderer-of-which-
   was-a-Subarean"[18]

When Enki had looked   68b
   the "Moron,-the-engenderer-of-which-
   was-a-Subarean"
   over,
he determined a way for it to be,   68c
   had it stand at attention
   by the head of the king.

Fifth she molded from it   69
   the "Man-leaking-urine."[19]

When Enki had looked   70
   the "Man-leaking-urine"
   over
he showered it
   with blest water
   and thereby drew out
   of its body
   the (former)
   mode of being.

16. Throughout antiquity the profession of rhapsodist was a standard one for gifted blind persons. It is likely, therefore, that the composer of this tale was himself blind and performed at the royal court. If so, that might account for the lengthy coverage of handicapped beings which, with its seven very similar tristichs, all of which are then repeated once more, badly overbalances the tale. Those tristichs, though, would have served as a kind of charter for himself and the other handicapped among the personnel at court, showing that they were there by divine decree.

17. In Sumerian ĝìr-min-hum-ĝìr-daba.

18. In Sumerian lú-lil-ùdúbi-šubur. Subartu was the area of later Assyria, in modern terms northern Iraq and eastern Syria. Apparently it was considered barbaric and backward to the storyteller.

19. In Sumerian lú-a-sur-sur.

Sixth she molded from it
  the "Woman-who-is not-
  giving-birth."[20]

When Enki had looked
  the "Woman-who-is-not-
  giving-birth"
  over
he determined a way for it to be,
  made it look (for orders)
  to a weaver,
  and entrusted it
  to the queen's household.

Seventh she molded from it
  the "Man-in-the body-of-which-
  no-male-and-no-female-organ-was-placed."[21]

When Enki had looked
  the "Man-in-the-body-of-which-
  no-male-and-no-female-organ-was-placed"
  over
he called it by the name
  "Nippurean-
  the-courtier"
and determined for it
  its mode of being
  so that it would stand
  in attendance
  before the king.

Ninmah threw the pinch of clay
  in her hand upon the ground
  and a great silence fell.

ENKI MAKES
A FREAK
FOR NINMAH
TO COPE
WITH

The great lord Enki   80
  said to Ninmah:
"I have determined modes of being
  for your creatures
  and given them
  (their) daily bread.
Well, then! Let me (now) mold
  (one) for you,

20. In Sumerian munus-nuʾùdú.
21. In Sumerian lú-suba-ĝiš-nuĝar-galla-nuĝar.

and do you determine
the mode of being
of that newborn one!"

Enki for his part
fashioned a creature
the secret purpose of which
was killing her city.
He said to Ninmah:
"The semen which the male member
is emitting,
when discharged
into a woman's womb
that woman
gives birth to it
from in her womb".
(So) Ninmah brought [a woman
to Enki]
to give birth to it.
but that woman [. . . . .]
aborted the fetus
in accordance with
its secret purpose,
so that its days [became not full.]
The first one, Ud-mu'ul,
("the-day-was-far-off")
—its scalp was sore,
its front was sore,
its eyes were sore,
its neck was sore,
the throat was closing up,
the ribs twisting
the liver was sore,
the insides were sore,
the heart was sore,
its hands, having the shakes,   90
could not put food
to its mouth,
the spine was crushed,
the anus closed up,
the hips were brittle
the feet (with their) skin breaking
unable to walk the fields.

Enki said to Ninmah:
"I determined modes of being
   for your creatures,
     gave them
    (their daily) bread
do you (now) determine
   for my creature
    its mode of being,
    that it may
    (have enough to) eat!"

Ninmah, when she had looked
   Ud-mu'ul over
    took back the pinch (of clay)
    into her hand.
She approached Ud-mu'ul,
   was questioning him,
    but it was not opening
    its mouth
she piled up loaves
   for him to eat,
    but he reached not out
    to her for it.
A seat to make (one) rejoice,
   a place to lie down,
    she laid out for him
    but he was unable
    to lie down.
Standing he was [un]able to sit down,
   was unable to lie down,
    was unable to [. . . . . .]
    he was unable to [. . . . . .]
    he was unable to eat bread.

Ninmah [re]plied to Enki   100
   to the word (he had spoken):
"The man, your handiwork,
   is not a live man,
    nor a [dead] man,
    I cannot support it!"

Enki replied to it to Ninmah
   (saying:)
"For the "Man-(unable-to-close-)

the-shaking-hand-
upon-an-arrow-shaft"
I determined a mode of being
and gave it thereby
(its daily) bread,
for the "Man-returning-the-lamp"
I determined a mode of being
and gave it thereby
(its daily) bread,
for the "Hobbled-by-twisting-ankles"
I determined a mode of being
and gave it thereby
(its daily) bread,

for the "Moron,-the-engenderer-of-which-
was-a-Subarean"
I determined a mode of being
and gave it thereby
(its daily) bread,
for the ["Man-leaki]ng-[urine"]
I determined a mode of being
and gave it thereby
(its daily) bread,
for the "Woman-who-is-not-
[giving birth"]
I determined a mode of being
and [gave it thereby
(its daily) bread,],
for the "M[an-in-the-body-of-which-
no-male-and-no-female-
organ-was-placed"]
I [determined] a mode of being
[and gave it thereby
(its daily) bread,]
My sister, you [. . . . .]   110
[. . . . . . .]
[. . . . .]

NINMAH   [N]inmah [replied to Enki to it (saying:)]
DESPAIRS   . [. . . . . . .]
                          . [. . . . .]
                          my [. . . . .]
                          . [. . . . .]
                          . [. . . . .]

. [. . . . . . .]
. [. . . . . . .]
    [. . . .] I am one lamenting,
. . [. . . . . .]   120
    [. . . .] I am one driven out of my house,
at my beer-pouring party [. . . .]
I am become one lingering outside (?),
    [cannot] enter at wish!(?)[22]

"Now I cannot dwell under heaven,
    cannot dwell on earth,
    cannot in the country
    get out of your sight.
Where you dwell not,
    in a house I shall build,
    I shall not hear your voice.
Where you live not,
    in a city I shall build,
    me myself (despairing) silence will fill.

"My city is destroyed,
    my house wrecked,
    my children taken captive.
I am a fugitive
    driven out of Ekur,
I myself, even,
    have not escaped
    out of your hands!"

CONCILIA-
TORY SPEECH
BY ENKI

Enki replied to it, to Ninmah:
"Who can gainsay   130
    a word
    issued from your mouth?
(But) hand (down) *Ud-mu'ul*
    clasped to your bosom
    from your lap!
He is lacking, in sooth,
    your work, Ninmah;
    was born to me
    incomplete,
    who could challenge that?

22. In the original independent version of the story the party at which the contest took place may have been given by Ninmah rather than by Enki.

"May men to the end of days
    in awe pay their respect to him,
and whenever, as is due,
    my male member
    may be extolled,
    may he be there
    as a (sobering) reminder!
May Enkum and Ninkum
(consolingly) respond
    [with cries of woe
    to your cries of woe,]
    may they relay widely
    word of your power!
My sister,
    may your warrior's arm
    be made [man]ifest to hea[ven]'s [borders].
Holy songs, softly and loudly,
    [. . . . .]
  . . . . *Ud-mu'ul* . . [. . .]
    may [. . . . .] do my. . . .

Ninmah did not equal   140
    the great lord Enki!
Father Enki,
    praise of you is sweet!

Enlil and Ninlil

In mythical times,[1] when its gods had not yet settled in it, Nippur was a town like any other town. The localities the tale mentions cluster around the temple Ekur suggesting the area of a small village only. The town well, the "Honey Well," we know to have been located in the main courtyard of Ekur, Kiur, where the gods sat in judgment on Enlil later in the tale. Kiur was the forecourt of Ekur, and the fateful Nunbirdu canal flowed just outside the town wall northeast of Ekur, not very far away.

The town in those days had only two young people growing up in it, Enlil and Ninlil, and only one matron, Ninlil's mother Ninshebargunu. At the time the story begins, Ninshebargunu very properly warns her daughter against bathing in Nunbirdu where she might be seen by Enlil and taken advantage of by him.

Ninlil listened carefully, but rather than obeying, she made straight for the forbidden canal to bathe and be seen. Everything happened as predicted. Enlil saw her and immediately propositioned her. She, however, demurred—albeit somewhat coyly—arguing that her parts were too small for copulation, her lips for kissing. Also, her mother would slap her hand if she knew, her father would give her a good shaking, and—last but perhaps not least—she would have to keep it secret from her girlfriend.

Enlil, understandably, was not too impressed with her arguments nor dissuaded by them from his purpose. He seems to have been on the other side of the canal from her, for he had his page Nusku get him something that would serve as a boat. Nusku provided the needed conveyance, and Enlil made love with Ninlil, who apparently had not moved from where she was. In their union the god of the waxing and waning moon, Suen, was engendered.

Words of what had happened must have got about quickly, for when Enlil passed through Kiur, where the gods sit in judgment, he was seized and condemned as a sex offender to banishment from the town—implying, it would seem, banishment from the country generally. He accepts the judgment and leaves for the mountains, and Ninlil follows him.

---

1. For earlier treatments see the edition by Hermann Behrens, *Enlil and Ninlil* (Rome, 1978) and the review by Jerrold Cooper, *Journal of Cuneiform Studies* 32/3 (1980): 175–88.

On his way out of town, Enlil stops at the city gate, where he orders the gatekeeper not to reveal to Ninlil where he is, when she arrives. Then, one must assume, he hides in the gatekeeper's chamber in the gate. When Ninlil arrives she asks, as expected, where Enlil has gone, having obviously lost sight of him when he hid himself. The gatekeeper answers, as instructed by Enlil, that Enlil never deigns to exchange pleasantries with him, meaning that Enlil has not troubled to tell him. Ninlil then, partly to establish her right to be answered, but obviously also to gloat over her own cleverness, boasts of how she lured Enlil to unite with her and get her with child. She points out at the same time that since Enlil is the gatekeeper's master, so is she now his mistress.

In answer Enlil has the gatekeeper make what is apparently an offer to swear an oath of allegiance to her as his mistress, but the type of oath he proposes is swearing while touching her genitals with his hand. What is involved, directly and by implication, is not easy to say with any degree of certainty except, perhaps, that the fact of the genitalia being the sacred power behind this type of oath suggests relation to generation and descent. It is difficult to imagine, though, that such a proposal between people of opposite sexes would always have been wholly free from sexual overtones.[2]

However this may be, Ninlil is clearly not taken aback. She tells of the child in her womb, the gatekeeper's future master, presumably the ultimate object of the oath of allegiance. The mention of Suen gives Enlil his clue. He has the gatekeeper suggest to Ninlil that she lie with him to conceive one more child who can take the place of Suen in the netherworld and thus preserve him for the world above. Ninlil agrees, but in the gatekeeper's chamber it is the concealed Enlil who lies with her and engenders upon her another child, this time the future king of the netherworld, Nergal or Meslamtaea.

Enlil then continues his journey until he comes to the "man of the river of the mountains," to whom he gives the same directions he gave to the gatekeeper. When Ninlil arrives, the same dialogue follows, with the same results. This time Enlil engenders the god Ninazu.

A third and last stop on the way is at the ferryman of the river, and in his chamber Enlil, posing as him, engenders the god Enbilulu. With that the rhapsodist has come to the end of what he had to tell, and concludes with a paean in praise of Enlil as a mighty god whose word has the power to come true—even if, as

---

2. This oath is demanded—as an erotic ploy—by the girl in the "Tavern Sketch," above, and in the Akkadian Gilgamesh epic Ishtar demands it of Gilgamesh as a binding acceptance of her offer of marriage. Oath by touching the genitalia of the one to whom the oath is made is mentioned also in the Bible, in Genesis 24:1–9, where Abraham's servant swears not to take a Canaanite wife to Isaac, and in Genesis 47:29–31, where Joseph swears to Jacob that he will carry his body out of Egypt and bury it with Jacob's forefathers. In both of these cases there are no erotic overtones, but rather a focus on line of descent, symbolized by the genitalia. It seems likely that some such concept originally played in as a background for Enlil's ploy.

here, it is spoken to deceive—and as a source of fertility, yields, and prosperity. The traditional closing words of praise also include Ninlil.

This story, as will be seen, is told in thoroughly anthropomorphic terms. Ninlil's all-engrossing craving for a child sets in motion a series of events gathering momentum from Enlil's lustfulness and Ninlil's concern for the welfare of the yet-unborn Suen. The scene is the everyday one of Nippur with its familiar landmarks and assembly administering justice.

Yet this should not blind one to the fact that the names of the characters in the tale identify them as major deities, and that the praise of Enlil's powers at the end presents these powers as divine and cosmic. His word has the quality of automatically coming true, his powers for fertility and prosperity are for fertility and yields in nature. We are thus clearly dealing with a myth; that is to say, with sacred knowledge about the powers that govern existence, their nature, and how they came about.

Attempting to understand the tale in such terms, one will probably do well to take as the clue the encomium at the end and see the aim of the myth as one of characterizing and celebrating the powers that bring cosmic fertility. With this fits that Enlil in one of his essential aspects is god of the wind as a productive force, for *en* means "productive manager" and *lil* means "wind." His name characterizes him thus as "productive-manager wind," that is, as the moist winds of spring—growing weather.

Since fertility in nature is usually seasonal in character only, the powers thought to bring it about tended to be seen as shortlived. Thus deities of fertility and natural abundance, of whatever kind, take on the character of dying and reviving gods. They die or disappear into the mountains, which to the ancients was the realm of death, to reappear again next year in their season. In the case of Enlil, the spring winds, growing weather disappears with the onset of the long, dry summer. In the myth this is expressed as Enlil's banishment and his going away to the mountains.[3]

Ninlil, according to her name, which means "lady wind," is simply the female counterpart of Enlil, the fertility and productivity in the spring wind taking the form mythopoeically of a productive divine couple. Since she and Enlil are thus merely parts of the same phenomenon, the spring winds, she naturally follows him when he goes into the mountains.

There is, however, also another side to Ninlil. The myth makes her the daughter of the goddess Ninshebargunu, the goddess of barley, and under her name Sud she is known elsewhere as a cereal goddess, most likely perhaps goddess

3. There is in Enlil's being banished to the mountains an odd ambivalence which was probably not lost on the ancient listeners, for in one of his aspects Enlil was the mountains. A frequently used name for him was Kurgal, "great mountain." His temple in which he lived was Ekur "house mountain," and the theriomorphic forms under which he could be envisaged were those of mountain goats or the wild bison of the mountains. The connection between this aspect of the god and his aspect as spring wind is conceivably that these winds were seen as cool and moist mountain air blowing in from the east.

of the cleaned, naked grains. Sud was the city goddess of Shuruppak, a city near Nippur, and was undoubtedly originally a goddess separate from Ninlil who was later identified with her. In mythological terms this was expressed by allowing Sud to be her original name and the name Ninlil that given her by Enlil when he married her.

In the myth here told Ninlil's going to bathe in the canal may reflect the irrigation of the ripening grain, and Enlil's taking her in spite of her weak protests the role of the wind in winnowing it.

Since the image of Ninlil thus differs significantly in the first half of the story, as here told, from what it is in the second—from grain goddess to wind goddess—it may well be that the story as we have it is a composite of two originally separate tales, as are so many other Sumerian myths.

Consistent with the theme of productivity and the related one of the mountains which become identified with the netherworld is the nature of the children Enlil engenders. Suen, the oldest, was god of the moon, but also a power for fertility. His special care is the growth of the marshes, filling them with water in spring, and the multiplying of the herds of cows grazing in them. Having been engendered in the world above and protected by having his younger brothers serve as substitutes for him in the netherworld, he is not of that dark realm. Wholly, though, he has not escaped it. One day every month he spends there, and during the month light and darkness struggle in him, now one, now the other having the upper hand. That the ancients saw this as a struggle between life and death is suggested by a curse at the end of the stela with the laws of Hammurabi; Suen is asked to afflict a possible violater of the stela with "life that is ever struggling with death," surely a reference to his own nature.

The second son, Nergal, or Meslamtaea, was thought by the ancients to be king of the netherworld. He is occasionally hailed as a producer of abundance, but mostly less benevolent aspects are stressed. He is god of death, of plague, and of war.

Ninazu, the third son, was a netherworld deity of the "dying god" type. Essentially he would seem to be a god of the spring rains which die when summer sets in. His name may be interpreted as "the water-pouring lord," and his Akkadian counterpart was Tishpak, whose name means "downpour."

Enbilulu, the fourth and last son, was god of irrigation, of dikes and canals, and so of agricultural yields. Relatively little is known about him, and evidence for his being a netherworld deity is limited to this myth.

Seen as a myth, then, the tale of Enlil and Ninlil tells how a great many powers for fertility and abundance came into being, why they are partly or wholly powers of the netherworld, and how they derive ultimately from Enlil, the

Lord of heaven, lord making yields be,
  and lord of the earth,
- - - - - - - - -
Lord of the earth, lord making yields be
  and lord of heaven.

PRIMEVAL
NIPPUR

It was just a city, just a city[4]
    but these chose to come to settle,
Nippur was just a city,
    but these chose to come to settle,
Durgishimmar,[5] was just a city
    but these chose to come to settle.

Just Idsalla[6] was its pure river,
just Kargeshtina[7] its harbor quay,
just Karusar[8] its mooring quay,
just Pulal[9] its well of sweet water,
just Nunbirdu[10] its shimmering canal,
if measured out, just fifty *sar*[11] each
    were its arable lands.

Just Enlil was its young man   10
just Ninlil was its young maiden
just Nunbarshegunu, was its matron.

NINLIL IS
WARNED BY
HER MOTHER

In those days
    did the mother who gave her birth
    advise the girl,
Nunbarshegunu
    advised Ninlil:
"May you not, o woman,
    bathe in the pure canal,
    in the pure canal,
may you not, o Ninlil,
    come stepping (back)
    unto the bank of Nunbirdu!
He who is all bright eyes,
    the master, who is all bright eyes,
    will be laying eyes upon you,

---

4. That is, it was just like any other town, having not yet attained to its later eminence and size.

5. Name for Nippur or possibly for a specific part of it around Ekur, where the storyteller located the early town.

6. Presumably a branch of the Euphrates which flowed through Nippur in antiquity. The name *Idsalla* means simply "the wide river." It was also used for the Tigris.

7. "The wine quay." Apparently the harbor closest to Ekur, since it was used by the goddess of nearby Isin on her ritual visits to that temple.

8. "The neighbor quay." Apparently a subsidiary harbor used for boats tying up for a longer stay.

9. This was a well located in the main courtyard of Ekur.

10. The Nunbirdu canal, as shown by an ancient map, flowed just outside the city wall northeast of Ekur.

11. A *sar* measured 35.28 square meters.

the great mountain, father Enlil,[12]
  who is all bright eyes,
  will be laying eyes upon you,
the shepherd, the decision maker,
  who is all bright eyes,
  will be laying eyes upon you.
Forthwith that cock   20
  will come burgeoning,
  he will be kissing you,
and, happy, will gladly leave with you
  the glorious sperm filled into the womb."

NINLIL DRAWS   To the mother who advised her
HER OWN   she on her part lent ear.
CONCLUSIONS   In that selfsame pure canal,
  in that selfsame pure canal,
  the woman came and bathed,
and Ninlil was about to come stepping[13]
  (back) unto the bank of Nunbirdu.

ENLIL SEES   He who is all bright eyes,
HER AND   the master, who is all bright eyes,
PROPOSITIONS laid eyes upon her,
HER   the great mountain, father Enlil,
  who is all bright eyes,
  laid eyes upon her,
the shepherd, the decision maker,
  who is all bright eyes,
  laid eyes upon her:

"Let me make love with you!"
  he was saying to her,
  but was not thereby able
  to make her agree to it.
"Let me kiss you!"
  Enlil was saying to her,

12. Mention of Enlil automatically calls up his standard epithets and titles even though, as here, they do not fit the situation. Enlil is not yet "father" Enlil, nor would the other titles have been applicable at the time spoken of. This feature seems to a survival from oral poetry, where it is very common.

13. To the ancient listeners the name of the place where Ninlil chose to disobey her mother may well have seemed ominous and boding nothing good. Nunbirdu means "Prince Birdu," and this Birdu was an infernal deity, so that the shadow of the netherworld already falls over the course of events narrated.

but was not thereby able
    to make her agree to it.

NINLIL
REFUSES

"My parts are little,   30
    know not how to stretch,
my lips are little,
    know not how to kiss!
If my mother learned about it
    she would be slapping my hand,
if my father learned about it
    he would be grabbing hold of me
    (harshly),
and it would not be for me,
    now, to tell my girlfriend,
    I should be drying up on her!"

ENLIL SEEKS
MEANS OF
CROSSING
OVER

Enlil said to his page, Nusku:[14]
"Nusku, my page!"
    "Yes, Pray!"
"Great trust of Ekur."
    "Yes, my master!"
"With a girl so nice, so shapely,
with Ninlil, so nice, so shapely,
one gets an urge   40
    to make love,
    one gets an urge to kiss!"

The page brought to his master
    the likes of a boat[15]
brought to him the likes of a towline
    of a small boat,
brought to him the likes of a big boat.
"My master willing,
    let me float him down on it,
so he can follow the urge
    to make that love,
    follow the urge to kiss those lips,
Father Enlil willing,
    let me float him down on it,

14. God of lamps, and Enlil's right hand and agent.
15. That is, something that would serve as a boat, perhaps an improvised raft or the like, which Nusku gradually made bigger as he collected more materials, until it would finally do.

so he can follow the urge
   to make that love,
   follow the urge to kiss those lips!"

ENLIL AND
NINLIL
UNITE

As he was hugging her
   he held her hands,
followed the urge
   to make that love,
   followed the urge to kiss those lips;
and she for her part   50
   was making lie up next to him
   the bottom and little moist place.
He followed the urge
   to make that love,
   followed the urge to kiss those lips,
and at his first making love,
   at his first kiss,
he poured into the womb for her
   the sperm, (germ) of Suen (the moon),
   the bright lone divine traveler![16]

ENLIL IS
OUTLAWED
FOR RAPE

Enlil was passing through Kiur,[17]
and as Enlil was passing through Kiur
the fifty great gods,
and the seven gods
   of (formulating) the decisions,
were seizing Enlil in Kiur:
"The sex offender[18] Enlil
   will leave the town!
The sex offender Nunamnir[19]   60
   will leave the town!"

16. "The bright lone divine traveler," ash-im-babbar, is a frequently used name for the moon god.

17. Kiur was the forecourt to Ekur. Here in later times Ninlil's temple was located. In a corner of Kiur called Ubshu'ukkina the gods met in assembly to pass decrees or sit in judgment. Cf. "The Eridu Genesis" above, n. 17.

18. The term translated "sex offender" denotes a person who for reasons connected with sex is, or has become, taboo; temporarily, as for instance a menstruating woman, or permanently, as here. The use of this term, and the penalty of banishment imposed, show that Enlil's offense was considered a crime, an act threatening society as a whole, probably because divine anger would bring retribution on the society unless the offender were removed from it.

Later Sumerian law took a more lenient view of the deflowering of a freeborn girl without her parents' knowledge—and presumably without her consent—and prescribed enforced marriage as the solution. Banishment was a severe penalty. It is prescribed in the code of Hammurabi (par. 154) only for a man having sexual relations with his own daughter.

19. A frequently used name for Enlil in literary texts. It means "Prince Authority."

ENLIL LEAVES
FOR THE
NETHERWORLD

Enlil, in accordance
   with what had been decided about him,
     left town.

NERGAL IS
ENGENDERED

Enlil was walking along,
   Ninlil was following,
Nunamnir was walking along,
   the girl was pursuing.
Enlil said to the man
   (in charge) of the city gate:
"Man of the city gate
   man of the bolt,
man of the lock,
   man of the holy bolt!
Your mistress Ninlil
   will be coming,
an she ask you about me,
do you not show her where I am!"[20]   70

Ninlil said to the man
   (in charge) of the city gate:
"Man of the city gate,
   man of the bolt,
man of the lock,
   man of the holy bolt!
Where did Enlil,
   your master, go?"[21]

Enlil had the man of the city-gate
   answer her:

MAN OF THE
CITY GATE

"My master never deigned
   to exchange pleasantries with me,
Enlil never deigned
   to exchange pleasantries with me!"

NINLIL

"Having decided in my mind,
   I made my plans,
and was filling from him
   my empty womb,
Enlil, king of all lands   80
   made love with me.

20. The place where he hid was obviously the gatekeeper's chamber, where Ninlil later lay with him thinking he was the gatekeeper.
21. Ninlil will have lost sight of Enlil when he hid himself.

As Enlil is your master,
    so also am I your mistress!"

MAN OF THE   "An you be my mistress
CITY GATE   let my hand touch your pudenda![22]

NINLIL   "A sperm, your (future) master,
    a lustrous sperm, is in my womb,
a sperm, (germ) of Suen (the moon),
    a lustrous sperm, is in my womb!"[23]

MAN OF THE   "May the sperm, my (future) master,
CITY GATE   go heavenward,
    and may my sperm
      go to the netherworld,
may my sperm
    instead of the sperm, my (future) master,
    come to the netherworld!"

Enlil, as man of the city gate
    had her lie down in the latter's chamber,
made love with her, kissed her;
and at his lovemaking,
    at his first kiss,
he poured into the womb for her   90
    the sperm, (germ) of Nergal,[24]
    the one issuing forth from Meslam!

NINAZU IS   Enlil was walking along,
ENGENDERED   Ninlil was following,
Nunamnir was walking along,
    the girl was pursuing.
Enlil drew near
    the river of the mountains,
    the man-nourishing river,
and to the man (in charge)
    of the river of the mountains,
    the man-nourishing river,[25]
    Enlil said:

22. Apparently an offer to swear an oath of allegiance. See the introduction, above.

23. Ninlil's mention of the unborn Suen as the gatekeeper's future master is presumably to have the latter include him in the oath of allegiance.

24. The name of the city gate by which Enlil left is not stated, but since the child engendered in it was Nergal, it seems likely that the ancient listeners would instinctively have thought of the Nergal gate, a gate which leads out through the city wall of Nippur a short distance due north of Ekur and Kiur.

25. The ancients identified the netherworld with the mountains to the east of Mesopotamia. The

"Your mistress Ninlil
      will be coming,
an she ask you about me,
do you not show her where I am!"

Ninlil was nearing
      the river of the mountains,
      the man-nourishing river,
and to the man (in charge)
      of the river of the mountains,
      the man-nourishing river,
      Ninlil said:
"Where did Enlil,   100
      your master go?"

Enlil had the man
      (in charge) of the river of the mountains
      answer her:
"My master never deigned
      to exchange pleasantries with me,
Enlil never deigned
      to exchange pleasantries with me!"

NINLIL   "Having decided in my mind,
                    I made my plans,
               and was filling from him
                    my empty womb,
               Enlil, king of all lands,
                    made love with me.
               As Enlil is your master,
                    so also am I your mistress!"

MAN OF THE   "An you be my mistress
RIVER   let my hand touch your pudenda!"

NINLIL   "A sperm, your (future) master,
                    a lustrous sperm, is in my womb,
               a sperm, (germ) of Suen (the moon),   110
                    a lustrous sperm, is in my womb!"

MAN OF THE   "May the sperm, my (future) master,
RIVER   go heavenward,

---

volume of water carried by the mountain streams in the spring as the accumulated snow melted caused the rise in the rivers of Sumer on which irrigation and yields depended. They were thus "man-nourishing."

and may my sperm
go to the netherworld,
may my sperm,
instead of the sperm, my (future) master,
come to the netherworld!"

Enlil, as the man
(in charge) of the river of the mountains,
had her lie down in the latter's chamber,
made love with her, kissed her;
and at his first lovemaking,
at his first kiss,
he poured into the womb for her
the sperm, (germ) of Ninazu,
owner of the (temple) manor Egida.[26]

ENBILULU IS
ENGENDERED

Enlil was walking along,
Ninlil was following,
Nunamnir was walking along,
the girl was pursuing,
Enlil drew near
Silulim[27] the ferryman,
and to Silulim the ferryman,   120
Enlil said:
"Your mistress Ninlil
will be coming,
an she ask you about me,
do you not show her where I am!"

Ninlil drew near the ferryman
and said to him: 125
"O ferry-man! Where did Enlil,
your master, go?"

Enlil had the man Silulim
make answer:
"My master never deigned
to exchange pleasantries with me,
Enlil never deigned
to exchange pleasantries with me!"

26. Egida was the name of Ninazu's temple in the city of Enegi(r), located on the Euphrates between Larsa and Ur.

27. *Silulim* means "staghorn." The stag, as an animal typical of the mountains, symbolized the mountain/netherworld character of the ferryman. He is, to the best of our knowledge, not mentioned elsewhere.

NINLIL	"Having decided in my mind, 130
	    I made my plans,
	and was filling from him
	    my empty womb,
	Enlil, king of all lands,
	    made love with me;
	As Enlil is your master,
	    so also am I your mistress!"

SILULIM	"An you be my mistress, let my hand touch your pudenda!"

NINLIL	"A sperm, your future) master,
	    a lustrous sperm is in my womb,
	a sperm, (germ) of Suen (the moon),
	    a lustrous sperm is in my womb!"

SILULIM	"May the sperm, my (future) master,
	    go heavenward,
	and may my sperm
	    go to the netherworld,
	may my sperm,
	    instead of the sperm, my (future) master,
	    come to the netherworld!"

	Enlil, as Silulim,
	    had her lie down in the latter's chamber,
	made love with her, kissed her, 140
	and at his first lovemaking,
	    at his first kiss,
	he poured into the womb for her
	    the sperm, (germ) of Enbilulu,
	    the river warden![28]

CONCLUDING
PAEAN
	Thou art Lord! Thou are master!
	Enlil, thou are lord! Thou art master!
	Nunamnir, thou art lord! Thou art master!
	A lord carrying great weight,
	    lord of the storehouse,
	    art thou!
	The lord making the barley sprout forth,
	    the lord making the vines sprout forth,
	    art thou!

28. Enbilulu was a god of irrigation, responsible for dikes and canals. Note that he and Ninazu, both of whom are gods connected with water, were conceived by Enlil at the mountain/netherworld river when he was posing as a figure connected with it.

Lord of heaven, lord making yields be,
   and lord of the earth,
     art thou!
Lord of the earth, lord making yields be,
   and lord of heaven
     art thou!
Enlil being lord, Enlil being master,   150
and inasmuch as a lord's word
   is a thing unalterable,
his sagacious word
   cannot be changed!

Give praise unto Mother Ninlil!
Father Enlil, praise!

Enki and Ninsikila/Ninhursaǧa

This odd composition is perhaps best understood as an occasional piece put together to entertain visitors from the island of Dilmun at a banquet at the royal court in Ur. Dilmun, modern Bahrein, was the intermediary for sea trade with India and Africa, and so was of sufficient importance for traders from there to be given official welcome when their ships docked at Ur.

The composition takes pains to flatter the visitors with praise of Dilmun's sacred origins and its god-given worldwide trade relations. It is also, one might venture, tailored to a sailor's robust sense of humor.[1] Apparently it was quite popular, for it has come down to us in no fewer than three different versions, a short one from Ur, a longer one from Nippur, and a fragment of a third one of unknown provenience.[2] The translation here given represents a composite text. It uses the Nippur version as a basis and adds from the other two versions the sections which the Nippur version does not have. The extent of such additions is indicated in the notes.

As will be seen, this composition, like so many others, consists of two originally separate and independent stories linked loosely to one another with no attempt at achieving any real integration and conformity.

FIRST STORY: ENKI AND NINSIKILA

The first of these stories deals with how Dilmun was supplied with fresh water. It begins in primeval Dilmun, where Enki lies with his consort Ninsikila, and where everything is still in the bud, pristine and unformed; nothing has yet settled into

---

1. The humorous character of the composition was missed by me in earlier attempts at interpretation. It should have been obvious.

2. The Nippur version was edited by S. N. Kramer, *Enki and Ninhursag* (New Haven, 1945) with a discussion of earlier treatments. See also his study of it in *ANET*. The version from Ur is published in *UET* VI/I (1963), no. 1, and the version of unknown provenience was published by de Genouillac in *TCL* XVI (Paris, 1930), no. 62 and republished with a new copy by J.-M. Durant in *RA* 71 (1977), p. 171. A new edition was given by P. Attinger in "Enki et Ninhursag" *ZA* 74 p. 1–52. The translation here given has also had the benefit of collations by S. N. Kramer and S. Lieberman, generously placed at my disposal.

its final being or behavior.[3] Also, the city of Dilmun, which Enki apparently has given as present to Ninsikila, may not be in its final form: it lacks fresh water for a riverine harbor quay, for irrigation agriculture, and for drinking water. Ninsikila points out this serious lack to Enki, as whose daughter she here appears. She begins her enumeration of what is missing somewhat oddly with the harbor quay, perhaps because the rhapsode thought that that would be what visiting sailors would worry most about. Enki readily agrees to set matters right. He brings fresh water underground from the Euphrates at the Sumerian port of Izin[4] and has it fill the large footprints made by the sun god as he steps from Dilmun up onto heaven[5] much as footprints in marshy ground will fill up with water. Thus Dilmun enjoys prosperity and becomes an emporium for the neighboring regions. The version from Ur has Enki expatiate further on this in a long series of blessings detailing Dilmun's far-flung trade relationships and outstanding agricultural products.[6]

Reading this story as it is presented in the text, one will notice that it is not really very well told. The description of primeval Dilmun in its inchoate state is not followed up but is left hanging without any attempt to clarify its import for what follows: Ninsikila's city appears suddenly and abruptly: "You have given a city!" without our having first been told about that city and about the circumstances leading up to Enki's giving it to Ninsikila. This is not normal style; rather, it is as if the storyteller only remembered disconnected bits of a longer tale, or as if he had ruthlessly cut a tale major parts of which did not serve his purpose.

LINKAGE WITH SECOND STORY

The linkage between the first and the second story in the composition is, as mentioned, very loose. Ninsikila's city and its waters are lost sight of completely, and so, probably, is Dilmun; for the scene of the second story is most naturally seen as the marshes in southern Mesopotamia. Thus, essentially, there remains as link merely the identity of the chief characters in the two stories, Enki and Ninsikila, and even that identity, at a closer look, is questionable.

The Ninsikila of the first story is, we noted, the spouse (ll. 6 and 9) and the daughter (l. 29) of Enki. It is quite otherwise in the second story. Here as Nintur

3. Cf. "The Birth of Man," above, l. 3, for the same idea of an initially inchoate world achieving, or being given, its present mode of being.

4. Izin has not yet been identified. The mention of bollards indicates that it was a harbor city, and the fact that Dilmun's fresh water came from there suggests a position on the Euphrates, perhaps near the outlet, where the river loses itself in the sea and could have been thought to have gone underground.

5. In Sumerian mythical geography Dilmun lay at sunrise, which is how it conceivably looked to an observer from the mainland west of it. The sun god was traditionally assumed to step up unto heaven over two mountains. In Dilmun those steppingstones would have been the central hills called Jabal Dukhan.

6. The text breaks off at this point, so one does not know how long he may have gone on.

(l. 64), she is yet unmarried and is pursued by Enki, whose advances she rejects until he makes a binding proposal and marries her. Even had the composer taken care to smooth over this incongruity, however, the basic independence and essential incongruity of the stories he chose to join would have stood out. Ninsikila or, to give her her correct name, Nin-sikilak, "lady of lustrations"[7] was a purely local goddess of Dilmun. There she was married to Ensak, who figures at the end of the second story as one born of Enki's body and as lord of Dilmun. She is not, however one looks at it, on a par with the great goddess of the second story, Nintur, or, by her other name, Ninhursaga, who was a member of the ruling triad of gods. In choosing to join the two stories the composer may, however, deliberately have accepted the incongruity as a means of flattering the visitors, who could not but be pleased to have their goddess so signally advanced in rank.

Even the identity of the Enki of the first story with the one of the second one may not be beyond doubt. The fact that he is introduced so incongruously as spouse of Ninsikila may well be a carry-over from a more original form of the story, in which Ensak was Ninsikila's husband and gave her her city, providing it with an underground flow of fresh water. In Islamic times there was a tradition reported by Yāqut that Hajar, from whom the capital of Bahrein was named, was married to the lord of the river that is in Bahrein.[8] Arab geographers likewise report that mainland Bahrein owes its supplies of fresh waters to an underground river draining the Nedj highlands.[9] Near the islands water wells up from beneath the sea in such masses and with such force that it entirely displaces the salt waters. It seems quite possible that similar traditions existed in earlier times, and if so the composer may have based his story on them, merely changing the name of the river god to Enki.

SECOND STORY: ENKI AND NINHURSAGA

The second story rather abruptly begins by telling how Enki—here clearly the personified river—tries to make love with Nintur by pushing his phallus into the canebrake, which is probably to be understood mythopoeically as the pubic hairs of the earth mother. She refuses him until he addresses her under oath as "great spouse of the prince," that is, of himself, and thereby formally takes her in marriage.

7. Why the composer changed her name from Nin-sikilak "lady of lustrations" to Ninsikila, which means "pure virgin lady," is not clear. It is possible that he confused the goddess with a Sumerian goddess Ninsikila, consort of the god Lisi in Adab, who may have been more familiar to him. It is also possible, however, that he changed the name deliberately to have it, as a pun on ki-sikil "maiden," designate the goddess before she was married to Enki. See below, n. 17. A similar punning change was apparently his change of ᵈNinkirida to Nin-kiri₄-e-dú "lady born of a nose" to fit in with her role in the story. See below, n. 26.

8. See Fr. E. Burrows, "Tilmun, Bahrain, Paradise," *Orientalia* 30/2 (Rome, 1928): 10.

9. Cf. ibid., p. 18, with n. 2.

Nintur gives birth to Ninnisiga,[10] who, when grown, goes to the riverbank, where Enki unites with her. She gives birth to Ninkurra, who in her turn goes to the riverbank and is made pregnant by Enki. In the version from Nippur she gives birth to the spider goddess, goddess of weaving, Uttu. In the version of uncertain origin there is one more generation; there Ninkurra gives birth to Nin-imma, and it is she who, after her visit to the riverbank, gives birth to Uttu.

This remarkable series of Enki's great-great-grandfatherly conquests is not without humor, especially since it ends with the "shapely and decorous" spider personified, and the rhapsodist very likely intended it to produce a smile in the listeners. It may, though, actually build on an older cosmic genealogy, such as is frequently found at the beginnings of incantations and of blessings of materials used in rituals. Water and the foothills, Enki and Ninhursaga, produce the mountain verdure (Ninnisiga) which in turn produces the high mountains behind (Ninkurra), and they, as pasture for sheep, produce the goddess of weaving, Uttu, another name for whom is Sig, "Wool."

By the time Uttu is grown up, it appears that Enki's long-suffering actual wife, Ninhursaga, has finally lost patience with his philandering. At any rate she warns Uttu against him, and when Enki approaches he finds Uttu securely ensconced in her house—apparently the blind spiders build at the center of their nets. To win her he has again to resort to a proposal of marriage, and so asks her which marriage gifts will serve to obtain her "Yes." She tells him. The things desired are all fruits and vegetables, and so Enki finds a gardener, whom he helps by filling his irrigation ditches with water. The gardener is delighted and readily gives Enki all he wants, and Enki, having spruced up his appearance, sets out with the gifts for Uttu's house.

Uttu, when she hears what Enki has brought her, happily opens the door to him and lets him in. Once in, Enki, apparently celebrating the occasion, gets Uttu drunk on beer and then takes her by force. Uttu's wails are heard by Ninhursaga, who comes to her aid, removes Enki's semen from her body, and plants it. From it eight plants grow up.

After a while Enki comes upon these plants and is annoyed at not knowing them. His page Isimu, however, suggests that he, Isimu, call each grass something and then hand it to Enki to eat. Enki agrees, and Isimu's suggestion is carried out. "Enki determined the nature of the grasses," says the story "had them know it in their hearts."

Exactly what this means may well have been more apparent to the ancients than it is to us. Tentatively we should suggest that one does not eat what one does not know. However, assigning a name means assigning an identity, namely the one already implied in the name. The names that Isimu suggests may at the time have been free invention on his part, but even so, each one will already have carried a meaning which, since they are names of actual plants, will have been known to the listeners.

10. This seems a better reading than either Nin-sar or Nin-mú.

The new identity imposed on the plants by Enki cannot, it seems, completely have replaced their original nature as Enki's semen, for once eaten and absorbed into his body, they make him pregnant. He, as a male, is of course unable to give them birth, and as a result suffers grievously, to the point of being near death.

The gods are greatly perturbed, but do not know what to do. However, the fox appears and offers to bring Ninhursaḡa. It makes good on its promise. Ninhursaḡa hurries to Nippur, is loosed from the oath with which she cursed Enki when she saw what he had done to the plants, and is ready to help. She places him in her vulva and gives birth to eight deities, each from a different part of Enki's body, each with a name in some way a reminder of that body part from which it was born. This would surely have been admired as a brilliant jeu d'esprit.

The composition ends with Ninhursaḡa assigning roles or status to the newborn deities. The last one is Ensak, who is made lord of Dilmun. Thus the composition both begins and ends with Dilmun.

ADDRESS TO
VISITORS FROM
DILMUN
	Pure is the city—
	   and you are the ones
	   to whom it is allotted![11]
	Pure is Dilmun land!
	Pure is Sumer—
	   and you are the ones
	   to whom it is allotted![12]
	Pure is Dilmun land!

DILMUN AT
THE BEGIN-
NING OF TIME
	Pure was Dilmun land!
	   Virginal was Dilmun land!
	Virginal was Dilmun land!
	   Pristine was Dilmun land!

When all alone
   he had lain down in Dilmun,
the spot where Enki
   had lain down with his spouse
that spot was virginal,
   that spot was pristine!
When all alone
   he had lain down in Dilmun,
the spot where Enki
   had lain down with Ninsikila
that spot was virginal,
   that spot was pristine!

10

11. Direct address to visitors from Dilmun.
12. Direct address to the court.

THINGS YET
IN INCHOATE
STATE

In Dilmun the raven
  was not (yet) cawing,
the flushed partridge
  not cackling.
The lion slew not,
the wolf was not
  carrying off lambs,
the dog had not been taught
  to make kids curl up,
the colt had not learned
  that grain was to be eaten.
When a widow had spread out
  malt on the roof,
the birds were not eating
  that malt up there,
the dove was then not tucking
  the head (under its wing).

No eye-diseases said there:
  "I the eye disease."[13]
No headache said there:
  "I the headache."
No old woman belonging to it
  said there:
  "I old woman."
No old man belonging to it
  said there:
  "I old man."
No maiden was as she is in
  her unwashed state
  in the city.
No man dredging a river
  said there:
  "It is getting dark!"
No constable made the rounds
  in his border district.
No singer was singing
  work songs there,
and no wailings were wailed
  in the city's outskirts
  there.

20

13. That is to say, there was nothing that could call itself an eye disease or a headache, no one who could call himself or herself old, etc.

<table>
<tr><td>DILMUN'S CITY
NEEDS WATER</td><td>

Ninsikila said
  to her father Enki:
"You have given a city!   30
  You have given a city!
  What avails me your giving?
You have given a city, Dilmun,
  You have given a city!
  What avails me your giving?
You have given a city, [Dilmun]
  You have given a city!
  What avails me your giving?
[A city] that has no river [quay!]
You have given [a city, Dilmun,]
  a city that has no river [quay!]
  [What avails me your giving?]

[You have given] a city, [Dilmun!]
  [You have given a city!
  What avails me your giving?
[You have given a city
  that has no fields] and glebe,
  [plo]wlands!
[You have given a city, Dilmun!
  You have given a city!
  What avails me your giving?
[You have given a city
  that has no ponds
  of sweet water!]

</td></tr>
<tr><td>ENKI PROMISES
WATER AND TO
MAKE THE CITY
AN EMPORIUM</td><td>

[Father Enki
  answered Ninsikila:
"At the stepping onto heaven   40
  by Utu
may, from Izin's shore's
  standing bollards,
from Nanna's radiant
  temple up high,[14]
from the mouth of the waters
  running underground
  sweet waters run out
  of the ground for you!]

</td></tr>
</table>

14. Nanna was god of the moon and city god of Ur, where he dwelt in a temple high on top of a stage tower or ziggurat. The temple is probably mentioned here so that the capital, Ur, which also was on the Euphrates, could share the credit for providing Dilmun's water.

May the waters rise up from it
    into both his great footprints!
May your city drink water
    aplenty from them,
may Dilmun drink water
    aplenty from them
may your ponds of salt water
    become ponds of sweet water![15]
[May your fields and glebe,
    the plowlands,
    produce grain for you!]
May your city become (an emporium,)
    a (store)house on the quay
    for the country's
    produce!
May Dilmun become (an emporium,)   50
    a (store)house on the quay
    for the country's produce!
May the land Tukrish[16]   x + 1
    [offer you for exchange]
    gold of the river-bends,
may it exchange lapis lazuli
    and clear [lapis lazuli!]
May the land Meluhha
    load precious desirable sard,
mesu wood of the plains,
    the best *abba* wood
up into large ships!
May the land Marhashi me[et] you

15. Probably the reference here is to the way fresh water at Bahrein wells up from the bottom of the sea, replacing sea water. The storyteller seems not to have been aware that this happens in the sea, and so takes for granted that ponds are involved.

16. The section from l. 51 to l. 70 is attested only in the version from Ur. It is not certain what directly preceded and followed it, but it seems natural to assume that it continued Enki's blessings, so we have tentatively inserted it at this point.

The countries mentioned are on the outer periphery of the world as known to the average Sumerian. Tukrish was situated north or northeast of the later Assyria; Meluhha and Magan were identified with Ethiopia and Egypt by the scribes of the Assyrian empire period. Many modern scholars, however, would like to identify one of them at least with India, which is known from archeological evidence to have had trade relations with Dilmun. Marhashi is probably to be sought in the region to the south and west of Lake Urmia. What the Sealands and the "Tent" lands were is not clear, possibly indefinite poetic terms for lands overseas and desert lands dotted with nomads' tents. The order of the names, to stress the far-flung nature of the trade involved, seems to be by diametrically opposed pairs, Tukrish-Meluhha for north and south, Marhashi-Magan for east and west.

with precious stones,
    topa[zes],
May the land Magan
    offer you [for exchange]
    strong copper gongs,
dolerite, pounding stones,
    and pounding stones
    for two hands!
May the Sealands   x + 10
    offer you [for exchange]
    ebony wood
    fit for a king's chest!
May the "Tent" lands
    offer you [for exchange]
    fine multicolored wools!
May the land Elam
    offer you for exchange
    choice wools, its produce!
May the manor Ur,
    the royal throne dais,
    city of hea[rt's delight,]
[load up into] large ships for you
    sesame, august raiment,
    and fine cloth!
May the wide sea
    [yield you] its wealth!"

All the city's dwellings
    are good dwellings!
All Dilmun's dwellings
    are good dwellings!
Its grains are little grains,
its dates are big dates,
its harvests are triple,   x + 20
its wood is . . . . . wood.

(gap of unknown length)

PROMISES   At this moment, on this day,
FULFILLED   and (under this) sun,
                       at the stepping onto heaven
                         by Utu
                       did from Izin's shore's
                         standing bollards,

from Nanna's radiant
[temple up high,]
from the mouth of the waters
    running underground,
    sweet waters run out
    of the ground for her.
Up into [both] his great footprints
    rose the waters.

Her city drank water
    aplenty from them
Dilmun drank water
    aplenty from them,
her pools of salt water
    became pools of sweet water only,
her fields and glebe,   60
    the plowlands,
    [produced] grain for her,
her city became (an emporium)
    a (store)house on the quay
    for the country's
    produce.
Dilmun became (an emporium)
    a (store)house on the quay
    for the country's
    produce.
At this moment, on this day,
    and (under this) sun,
    thus it verily became!

ENKI WOOS   The only one (with) her,
NINTUR   the wise one,
                            toward Nintur,[17]
                            the country's mother—

17. At this point the second story begins, and the change of name from Ninsikila to Nintur is
dictated by the identity of its heroine, Nintur or Ninhursaǧa. At the same time, however, the
storyteller makes a virtue of necessity by playing very ingeniously on the meaning of the names. Thus
the heroine of his combined tales is Ninsikila before Enki makes advances to her, reminding of *ki-sikil*
"maiden"; when he makes his advances, her future role is adumbrated in Nintur, the country's mother,
for Nintur is the name of the birth goddess preeminently. This play on names is contined in the
following "the august one," *mah*, in l. 86, which reflects the names Ninmah "august queen" and
Dingirmah "august deity" under which Nintur is also known and shows her stature as she refuses Enki's
advances. As Enki offers her marriage by declaration, he addresses her as *dam-gal-nun-na* "great spouse
of the prince," which is here an epithet, but is also the standard, and generally used, name of Enki's
spouse, who is, however, not elsewhere identified with Nintur/Ninhursaǧa. Finally, in telling about

Enki, the wise one,
 toward Nintur,
 the country's mother,
was digging his phallus
 into the levee,
plunging his phallus
 into the canebrake.
The august one, for her part,
 pulled his phallus aside
and cried out:
 "No man take me
 in the marsh!"

ENKI MARRIES
NINTUR BY
DECLARATION

Enki cried out: 70
"By the life's breath
 of Heaven
 I adjure you:
Lie down for me,
 lie down for me!"
 He had his mouth - - -
"Calm down O great spouse
 of the Prince,"
Enki had his mouth
 utter.

NINNISIGA
BORN

On Ninhursaĝa he poured
 semen into the womb,
and she conceived the semen
 in the womb,
 very semen of Enki.
But one day
 was her one month,
but two days
 were her two months,
but three days
 were her three months,
but four days
 were her four months,
but five days   80
 were her five months,

---

the conception of Ninnisiga the storyteller uses the name Ninhursaĝa, "mistress of the foothills,"
perhaps because, as suggested earlier, a mythological genealogy having "lady verdure" (Ninnisiga)
born of the "mistress of the foothills" (Ninhursaĝa) and the freshwater Enki existed.

but six days
　　were her six months,
but seven [days]
　　were her seven months,
but eight [days]
　　were her eight months,
but nine [days]
　　were her nine months!
　　In the month of womanhood
[like juniper oil,]
　　like [juni]per [oil,
　　like a prince's sweet butter,
did Nintur,
　　mother of the country,
[like junip]er [oil,]
give birth
　　[to Ninnisiga.]¹⁸

NINNISIGA GOES
TO THE RIVER

In turn Ninnisiga
　　went out to the riverbank;
Enki was able to see up there　　　　　　90
　　from in the marsh,
　　was able to see up there.
To his page Isimu he said:
"Is this nice youngster
　　not to be kissed?
Is this nice Ninnisiga
　　not to be kissed?"
His page Isimu
　　replied to it to him:
"Is this nice youngster
　　not to be kissed?
With a (favorable)
　　downstream wind
　　blowing for my master,
　　a downstream wind
　　blowing,
he has put his one foot
　　in the boat,
may he not stay the other
　　on dry land!"¹⁹

18. The name means "lady verdure."
19. The sense of the proverb is obviously that once one has taken a decisive first step there is no turning back.

He clasped her to the bosom,
   kissed her,
Enki poured   100
   semen into the womb,
and she conceived the semen
   in the womb,
   very semen of Enki.

NINKURRA
BORN

But one day
   was her one month,
but two days
   were her two months,
but three days   103a
   were her three months,
but four days   103b
   were her four months,
but five days   103c
   were her five months,
but six days   103d
   were her six months,
but seven days   103e
   were her seven months,
but eight days   103f
   were her eight months,
but nine days
   were her nine months.
   In the month of womanhood
like juniper oil,
   like juniper oil,
   like a prince's sweet butter,
[did Ninnisiga
   like juniper oil,
   like juniper oil,
give birth
   to Nink[urra.][20]

NINKURRA
GOES TO THE
RIVER

In turn Ninkurra
   [went out on the riverbank;]
Enki was able to see up there
   from in the marsh,
   was able to see up there.
To his page Isimu [he said:]   110

20. The name means "mistress of the mountains."

"Is this nice youngster
   not to be kissed?
Is this nice Ninkurra
   not to kissed?"

His page Isimu
   replied to it to him:
"Kiss this nice youngster!
Kiss this nice Ninkurra!
With a (favorable)
   downstream wind
   blowing for my master,
   a downstream wind blowing,
he has put his one foot
   in the boat,
may he not stay the other
   on dry land!

He clasped her to the bosom,
   kissed her,
Enki poured   120
   semen into the womb,
and she conceived the semen
   in the womb,
   very semen of Enki.

NIN-IMMA BORN

But one day
   was her one month,
but two days   122a
   were her two months,
but three days   122b
   were her three months,
but four days   122c
   were her four months,
but five days   122d
   were her five months,
but six days   122e
   were her six months,
but seven days   122f
   were her seven months,
but eight days   122g
   were her eight months,
but nine days
   were her nine months.

In the month of womanhood
like juniper oil,
   like juniper oil,
   like a prince's sweet butter,
did Ninkurra
   like juniper oil,
   like juniper oil,
   like a prince's sweet butter,
did Ninkurra in turn
   give birth
   to Nin-imma.[21]

NIN-IMMA GOES
TO THE
RIVER

Her young one
   growing up
   became full-bodied.
Nin-imma in turn [went out]
   on the riverbank;
Enki was towing (his boat)
   up from the marsh
   and was able to see up there,
he la[id] eyes on Nin-imma   130
   on the riverbank,
and to his page Isimu
   he said:
"One like the nice youngster
   should I not kiss?
With one like nice Nin-imma
   should I not
   make love?"

His page Isimu
   replied to it to him:
"A (favorable) downstream wind
   is blowing for my master,
   a downstream wind
   is blowing!
You have put one foot
   in the boat,

21. The name means "lady female genitals." The episode dealing with her is found only in the version of unknown origin. It covers lines 157 to 181. As suggested earlier, it may be an addition by a scribe who wished to prolong the series of Enki's conquests. Her name makes her a natural choice for a sexual partner for Enki.

put the other one up there
   like the first one."

He clasped her to the bosom,
   lying in her crotch,
plied the member
   in the youngster,
      and kissed her.
Enki was pouring on Nin-imma   140
   semen into the womb,
and she conceived the semen
   in the womb,
      very semen of Enki.

UTTU BORN   To the woman
                      its one day
                         was its one month,
                      no more,
                   its two days
                      were its two months,
                      no more,
                   its three days
                      were its three months,
                      no more,
                   its four days
                      were its four months,
                      no more,
                   its five days
                      were its five months,
                      no more,
                   its six [days]
                      were its six months,
                      no more,
                   [its seven days]
                      were its seven months,
                      no more,
                   [its eight days]
                      were its eight months,
                      no more,
                   [and at its nine days,]   150
                      in the month of womanhood
                   [like juniper oil,]
                      [like juniper oil,]
                      like a prince's sweet butter,

[did Nin-imma,
    like juniper oil,]
    like a prince's sweet butter,
give [birth]
    to a shapely and decorous woman,
    Uttu.

UTTU WARNED

Nintur said to Uttu,
    the shapely and decorous woman:
"Let me advise you
    and take you
    my advice!
Let me speak a word to you
    and may you [heed]
    my word!
From in the marsh
    one man
    is able to see up here,
    is able to see up here,
from in the marsh
    Enki
    is able to see up here,
    is able to see up here,
    from in the marsh,
He will [lay] eyes on you
. . . .   160

(gap of approximately ten lines)

[. . . . .]   170'

UTTU DEMANDS
MARRIAGE AND
MARRIAGE
GIFTS

Uttu,
    the shapely and decorous woman
[. . . . .
    . . .] . . [. . .]
[. . . . .
    . . .] . . . [. . .]
. . . .
    will give]
    what the heart desires
    to [obtain a 'Yes'!]"
"Bring [cucumber
    in . . . . .]
bring apples
    with their [stems
    sticking out,]

bring grapes
   in their clusters,
and you will verily
   have hold of my halter,
O Enki, you will verily
   have hold of my halter!"

Next, in filling with water,
he filled water into the dikes,   180'
filled water into the dikes
   with canals along their tops,
filled water into the fallows.

The gardener in his joy
   [rose(?)] from the dust,
and was embracing him:
"Who are you
   [who have watered(?)
   my] garden?"

Enki [said to] the gardener:
["Fill] my lap!
[Bring cucumber
   in . . . . ,
bring apples
   on their stems,
bring grapes   190'
   in their clusters!"]

[He] br[ought him
   cucumbers
   in . . . . .],
brought him apples
   with their stems sticking out,
brought him grapes
   in their clusters,
   filled his lap.

Enki touched up his face,
   took a staff in hand;
Enki came to a halt
   at Uttu's,
called out to her house:
   "Open up!"

"Who are you, you?"

"I am a gardener,
   let me give you
   cucumbers, apples,
   [and grapes]
   for (your) 'Yes!'"

UTTU'S MARRIAGE
CONCLUDED AND
ROUGHLY CON-
SUMMATED

Uttu, in her joy of heart
   opened the house[22]
and Enki was giving Uttu,   200'
   —the shapely and decorous woman—
cucumbers in . . . . . . ,
was giving her apples
   on their stems,
was giving her grapes
   in their clusters,
[poured] beer for her
   in the big quart measure
Uttu—the shapely and decorous woman—
   was swerving to the left
   for him,
   was waving the hands
   for him,
Enki had got Uttu
   feeling good.

He clasped her to the bosom,
   lying in her crotch,
was stabbing
   at her underbelly,
   began hitting the parts,
he clasped her to the bosom
   lying in her crotch,
plied the member   210'
   in the youngster,
   and kissed her.
Enki on Uttu
   was pouring
   semen into the womb,
and she conceived the semen
   in the womb,
   very semen of Enki!

22. The symbolic act that concluded a Sumerian marriage consisted in the bride opening the door to the groom who was bringing the specified wedding gifts. It was followed by the consummation of the marriage and a wedding banquet the next morning.

ENKI'S SEMEN
REMOVED AND
PLANTED

Uttu, the shapely and decorous woman
   was crying: "Woe, my underbelly!
   Woe, my outsides!
   Woe, my innards!"

Ninhursağa [removed] the semen
   from the underbelly,

(Gap of perhaps no more than a line telling that Nin-hursağa planted the semen in the ground.)

ENKI EATS
THE PLANTS

The "tree" plant she grew,
the "honey" plant she grew,
[the "vegetable" plant] she grew,
[the *a-pa* vegetable plant] she grew,   220'
[the *a-tu-tu* plant] she grew,
[the "fennel"(?) plant] she grew,
[the   .   .   .] plant she grew,
[the amharu plant] she grew.

Enki was able to see up there
   from in the marsh,
   was able to see up there.

To his page Isimu he said:
"Plants! Shall I not find out
   their nature?
What is this one?
   What is this one?"
His page Isimu
   replied to it to him:
"I shall say to my master   230'
   'the tree plant',
shall cut it off for him,
   and he can ea[t] it,
I shall say to my master
   'the honey plant,'
shall pull it up for him,
   and he can eat it.
I shall say to my master:
   'the vegetable plant,'
shall cut it off for him,
   and he can eat it.
I shall say to my master:
   'the a-pa vegetable plant,'

shall pull it up for him
        and he can eat it,
I shall say [to my master:]
        'the [a]-tu-tu plant,'
[shall cut it off for him,]
        and he can eat it,
[I shall say to my master:
        'the fen]nel(?) plant,'[23]
[shall pull it up for him,   240'
        and he can eat it,]
[I shall say to my master:
        'the . . . plant,'
shall cut it off for him,]
        and he can eat it,
I shall say [to my master:]
        'the amharu plant,'
shall [pull it up for him,]
        and he can eat it."
[Enk]i determined the nature
        of the plants,
        had them know it in their hearts.

NINHURSAĞA'S
CURSE

Ninhursaĝa
        cursed the name Enki:
"With life-giving eye
        until he is dying
        never will I look
        upon him!"

THE FOX OFFERS
TO BRING
NINHURSAĞA

The Anunnaki
        sat down in the dust,
and the fox[24] was able
        to speak to Enlil:
"If I bring Ninhursaĝa to you,   250'
        what will be my reward?"
Enlil replied to it, to the fox:
"If you bring Ninhursaĝa
        to me,
let me implant
        two standards for you

23. The translations of these plant names is uncertain and must be considered tentative only.
24. The fox to the rescue belongs in fable or fairy tale rather than in myth proper. Its appearance here is one more indication that the composition is meant as entertainment rather than as theology.

in my city,
may you be renowned!"

The fox first anointed
its skin,
it first shook
its hair(?)
it first put kohl
on its eyes,

(gap of some three or four lines)

[The fox said to Ninhursağa:]   260'
"I have gone [to Nippur,]
   but Enlil [. . . . . . . ,]
I have gone [to Ur,]
   but Nanna [. . . . . . ,]
I have gone to [Ararma,]
   but Utu [. . . .]
I have gone to [Uruk,]
   but Inanna . . [. . . ,]
With one
   who is [compas]sionate
   I am seeking refuge
[. . . . .]25
Ninhursağa li[stened
   . . . .]

(gap of some three lines)   270'

[Ninhursağa] said [to it:
"Let me] go with you
   [to Nippur!"]

RITUAL TO   Ninhursağa
RELEASE HER   came running.
FROM HER   The Anunnaki
CURSE ON   slipped off her garment,
ENKI   made warp threads from it,
                 put the curse thereon
                 and cut the warp.

THE PLANT   Ninhursağa laid Enki
DEITIES BORN   in her vulva,

25. The nature of the fox's successful plea is not altogether clear. It may be that, cunningly, it sneaks in the information about Enki's mortal danger by pretending it is seeking a protector, now that its former patron Enki is dying.

[placed(?)] cool hands
on [. . . . . .]
and [. . . .] on its outside (saying:)

"My brother,   280'
  what part of you hurts you?"
"My brainpan
  hurts me!"
She gave birth
  to Abu out of it![26]

"My brother,
  what part of you hurts you?!"
"The top of my hair
  hurts me!"
She gave birth
  to Ninsikila
  out of it.

"My brother,
  what part of you hurts you?"
"My nose hurts me!"
She gave birth
  to Ninkiriedu
  out of it.

"My brother,
  what part of you hurts you?"
"My mouth hurts me!"   290'

---

26. I base the translation of the section about the birth of the children on both the Nippur and the Ur versions, using whichever seems to me to have the better text.

The list of children comprises four male and four female deities, arranged so that the list begins and ends with a pair of males and groups the females together in the middle.

The deities, most of which are known from elsewhere, have been so chosen by the storyteller that the name of each has an element that corresponds with the name of the part of Enki's body from which the deity in question was born. In some cases this correspondence amounts to no more than a similarity in sound of a syllable, as when *ugu-dili* "brainpan" is resumed in the name ᵈAb-ú by their common syllable *u* only. Similar cases are *zi*, *ti*, and *zag*, for it is unlikely that the corresponding syllables in the names ᵈNa-zi, ᵈNin-ti, and ᵈEn-sa₆-ak are words for "throat," "rib," and "side."

More meaningful seem *pa-siki* "top of the hair" as producing ᵈNin-siki-lá "lord bearing wool" (perhaps an ovine deity)—*siki* denoting both "hair" and "wool"; and *ka* "mouth" producing ᵈNin-ka-si "lady filling the mouth," the goddess of beer. Happier still seem *á* "arm (or "branch") properly grown" and *kiri* "nose" giving ᵈNin-kiri₄-e-dú (variant ᵈNin-kiri₄-ù-dú), whose name, as the storyteller gives it, would mean "lady born of a nose." To achieve this he had to adjust the name slightly, though: its actual form is ᵈNin-giri_x-da.

The list as a whole, again, is most likely to be seen as a *jeu d'esprit* rather than an attempt at serious theology: The rhapsodist ends his performance with a scintillating display of wit.

She gave birth
  to Ninkasi
  out of it.

"My brother,
  what part of you hurts you?"
"My throat hurts me!"
She gave birth
  to Nazi
  out of it.

"My brother,
  what part of you hurts you?"
"My arm hurts me!"
She gave birth
  to Azimua
  out of it.

"My brother,
  what part of you hurts you?"
"My ribs hurt me!"
She gave birth   300'
  to Ninti
  out of it.

"My brother,
  what part of you hurts you?"
"My sides hurt me!"
She gave birth
  to Ensak
  out of it.
"For the little ones
  to whom I have
  given birth
  may food-portions
  not [lack!"]
May Abu become king of the grasses,
may Ninsikila become lord of Magan,
may Ninkiriedu marry Ninazu,
may Ninkasi be what satisfies the heart,
may Nazi marry Ninsu,
may Azi[mua marry Nin]gishzida,   310'
may N[inti] become lady of the month,
and may [Ensa]k become lord of Dilmun,
  Praise be to Father Enki!

Inanna's Descent

The joining together of two independent stories which makes up so many Sumerian compositions is here more ingeniously done than is usually the case.

The first story is a myth telling how Inanna unsuccessfully tried to take the rule of Hades away from her sister Ereshkigala, and had to be rescued. The second story, also a myth, deals with the capture and recapture of Dumuzi by a detachment of military police (rangers), originally probably for service in the army, as in other similar Dumuzi tales. In this composition, however, Inanna's release from Hades depends upon her providing a substitute to take her place there, and in a fit of jealousy she hands over Dumuzi.

As the story is told it seems to aim primarily at entertaining. The listener follows the dramatic chain of events as it unfolds and reflects the emotions of the characters as the innocent Dumuzi is made to bear the consequences of Inanna's ill-considered attempt at a coup d'état.

To some extent, though, the underlying mythical background still shows through. The very odd fate of Inanna, her going underground, her being stripped, and her ending up as a stored cut of meat going bad, does not fit well into a story of deities envisioned in human terms; but it parallels fairly closely the fate of the herds of sheep at the end of the grazing season, the animals being shorn, butchered and, the meat hung in underground cold-storage rooms. Since Inanna in her relation to Dumuzi is closely associated with the flocks, she probably stands for them in the myth. Her revival, effected by the water of life and the grass—or pasture—of life, may then represent the reappearance of the live flocks in the pastures in spring when the waters of the spring rains call vegetation to life in the desert.

The myth underlying the second story belongs to a well-known type dramatizing the disappearance of shepherds and flocks as the desert pastures wither in the hot, dry summer. The mythopoeic image is sometimes one of the raiding of the fold by bandits from the mountains, who carry shepherd and sheep off as spoils, sometimes, as apparently here, one of a detachment of military police serving as a press-gang. See "Dumuzi's Dream" and "In the Desert by the Early Grass" earlier in this volume.

INANNA PLANS
TO TAKE OVER
HADES

From the upper heaven
  she had her heart set
  on the netherworld,
the goddess had
  from the upper heaven
  her heart set
  on the netherworld.
Inanna had
  from the upper heaven
  her heart set
  on the netherworld. [1]

My lady forsook heaven,
  forsook earth,
  went down into Hades.
Inanna forsook heaven,
  forsook earth,
  went down into Hades.
Lordship she forsook,
  queenship she forsook,
  went down into Hades.

In Uruk she forsook Eanna,
  went down into Hades.
In Bad-Tibira she forsook Emushkalamma,
  went down into Hades;
in Zabalam she forsook Giguna,
  went down into Hades;
in Adab she forsook Eshara,   10
  went down into Hades;
in Nippur she forsook Ebaragdurgara,
  went down into Hades;

1. In one of Inanna's many aspects she was goddess of the planet Venus, the morning and evening star. As such she identifies herself at the gate of Hades, and that is clearly the aspect under which she is here seen. It is not, however, the aspect of her with which the myth basically deals, that in which she represents the herd animals, and its occurrence here is probably due to the composer, for whom the original myth and its meaning were no longer alive, and who saw a rhetorical possibility of contrast between above and below.

The stanza also differs by using terms expressive of that contrast: *an-gal* "greater heaven," a term for an upper heaven above the visible one, and *ki-gal* "the greater earth," a term for a lower earth beneath the earth, considered the abode of the dead. I have translated it as "netherworld." A different concept located the realm of the dead in the fearsome mountains in the east, *kur* "the mountains." I render this term as "Hades." It is the one regularly used by the composer and does not truly fit the myth either. In the basic myth, the realm of Death to which Inanna goes is underground in the earth, like the grave. The obvious inconsistency of these different concepts with one another did not, apparently, disturb the ancients in any way, the less so since the Sumerian verb for "to go up," *è*, also meant "to go down." The Sumerian phrase rendered "she had her heart set" means literally "had her ear stand."

In Kishi she forsook Hursag-kalamma,
    went down into Hades;
in Akkadê she forsook E-ulmash,
    went down into Hades.[2]

The seven powers of office
    she bundled,
hugged the powers,
    kept them handy;
fetched out
    the stored-away
mittu-weapon.

Kaffieh and aghal,
    the desert headdress,
    she put on her head;
the wig of her brow she took;
    held in the hand
    the pure yardstick
    and measuring line.
Small lapis lazuli beads   20
    she hung around her neck,
with yoked oval stone beads
    she covered her chest.
Gold bracelets
    she slipped over her hands;
and the breast-shields (named)
    "O man, come hither, come hither!"
    she drew over her chest.
With the robe of office,
    the robe of queenship,
    she covered her back;
the kohl (named)
    "O may he come, may he come!"
    she put on her eyes.

SHE PROVIDES   Inanna was walking toward Hades,
AGAINST   her page Ninshubur[3]
POSSIBLE   was walking at her side,
FAILURE   Holy Inanna
    said to Ninshubur:

2. This list of Inanna's major cult centers and temples suggests, by the order in which they are mentioned, a route east and then north from Uruk. Beyond Akkadê it may have turned northeast to enter the mountains.

3. Ninshubur is the name of a god as well as of a goddess. When it refers to Inanna's handmaiden and page, it is that of a goddess.

"My ever-loyal one,
my page   30
        of fair words,
my envoy
        of true words,
I am now going down
        into Hades,
if I stay gone
        to Hades
set up resounding
        wailings for me,
sound the tambourine[4] for me
        in the assemblies of administrators,
make the rounds for me
        of the gods' houses,
claw at your eyes (for grief) for me,
        claw at your mouth for me,
claw, in the places
        one goes not with a man,
        your big belly for me!
Dress in a one-ply garment for me
        like one who has no man![5]

"Wend first your foot   40
        to Enlil's temple Ekur,
and upon your entering
        Enlil's temple, Ekur,
weep before Enlil (saying:)

'O Father Enlil! Let no man put to death
        your child in Hades!
Let him not mix your good silver
        in among Hades' dust,
let him not cut up your good lapis lazuli
        in among the flint-arrowhead maker's stones,
let him not split up your good boxwood
        in among the carpenter's lumber,
let him not put to death in Hades
        the maiden Inanna!'[6]

4. An instrument typically accompanying lamentations.

5. I.e., who has no one who is responsible for her as head of a household to which she belongs. To dress in a one-ply garment was a mark of poverty. Here it is one of the signs of mourning.

6. The point of these metaphors would seem to be that Inanna, as a goddess, is too precious to be treated as are mere mortals. Silver is not to be mixed with dust, lapis lazuli not used for arrowheads as were it mere flint, boxwood not treated as mere lumber.

If Enlil stands not by you
   in this matter,
     go on to Ur!

"In Ur, the nations birth-chamber,[7]
upon your entering   50
   Ekishnugal,
   Nanna's temple
weep before Nanna (saying:)

'Father Nanna! Let no man put to death
   your child in Hades
Let him not mix your good silver
   in among Hades' dust,
let him not cut up your good lapis lazuli
   in among the flint-arrowhead maker's stones,
let him not split up your good boxwood
   in among the carpenter's lumber,
let him not put to death in Hades
   the maiden Inanna!'

"If Nanna stands not by you
   in this matter,
     go on to Eridu!

"Upon your entering
   E-engur, Enki's temple,
weep before Enki (saying:)
'Father Enki! Let no man put to death
   your child in Hades!
Let him not mix your good silver
   in among Hades' dust,
let him not cut up your good lapis lazuli
   in among the flint-arrowhead maker's
   stones,
let him not split up your good boxwood
   in among the carpenter's lumber,
let him not put to death in Hades
   the maiden Inanna!'

"Father Enki, a lord of vast intelligence,
knows the grass of life,

---

7. Sumer and Akkad, disorganized after the Gutian period, became a nation only with Ur-Namma and the Third Dynasty of Ur. Thus Ur was the "birth-chamber" of the nation. The phrase suggests that the version of the composition we have was put in this form during the time of that dynasty.

knows the water of life.
May he make me come alive!"

Inanna was walking toward Hades,
to her page Ninshubur
    she said:

"Go, Ninshubur,   70
and toss not your head
    at my orders I have given you!"

INANNA SEEKS   When Inanna had come close
ENTRY INTO   to Egalkurzagin,[8]
HADES   she wickedly rammed things
                    against the door of Hades,
                shouted wickedly
                    into Hades' palace:

"Open the house instantly!
    Gatekeeper,
    open the house instantly!
Open the house instantly!
    Neti, open the house instantly,
    and let me go in to my wailing!"

Neti, Hades' chief gatekeeper,
answered holy Inanna (saying:)

"And who might you be? You!"

"I am Inanna,   80
    toward where the sun rises!"

"If you are Inanna
    toward where the sun rises,[9]
why have you gone away
    to a land of no return?
How could your heart take you on
    a road that he who goes it
    travels not back?"

Holy Inanna replied to it to him:
"My elder sister Ereshkigala

8. Egalkurzagin is a name for the abode of the dead. It means "the lustrous mountain palace" and
apparently refers to the shining, snow-covered high mountains. As a name for the abode of the dead it
thus belongs with the concept of that abode as located in the mountains.
    9. See n. 1, above.

—to have the obsequies
    for Gugalanna,[10]
    her husband, who was killed,
(widely) viewed
is pouring grandiosely at his wake.
    That's why!"

Neti, Hades' chief gatekeeper,
answered holy Inanna (saying:)   90

"Wait for me Inanna,
    let me speak to my mistress,
let me speak to my mistress Ereshkigala,
    let me make [you known] to her!"

Neti, Hades' chief gatekeeper,
went in into the house
    to Ereshkigala, his mistress,
    and said to her:

"My mistress! A single maiden,
tall like a god,
    [has approached Egalkurzagin];
[she wickedly rammed things
    against] the door [of Hades,]
[shouted wickedly
    into Hades' palace,]
In Eanna [she . . . .] ,
the seven powers of office   100
    she has bundled,
has hugged the powers,
    kept them handy,
has fetched out
    the stored-away
    mittu-weapon.

"Kaffieh and aghal,
    the desert headdress,
    she has put on her head,
the wig of her brow she has taken,

10. The thunderstorms of spring were heard mythopoeically as a battle between a celestial lion or lion-bird and a celestial bull in which the bull was killed. This bull was called Gu(d)galanna(k) "the great bull of heaven." It is listed in ancient lists of gods as the husband of Ereshkigala.

holds in the hand
   a pure yardstick
   and measuring line.
Small lapis lazuli beads
   she has hung around her neck,
with yoked oval stone beads
   she has covered her chest.
Gold bracelets
   she has slipped over her hands,
the breast-shield (named)
   'O man, come hither, come hither!'   110
   she has drawn over her chest;
   the kohl (named)
   'O may he come, may he come!'
   she has put on her eyes.
With the robe of office.
   the robe of queenship,
   she has covered her back!"[11]

ERESHKIGAL   That day did Ereshkigala
DECIDES TO   smite her thigh,[12]
FACE HER   bite her lip,
   and cry out in anger.
To Neti, her chief gatekeeper
   she said:

"Come, my Neti, Hades' chief gatekeeper,
toss not your head
   at the order I am to give you!
Let the bolts be drawn
   on Hades' seven great gates,
and let the doorleaf of the Ganzir palace
   [the facade of Hades]
   be pushed (open) first.
After she has entered,
crouching down, having had the clothes stripped off,[13]
   [someone can usher] her in."

11. It is probably intentional that the composer of the tale fails to have Neti mention Inanna's pretended reason for her visit. Presumably it was clear to him, as to the listeners of the tale, that it was mere pretense.

12. This gesture is one accompanying and expressing arrival at a decision. Approximately it means, "Let us get on with it!" or "Go to!" Here it probably denotes that Ereshkigala wants to have it out with Inanna for good or bad.

13. The dead were buried naked and in a crouching position, so the inhabitants of Hades are

Neti, Hades' chief gatekeeper,   120
obeyed his mistress's orders,
[drew back] the bolts
    on Hades' seven great gates,
[and pushed (open)] first
    [the doorleaf] of the Ganzir palace,
    the facade of Hades.
To holy Inanna he said:

INANNA IS   "Come, Inanna, come in through it!"
STRIPPED   After she had entered in,
someone had slipped off her
    kaffieh and aghal,
    the desert headdress,
    of her head.

"Why was that?"

"Be quiet, Inanna,
    an office of Hades
    has been faultlessly performed.
Inanna, open not your mouth   130
    against Hades' sacred functions!"

After she had entered through
    the second great gate,
someone had slipped off her
    the pure yardstick
    and measuring line.

"Why was that?"

"Be quiet, Inanna,
    an office of Hades
    has been faultlessly performed.
Inanna, open not your mouth
    against Hades' sacred functions!"
After she had entered through
    the third great gate,
someone had slipped off her
    the small lapis lazuli beads
    of her neck.

---

typically naked and crouched down. Inanna, allowing herself to be stripped of clothes and accoutrements, submits to the authority of Hades, and so is on a par with ordinary mortals.

"Why was that?"

"Be quiet, Inanna,
  an office of Hades
  has been faultlessly performed.
Inanna, open not your mouth   140
  against Hades' sacred functions!"
After she had entered through
  the fourth great gate,
someone had slipped off her
  the yoked oval stone beads
  of her chest.

"Why was that?"

"Be quiet, Inanna,
  an office of Hades
  has been faultlessly performed.
Inanna, open not your mouth
  against Hades' sacred functions!"
After she had entered through
  the fifth great gate,
someone had slipped off her
  the gold rings
  of her hands.

"Why was that?"

"Be quiet, Inanna,
  an office of Hades
  has been faultlessly performed.
Inanna, open not your mouth   150
  against Hades' sacred functions!"

After she had entered through
  the sixth great gate,
someone had slipped off her
  the breast-shields (named)
    "O man, come hither, come hither!"

"Why was that?"

"Be quiet, Inanna,
  an office of Hades
  has been faultlessly performed.
Inanna, open not your mouth
  against Hades' sacred functions!"

After she had entered through
   the seventh great gate,
someone had slipped off her
   the robe of office,
   the robe of queenship
   of her back.

"Why was that?"

"Be quiet, Inanna,
   an office of Hades
   has been faultlessly performed.

Inanna, open not your mouth   160
   against Hades' sacred functions!"

INANNA ATTEMPTS
TO USURP ERESH-
KIGALA'S THRONE
AND IS PUNISHED

[Crouching down]
   having had the clothes
   stripped off,
she was led in by a man.
Holy Ereshkigala she made get up
   out of her chair
and in her chair she sat down.

The Anunnaki, the seven judges,
   rendered judgment to her face,
their verdict was a verdict
   griping the bowels,
they cried out against her,
   it was the call for punishment!
Killed she was, and turned
   into a slab of tainted meat,
and the slab of tainted meat
   a man hung from a peg.[14]

NINSHUBUR
FOLLOWS ORDERS

When three days and three nights
   had gone by,
her page   170
   Ninshubur,
her page
   fair of words,
her envoy
   true of words,
was setting up resounding
   wailings for her.

14. See the introduction to the composition.

The tambourine
    which she sounded for her
    in the assemblies of administrators,
she had make the rounds for her
    of the gods' houses.
She clawed at her eyes (for grief) for her,
    clawed at her mouth for her,
and in (the) places
    one goes not with a man,
    she clawed her big belly for her.
Like one who has no man,
    she dressed in a one-ply garment for her.

Her foot she wended first
    to Enlil's temple, Ekur,
and upon her entering   180
    Enlil's temple, Ekur,
wept before Enlil (saying:)

"Father Enlil! Let no man put to death
    your child in Hades!
Let him not mix your good silver
    in among Hades' dust,
let him not cut up your good lapis lazuli
    in among the flint-arrowhead maker's stones,
let him not split up your good boxwood
    in among the carpenter's lumber,
let him not put to death in Hades
    the maiden Inanna!"

Father Enlil answered Ninshubur:

"My child craved the upper heaven,
    craved (too) the netherworld;
Inanna craved the upper heaven,
    craved (too) the netherworld;
Hades' offices, demanding offices,   190
    demanding offices,
    have been performed effectively.
Who has (ever) been reached there
    and (re)claimed?"[15]

15. Enlil here, Nanna next, express a natural reaction to the news of Inanna. Hades lies outside the jurisdiction of the gods of the world above, so they can do nothing. Furthermore, what has happened is in the very nature of things. The offices of Hades have been realized, have been performed as is proper.

Father Enlil stood not by her
  in this matter;
  to Ur she went.
In Ur, the nation's birth-chamber,
upon her entering
    Ekishnugal,
    Nanna's temple,
she wept before Nanna (saying:)

"Father Nanna! Let no man put to death
  your child in Hades!
Let him not mix your good silver
  in with Hades' dust,
let him not cut up your good lapis lazuli
  in among the flint-arrowhead maker's stones,
let him not split up your good boxwood
  in among the carpenter's lumber,
let him not put to death in Hades   200
  the maiden Inanna!"

Father Nanna answered Ninshubur:

"My child craved the upper heaven,
  craved (too) the netherworld;
Inanna craved the upper heaven,
  craved (too) the netherworld;
Hades' offices, demanding offices,
  demanding offices,
  have been performed effectively.
Who has (ever) been reached there
  and (re)claimed?"

Father Nanna stood not by her
  in this matter.
  To Eridu she went.
Upon her entering
    E-engur,
    Enki's temple,
she wept before Enki (saying:)

"Father Enki! Let no man put to death
  your child in Hades!
Let him not mix your good silver   210
  in with Hades' dust,
let him not cut up your good lapis lazuli
  in with the flint-arrowhead maker's stones,

let him not split up your good boxwood
    in with the carpenter's lumber,
let him not put to death in Hades
    the maiden Inanna!"

ENKI PLANS TO   Father Enki answered Ninshubur:
TRICK ERESHKIGAL   "What has been done to my child
INTO MAKING A   down there?
RASH PROMISE   She has me worried!
                   What has been done to Inanna
                      down there?
                      She has me worried!
                   What has been done to the queen of all lands
                      down there?
                      She has me worried!
                   What has been done to heaven's holy one
                      down there?
                      She has me worried!"[16]
From under his fingernail
    he brought out dirt,
    and fashioned from it
    a myrmidon.
From under another fingernail of his   220
    he brought out dirt,
    and fashioned from it
    a young elegist.[17]
To the myrmidon he gave
    the grass of life,
to the young elegist he gave
    the water of life.
Father Enki said to the young elegist
    and the myrmidon:

"Go! Lay the foot toward Hades!

16. Enki is more personally and deeply disturbed, and so—unlike Enlil and Nanna—he does not think only in terms of power to command, but goes on to explore ways to achieve his goal by guile. Enki's special emotional involvement is a given, since he is Inanna's father. In this the composition follows a variant tradition attested also in other myths. The official view has Inanna as daughter of Nanna and granddaughter of Enlil, the two gods approached for help first. Whether there was some special point to this or not is difficult to say.

17. What Enki creates is two types of professional mourners, as is clear in the case of the elegist. The myrmidon, *kurgarû*, was a member of the cult personnel around Inanna at Uruk. Originally an armed guardsman, he seems to have become a general performer of a variety of ritual dances, songs, and music. His flute playing is mentioned as soothing grief, so he may well have had a role in mourning ceremonies too.

When you have flown like flies
    over the doorleaves,
when you have wiggled like lizards
    past the door-pivots,
lo!
    The mother who gave birth,
Ereshkigala, lies sick (with grief)
    for her little ones.
Her holy shoulders
    no linen veils,
her bosom, like oil cruses   230
    has nothing drawn over it,
her [nails] are
    like a copper rake upon her,
her hair?—Leaks
    she has on her head![18]

"When she is saying
    'Woe, my heart!'
[Say to her:]
    'You are [awe]ary, my lady,
    woe your heart!'
When she is saying:
    ['Woe,] my liver!'
Say to her:
    ['You are aweary,] my lady,
    Woe your liver!'

("She will ask:)

['Who] are you
    to whom I have spoken
    [from my] heart to your hearts,
    from my liver [to your livers?]
[An you be gods,]
    let me ta[lk with you,]
[an you be humans,   240
    let me] determine [your circumstances
    for you!'[19]]

18. Ereshkigala is presented as a typical mourner, a mother lamenting the death of her young children; she has rent her clothes, clawed herself with her nails, pulled her hair in the established gestures of grief.

19. Lament for somebody, or with somebody, was a highly valued kindness; so Ereshkigala will be certain to feel beholden to two strangers who take pity on her in her lone mourning and will offer to do something for them in return.

Adjure [her
  by the life's breath of heaven,
  by the life's breath of earth,]
[and sa]y [to her . . . .]

"They will offer you
  [the river at its (high) water;]
  may you not accept it.
They will offer you
  the field when in grain;
  may you not accept it.[20]
Say to her:
  'Give us the slab of tainted meat
  hanging from the peg!'
Throw on it
  one the grass of life,
  one the water of life,
and may Inanna rise!"

THE RUSE
SUCCEEDS

The young elegist and the myrmidon
  obeyed Enki's orders.
Over the doorleaves
  they flew like flies,
wiggled like lizards   250
  past the door-pivots,
lo!
  The [mo]ther who gave [bi]rth,
Ereshkigala, lay sick (with grief)
  for her little ones.
Her [holy shoulders]
  no linen veiled,
[her] bosom, like oil cruses,
  had nothing drawn over it,
her nails were   254a
  like a copper rake upon her.
Her hair?—Leaks   254b
  she had on her head![21]

When she said
  ["Woe, my heart!"

---

20. The gifts offered fix the time of year as late spring, just before harvest, approximately June.
21. Lines 254a–b were omitted by the ancient copyist by mistake. They are not included in the line count.

they said to her:
    "You are aweary, my lady,
    woe your heart!"
When she said,
    ["Woe,] my liver!"
they said to her:
    "You are aweary, my lady,
    woe your liver!"

(She said to them:)

"Who are you
to whom I have spoken   260
    from my heart to your heart
    from my liver to your liver?
An you be gods
    let me talk with you
an you be humans,
    let me determine your circumstances
    for you!"

They adjured her
    by the life's breath of heaven
    by the life's breath of earth
    [and said to her . . . . . .]

They offered them
    the river at its (high) waters,
    but they accepted it not.
They offered them
    the field when in grain,
    but they accepted it not.

"Give us the slab of tainted meat
    hanging from the peg!"

Holy Ereshkigala replied to it,
    to the young elegist and the myrmidon:

"The slab of tainted meat
    is the property of your mistress!"
"Though the slab of tainted meat
    be the property of our mistress
    give it to us!" they said to her.

They were being given   270
    the tainted slab of meat
    hanging on the peg

and threw upon it,
   one the grass of life,
   one the water of life,
and Inanna rose.

THE REVIVED
INANNA MUST
PROVIDE A
SUBSTITUTE

Inanna was about
   to ascend from Hades,
but the Anunnaki
   laughed at it (saying:)

"What man has ever,
   ascending from Hades,
   ascended scot-free?
If Inanna is
   to ascend from Hades,
let her give it one head
   in lieu of her head!"

Inanna was ascending
   from Hades.
Little rangers,
   like unto reeds
   for lance-shafts,
big rangers,
   like unto bamboo(?),
walked beside her.
The man in front of her,
   though no herald,
   held a staff in the hand,
(the one) behind her
   though not an envoy,
   had tied a weapon
   unto the hip.

280

The men who followed her to him,[22]
the men who followed Inanna to him,
knew not food, knew not drink,
ate not (offerings of)
   flour strewn,
did not drink
   libated water,
They took the wife
   from a man's lap,

22. "to him" refers to the substitute to be designated.

took the child 290
   from the wet-nurse's breast.

Inanna was ascending from Hades.

When Inanna had ascended
   from Hades,
her page Ninshubur
   threw herself at her feet;
she had sat in the dust
   was dressed in dirty clothing.

The rangers said
   to Holy Inanna:

"Inanna, go on to your city,
   and let us carry her off!"

Holy Inanna answered the rangers:
"My page,
   fair of words,
my envoy
   true of words,
was not letting go 300
   of my instructions,
did not toss her head
   at the orders I had given!
She set up resounding
   wailings for me.
The tambourine
   which she sounded for me
   in the assemblies of administrators,
she made go for me the rounds
   of the gods' houses.
She clawed at her eyes (for grief) for me,
   clawed at her mouth,
and in the places
   one goes not with a man,
   she clawed her big belly for me.
Like one who has no man
   she dressed in a one-ply garment for me.
To Enlil's temple, Ekur,
to Nanna's temple in Ur, and
to [Eri]du and Enki's temple, 310
she went for me
   and had me come alive.

How could you give me (another) such?"   311a

"Let [us go] for him,
   let us go for him,
   to Sigkurshaga
   in Umma!"

In Umma,
   from Sigkurshaga,
Shara[23] [threw] himself
   at her feet;
he had sat in the dust,
   was [dressed] in dirty clothing.

The rangers said
   to holy Inanna:

"Inanna, go on to your city
   and let us carry him off!"

Holy Inanna answered the rangers:

"My [singer] of songs, Shara,
my one who clips my nails,   320
   my one who ties
   (the hair-bunch on) my neck,
how could you give me (another) such?"

"Let us go for him,
   let us go for him,
   to Emushkalamma
   in Bad-Tibira!"

In Bad-Tibira,
   from Emushkalamma,
Lulal threw himself at her feet;
   In his city
he had sat in the dust,
   was dressed in dirty clothing.
The rangers said to holy Inanna:

"Inanna, go on to your city,
   and let us carry him off!"

Holy Inanna answered the rangers:

23. Shara, the city god of Umma, counts usually as Inanna's son. That seems not to be so here, where he is spoken of rather as a personal servant, Inanna's "beautician."

"Preeminent Lulal,
  leading my right and left wings
  (of the army),
How could you give me (another) such?"   330

"Let us go for him
  to the maimed apple tree
  in the Kullab desert!"
To the maimed apple tree
  in the Kullab desert
  they followed in her footsteps.

DUMUZI, FOR NOT   Dumuzi had dressed
SORROWING, IS   in a grand garment
DESIGNATED   and sat seated in grandeur.[24]

The rangers swept into his fold,
and pouring out the milk
  from (all) seven churns,
they bumped him seven strong,
  as were *he* the intruder,
starting by hitting the shepherd
  in the face
  with the reed pipes and flutes.

She looked at him,
  it was a look to kill;
she gave them orders,
  it was an order
  griping the bowels;
she called out to them,   340
  it was a call for punishment:

"How long (must you dawdle)?
  carry him off!"

Holy Inanna gave the shepherd Dumuzi
  into their hands.

They, the men who had escorted her,
the men who went for Dumuzi,
knew not food, knew not water,

24. Dumuzi's festive attire—contrasting so glaringly with the mourning garb he should have been wearing, desolate at the loss of Inanna—understandably triggers Inanna's jealousy in a flash of hot anger.

ate not (offerings of)
 flour strewn,
did not drink
 libated water.
They bent not over
 to that sweet thing,
  a wife's loins,
they did not kiss
 that dainty thing,
  a child.
They would make a man's child   350
 get up from his knee,
would make a daughter-in-law
 leave the father-in-law's house.

DUMUZI   Dumuzi knit the brows,
ESCAPES   he burst into tears,
       the lad lifted his hands
        heavenwards to the sun god:

"Sun god! You are my brother-in-law,
 I am your brother-in-law,[25]
I carry the butter to your mother's house,
I carry the milk to Ningal's house.[26]
When you have made my hands
 like unto the feet of a skink,
when you have made my feet
 like unto the feet of a skink,
let me escape from my rangers,
 and may they not catch me!"

(The text has a lacuna here. It must have told how the sun god granted Dumuzi's wish, changed him into a skink—more precisely probably, into a waran—and how he escaped. Presumably he fled to Uruk to Inanna. The rangers follow.)

The little ranger opened the mouth
 and said to the big ranger:

"Come! Let us go with him
 to Inanna's holy loins!"[27]

25. The sun god, Utu, was the guardian of justice and fairness. He was also, as Inanna's brother, Dumuzi's brother-in-law. It may be noted that the myth underlying the second part of the composition apparently followed the standard pattern of Inanna as sister of Utu, both of them children of Nanna and Ningal. She is not, as in the first part, seen as the daughter of Enki.

26. Dumuzi, as shepherd, would naturally supply his mother-in-law's house with these delicacies.

27. The "holy loins" seem oddly out of place in the context. It may be that the gendarme envisioned

The rangers entered Uruk
and seized holy Inanna:

"Come Inanna!
Get started on your journey,
get going
descending into Hades!
go to the place your heart desired,
descending into Hades,
go to Ereshkigala's place
descending into Hades!
May you not dress in your queenly robe,
the holy robe of office,
the robe of queenship,
descending into Hades!
And when you have taken off
the decorous and illustrious
holy crown of your head,
descending into Hades;
you should not take your gay wig,
descending into Hades;
unstrap your [shoes]   10'
the 'wild-dog puppies' of your feet,
descending into Hades.
Where you are descending no [. . . . . .] . . !'"

RECAPTURE AND   They reviled holy Inanna,
SECOND ESCAPE   they [. . . . . .] her,
and Inanna in her panic
gave them Dumuzi in hand.

As for the lad,
they were putting
huge hobbles on his feet;
as for the lad,
they were ensnaring him,
were putting a neck stock
on (his) shoulders,
henzir weapons, *kibir* axes,
huge copper spears,
they were carrying up
before him,

Dumuzi as forgiven and in Inanna's embrace. More likely though, the phrase—a stereotype—was
mechanically taken over from standard descriptions of movement toward Inanna in different that is,
marital, situations.

great axes they were sharpening.
They made the lad stand up,
    made him sit down,
the clothes of his back they threw down
    set up. . . .
As for the lad, they tied his arms,   20'
    and valuing his clothes
    at thirty shekels (only)
covered his eyes with his own clothes.

SECOND ESCAPE   The lad lifted his hands
    heavenwards to the sun god:

"Sun god, I am your comrade,
    you are a gallant, you know me!
Your sister, whom I took to wife,
she, having descended into Hades,
so as to ascend from Hades,
wants to give me to Hades
    as substitute.
O sun god, you are a fair judge,
    let her not wrong me!

When you have changed my hands,
    when you have switched my frame,
let me slip out of   30'
    the hands of my rangers,
    and may they not catch me!
Like a noble serpent
    I shall traverse plain and hills,
let me flee for my life
    to (my) sister Geshtinanna's place!"

The sun god accepted his tearful plea
changed his hands,
    switched his frame.
A noble serpent he traversed
    plain and hills,
like a bird in flight
    (from) a falcon's talons
Dumuzi tended to his life,
fled for his life
    to Geshtinanna's place.

GESHTINANNA
PROTECTS HER
BROTHER

Geshtinanna, looking at her brother,
clawed at her cheeks (for grief),
    clawed at her mouth,
pulled out the pin of the front   40'
    (of her dress), and rent
    her dress with it;
over the ill-used lad
    she was voicing bitter lament
    forsooth:

"Woe, my brother! Woe, my brother!
    the lad who that day was not
    [wrapped for burial!]
Woe, my brother, the shepherd Ama-ushumgal-anna,
    the lad who that day was not
    amid wails
    wrapped for burial!
Woe, my brother, the lad who will not wed a wife,
    will not have a child!
Woe, my brother, who will have no comrade,
    will have no friend!
Woe, my brother, the lad for whom his mother
    will see no good fortune!"[28]

The rangers were seeking Dumuzi
    cast around for him.
The little ranger said to the big ranger:
"Rangers have no mercy,
    have no fathers, mothers, wives,
    brothers, sisters, or children;
ever since the days the nation was founded,   50'
    since heaven was removed from earth,
you have been rangers
    for shoving people along,
(such) have no clemency or kindness,
    know not good and evil!

28. The composer apparently used a standard Geshtinanna lament in which she mourned her brother who lay slain by bandits in the desert without decent burial and who was yet a young boy unmarried and not father to a child. In its present context it requires that one see the pursuit by the rangers as implying that Dumuzi was already dead and was lying unburied in the desert, which is not without serious difficulties. Also, he would have to be considered engaged only, not married, to Inanna. Nevertheless it is almost certainly the correct interpretation, cf. above, "Dumuzi's Dream" nn. 18 and 20.

"Whoever saw a man find safety for his life
   in a house not his own?
We will not go for him
   to the place of his comrade,
   we will not go for him
   to the place of his father-in-law,
let us go for the shepherd
   to Geshtinanna's place!"

The gendarmes had let him
   slip out of (their) hands,
   they were seeking him,
and before she had finished
   that wailing
the rangers followed him
   to Geshtinanna's place.

"Show me where your brother is!"
   they said to her,
   but she was not giving out
   that information.

She came up to the wool,   60'
   plucked (?) it in the shearing (!) place,
   but she was not giving out
   that information.
She came up to a piece of ground,
   dug with her hoe there,
   but she was not giving out
   that information.
she came up to the skins,
   was tying them up on the ground
   with her string,
   but she was not giving out
   that information.
She was pouring out
   her loins' bedding of chaff,
   but she was not giving out
   that information,
and they did not discover Dumuzi
   in Geshtinanna's house.
The little ranger said to the big ranger:

DUMUZI CAPTURED IN FOLD	"Come, let us go for him to the holy sheepfold!"

In [his holy sheepfold] they seized Dumuzi,
they surrounded him
  and seized him,
    they sought him and they saw him.
The house protected not the lad,   70'
  an axe was taken to the door,
they sharpened (their) hip-daggers
  and surrounded him
    in the enclosed space.

GESHTINANNA
SEEKS HIM
	The sister, for the sake of her brother,
	  tore around the city
	    like a (circling) bird.

"Let me go to my brother
  (so) ill used!
  I will enter any household!"

(The text has a second lacuna here. A relevant passage in a Dumuzi lament indicates that the fly told Geshtinanna that her brother was held in the brewery with the wise brewmasters. Geshtinanna must have joined her brother there. When the text resumes, the fly is mentioned, and one may conjecture that it pleaded with Inanna on Geshtinanna's behalf.)

    . . [. . . . . .]

INANNA'S EASEMENT OF TERM	The fly [. . . .] The maiden Inanna [ans]we[red the F]ly:[29]

"In the beer brewery . . . [. . . ,]
as with the doers of equal (tasks),
  let me determine conditions for them!"
(So) now, by Inanna's determining conditions,
  thus [it verily is.]

[Dumuzi br]oke into tears thereat:

---

29. The section of the tale dealing with Geshtinanna's search for Dumuzi and joining him in Hades does not belong with the myth dealing with Dumuzi as shepherd, but to another, variant, group of myths in which he is god of barley and beer and brother of the goddess of the grapevine stock and its wine, Geshtinanna. Both at different times of year go underground in storage as, respectively, beer and wine.

"My [sist]er has come,
  she has been [given] into (their) hands
  together with me!
Alas now! Her life [is lost!]"

(to which Inanna seems to answer:)

"[Y]ou half a year only,   10'
  your sister half a year only.
[When yo]u demand it
  she will [spend] the days in question.
When your sister demands it
  you will [spend] the days in question.
Holy Inanna was giving Dumuzi
  as substitute for her(self).
O holy Ereshkigala!
Praise of you is sweet!

The Ninurta Myth Lugal-E

The composition known from the word with which it begins as *Lugal-e* has been admirably edited by J. van Dijk. It is a myth—or combination of myths—cast in epic form. It deals with the god of the spring thundershowers and floods, Ninurta, telling of his war against a rival in the mountains, his regulation of the river Tigris, and how he determined the character and use of various kinds of stones.

The story begins with the young warrior-king, Ninurta, feasting quietly at home, when his weapon Sharur brings him disturbing intelligence. A rival has risen in the mountains, a certain Azag, whom the plants have chosen king and who with his warriors, the stones, raids the border cities. Azag plans to attack Ninurta and take over his domain.

This news thoroughly rouses Ninurta, and he immediately sets out with his army for a preventive strike. Before Ninurta meets the enemy's main forces Sharur reconnoiters and, impressed with what it learns about the enemy strength, counsels prudent retreat. Ninurta, though, recklessly disregards the advice and orders an attack. The decision proves disastrous. Azag raises a dust storm that chokes Ninurta, and defeat seems imminent. Sharur, however, quickly makes its way back to Nippur to seek help from Ninurta's father, Enlil. Enlil provides a rainstorm to be sent in over the dust to lay it and clear the air so Ninurta can breathe. Thus helped, he gains victory.

Azag, though, is still alive and free, so the prudent Sharur pleads with its master to have him finish it off and not leave it as a constant threat. This time Ninurta follows its advice, launches a second attack, and succeeds in killing and dismembering Azag, thus ensuring that he will meet with no resistance when he takes over its realm.

After the victory, Ninurta attends to internal matters. The waters of the yearly flood were at that time going into the mountains, where they froze and piled up as ice. Ninurta collected them and threw them into the Tigris, thus creating the flood. To prevent the waters from going back into the mountains as before, he built a levee of stones, named Hursag, "the foothills."

By this time Ninurta's prolonged absence had become too much for his mother, Ninlil. She longed for him, and eventually she decided to undertake the long and arduous journey to visit him in the mountains. Ninurta was overjoyed when he saw her and, moved by this proof of her love, he presented her with the Hursag which he had just built and renamed her Ninhursağa "mistress of the Hursag."

Shortly afterward, however, since he had to pass judgment on his captive enemies, the stones, he asked her to leave and return to Nippur. This she did willingly, not wishing, by her presence, to have any part in the proceedings and their predictably grim outcome. The judgments passed by Ninurta are reported in detail and constitute the major part of what remains of the composition. Guiding for Ninurta is the greater or lesser virulence with which the individual stones have fought him. The more vicious ones are cursed and given severe sentences, the less hostile ones are appointed to offices in his newly won domain.

Eventually, with the administration of his conquests seen to, Ninurta embarks with his troops to return to Nippur, where he is greeted by the gods and receives warm praise from his father, Enlil. The composition ends with praise of the goddess of writing, Nidaba, whom Ninurta has charged with recording his great deeds for posterity.

As to where and when this composition was put in its present form, one may with a fair degree of probability fix on the city of Girsu in the Lagash area, and a time after, but probably not too long after, the time of its famous ruler Gudea (ca. 2150 B.C.). It will, correspondingly, originally have called its hero by his local name, Ningirsu, rather than by his Nippur name, Ninurta.

For Girsu as origin of the composition speaks clearly the fact that the section on the dolerite directly mentions Ningirsu's temple in that city, Eninnu, and has unmistakable reference to Gudea's statues of dolerite set up in it. We also have at least one version of the composition which still retains the name Ningirsu. However, since Ningirsu and Ninurta were identified quite early, important lore referring to the god under one of his names would naturally be valid for him also under the other. One can therefore not wonder that the scribes in Nippur copying the composition preferred to use the name more familiar to them, Ninurta. With a dating to slightly after Gudea agrees also the rather wordy and bombastic style in which Ninurta's military prowess is described; it has its closest parallel in hymns celebrating Shulgi, the second king of the Third Dynasty of Ur. (ca. 2050 B.C.) and his martial deeds in those same mountains in which Ninurta fought.

The epic form in which the composition is cast tends to overshadow somewhat the myths that underlie the tale and their cosmic reference. Nevertheless, it is not too difficult to recognize the burden of the myth that informs the first part of the story, for it is the vision of the spring thundershowers as a young divine warrior, Ninurta/Ningirsu, going to battle in the mountains in a fury of thunder and lightning. The precise nature of Ninurta's opponent in that battle, Azag, is more problematic. The text suggests a tall hardwood tree, meant, perhaps as a symbol of the mountains. A certain degree of vagueness is perhaps to be expected here, for while the mythopoeic imagination may quite readily see the thundercloud as a young warrior riding to battle in a rumbling war chariot and shooting lightning arrows, there is little or nothing to indicate what or whom he is battling, thus leaving imagination free play for any number of possibilities.

The second myth, underlying the tale of Ninurta's irrigation engineering, is clearly a culture myth. The spring rains in the mountains and the melting snows fill the tributaries of the Tigris, which then empty into the river itself, creating the yearly flood. Mythopoeically, this takes form as Ninurta—the numinous power behind those waters—instituting the flood and thus making irrigation agriculture, and its high yields, possible.

The last section, dealing with Ninurta's judgment of the stones, explains the various properties and typical uses of the different kinds of stones as due to the sentence Ninurta on this occasion passed on them.

It seems only reasonable to assume that these different sections of the composition, the battle with Azag, the institution of irrigation agriculture, and the judgment on the stones originally formed three separate and independent stories, presumably each with its own setting.

INTRODUCTORY PAEAN TO NINURTA	O (warrior-)king! (Thunder)storm, whose fulgur compels compliance, Ninurta,[1] leader, possessing august strength, raiding the highland by himself alone. Floodstorm, restless serpent swaying (to strike) at the rebel country. Warrior, striding into battle, trampling down (all before him). Lord, putting a fighter's hand to the *mittu*-mace reaping like grain the necks of the insubordinate.

1. The name of the hero of the story in its original form was, as mentioned above, Ninĝirsu. Ninĝirsu and Ninurta were considered mere different names for the same deity, the former his name in Girsu, the latter in Nippur. Basically he was a god of nature, the power in the thunderstorms over the eastern mountains in spring, and in the flood of the Tigris caused by these rains as the mountain streams poured their waters into it.

He was envisioned originally as the thunder cloud, seen as an enormous bird; and because its thunderous roar could come only from a lion's maw it was given a lion's head. The two forms, bird and lion, tended to compete in the image of the god, who was sometimes the lion-headed bird, sometimes a winged lion with bird's tail and talons, sometimes all lion. In time the animal forms were rejected in favor of imagining the god in human form only, yet down to the time when this work was presumably composed he still retained some of the theriomorphic features such as the bird wings. In his human form his image was that of a young warrior-king riding to battle in his loudly rumbling war chariot.

In the opening paean these various conceptions of the god inform the imagery: flood storm, warrior, (warrior-)king, south storm, etc.

Ninurta, (warrior-)king,
   son in whose strength
   his father rejoices,
warrior who,
   like a south storm,
   blankets the highland,
Ninurta,
   behind you the grain goddess,
   in front lightning,
   branch out![2]
Darkness, yet engendered   10
   in bright waters
   by a prince,[3]
   bringing, as rain,
   verdure back.

Right forepaw that a lion
   puts out toward a snake
   against the tongue,
   roaring roars
   that fill the heavens.
Ninurta, (warrior-)king,
   whom Enlil made greater
   than (he) himself (is).
Warrior, throw-net
   flung over the foe!
Ninurta, awesome aura,
   your protective shadow
   is stretched over the country,
bringing distress
   to the rebel country,
   overwhelming its host.

SHARUR'S   As Ninurta, the (warrior-)king
REPORT   who had his father acclaimed
                far (and wide),[4]

2. The image is that of the thunder cloud and its branching lightning being followed by luxurious growth of grain after the rain—the grain goddess sending out shoots.

3. The thunder clouds were seen as engendered by vapors rising from the pools in the marshes of southern Mesopotamia. See "Lugalbanda and the Thunderbird" below, ll. 115–17. The prince is the water god, Enki.

4. Under the early political forms, which are here reflected, the king (*lugal*) was usually a young man whose task it was to lead the army in war. The supreme ruler was an older, experienced administrator, here Ninurta's father, Enlil. Thus his military exploits serve to impose and maintain Enlil's authority.

was occupying the throne
  on the august throne dais,
  was carrying great fearfulness;
as he sat broad, enjoying
  the feast set out for him,
as he rivaled An and Enlil
  by his having the prime beer (brewed) sweet,[5]
as Baba[6] was pleading petitions to the king   20
  before him,
and Ninurta, Enlil's son,
  was handing down decisions—
then did his weapon have the lord
  consider the highland,
Sharur[7] was calling to its owner
  from up high (saying:)

"Lord of lofty station, foremost one,
  Lord resplendent on the throne dais,
Ninurta, your orders are not changed,
  your decisions are truthfully deputed—
My master! Heaven copulated
  with verdant Earth,
Ninurta, it bore him
  a fearless warrior, Azag,[8]

---

5. Apparently a ruler's privilege. Among the Bedouins of modern time serving coffee was considered a way of competing with the sheikh for authority.

6. Baba (also read as Bau) is Ninurta's (actually Ninĝirsu's) wife. As a woman and mother she was considered more approachable than her formidable husband, and so she would be asked to transmit prayers and requests to him—choosing, of course, a moment when he would be in a generous and responsive mood.

7. Sharur is Ninurta's weapon. Its name means "the one who lays low multitudes," and it is termed "flood storm of battle." Consonant, with its storm character it was envisioned as a bird, in this tale even as a bird with a lion's head, which makes it indistinguishable from the thunderbird, Imdugud or Anzu, Ninĝirsu/Ninurta's old form as personification of the thunder cloud. In this tale Sharur is personified, moves about freely on its own initiative, and acts as a devoted servant and friend rather than as a mere weapon.

8. The precise nature of the opponent Ninurta fights in the mountain, Azag, is not, as mentioned in the introduction to the tale, immediately clear. It is referred to grammatically as a non-personal, a thing, and is said to have been engendered on Earth by the Sky. That suggests a plant or tree springing up from the soil after the rains in spring. With this agrees that it was chosen king by the plants, and the description of Azag in ll. 62–63 points specifically to a tree: "and the hardness of it is impenetrable, no weapon can stab into the wood, Ninurta, neither axe, mace, nor great spear cleaves its body," where its body apparently consists of wood. With its being a tree fits further that it has spread far and wide its seed (l. 34) and that its seed will drop from it when it is shaken (l. 294). It also explains its entirely passive role when Ninurta "tore it out like rushes, plucked it out like sedge" (l. 292). Its only weapon seems to be its "dreadful aura" (l. 289), which probably reflects the desert-dwelling Sumerians' awe of

a child not dwelling with the mother,
  nursed by wild beasts,
a foster child, my master,
  not knowing the father,
  a killer (out) of the highland,
a young brave, come out of the insubordinates,   30
  impudent of eye,
a towering he-man, Ninurta,
  enjoying the stature,
a true fighter, my (good) warrior,
  whom I fain would tackle.

"A ruler, my master,
  advertent toward his town,
  an old hand with his army.
It has sired offspring in the highland,
  spread far and wide its seeds,
and the plants have unanimously
  named it king over them;
among them, like a great wild bull,
  it tosses (its) horns.
The Basalt, the Diorite, the Dolerite,
  the "Duck"-stone, the Haematite,
and the warrior Alabaster, its warriors,
  constantly come raiding the cities,
for them a monster's tooth has grown up
  in the highland,
  and they tremble before it!

"Before its might the gods of those cities   40
  bow toward its place.
My master, that one perches on the throne dais,
  draws not back the arm and lets go;
(as) a lord, Ninurta, it decides like you
  the country's lawsuits;
who could put a hand
  into Azag's dread glory?
Who strip it
  from its great brows?

---

forests and tall trees. Very curious and surprising are, however, lines 326–29 in which Ninurta does away altogether with the name Azag, renames it "stone," more precisely "*zalag* stone," in order to deprive it of any posthumous fame and thus make its defeat and death doubly bitter for its shade in the netherworld.

It makes kith tremble,
    has fear dog kin.
It has made them look to its place
    (for orders),
the mountains, my master,
    have taken their deliveries
    to its place.

"Warrior! It has gathered intelligence
    about you, about your father,
son of Enlil, it has gathered intelligence
    about you, about your august power,
has taken counsel, my master,   50
    about you, about your strength,
and has been told, Ninurta,
    that except for you there dwells (here)
    not a single warrior!
It has given instructions concerning you
    for an encounter,
Warrior, there have been consultations
    with a view to taking away your kingship.
Your sacred offices of the Apsû, Ninurta,
    are (already) entrusted
    to its outstretched hands.
It is slapping faces,
    relocating dwelling-places,
daily the Azag is turning the border (district)
    over to its side!

"(O you), the gods' (restraining) yoke,
    may you not sit (idle by)!
(O you), heaven's wild buck,
    who have trampled the mountains
    under your hoofs,
Ninurta, Enlil's son,
    what will repel its attack?
The Azag's attack no hand can stay,   60
    it is very heavy.
Reports come from its host,
    but no (spying) eye gets near its crack troops,
and the hardness of it (itself)
    is impenetrable; no weapon
    can stab into the wood.

Ninurta, neither axe, mace, nor great spear
   cleaves its body,
warrior, you may not find it
   like anything (else)!
Lord who stretches wings and forearms[9]
   (protectively) over august sacred offices,
refulgent as befits gods,
fighter—in appearance a great wild bull—
   endued with strength, honey ably encombed,
O my Ninurta, at whose form I look
   as were it Enki's,
Uta-ulu, lord, son of Enlil,
   what is to be done?"

NINURTA ROUSED   The lord cried woe! It shook heaven,
TO ACTION   made earth shiver under his feet,
he let it out again unto their borders,   70
   and Enlil grew perturbed, left Ekur,
mountains were shattered,
   and the Anunnaki[10] scattered then and there,
the warrior slapped his thigh,
   and the gods dispersed,
like sheep the Anunnaki ran out
   in (all) the world.

Rising, the lord abutted heaven,
Ninurta marching to battle
   kept abreast of the (hurrying) hours,
a very storm he went to war,
   rode on seven gales against the rebel country.
Javelins he held cradled in the arm,
the *mittu*-mace opened (in a snarl)
   maw at the mountains,
the weapons raged at the hostile horde.   80
The evil wind and the south storm
   were tethered to him,
the flood storm strode at their flanks,
and before the warrior went a huge
   irresistible tempest,

9. As shown by the form in which the god appeared to Gudea in his dream (See below, "Cylinder A of Gudea"), he was still envisioned as winged at the time of Gudea. The gesture described is that of a mother bird protecting its young.

10. The high gods. The term means "the sons of princes," i.e., the high born, the aristocracy, among the gods.

it was tearing up the dust, depositing it (again)
evening out hill and dale,
    filling in hollows;
live coals it rained down, fire burned, flames scorched,
tall trees it toppled from their roots,
    denuding the forests.
Earth wrung her hands against the heart,
    emitting cries of pain,
disturbed was the Tigris river,
    it became constricted, roiled, stirred up.

In (the barge) Makarnuntaea[11]   90
    he was hastening toward battle,
The people (in) its (path) knew not
    where it was going,
    they were building (defensive)
    adobe walls;
the flying birds
    had their heads beaten in,
    their wings trailed the ground;
the fishes (down) in the deep
    the storm smote,
    they were gaping (in death),
the gazelles and wild asses of the desert
    (in) its (path) were famished,
    (the desert) was burnt off as if (denuded) by locusts,
the wave rising (in) its (path)
    was shattering the mountains.

The warrior Ninurta had couriers slipping
    into the rebel country,
its (own) couriers he slew in the highland,
    and cut off (communication between) its cities.
Chasing its oxdrivers[12] like moths
    he crushed their skulls,
its hands were wrung into each other
    (in grief) like crabgrass,
its head it was saving,   100
    slipping it in (behind) walls.
The highland was not setting out its lamps,
    not a single lit one,

11. The name means "boat issuing out from 'the princely quay.'" Since southern Mesopotamia was crisscrossed by irrigation canals, almost all traffic was by boat.

12. The drivers of the oxen that hauled the boats of the couriers along the canals.

it held its breath in its chest;
its people, sick, linked arms (for support),
they were cursing the place
and were designating the day Azag was born
    as the day of their destruction.

SHARUR RECON-   The lord spewed bitter venom
NOITERS   at the rebel country,
the gall adhered to the travelers,
    penetrated angrily into the heart;
like a mighty river he sounded,
    swept toward the hostile horde,
the heart was brightening for him
    from (pleasure in) his lion-headed mace,
birdlike it was flying off,   110
    was tramping up the highland for him,
to bring a dissident one (back captive)
    it beat its wings,
to learn what was being done
    it circled heaven's base,
it confronted the ones going to war,
    brought word of them,
untiring, it sat not down (to rest),
    its wings going like a flood storm.

COUNSELS   What did Sharur up above
RETREAT   bring along for lord Ninurta?
It reported the deliberations
    of the highland,
was explaining the planning to lord Ninurta,
cut, like the string of a snare,
    what Azag had ordered:
"Warrior, (watch out) for yourself!"
    it well-meaningly told him.
The weapon embraced the beloved one,   120
Sharur called out to lord Ninurta (saying:)
"Warrior, overwhelmer, throw-net of battle,
Ninurta, (warrior-)king, An's mace,
    drawing not back the fist
    raised against the foe,
strong one, heat of day scorching the rebel country,
    flood drowning the harvest,
(warrior-)king! Having faced up to battle,
    gone nearly into its (very) maw,

do, Ninurta, after you have made
   the netlike enclosure
   and have put down the (cultic) reed hut
rinse, (o) adder of heaven,
   arrow and weapon with water![13]
O Ninurta, may the names of the warriors
   slain by you be mentioned:
The Kulianna, the Basilisk, the Gypsum,
the "Strong Copper," the warrior "Six-headed Buck,"   130
Magilum, the lord "Heaven's Hobble,"
the Bison, king Datepalm,
the Thunderbird, and the "Seven-headed Serpent"
you verily slew, (o) Ninurta, in the highland.[14]
But, (o) lord, to a battle so uneven
   you have never gone.
In a clash of weapons,
   the festival of manhood,
Inanna's dance,[15] lift not your arm!
Lord, go not into battle, be not hasty,
   keep the feet on the ground!
Ninurta, Azag awaits you
   in the highland,
but, warrior, very comely in his crown,   140
first child—unendingly attractive to Ninlil[16]—
right lord, born by a princess to a lord,
growing horns like the warrior Suen,
prolonging the lifetime for the nation's king,
who has it in him to open up for some
   out of heaven's august powers:
the one ordering the gathering of waters,
   the gathering of the bank in nets,

13. Rinsing the weapons in water was done after the battle or campaign was over.

14. Little is known about the myths in which these traditional vanquished foes of Ninurta/Ninĝirsu figured. The thunderbird is a later addition. It was the pre-anthropomorphic form of Ninĝirsu himself, but as the human form of the god gradually superseded the animal ones, these latter—since they could not easily be disassociated from the god—were degraded to emblems, weapons, or captive foes. As is the case with the Thunderbird here, it has become a captive enemy.

15. Inanna was, among many other things, goddess of war. The battle, with its two opposing lines moving back and forth against each other in hand-to-hand fighting, as if they were lines of dancers in a dance, was called "Inanna's dance."

16. Ninlil is the consort of Enlil and mother of Ninurta. Other names for her in this composition are Ninmah, Ninhursaĝa, Dingirmah, Nintur, Ninnagarshaga, and Aruru. See below, n. 26, and following notes.

(o) Ninurta, lord endued with awesome aura,
    about to rush at the highland,
great warrior having no compeer,
alas!—One who will prove no match
    for Azag,
knowing, o Ninurta, about the Diorite,   150
    one ought not to enter the highland!
(O) warrior, son who is a credit to his father,
wise one, who should come up with
    counsel from shrewdness,
Ninurta, lord, son of Enlil,
    bethink yourself amply about it!"

NINURTA DISRE-
GARDS THE
ADVICE AND
ATTACKS

The lord stretched the thigh,
    the donkey steeds were mounted,
he girded himself with [sword]belt[weapons,]
cast over the highland
    his long august [shadow,]
issued forth into its people
    like [. . . . .]
Unto [Azag's] stronghold
    he attained,
stood in the front line of battle
    in the rebel country,
gave his long spear instructions,   160
    wound fear (in)to its bindings,
the lord called upon his weapons,
    set out most completely arrayed.

Into the fray the warrior rushed,
    —and the sky sank down unto the tilth,[17]
bow and battle-sling he wielded well,
    shattered was the highland, it dissolved;
    and alongside of Ninurta's battle array,
as the warrior ordered his weapons,
    "Gird yourself!"
the sun marched no (longer),
    it had turned into a moon;[18]
in the highland the peaks (?)
    were wiped out from . . . . . .
    the day was made (black) like pitch.

17. The onrush of the army raises a cloud of dust that cuts off the view of the sky and makes it look as if the sky had sunk down toward the earth. A dust storm has the same effect.
18. The dust obscures the sun so that it looks like the moon.

The Azag rose to attack
    in the front line of the battle,
The sky it pulled down as a weapon
    for its hip, took it in hand,
into the earth it struck the head snakelike.   170
The frenzied dogs were wagging tails
    before the enemy: "Have you killed
    a(ny) victim?"
were drooling slaver on their forepaws.
The Azag was going to crash like a wall
    (down) on Ninurta, Enlil's son;
as were it a day of doom,
    it screamed wrathfully,
like a formidable serpent
    it hissed from among its people,
it wiped up the waters in the highland,
    swept away the tamarisks,
it gashed the earth's body,
    made painful wounds,
gave the canebrake over to fire,
    and bathed the sky in blood,
the interior it knocked over,
    scattered its people,
and till today black cinders are in the fields,   180
and ever heaven's base becomes to the observer
    like red wool—thus verily it is.[19]

THE GODS ARE   An shivered, sat down,
THROWN INTO   wrung the hands over the heart.
DESPAIR   Enlil trembled, leaned against the wall,
the Anunnaki hugged the walls,
and mourned in the house like doves out of fear.
The great mountain Enlil
    cried out to Ninlil:
"O my bride, my son is not here,
    what can I start up?
The lordly plowman of Ekur,
    his father's master of abundance,

19. The rather purple prose of this description of Azag's counterattack suggests the onset of a dust storm, which makes it seem that heaven has been pulled down. The dry wind dries up everything, its violence erodes the surface of the earth, the dry canebrake catches fire, and the flames—combined with the eerie light during a dust storm—makes the sky seem reddened. How the black cinders fit in with the dust storm is not clear.

a cedar grown forth out of the Apsû
    a storm cloud of broad shadow,
a son, sits not where I (take my) rest,   190
    who is going to hold my hand?"

SHARUR SEEKS   The weapon loving the lord,
HELP   heeding its master,
Sharur, for the lord Ninurta
took [the matter of b]reathing
    to Nippur, to his father.
awesome aura and fulgur had enveloped
    Enlil's son like a cloth,
    uprooted him like a tree.
[. . . . .] . . . therefore the lord
   [. . . . .]
[Sharur] said to (En)lil (as follows:)
". . . . . the Azag . . .

(gap from line 198 to 210, inclusive)

ENLIL ADVISES   [. . . . . .] all lands [. . . . . .]   211
[. . . . . .not] compare, the foot into the
    rebel country [. . . . .]
[. . . . . . .] who [. . . . .] does not wander,
    away to which my face [. . . . .]
[Azag] was verily (too) strong to be
    [. . . .] the prudent lord turned back.
[. . . . .] Ninurta trusted to himself
[from the highland], where it had put an end
    to [the rivers (?)], it came and dried up
    the waters like a strong wind,
[but] by my [gi]ft [the floodstorm] he can freely breathe,
    go happy of heart,
the evil winds rising be[low] the [warr]ior
    Ninurta.
[. . . . .] the highland will decide to
    bring [gi]fts to him only, it will see
    his power.
[Thus] I instruct him and he will grasp the matter,[20]   220
[let him] rain down fire [on the country,]
    but may he not strike with the lightning
    those in whom I trust.

---

20. Enlil's gift, the flood storm, will clean the air with its rain, so that Ninurta can breathe freely and win.

May his [plow (?)] pass over (?) the field
    that the nation be not reduced,
nor also that seed corn for the (fiel]ds become
    rare for me.
I a[m Enlil,] and the fame of the role
    I have decreed for him shall not
    be forgotten (ever)."

SHARUR   The weapon took the . . . , slapped the thigh
REPORTS   (to get going)
BACK   Sharur made tracks, made its way into the
    rebel country
and joyously spoke to Ninurta (as follows):
["My mas]ter, out of love,
    what said yo[ur father?]
'Keep spurting against the foe
    the flood storm, before which the [dust] will be laid.
May, when he has captured the Azag   230
    in (all) its strength, and speared it
    in (all) its venom,
my son enter Ekur with it,
may my nation duly praise Ninurta
    far (and wide).'
O lord who heeds his father's word,
O Enlil's august strength, do not
    hold back!
Storm, ready to spread out the rebel country,
    the highland as were it flour,
Ninurta, Enlil's bruiser, go!
    hold not back!
My master, the Azag, which has built
    (defensive) pisé and adobe walls,
is no leaning wall to be pushed over,
it is not cutting down on its bivouacs,
it is not removing its camps,   240
[men] disdainful of death
    it has pushed up into its front line against you,
[evil . . . . . .] it is having march (?)
    in front
my master, it is keeping safe
    against battle in its . . . ."
Ninurta . . . . . the weapon . . . . .
the long spear against the highland
    he . . .

the sun [went] into a cloud . . . .

   . . . .

[the light of day] turned into darkness,

like a [storm] he howled . . .

   . . . . the long spear . . .

Ninurta . . [. . . . . .]   250

the lord [wound] fear [into] the binding

   of [. . . . .]

rammed his battalion (like) a prod

   into the highland.

Sharur [sent] a storm up on heaven,

   it scattered its people,

like a chastiser

   it swept along,

its venom (all) by itself

   destroyed cities.

The weapon, going to reconnoiter

   the border areas, cast fire upon the highland.

The *mittu*-mace smote heads

   with (its) bitter teeth,

the *shita*-weapon, which plucks out hearts,

   gnashed (its) teeth,

the long spear was stuck into the ground,

   and the blood (from it) fitted

   the hole (it made),

the rebel country was poured out   260

   like milk for dogs,

the foes got up (to leave), called their

   wives and children,

lifted not the arm against lord Ninurta.

The weapon tumbled the highland

   in the dust, (and) the Azag had no smiles.

(Yet) Sharur wrung its hands against its shoulder

   over the lord (saying):

"Hey warrior, what has got into you?

You never (yet) touched the highland's

   high constable!

Ninurta, son of Enlil, who also

   is firmly grounded like a storm cloud:

That pustule—a breaking out of which

   (on the skin) is bad—

that Baghdad boil—a breaking out of

   which on the nose is not pleasant—

that twisted tongue—(o) Lord— 270
   have you not taken it to heart?
O my master, like an awning it will be nailed down
   above you, who could make you
   lift the head?
Warrior, (like) a heavy storm cloud it will lie
   on the ground (as a perennial threat)
   for you, (like) a soap-plant it [covers (?)]
   the ground.
"Ninurta, it is chasing the donkey foals
   into the highland,
with winds having halos (of heat) it gathers the dust,
   rains down clay pellets for rain.
In the rebel country the lions howl bitterly,
   no man passes through there.
With all gales, with the wind demons
   coming pounding as one,
   that one will be battering you
in the sheepfolds that are torn away
   with the wind demons,
   it will dry up the water in the wet spots.[21]
The storms blowing in unison
   make an end of the people
   before wings are full-fledged.[22]
The enemy (even), who cannot sustain (his) life,[23]
frenziedly says: 'Great warrior, lord, 280
   turn back your chest (to depart!)'"

The lord growled at the highland,
   could not keep back a roar,
The warrior set up a howl
   loudly in the highland,
what the evil winds had sent hither
   was paid them back,
heads he battered on the enemy horde,
   the highland was brought to tears,
the lord baled up soldier teams
   like looted goods.

21. The reference is to low-lying places where rain collects and where pasture lasts longer.
22. That is, while still children. The image is taken from young birds in the nest.
23. The devastation is too much even for Azag's own people, who cannot make a living in the burnt-up country.

AZAG   In the highland Azag looked
KILLED   balefully at him like an owl,
    the good judgment of the rebel country,
        which used to speak sensibly,
        was being destroyed.
    Ninurta passed through the enemies,
        laid them out as were they fatted calves(?)
    to Azag waiting in its dreadful glory.
    he strode southward, looked northward,   290
    strode northward, looked back southward,
    roiled it as one would water,
        scattered it over the mountain,
    tore it out like rushes, plucked it out like sedge,
    his dreadful glory
        covering the country;
    like ripe grain he shook Azag,
        made its seed (cones) drop off it,
    piled them up together
        like broken mud brick,
    its capable "hands,"
        as were they but ashes,
        he strewed like flour;
    like clay pulled out of a terre pisée wall,
        he heaped them together.[24]

    The warrior had accomplished
        what he had at heart,
    the lord Ninurta, Enlil's son relaxed,
        calmed down,
    came out of the storm in the highland,   300
    and hailed Utu (the sun).
    The lord rinsed belt and weapon in water,
        rinsed the *mittu*-mace in water,
    the warrior wiped his brow—
        and sounded the victory cry over the corpse;
    and as he carved up Azag,
        which he had killed like a fatted calf(?),
    the lads of the country came up to him
    and fell down before him,
        like tired donkey (steeds).

---

24. The "hands" of Azag are probably the pine twigs at the ends of branches, with their needles which could be "strewn" and "piled." Note that the Sumerian term for "branch," á, also is used for "arm." The reference to bits of a *terre pisée* wall may be to fallen bits that would be swept up.

At the lord—for the magnificent way
    in which he had conducted himself—
at Ninurta, Enlil's son, they were waving
    their hands.
Sharur gave praise to the lord Ninurta (saying:)
"Lord, chief steward irrigating the fields,   310
    and warrior—who can be likened to you?
My master, except for you no other (such)
    lives, no other resides, no other
    has been born!
Ninurta, from today on no man will rise
    up (against you) in the highland.
O my master, at your first roar"

(lines 314–22 too badly damaged for translation)

[With the rebel country harrowed
    as with] a harrow,
with Azag torn out from the rebel country
    like rushes,
    plucked out like sedge,
the lord Ninurta stood his *mittu*-mace in the corner,
standing as one unrivaled, as the only one,
    he full of gratification demanded:
"From this day on may (the name) Azag
    not be spoken, let 'stone' be its name,
let 'stone,' '*zalag* stone,' be its name,
    let 'stone' be its name!
May thus its extinction be bitter
and its warrior status be for the lord!   330
As status to be decreed for the weapon
    which is standing in the corner:
may its name be spoken in the highland
    as 'Thunderstorm unleashed
    against the foe
in the great battle that pared the
    country down!'"

NINURTA BUILDS   In those days the waters of the ground
THE FOOTHILLS   coming from below did not flow
    out over the fields.
(Nay!) As ice long accumulating
    they rose in the mountains on the far side.
The gods of the country, having gone there,
carrying pickaxes and baskets

—thus being their appointed task—
poured on a man's field
   according to what they would
   have chopped off (of the ice).
The Tigris river did not grandly rise up,   340
its outlets did not [take it straight out]
   into the sea, it carried not fresh waters,
(so) men could not dip (?) water pails
   at the quay;
in dire famine nothing was produced,
no man cleaned minor canals,
   nor dredged the silt from them,
water was not let down unto fertile fields,
   nor was there any construction of canal dikes.
In (all) the country no seed-furrow was drawn,
   grain was broadcast (only).
The lord directed his august intelligence
   thereunto,
Ninurta, Enlil's son, wrought grandly.
He made a bank of stones against the
   highland,
—like drifting clouds they (came floating on)   350
   outstretched wings—
and placed it as a bar before the country
   like a great wall.
At hundreds of places he set up well-sweeps,
—the warrior was shrewd, accorded the cities
   equal importance—
and the mighty waters followed along the stones.
Nowadays these waters do not (any more)
   rise up from in the earth up into the
   highland for good.
What (once) was scattered he gathered together,
what had been absorbed by swamps
   in the highland
he gathered and threw into the Tigris,
had the carp-flood[25] flow out over the fields.
Nowadays all the world   360
rejoices far (and wide) in the country's king,
   lord Ninurta.

25. Carp-flood was the Sumerians' term for an early flood during which the rivers would have carp swimming up them. The waters of this flood were important for irrigation.

He made the fields bear mottled barley,
made the orchard irrigation beds bear fruit
    at harvest,
heaped up grain piles;
high over the (surrounding) country
    the lord piled them up (on) the harbor quays,
made the gods' livers feel good,
and they duly praised Ninurta
    to his father.

NINMAH   On that day the queen took compassion,
MISSES   in (her bed) where he had been engendered,
HER SON   Ninmah[26] could not fall asleep.
            She covered the back with wool,   370
    (looking) like a stately ewe,
and greatly wailed about the highland
    in (all) its tracklessness:

"The lord for (all) his huge strength
    will not get up into the highland
the great warrior, like An in his wrath,
    any man, draws not nigh
    to its flanks.
It is an angry storm cloud
    standing on the ground,
    dust laid down in front of it!

"The lord, Enlil's (very) life's breath,
    worthy of a crown for the head,
a warrior whose strength
    recognizes no ordering (around),
who compellingly rushed to me,
    and whom I planted for my spouse,
to whom I gave birth for my bridegroom,
    but who has gone off
    paying me no heed,
Enlil's son, who has taken leave
    and not turned his face toward me!"

26. *Nin-mah* "august lady" is a name for Ningirsu's mother. This and the names used for her in the following lines reflect the mythology of Ningirsu and Girsu rather than that of Ninurta and Nippur. In Girsu Ningirsu's mother was the mountain and birth goddess Ninhursaga/Nintur; in Nippur Ninurta's mother was Ninlil, originally a grain goddess. This composition, however, treats them as names of one and the same divine figure. The plethora of names the Sumerians gave their deities may seem disturbing to a modern reader. The ancients, however, saw in each name the expression of a quality or power of the deity so designated, so that to have many names reflected high and important standing.

SHE DECIDES Unto the sterling champion   380
TO VISIT   she did truly a loving kindness
HIM   in that she went to them
                 at the place of (their) dividing (the booty)
                 on which he had (his) eyes:
             "Let me cut (any and all) strings
                 (to go) to him, to the valiant lord,
             let me, the queen, go by my(self) alone
                 to the lord with whom I would ever be!
             Could I but see him there!
             O may I meet with him,
                 the righteous child, Enlil's judge,
             the great warrior, his father's delight!"

SHE ARRIVES (As) the queen was chanting plaints silver-toned,
             Ninmah was catching sight
                 of the lord Ninurta,
             and he cast his life(-giving) eye upon her
                 and called out to her:

             "Queen, as you have come to the highland—   390
             Ninmah, as for my sake
                 you have entered
                 the rebel regions,
             as you have not shied away
                 from my battle (array),
                 over which hovers its dread aura,
             let the name of the bank
                 I, a warrior, have heaped up
             be Hursag,27 and be you its owner!"
             —At once, by Ninurta's decree,
             thus it verily became;
                 she is today to be spoken of
                 (as) Ninhursağa—
             "May its meadows grow herbs for you,
             may its ledges grow grapevines
                 and (yield) grape sirop for you,
             may its slopes grow cedar, cypress,
                 supalu-trees and box for you,
             may it adorn itself for you   400
                 with tree fruit like an orchard,

---

27. *Hur-sağ*, literally "head of the valleys," denotes the near mountains, the foothills, and contrasts with the more daunting, less accessible high mountains farther in, the "highland" (*kur*).

may the foothills make great
    scent of godliness for you,
may gold and silver be mined for you,
    and may HI-IB-LÀL be made for you.
May it smelt copper and tin for you,
    may it pay you its tribute,
may the highland make goats
    and wild asses numerous for you,
may the Hursag have the four-legged beasts
    bring forth offspring for you.
You are a queen, one comparable to me,
    carrying like heaven dread aura,
O Dingirmah,[28] hating boasting,
able woman, owner of the foothills,
    a (pristinely) pure place,[29]
Nintur![30] Cross over its snowy sides!
Come nigh unto me, Queen,   410
    I have bestowed on you a great office,
    have verily elevated you thereunto;
(but) while I am passing sentence
    upon the highland
    go (you) to Nippur!"
The able woman,
    whose offices surpass (other) offices,
    Ninnagarshaga,[31]
Aruru,[32] Enlil's older sister,
    stood up confronting him (and said:)
"Great warrior,
    on the warriors (to be) killed by you,
O lord, whose commands,
    like those of his father,
    can not be countermanded,
    I shall not have passed sentence!"[33]

28. *Dingir-mah* is still another name for Ninĝirsu's mother. It means "august deity."

29. I.e., wilderness, untouched—and so undefiled—by man.

30. Name of Ninĝirsu's mother as goddess of birth-giving. It means "lady birth hut" and designates the goddess as the numinous power in the birth huts of fold and pen, in which the pregnant animals were sheltered and attended to while giving birth.

31. Still another name for Ninĝirsu's mother in her capacity of birth goddess. It means "the womb's carpenter" and refers to the power of the womb to give shape to the embryo.

32. One more name of Ninĝirsu's mother as birth goddess. *A-ru-ru* means "The one who lets the water out," and refers to the amniotic fluid. The goddess in question, whether termed Ninhursaĝa, Nintur, or Aruru, was generally considered Enlil's sister, but some traditions made her his wife as well.

33. She does not wish to incur any responsibility for the sentences, some of which are certain to be severe. If she had been present she would have been sure to have been appealed to for mercy.

NINURTA HOLDS
COURT: THE
"PLANT" STONE

The lord called to the "Plant" stone,[34]
    thundered harsh invective at it.
The lord in anger spoke to it before the nation,
Ninurta, Enlil's son, passed sentence on it (saying:)
" 'Plant' stone, as you rose up against me
    in the highland,
as you incited to having me   420
    taken into custody,
as you passed sentence on me
    for me to be executed,
as you startled me, the lord Ninurta,
    out of my august seat,
may a strong one,
    a champion having (powerful) build
    exceeding you(rs),
    pare off from your shape,
may a great storm, trusting to its strength,
    wear you away,
may one possessing strength
    drag you in lead (to polish you).
'Plant' stone, lad, may your brothers
    heap you up like flour,
may you raise the hand
    against your (own) offspring,
    have (your) teeth go berserk
    in their carcasses.[35]
You are a lad! May there be
    a call to you (for service),
    but instead of you being entrusted
    (with any task),
    may you be put an end to;
like a big wild bull
    killed by a multitude of men
    be set out in portions!
'Plant' stone! (Off with you) from the weapons!   430
    Dog! (Off with you) from the battle,
like one a shepherd boy chases!
I am lord! Stone, be called
    by the name of your hollow
    that is hollowed out in you!"[36]

---

34. This stone has not been identified.
35. Supposedly crushed "plant" stone was used to grind and polish other hard stones.
36. The word for "hollow" is *gug*, which is the name of the stone.

Now, at the sentence passed by Ninurta,
today, when the "plant" stone has been cut
   a hollow is to be drilled in the stone.
   Thus verily it became.

THE GRANITE   The warrior called out
AND THE   to the Granite (?) and the Basalt,
BASALT   the lord counted them
   among the enemies,
Ninurta, Enlil's son,
   cursed them (saying:)
"Granite (?) as you (two) charged against my weapons,
Basalt, as you (two) came at me,
   roaring like bulls,
as like wild bulls you stabbed (your) horns   440
   into the dust,
I might have broken you
   as (one would) butterflies,
but my terrifying aura and glory
   overspread you,
and as you did not stand up
   against my august power,
may you be as the air he breathes
   to the silversmith
and may the foundryman love the two of you
   for his small work![37]
At the gods' "early grass" (festivals)
may they seat the two of you
   new-moon day by new-moon day,
   on the broad side (of the table)."[38]

"HARDHEAD,"   My king stepped over
"CRUSHER," AND   to the stone "Hardhead"
"FAMINE"   called out to the "Crusher" stone,
STONES   and the "Famine" stone,[39]
Ninurta, Enlil's son,   450
   passed sentence on them (saying:)

37. Molds for small items were often made of stone. The silversmith's use of granite and basalt is not specified. Tentatively one might consider whether, perhaps, the Sumerians classified the touchstone with either granite or basalt.

38. The "early grass," mentioned also below in l. 544, was presumably a spring festival, one celebrating the opening of the pasturing season for the flocks in the desert. To be seated on the broad side of the table was an honor. Reference here is probably to the bowls of granite or basalt in which the food was served.

39. These stones have not been identified.

"Stone 'Hardhead,' as you sent arrows
    flying at me,
'Crusher' stone, as you threw
    (the elite) troops against me
    like (bolts of) lightning,
'Famine' stone, as you made me
    shake the head (in distress),
as you bared the teeth at me, the lord,
may the stone 'Hardhead'
    smoothen you, 'Famine' stone,
and may the able young gallant, the 'Crusher' stone,
    hollow you out,
may one not hard headed
    pluck you![40]
Be set out for the country's famines,
    may the hands of your city
    be filled there.[41]
Verily, you are held in low esteem,
    verily you are slaves' and slave women's dog!
May they tell you: 'Hasten! Run!'   460
    and be you called by that name!"[42]
(So), by the sentence passed by Ninurta now,
today, for the country,
    to one doing an irksome task
    it verily became so.

THE DOLERITE   My king stepped hither to the dolerite
and, though in a rage, held in fairness
    (his) tongue,
    spoke with restraint to it,
Ninurta, Enlil's son,
    passed sentence on it (saying:)
"Dolerite, as, transferring your battalions
    to the rear,
and throwing up (dust)
    like a heavy smoke before me,
you raised not the arm,
    stormed not against me,

40. What is here described is not clear. Conceivably it is the cutting of ridges in a quern stone and the cleaning of the valleys between them.

41. If a hand mill of quern type is involved, this could refer to the upper millstone, to its being shoved back and forth fast.

42. A stone of that name (*ullalesarre*) is not otherwise known.

but said: 'It is wrong!
    The lord alone is the warrior!
Who can vie with Enlil's son,   470
    Ninurta?'
May they cause you to set out
    from the Northlands,
and may they have you alight
    from Magan.
May you—when the strong copper
    has encircled (?) you like a skin—
be grandly suited
    for mine, the lord's, warrior arm.[43]
The king who is establishing for his name
    life unto far-off times,
after he has fashioned out of you
    a statue (inscribed) with it
    for future days,
and has stood you in Eninnu,[44]
    temple laden with delight,
at its libation place,
    may you be suited for it!

THE COMMON   My king stepped hither to the (Lime)stone[45]
LIMESTONE   was flaying the skin   480
    off the (lime-)stone,[46]
Ninurta, Enlil's son,
    passed sentence on it (saying:)
"(Lime)stone, as you said:
    'Now *I* am it!'
(Lime)stone, as you cast lots
    about my offices,
be you made to lie for building purposes
    like a pig,

43. The reference is probably to a weapon consisting of a mace which had a stone macehead that was surrounded by bronze blades in the shape of lions. It is pictured on boundary stones and cylinder seals as an emblem of Ninurta/Ningirsu.

44. É-*ninnu* was the temple of Ningirsu in Girsu. The passage very clearly refers to the famous statues of Gudea set up in Eninnu, dolerite for which was imported from Magan.

45. This, apparently, is the "stone" (*na*) into which, according to lines 326–29, Azag was changed. Here there is no mention of this, or any reference to its leading role in the war with Ninurta. Most likely the section dealing with the judgment of the stones came unchanged from a separate source that had no relation to the war with Azag. See also n. 58, below.

46. Reference may be to a thin layer of vegetation on top of the stone, which would have to be removed before it could be quarried, or, possibly, to taking off the weathered top layer of the stone itself.

lie thrown—not to be worked—
  and be put an end to
  by being (broken) into bits.
May the one who knows (all about) you
  pierce you with water!"[47]

THE ELALU   My king stepped up to the "Waterbearer" stone.[48]
Ninurta, Enlil's son passed sentence on it
  (saying:)
"Wise 'Water-bearer' stone, though grown up
  in the hostile highland,
  you were endued, verily, with awe of me,
in the regions rebelling against me   490
  and in my country jointly as one
  you verily proclaimed ny name!
May your haleness suffer no attrition,
may your bulk be hard to diminish,
and may my sacred office (of warrior)
  find correct execution in your body
  for you;
going into battle, may you be grandly perfect
  for my killing warriors!
In my main courtyard
  may a pedestal be set up for you
and may the nation admire you,
  and all lands praise you!"[49]

THE HEMATITE   The warrior stepped over to the "Truth" stone,[50]
called out to (it in) its strength,
Ninurta, Enlil's son,
  passed sentence on it (saying:)
"(God-)fearing youth,   500
  shedding light to (all) sides,
'Truth' stone, whom I reclaimed
  from the rebel region,
(l. 502 not in older texts)

47. Limestone blocks were used from early times as fill for foundations and could remind, seen from above as one looked into the foundation ditch, of the backs of pigs wallowing in mire. The stone is, of course, highly soluble in water.

48. A kind of hard brownish limestone.

49. Reference is to the use of stone for maceheads. It is not unlikely that a ceremonial mace of this stone actually stood in the courtyard of Eninnu in Girsu.

50. That is, hematite. The Sumerian name for this stone comes from its use for stone weights, for which its heaviness made it specially suited.

not in violence did my hand reach you,
nor did I fetter you
    along with the defiant ones,
but united the nation at your feet.
May Utu's[51] office be your sacred office,
righting as judge all countries.
Among the wise ones knowing everything
may you be dear to them like gold!
Young gallant who had been taken captive,   510
    on account of you I could not sleep
    until you were (rescued all) hale!"
Now, by the sentence passed by Ninurta
today the hale (undamaged) "Truth" stone
    is verily thus.[52]

THE ALABASTER   The warrior stepped over to the great "Lamp" stone,[53]
Ninurta, Enlil's son,
    passed sentence on it (saying):
" 'Lamp' stone, of body of brilliance like daylight,
refined silver, young gallant fit for the palace,
in (whooping) your war whoops
    you were lifting hand against me,
but in your mountain
    you kissed the ground,[54]
(so) I did not do battle with you,
    bent not the arm against you,
and, warrior, I stayed my roaring!   520
May you be nominated for favors,
may the nation's treasuries
    be put in your hands,
        may you be their keeper of the seal."

(lines 522a and 523 omitted; not in the older texts)

THE STEATITE   My king stepped over to the steatite,
    frowned at it,
the lord spoke to it in anger
    in the country,

---

51. Utu was god of the sun and of justice and fairness.

52. Tentatively I have assumed that the reference is to the use of hematite for weights, where it must be undamaged to weigh true.

53. The "Lamp" stone is the alabaster, a stone much used for making oil lamps. Its translucency made it a symbol of light in itself.

54. Presumably this means that it changed its mind and went over to Ninurta.

Ninurta, Enlil's son, cursed it (saying:)
"O, how you enquired about my movements!
Go forward, in among my craftsmen,

(line 529 omitted; not in older texts)

and carrying the daily regular offering   530
    may you, steatite, be worked!"[55]

THE TOPAZ

My king stepped over to the Topaz,
called out to the *Hulalu* stone,
    the Carnelian, and the lapis lazuli,
to the Jasper, the *Shaba* stone, the *Hurizum* stone,
    the Carnelian, the *Marhalum* stone,
the *Egizanga* stone, the *Girin hiliba* stone,
    the *Anzugulme* stone, and the *Nir-muš-ul₄*^{ki} stone.[56]
The lord, life's breath of the waterskin
    [carried in the desert,][57]
Ninurta, Enlil's son,
    passed sentence on them (saying:)
"What has brought you,
    (stone) created male and female,
    one such as you,
    to my place too?
You have (committed) no offense,
    your hands picked me up at the wall,
in the presence of witnesses
    you adopted me,
and brought me up to give counsel,   540
and as you had me installed (as) general
    in the assembly,
O *Hulalu* stone, may you be found
    in honey and wine,
and may you all rightfully be decked out
    with gold,
at the "early grass" festival of the gods
may all lands salute you
    by lowering nose to the ground for you."[58]

55. The steatite will serve for bowls in which to carry temple income destined for food for the craftsmen as well as for working material for them.

56. Most of these seemingly precious stones have not been identified. It seems possible that the section originally concerned only the *hulalu* and a few others but has been added to for completion.

57. Ninurta, as god of the thundershowers, provides pools of rainwater in the desert from which the waterskins can be filled when empty.

58. This section apparently refers to an otherwise unknown myth according to which Ninurta or Ningirsu was abandoned as a child and left to die at the city wall, where the *hulalu* stone found him,

THE FLINT	My king stepped over to the great blade-flint,
(ITS FLAKES,	frowned at it,
BROKEN, WERE	the lord spoke to it in anger
USED AS	in the country.
TEETH IN	Ninurta, Enlil's son,
WOODEN SICKLES)	cursed it (saying:)

"Ah! What are (even) two men
    for the great blade-flint (to take on)?
May a wild bull be stabbing at you   550
    in your mountains,
      and you stay lying asleep thereat,
it being no match for you!
    (Lo!) it thrust the tip against you
and slit you like sacking!
    May man slim you down by that means,
may a craftsman doing inlays
    be assigned to you,
    and may he touch the chisel to you.
Young gallant, may a carpenter,
    one offering sickles for sale,
flood, as in irrigating (a field),
    your flesh, laden with hostility,
      crush you in the manner of malt!"[59]

THE IMMANAK	My king stepped over to the *Immanak*,
AND ALLIGA	called out to the *Alliga* stone,
STONES	Ninurta, Enlil's son,

    passed sentence on them (saying:)
"O *Immanak* stone, as the two of you   560
    roared at me in the highland,
as you dreadfully yelled
    the dread battle cry,

---

legally adopted him, and reared him until eventually he was chosen general by the assembly. As such he was sitting in judgment on his captured foes when, to his surprise, he found his foster father included among them. This myth—built on the well-known motif of the future hero as foundling of unknown parentage—can obviously not meaningfully be fitted in with the normal view of Ninurta/Ningirsu as son of Enlil and Ninlil/Ninhursaga which the composition as a whole follows. It must have been taken over mechanically by the composer from a separate source. Most likely it formed the frame story of the original tale of Ninurta/Ningirsu's judgment of the stones, part of which the composer of Lugal-e used for his section on them. The "early grass" festival is mentioned also in l. 446, above.

59. Flint flakes under the pressure of the tip of a horn. A common use for flint was to serve as cutting edge in sickles of wood and bitumen. The two sides of such sickles were of wood, the middle of bitumen which had been melted and poured over a row of square broken bits of flint blades—not unlike teeth in a jawbone—then allowed to harden. The flooding and crushing mentioned presumably has reference to this process.

you will be set aglow like fire,
piled up as (dust) by a storm,
torn out like rushes,
plucked out like halfa grass,
who has (ever) reached out the hand
    for you?
Immanak stone, may a request for you
    not be (thought) worthwhile,
    may no enquiries be made about you,
Immanak stone and *Alliga* stone,
    may your (summons:) 'Come to the palace!'
    never be uttered."

THE "GAZELLE" STONE

My king stepped over to the "Gazelle" stone
    called out to the *Dubban* stone   570
        and the *Urutum* stone,[60]
Ninurta, Enlil's son,
    thundered harsh invective
    at them.
" 'Gazelle' stone and *Dubban* stone,
    blazing holocausts,
and *urutum* stone,
    to which no one can stand up,
who, throwing the basalt
    to those baring the teeth at (its) throat,
    verily came raging hither from it,[61]
and flared up against me
    in the rebel regions like a conflagration,
as (the three of) you
    resisted me in the Sabum mountains,
O 'gazelle' stone, may you be bled (dry)
    like a (butchered) sheep!
O *Dubban* stone, may you be battered,
    a thing to be demolished!
O *Urutum* stone, may you be sharpened
    like a mittum-mace,
to (shape you to) hone a fierce point   580–81
    on the bronze of the gods' arrowheads.
May you be hewed by the axe!"[62]

60. These stones have not been identified.
61. The incident here referred to is not otherwise known.
62. The *urutum* stone must have been a stone suitable for use as a hone. A special shape of hone seems to have been needed for honing arrowheads.

THE SHAGARA
STONE

My king stepped hither
    to the *Shagara* stone[63]
Ninurta, Enlil's son,
    passed sentence on it (saying:)
"*Shagara* stone, who knocks
    the lone traveler on the head
    in the desert,[64]
as you tramped the highland to pinion me,
as you lusted after that battle,
may the reed worker make you leap
    from the reeds
    and throw you onto your bed,[65]
may he narrow the vulva
    of the mother who bore you,
    and not say of you: 'Extract it!'[66]
May no man live in need of you,
and may the nation not mention   590
    the loss of you!
(Yet) when in Ninhursaǧa's place of tranquility,
    lastingly built for sacred offices,
you have been cast upon its throne dais
    to sing (her) praise,
may men boil light beer
    for (a) mutton (dish) for you,
and may you enjoy
    the flour strewn by them,
    be that your place of absolution!"[67]

THE MARHUSHA
STONE

My king stepped hither to the *Marhusha* stone[68]
Ninurta, Enlil's son,
    passed sentence on it:
"*Marhusha* stone, a snare was [set]

63. The *shagara* stone has not yet been identified.

64. Presumably indicating that it could be used for maceheads, which might then be used by bandits in the desert.

65. The *shagara* stone was termed "the stone of the reed worker" by the ancients. Reference here is probably to a stone swathed in thread, which the maker of reed blinds throws from one side of the blind to the other as he is weaving the thread in over reed after reed.

66. Reference may be to the name *shagara*, which could represent a contracted form of *shag.a-ri.a* "engendered in the womb," that is to say, "yet unborn." Such a reading of the name might have reference to the enclosing of the stone in thread.

67. What this refers to is obscure.

68. The *marhusha* has not yet been identified. It was named from a country Marhashi which seems to have been located in the region around Kerman in Iran.

for where I was,
   you drew near and were caught,
fell (a victim) to your city's criminal act,
   [. .] . . [. .] . . [. .]
May you become an oil cruse,
   may water be poured (?) off it,
and, *Marhusha* stone, may ointment [fill it,]   600
   and may the lord [take] from the best of it!
Greatly suitable you are
   (also) for a pin, for silver,
and, *Marhusha*, you are seemly
   for the god's temples!"

THE "RAVINE"   The warrior stepped over
STONE   to the "ravine" stone,[69]
the lord spoke to it in anger
   in the nation,
Ninurta, Enlil's son,
   passed sentence on it (saying:)
" 'Ravine' stone, you roared at me
   in the highland,
yelled dreadfully the dread battle cry,
had your roar, a very gale,
   rend the highland,[70]
you are a lad, be you called by the name
   of your mauling the ground: 'ravine!' "
Now, by the sentence passed by Ninurta,   610
today the "ravine" stone is verily so to the speaker.

THE TURAN   My king stepped hither
STONE   to the *Turan* stone[71]
Ninurta, Enlil's son,
   passed sentence on it (saying:)
"*Turan* stone, keeping a festering (wound) clean,
   youth with the eyes gone,
   men gouged them out,
who made obeisance in the highland,
   as if I might sunder (your) fetter;

69. The "ravine" stone has not yet been identified. The name means "pit," "ravine."
70. The roar, and the breath that goes into it, amount to a gale strong enough to erode the mountains, as a strong wind erodes the soil of the alluvial plain of southern Mesopotamia.
71. This stone has not been identified. The name is identical with the ancient name of the Diyala River.

to match that you said: 'O that I might wait on
   my master Ninurta!'
May those who call your name
   prosper,
those saying 'Let me buy the maestro (free)
   with silver!'
and may all lands—as were they musicians—   620
   play (joyous) reed pipes thereat![72]

THE STONE OF THE ELAMITIC CITY SHIGSHIG TO FORM A BORDER GUARD	My king stepped over to the *Shigshig* stone

THE STONE OF   My king stepped over to the *Shigshig* stone
THE ELAMITIC   called out to the *engen* stone
CITY SHIGSHIG   and the *ezemma* stone
TO FORM A   the *madanum* stone, the *saĝ-gir₁₁-mud* stone,
BORDER GUARD   the . . . . stone, and the . . . . stone,[73]   625
                        Ninurta, Enlil's son,
       passed sentence (saying:)
"[Shigshig stone], who made [obeisance to me
   in the highland],
The [troops,] whether associates
   or followers of blood relatives,
   that have made obeisance,
whether of a sparing heart
   or bone-crushing like bears,
amid whom you have gone raiding,   630
   you will bring to me.
May you (all) now, from the borderlands   630–31
   of your protective comrades,
   move near unto me!
   Who could lay a hand on you?
May you be a pivot-stone,
   and the door be
   set up on you![74]
May the strong one bend down
   his neck to you,
have them run (scared) from the bruiser!
   May the dawn that is approaching the place,
daily make the one to have the water clock
   get up,

---

72. The stone, having had its eyes gouged out, would have become a rhapsodist, one of the typical professions for the gifted blind in antiquity.

73. None of these stones has been identified. The Shigshig stone seems to owe its name to an Elamitic city of that name.

74. The image is the popular one of a border stronghold keeping out intruders like a door.

and may the eternal young gallant (Utu)
　　cast a sidelong glance (down) at you
　　in the country!"

THE KURGARĀNU
(LIKE AN EFFEM-
INATE CULT-MIME)
STONE

The warrior stepped over
　　to the Kurgarānu stone
was calling out to the "spindle whorl" stone[75]
the lord—(dear to them like) their yellow cosmetics—
Ninurta, Enlil's son,　　　　　　　　　　　　　　　　640
　　passed sentence on them (saying:)
"You of whom the master of the house said:
　　'Let me expel him!'
who went to me
　　as the truest of followers,
you, as a lad whom the master of the house
　　had eat in the corner,
　　lived like a servant,
may you (here) be treated properly
　　among the young professionals,
may they celebrate well
　　the [festival of the sha]des,
and at the day of the new moon
　　may lads engage for you in (athletic) contests,
　　for nine days [in their city quarters,][76]
[and may you be in attendance]
　　for the rites of Ninhursağa!"

NINURTA RETURNS
TO HIS BOAT

The lord rode roughshod over the highland,
　　traveling the desert [he swept along like a st]orm,
like a standard he stood out tallest among them,
　　august strength he [. . . . .]
Rejoicing, Ninurta came to his beloved barge,　　　650
the lord set his foot in Makarnuntaea,
and the sailors broke into song
　　sweetly from it,
were sin[cerely hono]ring the lord,
were having [Ninurta,] Enlil's so[n]
　　accla[imed] far and wide (saying:)

75. These stones have not been identified. The kurgarānu, however, is named from kurgarû "myrmidon," originally a guardsman of the goddess Inanna, but later serving in various roles in her service. Inanna changed the kurgarûs from male to female, which explains why the kurgarānu stone is grouped with the "spindle whorl" stone. The spindle, typically an emblem of femininity, was carried by the kurgarû on occasion.

76. The kurgarû typically took part in war games, often quite bloody ones.

SONG OF
THE BOATMEN

"God preeminent among warriors,
[Lord] Ninurta, the Anunnaki gods' warrior-king,
effective goad, bearded one,
you fall upon the enemy horde
    (like) the waters bursting forth
    (through a break in a dike)!
Who can compare with you
    in all your great augustness,
warrior, floodstorm not to be opposed,   660
whom Enki and Ninki,[77]
    pay [homage(?)].
Warrior, raiding cities,
    subjugating the highland,
(O) son of Enlil,
    who compares with you?
Ninurta, Enlil's son, warrior,
    who is like you?

"My master, the warrior who is on hand
    for your arrival[78]
will, consonant with his name,
    straightway lay hold of your feet.
In your temple,
    for which he has made the proper thing appear,
on your temple terrace,
    which he raised for you with earth (as fill),
may he provide a largesse of food
    for your festival,
may he carry out your sacred rites   670
    to perfection for you!
He is worthy of (you,) the ordainer
    of his years of life,
    may he praise you to the country!

"May the heart of An
    be appeased toward the lord!

77. I.e., Lord and Lady Earth.

78. The reference is to Lugal-si-sá, the counselor of the original hero of the composition, Ningirsu. Lugal-si-sá greeted him, according to Gudea Cylinder A, viii. 10–22, when he returned from his yearly ritual journey to Eridu, having acted as his regent during his absence. He is thus the logical one to greet Ningirsu/Ninurta on his return from his victorious campaign. The text makes it clear that he is meant by its play on his name. "Straightway" is *si-sá* in Sumerian. It also, by listing his achievements, makes it clear that he was thought to be incarnate in the human ruler Gudea, for what is credited to him are the beginnings of Gudea's building of the temple Eninnu.

and may unto Enlil's fighter,
    Ninurta,
the maiden, dame Baba,
    come out like dawn!"

In the bow of the boat
    (thus) they were singing to the lord
and unto the boat, floating (downriver) by itself,
    (people) flocked,
pure arms were stretched out
    toward Makarnuntaea.

HOMAGE BY   To meet the warrior
THE GODS ON   coming safe from battle,
RETURN   into the house came the Anunnaki gods,
prostrated themselves   680
    and [laid] hand on the breast,
prayerfully they saluted the lord,
and verily soothed thereby
    the heart for the lord in (its) raging.

BENEFITS   Ninurta, king Uta-ulu,[79]
CONFERRED   lifted up the head,
BY ENLIL   and his father, Enlil,
    conferred (new) status on him (saying:)
"(Warrior-)king, surpassing as to your august name
    in heaven and on earth,
lord, settled, verily,
    amid sacred offices (productive) of abundance,
broad-chested one, fair of locks,
O king of battle, in rebel regions
    a storm . . . .
    has verily been accorded you,
the flood storm weapon
    hurling fire upon the highland,
o heaven and earth's warrior,   690
    has verily been accorded you,
for your storm, o (warrior) king,
    roads are verily (too) narrow!
Ninurta, your going into the highland
    has verily compelled compliance there;
as if unleashed to catch a wolf

79. "South storm," a frequently used other name for Ninurta.

you truly highstepped it
    to the rebel region to your battle royal!
May such as you have rushed at
    never (be able to) return home,
may their cities be counted mounds of ruins,
their highly placed ones
    hold (their) breath because of you!
May a pleasant reign not to be changed,
    (o) server of An,[80]
and life unto distant days,
    (o) trust of Enlil,
be your gift, king of towering strength!   700

As for that the warrior, killed Azag,
as for that the lord made that bank,
as for that he said: "May stones go into it,"
as for that the uniquely great one
    roared at them
    and made them bow,
as for that the warrior made the waters
    wend the foot off from the heights,
as for that he set boundary truthfully
    for the fields,
as for that he had plow furrows
    produce abundance,
as for that the lord instituted
    planting (in) furrows,
as for that Ninurta, son of Enlil,
    heaped up piles and heaps of grain,
did Ninurta, son of Enlil,
make the damsel who was raised   710
    amid sacred offices,
    and augustly instructed,
Nidaba,[81] the able woman,
    surpassing the experts in all lands,
who understands the preeminent tablets,
    the series (with the rites) of
    enship and kingship,

---

80. One of Ningirsu/Ninurta's offices was to serve his grandfather, An, the god of heaven, at table.
81. Nidaba was the goddess of grasses, grains, and reeds. Since the stylus of the scribe originally was cut from reeds, she became also the goddess of writing and literature generally.

endowed with august intelligence
    by "Lord Earth" from Duku(g),[82]
tend to it.

POET'S
PRAISE OF
NIDABA

Queen, heavenly star,
    grandly engendered by the prince in Apsû,[83]
damsel who releases for the (understanding) heart
    Nidaba's house of wisdom,[84]
unique adviser, adept counselor,
powerful [. . . . . .] of the dark-headed people,
    keeper of the seal,
    (thus) possessing her father's name,[85]
whose trap the flattened bird in it
    cannot open,
its construction being too much   720
    (for it) to open,
it counting the days by the moon
    in a braided cord not to be unraveled,[86]
wall of brass which no man can scale,[87]
expert at (sage) counsel, sage of the realm,
queen taking care of the dark-headed people,
    setting matters straight for the nation,
you are a [. . . . .] counterpart of Enlil,
[a queen,] consulting with the stars above.
    Nidaba, praise (be unto you)!

POET'S PRAISE
OF NINURTA

Ninurta, chief [plowman] of Enlil,
    august denizen of Ekur
the trust of the father who begat him,
    praise of you is sweet!

(A [*sìr-gí*]d (song) of Ninurta.)

---

82. "Lord earth" (*En-ki*) counted as one of an older generation of gods, now residing in the netherworld. *Duku*, the "holy mound," was a term for a grain pile covered with plaster to protect it, the usual way of storing grain. Here it may merely stand for the netherworld.

83. *Apsû* was the sea of fresh water thought to underlie the earth, the watertable. It came to the surface in pools and marshes. Nidaba, like the reeds of which she is the goddess, grows out of it.

84. Presumably a term for the library of inscribed tablets, her domain.

85. The seal would carry the name of her father.

86. I understand this to refer directly to fowlers' snares made of reeds or tough grass, and to serve indirectly as an image for the fleeting word caught and held fast in writing. Here it would refer directly to her responsibility for guarding the memory of Ninurta's great deeds.

87. Another image for the firmness with which the written word preserves a content.

PART FIVE

Epics

Enmerkar and the Lord of Aratta

The story of Enmerkar and the Lord of Aratta begins in legendary times, when trade and barter were still unknown and when many other achievements of civilization—such as written communication by letter—had not yet been invented. In Uruk ruled the "lord" or "priest-king" (en) Enmerkar. By virtue of his office he was the human husband of the goddess of the city, Inanna, with whom he united in the yearly rite of the sacred marriage. On him rested the responsibility for establishing the proper relations to the gods in cult, and rites on which the welfare of the community and its prosperity depended. And on him rested the responsibility for guiding the community and finding constructive solution to all problems and difficulties. As Enmerkar ruled in Uruk, so ruled the Lord of Aratta in the fabled city of Aratta which lay in the mountains far away to the east. He too was the spouse of Inanna, and he too had the same responsibilities for the welfare and prosperity of Aratta that Enmerkar had for Uruk. But Inanna, we are told, loved Enmerkar best.

Enmerkar's ambitions for the cult in Uruk made him feel acutely the need for stone and precious metals for the temples in Uruk and Eridu. These materials were not available in the Sumerian alluvial plain, and it therefore occurred to him to use Inanna's greater love for him to make her withhold rain from Aratta and, through the threat of starvation, force that city to submit to Uruk. As the corvée work due the victor it would bring stone and precious metals to Enmerkar and labor on his temple-building.

To such an extent had Enmerkar bewitched Inanna that she readily agreed to forsake her other husband, the Lord of Aratta, and to give him into Enmerkar's hands. An envoy was therefore dispatched to demand the submission of Aratta and to threaten it with destruction by famine if it did not obey.

The Lord of Aratta, secure from military attack in his mountain stronghold, at first scoffed at the thought of submission; but when he was told of Inanna's faithlessness, he realized the seriousness of the threat. Unable to defend himself with weapons, he decided on a duel of wits, a challenge to Enmerkar's intellectual pride, to the ability which the superior en must have to find ways and means when nobody else can. He therefore made his submission contingent on what he considered an impossible and mocking condition. Enmerkar was to bring grain to

Aratta to keep its people alive in the famine; but this grain was to be carried on donkey-back in the usual open carrying-nets, not in sacks.

Enmerkar accepted the intellectual challenge and solved the problem by filling the nets with malt, germinated grain felted together in solid lumps. As sign of submission he demanded that the Lord of Aratta accept a scepter cut from Enmerkar's own scepter—symbol that he derived his power from Enmerkar.

The people of Aratta, who had suffered under the famine and had been relieved by Enmerkar, were now ready to submit to Uruk, but the Lord of Aratta still held out. Though he formally declares himself ready to accept his scepter from Enmerkar, that sceptre must be of no known wood, nor of metal and precious stones. Enmerkar accepts this challenge also and grows a costly, resplendent reed which he sends as the scepter demanded.

By now the Lord of Aratta is near despair; Enmerkar has shown his intellectual superiority by twice doing what the Lord of Aratta thought could not be done, and yet he makes a last attempt: he proposes a duel between Enmerkar's and his champions, but Enmerkar's champion must have none of the known colors. Enmerkar finds a solution immediately. Natural, undyed cloth has no named color.

But by now Enmerkar's long patience is at an end, and he repeats his earlier threat of completely destroying Aratta if it does not submit. His long message is too much for the envoy to remember, and Enmerkar is equal also to this difficulty: he invents the letter, writes the message on a tablet of clay, and gives it to the envoy to take along.

When the envoy arrives in Aratta and the Lord of Aratta ponders the letter, despairing at this new proof of Enmerkar's superiority, the reward for his unremitting courage and fortitude at last comes. He has gained time and so has not yet submitted when by accident Inanna's brother, the god Ishkur, also a god of thunderstorms, happens to bring rain to Aratta. The mountainsides sprout with wild barley, the people harvest it, and the Lord of Aratta is no longer under the terrible pressure of the famine. His self-assurance returns, for he is certain that Inanna has not forsaken him. He twits the envoy and proudly relates the miraculous origin of Aratta's population.

At this point in the story, however, the text available to us appears to have suffered in the tradition and to have been handed on in a somewhat fragmentary state. One gathers that Enmerkar, his champion, and other members of his court, his singer (?) and a woman sage, arrive in Aratta. The woman sage, it seems, then suggests to Enmerkar that he try bartering his flocks and various fruits for Aratta's wealth of stone and metal. The story ends with Enmerkar listing his achievements.

There remains the question why this particular story was told, and what it was intended to convey. Two distinct aspects seem to stand out. Seen from one angle the story looks very much like a piece of political propaganda, and yet it clearly also can claim to be viewed as a work of epic poetry. We may consider the political implications first.

A major portion of Sumerian Literature as we have it traces back to the court of the kings of the Third Dynasty of Ur, where it was composed and performed by the royal bards who—as we know from the court accounts—would be rewarded with gifts of silver rings. Their works included hymns in praise of the king and epics celebrating the deeds of the king's ancestors, and among the epics there are several that deal with relations with Iran, or more precisely with the independent Iranian states which then bordered Mesopotamia. These states were highly important economically, for the major trade route eastward into Asia passed through them. The kings of Ur therefore constantly sought to achieve a measure of control over them to keep that trade route open, sometimes by force of arms, sometimes by diplomacy, and we have evidence of constant coming and going of envoys from there. The importance of these envoys, and of keeping on their good side by subtle flattery, is reflected not only in frequent royal gifts to them, which we find listed in the court accounts, but also, it would seem, in the choice of entertainment at court banquets. The so-called "Lugalbanda Epic,"[1] which deals with a royal ancestor and king of that name, surprises by celebrating him as a supernaturally endowed envoy bringing messages from Aratta to Uruk and back, and the story just retold actually pays exceptional attention to the envoy, praising his speed and devotion and telling of the deference shown him wherever he goes. Since the story deals with the peaceful solution of a conflict by mutually advantageous trade, it would clearly have been well suited to entertaining an Iranian envoy visiting Ur on a delicate diplomatic mission.

So much, then, for the propaganda aspect of our tale. That still leaves us with its other aspect. What can one say about it as an epic poem? Here it may be well to remember that to the Sumerians epic poetry was essentially poetry of praise. It celebrates persons, and in these persons the larger values for which they stand and which they embody. We must therefore turn to the persons in our tale, Enmerkar himself and the lord of Aratta, and ask what they stand for. Here it is important that they both are "lords" or "priest-kings," Sumerian *en*, and that they act as *ens* in the tale, not as private persons. What *is*, therefore, an *en*, and what values does he represent?

In the briefest compass one may perhaps say that he is a ruler responsible for the total welfare of his people, economically and socio-politically. He is the one who establishes the proper relations to the gods on which good years and prosperity depend, and who provides, by his superior knowledge and intelligence, effective solutions for all difficulties which may threaten the community. His powers are more subtle and in some ways more terrifying than the simple brute force of the warrior. He stems as a type from the magician-priest, the original wizard. Seen in this light the figures of Enmerkar and the Lord of Aratta gain background and outline. Enmerkar is the ideal of the *en* at the highest summit of potentiality. He is able, through his commanding personality, to enlist unlimited divine support. To the truly formidable intellect of his towering genius no problem is insoluble.

1. Here translated under the title "Lugalbanda and the Thunderbird."

His opponent, the Lord of Aratta, represents the other extreme: he is the *en* forsaken by the gods. His divine spouse, for no fault of his, has left him and withdrawn her favors, on which the life of his community depend, and that community has lost faith in him and no longer supports him. He is thus thrown entirely upon his own resources: his purely human qualities of shrewdness, fortitude, courage in adversity, and strength of character; and as the story pits him against Enmerkar it becomes apparent that these qualities are by no means negligible. He shows acute psychological insight in realizing that Enmerkar can not afford to ignore a challenge—and a mocking challenge at that—to his pride and competence, and he is deft in his use of that weapon. And though he loses out again and again, by courageously holding out he gains time, the situation changes, and he achieves victory. Aratta retains its freedom. Our story deals thus with the qualities that make a ruler, with the highest potential he can achieve, and with the strength of character with which he may face adversity. It deals with genius and with fortitude both.

In the presentation of these characters Enmerkar is, of course, by far the most difficult; not least because the difficulty of an achievement can only be effectively suggested in a tale by means of the effort that goes into it—and Enmerkar's achievements are, and must be presented as, effortless. Thus one must admire the very real skill with which the poet gradually enfolds his greatness. At first we learn only of a towering ambition: precious stones and metals must be brought to make a temple in Eridu shine "like silver in the lode," and the ritual procession of Enmerkar must be enriched so that his father, the sun god, will look at him joyfully. For this, faraway Aratta must submit, give up its riches, slave on the buildings; and the goddess Inanna must betray her other spouse, the Lord of Aratta, to further Enmerkar's interests.

Our first inkling that the stature and power of Enmerkar are as great as his ambition comes when Inanna readily grants his wish. He has conquered her completely, is as precious to her as her costliest jewels:

> "Shine forth like a sun disk on my holy breast!
> Truly you are (as dear as) the jewels of my throat!
> Praise be unto you, Enmerkar, son of Utu!"

she says to him, as she gives in to his request.

Our insight into the man grows as he is challenged. When he is faced with the impossible task of transporting grain in nets, he ponders calmly at the fire at night, turning now one, now the other side to it to keep warm, never losing confidence. And in the morning, as he attends to the daily cult rites, he has an inspiration— the goddess of the grain, Nidaba, opens his mind, and he thinks of malt, the cohesive germinated grain. What is here told poetically we might perhaps render more prosaically saying that he contemplated the nature of the grain, its various forms, and was arrested by the nature of malt, which would serve his purposes.

Quite similarly we can follow his intellectual processes in the case of the scepter. This time it is Enki, god of the sweet waters in rivers and marshes, who grants Enmerkar wisdom. We should say more prosaically that he thought of that region which would not be familiar to the Lord of Aratta in his mountains—the marsh and its products—and there found a reed which suited his purposes.

When the last challenge comes—to find a champion—it is simple compared with that of conveying his long message. And with characteristic ease of genius he solves that by inventing the letter.

In all these cases, it will be noted, Enmerkar solves specific problems which arise in the pursuit of his single quest, but as is characteristic of all intellectual genius, the solutions have value and are applicable far beyond the immediate purpose for which they were intended. For there can be little doubt that we are to consider the mode of transporting grain as malt, the cultivation of the "resplendent reed," and the letter, as important and lasting contributions to human civilization.

The last, and perhaps most impressive, accolade to his genius is Enmerkar's ultimate victory, when accident has deprived him of his powerful means of coercion, and starved Aratta again finds itself prosperous, under no compulsion to submit. There human intelligence achieves, by pointing to mutual advantage, what mere use of force had been unable to attain, and with the institution of trade and barter civilization is once more permanently enriched.

Compared with the difficulties inherent in the effective presentation of the figure of Enmerkar, those implied in the presentation of the Lord of Aratta are relatively simple, and it is far easier for us—even over the thousands of years which separate us from the story—to understand him immediately and in sympathy. The sudden shattering of all he trusted to, his courageous refusal to admit defeat, his despair and his persistence in the face of despair—

> Then did the heart
>> burn in the lord,
>> the throat choked up,
> no retort had he,
>> kept seeking
>> and seeking
>> for a retort.
> At his own feet
>> he was staring
>> with sleepless eyes.

We also know immediately what it is when he

> was wading around in words
> as in donkey-feed

and we know the triumphant feeling of

> he
>> began finding a retort,
> found the retort,
>> let out a shout,

loudly like a bull
    he bellowed
the retort to the message at the envoy.

And we find it just that his fortitude should be rewarded and that he should be victorious in his courageous fight to retain his and Aratta's freedom.

EARLY
URUK/KULLAB
	In that fierce bull of a city,
	    imbued with dignity
	    and great awesomeness,
	Kullab,[2]
	    [bellowing holy] hymns,
	place where at dawn
	    decisions (by the gods)
	    are made,[3]
	in Uruk
	    the great mountain
	    carried [in Inanna's] heart,
	des[tined]
	    in the days of yore
	    to be at workday's end
	    An's[4] dining hall:
	In Uruk, in Kullab,
	    in Urugal,[5]
	proudly the great princes
	    of the gods [convened,]
	and plenteous precipitation,
	    producing carp-floods
	and rainshowers,
	    producing mottled barley,
	they joined together
	    for Uruk and for Kullab
	    (in their decisions).

10

TRADE DID
NOT YET
EXIST
	The (emporium) country Dilmun[6]
	    did not exist,
	so—although,
	    seeing that the boundary

2. Kullab, originally a separate town, became a part of Uruk.

3. Refers to decisions by the gods sitting as a court presided over by the sun god to hear human complaints.

4. God of Heaven.

5. An's temple in Kullab, which is in Uruk.

6. For Dilmun, see the myth "Enki and Ninsikila/Ninhursaĝa," above.

of the house come down from Heaven[7]
was marching with
the boundary dike of Kullab.
holy Inanna wished
to make the *gipāru* temple[8]
stand out against Kullab's mudbrick
like silver in a lode—
[no merchant carried wares]
nor traded,
no [sea trader] carried [cargo]
nor plied sea trade,
gold and silver,
copper, tin, slabs of lapis lazuli,
[and simple mountain stone]—
neither of these
was brought down from its mountains.
[The people] bathed not for the feasts
[under copper ewers]
[the . . . .] who sat [not]   20
on [. . . . .]
spent the day in [. . . . .]
[. . . . .]
[. . . . .]

ARATTA

[In Aratta the Lord of Aratta]
[made for holy Inanna]
[an ornate bed,]
[had it, like the rising sun]
[send out] many-hued [rays,]
[built a house for her]
made of clear lapis lazuli,
green it was, and flower[ing,]
like a white *mēsu* tree.[9]

INANNA
PREFERS
ENMERKAR

The Lord of Aratta
set on the head
a golden crown for Inanna,
yet pleased her not as well   30
as did the lord of Kullab,

---

7. That is, Inanna's main temple in Uruk, Eanna, which, according to tradition, had descended
from heaven.
8. Traditional residence of an *en* priest, a "lord," or a priestess.
9. The *mēsu* tree has not been identified.

for in Aratta
   the like of the Eanna close
   and of the sacred place, the *gipāru*,
or of Kullab's brickwork,
   he built not
   for holy Inanna.

ENMERKAR WANTS   In those days did the lord
ARATTA TO   envisioned in the heart
SUBMIT   by Inanna,
envisioned
   from the mountain crests
   in the holy heart
   by Inanna,
Enmerkar, son of the sun god,[10]
   make entreaty
unto his sister,
   the queen who emits roars
   that fill the heavens,[11]
unto holy Inanna, (saying:)

URUK TEMPLES   "O sister mine! May Aratta
skillfully work me
   gold and silver for Uruk,
may it cut me clear lapis lazuli   40
   in its blocks,
and with amber
   and clear lapis lazuli
may Aratta in Uruk
   build a pure mountain!
May Aratta build in a high place
   the exterior
of your abode,
   the house come down from heaven,[12]
may Aratta skillfully do up for me
   the interior
of your seat,
   the holy *gipāru*,
—let me skip about there
   like a calf!

10. Enmerkar was considered a son of Utu, the sun god, and so a brother of Inanna, who was Utu's daughter. He was also, as *en* of Uruk, Inanna's husband.

11. Inanna's roars are the thunder, which she emits as goddess of thundershowers.

12. I.e., Eanna.

KULLAB TEMPLE

"May Aratta submit
[to U]ruk for me,
may the people of Aratta
fetch [d]own for me   50
    mountain stone [from their mounta]ins,
may they build the Urugal for me,
    and may they set out
    great banquets for me,
produce for me
    great banquets,
    ban[quets of the gods,]
and make for me
    my sacred office in Kullab
    what rightly it should be!

ERIDU TEMPLE

May they make the Apsû temple
    shoot up for me
    like the pure mountains,
may they make Eridu
    pristine for me
    like the foothills,
may they make the Apsû close
    stand out
    like silver in the lode!

RITUALS

"As for me,
    when I have said praise
    from the Apsû temple,[13]
have brought the sacred office
    from Eridu,
have made
    the priest-king crown agreeing
    as were it
    a crown of green basalt,[14]
when in Uruk and Kullab   60
    I set the holy crown on the head,
may then Urugal's . . . .
    convey me to the *gipāru*,
the *gipāru's* . . . .
    convey me to the Urugal,

13. The temple of Enki in Eridu.
14. The crown of the *en* as pictured on reliefs seems to have had a shoot of a palm, a grainstalk, or some other emblem of thriving vegetation set in it.

may the people look at me admiring,
and Utu joyfully watch me!"

INANNA REPLIES

At that time
    did the delightful one
    in the pure sky,[15]
    the queen keeping an eye
    on the mountains,
the young lady
    whose kohl
    is (put on) for Ama-ushumgal-anna,[16]
Inanna,
    queen of all lands,
say to Enmerkar
    son of Utu.

"Come here, Enmerkar,
    let me instruct you,
    and may you take
    my advice,
let me say a word to you,   70
    and may you listen!

"When you have chosen
    from out of the troops
    a word-wise envoy
    having (sturdy) thighs,
whither should he take
    the great message
    for wordwise Inanna?
May he go up
    into the Zubi ranges,[17]
may he come down with it
    out of the Zubi ranges,
may (the people of) Susa
    toward Anshan's mountains[18]
salute him,
    like tiny mice,

15. Inanna was goddess of the morning and evening star.
16. I.e., who makes herself look pretty for her beloved, Ama-ushumgal-anna, the name of Dumuzi as god of the dates.
17. Presumably the mountains around Mandali.
18. Anshan is Tell Malyan in Fars. From high up on the mountain road the inhabitants of Susa hailing the envoy look like tiny mice.

and may (the people
 of) all the great ranges,
 grown populous on their own,
at (word of) it
 grovel in the dust for him!

"Aratta will submit
 to Uruk for me,
and may the people of Aratta,   80
when they have fetched down
 mountain stone
 from their mountains,
build the Urugal for you,
 may they set out
 great banquets for you,
produce for you
 great banquets,
 banquets of the gods,
may they make for you
 your sacred office in Kullab
 what rightly it should be!
May they make the *Apsû* temple
 shoot up for you
 like the pure mountains,
may they make Eridu
 pristine for you
 like the foothills,
may they make the *Apsû* close
 stand out
 like silver in the lode!

"As for you,
 when you have said praise
 from the *Apsû* Temple,
[have] brought the sacred office
 from Eridu,
have made   90
 the priest-king crown [agreening]
 [as were it]
 a crown of green basalt,
when in Uruk and Kullab
 you [set] the [holy] crown on the head,
may then Urugal's [. .] . .
 convey you to the *gipāru*,

the *gipāru*'s [. . . .]
    convey you to the Urugal,
may [the people] look at you admiring,
and Utu joyfully watch you!

"May the people of Aratta
[da]ily after sunset,
    after they have carried
    workbaskets,
daily at evening,
    after they have [. . . . . .]
at the place where Dumuzi
    keeps his ewes, goats and lambs,
in Akalaga,[19] the field of Dumuzi,   100
kneel down for you (to sleep)
    like mountain sheep.
Shine forth like a sun disk
    on my holy breast,
truly you are (as dear as)
    the jewels of my throat.
Praise be unto you
    Enmerkar,
    son of Utu!"

ENMERKAR   The lord obeyed
OBEYS   holy Inanna's words,
chose [from out of the troops]
    a word-wise messenger
    [having] (sturdy) thighs,
and to his messenger
    the lord said:
"Whither will you take
    the great message
    for word-wise Inanna?
May you go up
    into the Zubi ranges,
may you come down with it
    out of the Zubi ranges,
may (the people of) Susa   110
    toward [An]shan's [mountains]
salute you
    like tiny mice,

19. The name means "flood," "high waters." It probably designated an actual field in Uruk.

and may (the people of)
  all the great ranges,
  grown populous on their own,
at (word of) it
  grovel in the dust for you!

ARATTA MUST
SUBMIT AND
DO CORVÉE

"Envoy,
  when you have spoken
  to the Lord of Aratta
  and elaborated on it (say:)[20]
'May I not have to
  make his city
  fly off from him
  like wild doves from their tree,
may I not have to
  make it fly
  like birds out of their nests,
may I not have to appraise it
  at current market rate (for slaves),
and may I not have to
  scoop up dust in it
  as in a destroyed city.[21]
May Enki not have to
  curse Aratta
  and the settlements,
may he not have to   120
  destroy *it* too
  like places he has
  (at other times) destroyed.
Inanna has set out after it,
has scre[amed at it,]
  [has ro]ared at it,
may she [not] have to
  drown it [too]
  with a flood wave

20. This awkward phrase was standard for entrusting an oral message to a messenger, and from there it was taken over as the introductory phrase of written letters. Since normally the carrier of a message was a person who happened to have business of his own with the addressee and carried the message as a favor, the phrase is obviously a bit of politeness saying: "Only when you have attended completely to your own business, please convey this message!" In the story it has already become a petrified formula devoid of its original meaning.

21. A gesture symbolic of conquest and destruction.

[like] the flood waves
[with which she drowns.[22]]
Rather, when it has packed
  gold in its [native form]
  into leather pouches,
has aligned with it
  purified silver
  in d[ust form;]
when it has done silver up
  into pac[ks,]
strapped saddlebags
  on the asses of all the mountains,
may then for me,
  envisioned in the holy heart
of Sumer's junior Enlil,
  lord Nudimmud,
the highland   130
  of immaculate
  sacred offices[23]
  begin building
  for me.
May it be making it
  attractive for me like the boxwood trees,
make it glow for me
  with many-hued rays
  like Utu emerging
  from (his) chamber
  (at morn,)
and make doorposts[24] branch for me
  at doorjamb after doorjamb!
In all its chambers
  intone holy songs
  and incantations

NUDIMMUD'S   recite Nudimmud's spell[25]
SPELL   to him:

---

22. All of these images seem to refer to Inanna as the numinous power in the thundershower, drowning out everything. Possibly she is here seen as the thunderbird.

23. A standing epithet for Aratta.

24. The word translated "doorpost" refers to ornamental posts—sometimes with rows of volutes at the top—placed at either side of doors.

25. "Nudimmud's spell" quoted at this point in the tale seems gratuitous. It has no bearing on the

"In those days,
  there being no snakes,
  there being no scorpions,
there being no hyenas,
  there being no lions,
there being no dogs or wolves,
there being no(thing) fearful
  or hair-raising,
mankind had   140
  no opponents—
in those days
  in the countries Subartu,[26]
  Hamazi,[27]
bilingual Sumer
  being the great country
  of princely office,
the region Uri[28]
  being a country
  in which was
  what was appropriate,
the country Mardu[29]
  lying in safe pastures,
(in) the (whole) compass
  of heaven and earth
  the people entrusted (to him)

---

situation, is mentioned only, is not repeated later on by the envoy, and plays no role whatever in the plot. Most likely it was a separate, independent myth added by some copyist who thought it might fit.

As it stands, it has been so severely abbreviated that it is difficult to determine either occasion or reason for the act of Enki/Nudimmud which it celebrates: that when mankind had one common language Enki replaced it with the present multiplicity of tongues. Presumably, since Enki is regularly presented as the protector of man—and very particularly so as Nudimmud, man's creator—this act of his will have served to shield mankind. One may conjecture, therefore, that a unilingual mankind somehow had become a threat or a nuisance to Enlil, so that he planned to wipe man out, a catastrophe averted by Enki's clever solution. This would put the story in line with the biblical story of the confusion of languages, where the building of the tower represents a threat to God, and with the myth of Atrahasis, where the noise made by proliferating mankind bothers Enlil to such an extent that he seeks recourse in sending the Deluge.

Here the mass of proliferating unilingual mankind's appeals to Enlil may have become too much for him and Enki, by instituting wars and by dispersing man by his confusion of tongues, will have forestalled a Deluge.

26. In modern terms, approximately northern Iraq
27. Not located with any certainty.
28. The northern part of southern Mesopotamia. The Akkadian term for it was Akkad.
29. The region east of Mesopotamia, also called Amurru.

could address Enlil,
  verily, in but a
  single tongue.

"In those days,
  (having) lordly bouts,
  princely bouts, and royal bouts—
(did) Enki, (having) lordly bouts,
  princely bouts, and royal bouts—
having lordly bouts fought,
  having princely bouts fought,
  and having royal bouts fought,
did Enki, lord of abundance,   150
  lord of effective command,
did the lord of intelligence,
  the country's clever one,
did the leader of the gods,
did the sagacious
  omen-revealed[30]
lord of Eridu
estrange the tongues
  in their mouths
  as many as were put there.
The tongues of men
  which were one".'"
Once again the lord
  added a word
to the envoy going to the mountains
  to Aratta:
"Envoy, fall down at night
  like the rain,
rise up by day   160
  like a rising storm."

ROAD TO   The envoy heeded
ARATTA   the word of his master.
By night he went
  just by the stars.
By day he could go
  by heaven's sun divine.
Whither did he take
  Inanna's great words

30. The accepted candidate for the office of *en* was revealed by the taking of omens.

in the reed canister
  for her?
He had to go up
  into the Zubi ranges,
had to come down with it
  out of the Zubi ranges,
(The people of) Susa
  toward Anshan's mountains
saluted him
  like tiny mice,
and (the people of)
  all the great ranges,
  grown populous on their own,
at (word of) it   170
  groveled in the dust for him.
Five mountain ranges,
  six mountain ranges,
  seven mountain ranges,
  he crossed over,
lifted up his eyes,
  he was approaching Aratta;
and joyfully he set foot
  in Aratta's courtyard.

MESSAGE   His master's preeminence
DELIVERED   he proclaimed,
                 and was decorously speaking
                   the words he had by heart,
                 the envoy was translating them
                   for the Lord of Aratta.
                 "It being that your father,[31]
                   my master,
                   has sent me to you,
                 it being that the lord of Uruk,
                   and lord of Kullab
                   has sent me to you. . . ."[32]

LORD OF   "What is to me
ARATTA   your master's word?
SCOFFS   What is to me
                   what he said further?"

31. The term implies Enmerkar's claim to superiority. A ruler of equal status would have been addressed as "brother."
32. The dots here merely indicate that the envoy was being interrupted.

MESSAGE
RESUMED

"My master—what did he say,   180
  what did he say further?
Being that my master, fit for the crown
  from his birth,
lord of Uruk,
  the (most) honored
  (wearer of the) diadem[33]
  living in Sumer,
  grinding mountains
  as flour,
a wild goat
  of the high mountains
  with noble horns,
  . . . . a buck
  wiping the hooves
  in pure soapwort,
born in the heart of the highland
  by a good cow,[34]
Enmerkar, son of Utu,
  has sent me
  to you;
what my master
  has to say (is:)
'May I not have to
  make his city
  fly off from him
  like wild doves from their tree,
may I not have to
  make it fly
  like birds out of their nests,
may I not have to appraise it   190
  at current market rate (for slaves).
May I not have to
  [scoop up] dust in it
  as in a destroyed city.
May Enki not have to
  curse Aratta
  and the settlements,

33. The *en* wore a characteristic headdress called *muš* "crest," "diadem," different from the crown worn by a king.
34. Presumably Utu's consort Aia. However, there are no indications elsewhere that she was envisioned in cow shape.

may he not have to
　　destroy it too,
　　like places he has
　　(at other times) destroyed.
Inanna has set out after it,
has screamed at it,
　　has roared at it.
May she not have to
　　drown it too
　　with a flood wave
　　like the flood wave
　　with which she drowns.
Rather, when it has packed
　　gold in its native form
　　into leather pouches,
has aligned with it
　　purified silver
　　in dust form,
when it has done silver up
　　into packs,
strapped saddlebags　　　　　　　　　　　　　　200
　　on the asses of all the mountains,
may then for me,
　　envisioned in the holy heart
of Sumer's junior Enlil,
　　lord Nudimmud,
the highland
　　of ritually pure
　　sacred offices
　　begin building
　　for me.
May it be making it
　　attractive for me like the boxwood trees,
make it glow for me
　　with many-hued rays
　　like Utu emerging
　　from (his) chamber
　　(at morn),
make doorposts branch for me
　　at doorjamb after doorjamb,
and as in all its chambers
　　the holy songs
　　and incantations
　　are intoned,

rec[ite] for me
  Nudimmud's [spell].'[35]
When you have said
  what you have to say to me
  about that,
let me unto the scion   210
  [wearing] a lapis-lazuli beard,[36]
[unto] him who was [borne]
  by his sturdy [cow(-mother)]
  in the highland
  of pure sacred offices,
unto him who was reared
  on Aratta's soil,
unto him who was suckled
  with milk
  at a good cow's udder,
who befits lordship in Kullab,
  country of great sacred office,
unto Enmerkar,
  son of Utu,
in the Eanna close,
  announce that message,
in his *gipāru*,
  bearing flowers
  like the new shoots
  of a *mēsu* tree,[37]
let me report
  to my master
  the lord of Kul[lab!]"
After thus
  he had been telling him:

REQUEST   "Envoy,   220
DENIED   when you have spoken
                    to your master,
                    the lord of Kullab,
                    and elaborated on it (say:)

35. At this point ends the messenger's message from Enmerkar and he speaks as himself, asking what reply he is to take back.
36. That is, bluish black and shiny.
37. The outer walls of the *gipāru* may have been decorated with rosette-headed clay nails set into the plaster, suggesting the flowering *mēsu* tree image.

'Me, a lord,
   carried in the
   immaculate hands,
did heaven's (restraining) curb,[38]
   the queen of heaven and earth,
the damsel of myriad offices,
   holy Inanna,
verily bring to Aratta,
   the highland
   of immaculate
   sacred offices,
made me be a bar,
   like a great door,
   before the highland.[39]
How could Aratta
   bow to Uruk?'
Tell him:
   'There will be no bowing
   of Aratta to Uruk!'"

After thus
   he had been telling him,

ENVOY REVEALS
INANNA HAS
COME TO URUK

the envoy
   replied to it
   to the Lord of Aratta:
"Heaven's great queen   230
   riding on high
   in ruddy robe,
enthroned on the range
   of mountain crests,
arrayed
   on the throne dais
   of the mountain crests,
—the lord my master,
   being her servant,
An and the queen
   have moved in with him
   in Eanna!

38. The word translated "curb" denotes a neck stock, a board with holes for the neck clamped around the necks of prisoners to secure them. It therefore comes to serve as a symbol of restraint and policing as well. Here it indicates Inanna's powers as ruler.

39. That is, a border fortress.

'The Lord of Aratta
bowed down!'
May I thus tell him
in Kullab's brick structure?"

LORD OF
ARATTA CHAL-
LENGES TO A
DUEL OF WITS

Then did the heart
burn in the lord,
the throat choked up,
no retort had he,
kept seeking
and seeking
for a retort.
At his own feet
he was staring
with sleepless eyes—
began finding a retort,
found the retort,   240
let out a shout—
loudly like a bull
he bellowed
the retort to the message
at the envoy.
"[Envoy,]
when to your [master,]
the lord of Kullab,
[you have] spoken,
and have enlarged upon it
for him (say:)
'The [great] mountain range,
[a *mēsu* tree] grown sky-high,
its base the root net,
its summit the spreading tree,
therein the thunderbird eagle,[40]
shackled knee and beak
with Inanna's fetter,
has the highland's blood
dripping down
the mountain crest
from its eagle talons.[41]

---

40. The thunderbird is the thundershower personified.

41. The imagery is taken from falconry and its leashed and hooded bird. The blood would be from a previous kill, so the image does not carry through consistently, since it is the shackling of the bird, the absence of rain, that hurts Aratta.

In Aratta laughter
   is become lament,
is become libations of water   250
   and strewing of flour![42]
In the highland
   libation and prayer
   are become
   the humblest of supplications!'

"How could,
   even with but ten men,
   but five men,
the Urukian levy
   (ever) press ahead
   into the Zubi ranges?
O that your master
   would rush against my weapons
and I could rush
   into single combat with him!
He does not know
   single combat
   does not dogfight,
the bull knows [not]
   the bull, its neighbor.
When he had come to know
   single combat
   when he had
   been in a dogfight,
when the [bull]
   had come to know
   its neighbor,
I should have made [hi]m   260
   leave single combat alone!
Yet also [with my wits,]
   the which no man can match,
I'll make [h]im leave it alone.

"Once more, envoy,
   I speak to you.
I on my part
   shall frame a [r]equest
   skillfully for you,

42. The standard offerings to the dead.

may it get across to you
intact,
and in [E]anna,
a lion lying on its paws,
or being—to judge from its interior—
a loudly bellowing bull,[43]
in his *gipāru*,
bearing flowers
like the new shoots
of a *mēsu* tree,
report to your master,
the lord of Kullab, (saying:)
'If the mountain range,
—a warrior deeply stained
like unto the sky   270
repairing to its home at eve,
with drops of blood
hanging from its face,
august as Nanna[44]
in heaven's heights,
its forehead set
with awesome glory,
and lying blocking
for the mountains
like a tree(trunk),
the crest upon Aratta's head—
will send on straight
unto the kindly genius
of the highland
of immaculate
sacred offices
Aratta's breeze,
the like of heaven's holy north wind,
let me that day
make known my superiority!

FIRST TEST: 'Meanwhile,
GRAIN FOR   as to the relief grain due us,
ARATTA   let him not load it
                      into carts,

43. Reference is to the music and singing issuing from inside it.
44. I.e., the full moon.

let him not take it   280
   by portage into the mountains,
and when he has cut it,
   let him not place it
   in (carrying) yokes,
but if,
   having filled it
   into carrying-nets,
loaded it onto packasses,
and provided spare asses
   beside them,
he piles it up
   in Aratta's courtyard,
then *he* says true,
   and (Inanna),
   the power of rain,
   the granary's delight,
(will have flung Aratta),
   the placer of beacons on all mountains,
   well suited for settlements,
adorned with seven city walls—
then he says true: the queen,
   the warrior fit for battle,
Inanna, the warrior all set   290
   to vie in dusty battle,
in Inanna's dance,[45]
will have flung from the hand
   Aratta
as were it a "dog-cadaver" plant.[46]
On *that* day I on my part
   shall bow to *him,*
I, on my part, shall,
   like the city,
   submit as the lesser one
   say unto him!' "

After thus he had been telling him,
the Lord of Aratta
   had the envoy
reproduce with his mouth
   his words.

45. A kenning for "battle."
46. This plant—obviously an evil-smelling one—has not been identified.

REQUEST
REPORTED

Like a wild bull
   he slept on his haunches,
resting like a sandfly,
   at dawn he was ready to go.
Into brickbuilt Kullab   300
   he joyously set foot.
Into the main courtyard,
   the courtyard of the council,
   the envoy made his way
and to his master,
   the lord of Kullab,
he reported
   in the manner of his message,
bellowed it at him
   like a bull,
and he—like the oxdriver—
   paid attention.[47]

The king turned his right side
   to the fire,
turned his left side
   back to it.
"He says true!
   Aratta must know
   that (divine) instructions were given!"
   he said.

MORNING
RITUAL

The day dawned,
   and unto Utu,
   who had risen,
it made the country's   310
   "Utu", (the king)
   lift up the head.
The king matched
   Tigris (water) with Euphrates (water),
matched Euphrates (water) with Tigris (water)
set up the great jars
   unto An,
leaned the little jars
   against their sides
   like hungry lambs,

47. The envoy imitates for Enmerkar the Lord of Aratta's loud and aggressive way of delivering the message. Enmerkar listens calmly, no more upset or intimidated than an oxdriver listening to his animals.

and stood An's shiny jars
  beside them.
The king, Enmerkar, Utu's son
  was hurrying up
to the gold inwrought
  eshda chalice—

INSPIRATION   That day did she
FROM GRAIN   who is (like) shining brass,
GODDESS   the refulgent reedstalk,
the aureate shape,
  born on a propitious day,
borne   320
  by green Nanibgal,[48]
Nidaba,
  the lady of vast intelligence,
open for him
  her "Nidaba's holy house
  of understanding,"[49]
and entering An's palace
  he was paying heed.
The lord opened the door
  to his huge granary
and set on the ground
  his huge standard measure.
The king took out from the grain
  his old grain,
soaked with water
  the malt spread on the ground,
and its lips locked together
  like *sassatu* and *hirinnu* weed.
On the carrying-nets
  he reduced in size the meshes,
and the stewards filled the grain   330
  of the grain piles into them;
  and the stewards
  added to it for the birds.

48. Little is known about his goddess, who is mentioned often with Nidaba. According to this passage she was Nidaba's mother.

49. Goddess of grasses, grains, and reeds and—since the scribe's stylus originally was of reed—of literature. The precise meaning of "Nidaba's holy house of understanding" is not clear. Normally one would think of "library," a meaning that seems possible in other of its occurrences. Here it seems to mean simply that she inspired Enmerkar, gave him an idea.

<table>
<tr><td>FIRST TEST
PASSED</td><td>When he had loaded up
    the packasses,
and placed spare asses
    at their sides,
did the king of vast intelligence,
the lord of Uruk,
    the lord of Kullab,
direct them
    unto the road to Aratta;
and the people,
    like ants of the cracks
    in the ground,
wended their way by themselves
    to Aratta.</td></tr>
</table>

<table>
<tr><td>VASSAL
SCEPTER
FOR ARATTA</td><td>The lord gave the envoy
    going to the highland
a further message for Aratta
    (saying:)
"Envoy, when you have spoken
    to the Lord of Aratta,
    and elaborated thereon
    for him, (say:)
'The base of my scepter
    is in the sacred office
    of princedom,
its crown gives shade
    for Kullab,
under its ever-branching crown
    does the Eanna-close—
does holy Inanna—
    cool off.
When he has cut from it a scepter,
    may he carry it,
may it be in his hand
    as were it (one of)
    carnelian sections
    and lapis lazuli sections,
and may the lord of Aratta
    bring it before me!'
    say to him."⁵⁰</td></tr>
</table>

340

50. Enmerkar here describes his scepter in terms of a large shadetree, shade standing, as so often, for protection. Its base, that is, its claim to authority, grows out of his princely office. Whether the

After thus he had been telling him,
the envoy going to Aratta
plunged his foot   350
    into the dust of the road,
sent rattling the little stones
    of the mountain ranges,
like a basilisk[51] prowling its desert,
    he had none opposing him.

ARATTA   To the envoy,
RELIEVED   when he had neared Aratta,
came Aratta's people
to admire the packasses.
In Aratta's courtyard
    the envoy
had the stewards fill the grain
    into grain bins,
    had the stewards
    add to it for the birds.
As if there had been
    rains of heaven and storms,
abundance filled Aratta,
as if the gods   360
    had returned to their abodes,
the Arattans' hunger
    abated by and by.
The people of Aratta
sowed the fields
    with his water-soaked malt.
The shepherds, the despatch riders
    . . [. . . .]
[the grain,] as it was left on the ground
    [. . . . .]

(gap of several lines)

---

description is figurative or realistic is not altogether clear. One would expect the former, but the Lord of Aratta is supposed to cut a branch from it to use as his scepter, which suggests a real tree. On the other hand, the idea of a huge live tree as scepter seems unacceptable. The cutting may therefore be from Enmerkar's actual scepter, which may have been of sufficient length for it.

51. The word translated "basilisk" denotes a much-feared wild animal. Mentions of it would make one think of a lion or tiger, but the ancients classed it with serpents. In translating "basilisk" I suppose that by the time this passage was composed the word had come to denote a purely mythical frightful creature.

ARATTA'S
PEOPLE
WOULD
SURRENDER

The citizens of Aratta list[ened.]
He[52] explained the matter
    to Aratta (saying:)
"As were it a 'dog-cadaver' plant   370
    Inanna [has flung]
    Aratta from the hand,
has [given] her hand
    to the lord of Uruk,
let us, in direst of want,
in [our dir]e hunger,
    crawl to the lord of Kullab!"
All the word-wise elders
folded (their) hands,
    le[aned] (their) shoulders
    (back) against the wall,
and were actually
    placing their treasuries
    at the disposal of the lord.

SCEPTER
MESSAGE
DELIVERED

The [en]voy(?) [was] waiting,
    and in the palace
he was [decorously speaking]
    [the words] he [had by heart:
"Being that your father,
    my master,
    has sent] me to you,
being that [Enmer]kar,   380
    son of Utu,
    has sent me to you. . . ."[32]

THE LORD OF
ARATTA
INTERRUPTS

"Your master?—His word,
    what is it to me?
    What he said further,
    what is it to me?"

"My master—what did he say?
    What did he say further?
'The base of my scepter
    is in the sacred office
    of princedom,
its crown gives shade for Kullab,
under its ever-branching crown
    does the Eanna-close—

52. That is, the Lord of Aratta.

does holy Inanna—
   cool off.
When he has cut from it a scepter,
   may he carry it,
may it be in his hand
   as were it (one of)
   carnelian sections
   and lapis lazuli sections,
may the Lord of Aratta
   bring it before me!'
   he verily said to me."

LORD OF ARATTA After thus he had been telling him   390
SEEKS NEW TEST he went into the back
         of his bedroom
         and lay there
         eschewing food.[53]
       Day dawned,
         he was wallowing and wallowing
         in words,
       spoke words one does not
         take in one's mouth,
       was wading around in words
         as in donkey feed, (musing:)
       "Now, what will man
         have said to man?
       And what else will man
         have said to man,
         one like the other?
       Verily as man says to man
         thus be it!"

SECOND TEST: "Envoy, when you have spoken
SCEPTER OF   to your master,
NO KNOWN   and elaborated thereon, (say:)
MATERIAL   'May the scepter not be of wood,
         nor called by the name of wood,
       when a man has placed it   400
         in his hand,
         and has scrutinized it,
       be it not poplar,
         be it not *kanaktu* wood,

---

53. Typical reaction to deep distress. Cf. "The Cursing of Akkadê," l. 209.

be it not cedar,
   be it not cypress,
[be it not] *hashur* cedar,
   be it not [boxwood,]
be it not ebony,
   be it not [. . . . . .],
be it not strawberry-tree wood,
   be it not *gigirra* wood
be it not *kidda* wood,
   be it not *usanna* wood,
be it not gold,
   be it not copper,
be it not good refined silver,
   or white silver,
be it not carnelian,
   be it not lapis lazuli!
When he has cut the scepter   410
   may he carry it
may he place it in his hand
   as were it (one of)
   carnelian sections
   and lapis lazuli sections,
and may the lord of Kullab
   bring it before me!'
   say to him.' "

After thus he had been telling him,
the envoy went off,
   giving praise
   like a colt
   whose whippletree
   has broken.
Like a (wild) ass of the desert
   galloping on dry soil
   he made tracks,
kept lifting his nose
   into the wind,
like a long-tufted wool sheep,
   a sheep trotting into its fold,
   he moved along
   amid (his) companions,[54]

---

54. The envoy longs to get home. His eagerness and the sheepskin coat he will have been wearing suggest the image of the sheep returning to the fold.

and into Kullab's brickwork
    he joyfully set foot.
Unto his master,
    the lord of Kullab,
he sang it out   420
    word for word.

INSPIRATION
FROM ENKI,
GOD OF RIVERS
AND MARSHES

Enki lent Enmerkar
    understanding,
and the lord gave instructions
    according to his august
    indications
his house [. . . . .]
the king picked out

    . . . .

came up, too[k] it in hand,
    scrutinized it,
it bit into stone
    as into an herb,
the gleaming reed

    . . . .

from the sun
    he was taking it
    out into the shade,
from the shade
    he was taking it
    out into the sun.
After five or ten years   430
    had passed,
he cut the gleaming reed
    as with an axe.

SECOND TEST
PASSED

The lord looked at it
    joyfully,
juniper oil,
    pressed-out oil
    of the mountain crests
    he poured on its stem,
and into the hands
    of the envoy going to the highland
the lord placed the scepter.

The envoy,
    in his going to Aratta,

having passed over the mountains,
   —over the mountain ranges
   like an owl,
   over the sand dunes
   like a fly,
   through the pools
like a carp—
   approached Aratta,
set foot joyfully
   in Aratta's courtyard.
The scepter he carried   440
   in his fingertips
he had polished it right,
   had been doing the work.

LORD OF   The Lord of Aratta,
ARATTA PRE-   having shielded the eyes
TENDS TO   from the scepter
GIVE UP   as wailing he burned with fear
                           on his holy seat,
                         cried out, he the lord, to his seneschal
                           (saying:)
                         "Aratta is verily become
                           like scattered ewes,
                           verily, its road lies
                           into hostile country.
                         Ever since holy Inanna
                           delivered up august Aratta
                         unto the lord of Kullab,
                         his envoy whom he sends
                         makes, (like) a rising sun,
                           beclouded meanings
                           apparent.
                         Now holy Inanna   450
                           is eyeing us,
                         so where, o seneschal,
                           could Aratta run from her?
                         How long will it be
                           before hand is put to hoe again?
                         Let us, in direst of want,
                         in our dire hunger,
                           crawl to the lord of Kullab!"

<table>
<tr><td>

THIRD TEST:
CHAMPION OF
NO KNOWN
COLOR

</td><td>

The Lord of Aratta
   entrusted to the envoy
a great seal, as it were,
   on the matter:[55]
"Envoy, when you have spoken
   to your master,
   the lord of Kullab,
   and elaborated thereon
   to him, (say:)
'May the champion not be black
   may the champion not be white,
may the champion not be brown,
   may the champion not be pied,
may the champion not be green,
   may the champion not be iridescent,
   but may he give me a champion!
May my champion
   do single combat
   with his champion,
and may the stronger
   become known!'
   say unto him."
After thus he had been telling him,
the envoy went
   through thorns and thistles,
when to the brickwork of Kullab
   like a . . . . .
   he brought back the word,
he lifted up his eye
   unto the highlands'
   . . . . . . ,
like one scared up
   from a huge fast serpent
   he . . . . . .

</td><td>

460

</td></tr>
<tr><td>

THIRD TEST
PASSED: ENMER-
KAR LOSES
PATIENCE

</td><td>

[Enmerkar, son] of [Utu,]
   lifted the head
[. . . . .] of Aratta, [. . . .]
and from his seat
   like a mighty

</td><td>

470

</td></tr>
</table>

55. That is to say, a statement that would be final and close the matter.

burst of a dam,
he said to him:
"Envoy, when you have spoken
to the Lord of Aratta,
when you have elaborated thereon
for him, (say:)
'Let the clothes not be black,
let the clothes not be white,
let the clothes not be brown,
let the clothes not be pied,
let the clothes not be green,
let the clothes not be irridescent,
let me give him (undyed) cloth!
My champion, Enlil's alert champion,
I shall leave for him
as champion,
and let my champion
do single combat
with his champion,
and may the stronger become known!'
say to him!
Next, when you have spoken to him,
and have elaborated thereon
for him, (say:)
'Quickly may he pass
from subterfuge into "when?"[56]
From in his city   480
may the men walk like sheep,
and may he follow after them
like their shepherd.
On his way,
in the mountains
of silver and lapis lazuli,
let them gather for him
the likes of a pile
one rod (high),
and gold, white silver, and amber
for Inanna,
mistress of Eanna,
let them pile up
in Aratta's courtyard.'

56. That is, "May he cease his evasive tactics and set a date for performance."

Thirdly, when you have spoken to him,
  and elaborated thereon for him, (say:)
'May I not have to
  scatter his city
  like wild doves from their tree.
May I not have to smash it li[ke]
  [. . . . . .]
May I not have to appraise it   490
  at [the current market rate
  (for slaves).]
May I not have to
  let the wind-[maiden]⁵⁷
  haunt it.
When he comes,
  after he has taken mountain stone,
may he be building for me
  the Urugal, Eridu, . [. . .]
  and the storehouse;
may he be decking out [for me]
  their outer chambers
  with whitewash,
may he be making their shadows
  stretch out over the coun[try]
  [for me]'⁵⁸
So that [you may br]ing back
  his promise
  give [him] notice."

THE LETTER
INVENTED

That day the words
  of the lord [. . . . .]
seated on [. . . . . . . ,]
  the seed of princes,
[a *mēsu* tree (?)]   500
  grown up singly,
were difficult,
  their meaning not to fathom,
and, his words being difficult,
  the envoy
  was unable to render them.

---

57. An evil wind spirit. With the city abandoned, the houses crumbled, the place would be a playground for the winds.
58. I.e., build them high.

Since the envoy
   —his words being difficult—
   was unable to render them,
the lord of Kullab
   smoothed clay with the hand
   and set down the words on it
   in the manner of a tablet.
While up to then
   there had been no one
   setting down words on clay,
now, on that day,
   under that sun,
   thus it verily
   came to be;
the lord of Kullab
   set down wo[rds on clay,]
   thus it verily
   came to be!

The envoy, like a bird,
   was beating the wings,
like a wolf
   closing in on a buck
   he was hurrying
   to the kill.
Five mountain ranges,   510
   six mountain ranges,
   seven mountain ranges,
   he crossed over,
lifted up the eyes,
   he was approaching Aratta;
and joyfully he set foot
   in Aratta's courtyard.

His master's preeminence
   he proclaimed,
and was decorously speaking
   the words he had by heart,
the envoy was translating them
   for the Lord of Aratta:
"It being that your father,
   [my] master,
   has sent me [to you,]

it being that the lord of Uruk,
    and lord of Kullab,
    has sent me to you. . . ."

THE LORD OF
ARATTA INTER-
RUPTS

"What is to me
    your master's wo[rds?]
    What is to me
    what he said further?"

"My master—[what] did he say?
    what did he say further?
My master,   520
    [des]cendant (?) of Enlil,[59]
grown as high as . . [. ,]
abutting [. . . . ,]
the [. . . . of . . . . ,]
who is outstanding
    in lordship and kingship,
Enmerkar, son of Utu,
    has given me a tablet.
When the Lord of Aratta
    has looked at the clay,
    and understood from it
    the meaning of the words,
and you have told me
    what you have to say to me
    about it,[60]
let me unto the scion
    wearing a lapis lazuli beard,
unto him who was born
    by his sturdy cow(-mother)
    in the highland
    of immaculate offices,
unto him who was reared   530
    on Uruk's[61] soil,
unto him who was suckled
    with milk
    at a good cow's udder,

59. Enlil would be Enmerkar's great-grandfather as father of Suen, the moon god, who in turn was father to Enmerkar's father, Utu.

60. The messenger addresses the lord of Aratta with his titles and in the third person as a matter of politeness. Thereafter he changes to second person.

61. Most likely an ancient scribal mistake for "Aratta's."

unto him, who befits
  lordship in Kullab,
    country of great sacred office,
unto Enmerkar,
  son of Utu,
in the Eanna close
  announce that message,
in his *gipāru*,
    bearing flowers
    like the new shoots
    of a *mēsu* tree,
let me report
  to my master
  the lord of Kullab."

After thus he had been telling him,
the Lord of Aratta took
the envoy's piece of clay.
The Lord of Aratta   540
  looked at the clay.
The words were fierce words,
  were frowning,
the Lord of Aratta
  kept looking
  at his piece of clay—

ISHKUR
BRINGS
RAIN

That day
  did the crowned lord,
  fit for lordship,
  Enlil's son,
Ishkur,[62]
  the thunderer
  of heaven and earth,
the whirling storm,
  the great lion,
  see fit to come by.
The mountains were shaking,
the mountain ranges
  roaring with him
  in laughter.
As they met his awe and [g]lory

---

62. The storm god Ishkur usually counted as Inanna's brother and grandson of Enlil, so "father" may here stand for "grandfather."

the mountain ranges
   lifted their heads
   in delightful verdure,
and on Aratta's parched flanks,   550
   inmidst the mountains,
wheat was sprouting of itself,
   and vines also were sprouting of themselves.
The wheat, that had sprouted of itself,
   they [piled] in piles and heaps
and bro[ught] it in
   to the Lord of Aratta,
piled it up before him
   in Aratta's courtyard.

RAINS
ATTRIBUTED
TO INANNA

The Lord of Aratta
   took a look at the wheat,
and in front of all his overseers
   was twitting the envoy,
the Lord of Aratta
   said to the envoy:
"Most magnificently
   Inanna,
      queen of all lands,
has not abandoned
   her home, Aratta,
   has not delivered it up
      to Uruk
has not abandoned   560
   her lapis lazuli house,
   has not delivered it up
      to the Eanna close,
has not abandoned
   the mountain
   of immaculate offices,
   has not delivered it up
      to Kullab's brickwork,
has not abandoned
   the ornate bed,
   has not delivered it up
      to the *girin*-flowered bed,
the lord,
   her one of the clean hands,
   she has not abandoned,

has not delivered him up
to the lord of Uruk,
to the lord of Kullab!
Aratta, right and left,
has Inanna,
    queen of all lands,
surrounded for him
    as with the waters
    of a mighty
    burst of a dam.

MIRACULOUS   Its men are men
ORIGINS OF   chosen from out of men,
ARATTA'S   are men whom Dumuzi
PEOPLE   picked out from men,
they carry out
    holy Inanna's commands,
alert champions,   570
    houseborn slaves of Dumuzi,
    they verily are,

. . . .

They stood in the Deluge's waters;
but after the Deluge
    had passed over,
Inanna, queen of all lands,
for great love of Dumuzi,
sprinkled them
    with the water of life,
and subjected the country
    to them.[63]

ENMERKAR'S   When the alert champion came
CHAMPION   he wore on his crown
ARRIVES   a pied (skull)cap,
was wrapt in lion(skin) cloth,[64]   580
    [. .]. . . . .
    [. .]. . . . .
    [. .]. . . . .

ENMERKAR'S   When [the singer (?) came to Aratta]
SINGER   [. . . . .] Inanna.
ARRIVES   His songs pleased Dumuzi, Ama-ushu[mgal-anna]

63. A section of the text was apparently lost here in the course of its transmission.
64. One may assume that Enmerkar thought it enough that he had given the solution to the colorless champion—one clad in undyed cloth—and did not feel he had to carry it out when he sent him.

and from that time on
　　for the holy ears, the [. . . . ea]rs
of Dumuzi,
　　they have been suitable,
　　he taught the tune,
　　he taught the words.

ENMERKAR'S
WOMAN SAGE
ARRIVES

When the woman sage came
　　to the mountain
　　of immaculate offices,
she came out to him   590
　　like a maiden
　　when her days are over,[65]
on her eyes
　　she had painted kohl
was wrapped
　　in a white [garment,]
the right [arm]
　　she had out
　　like moonlight.
[The hair she had] combed,
　　had straightened her head.

ENMERKAR
ARRIVES. SHE
SUGGESTS
BARTER

When Enmerkar came
　　he sat down with her
　　on the throne dais.[63]
"When you have called up
　　Uruk and Kullab,
[may] they drive to Aratta
　　the ewes with their lambs,
[may] they drive to Aratta
　　the goats with their kids,
[may] they drive to Aratta
　　the cows with their calves,
[may] they drive to Aratta   600
　　the asses with their foals;
what will the lord of Aratta
　　have to say to that?
May he pour out [stone,]
　　may he pile them,
and when you have made
　　the lord of Aratta
barter [the wealth] of stones
　　with your wealth,

65. I.e., her monthly period.

[may the high]land
 [get to know your]
 [desirable things,]
and it will bring along
 [its silver (?) to Aratta."]
 [. . . . . . .] come out thereof
When thus she had told him
 [. . . . .]
 [. . . . .]   610
 [. . . . .]
 [. . .] . .
 [. . .] . .

<table>
<tr><td>ADVICE TO
THE LORD
OF ARATTA</td><td>

"Your wealth is tin
 and clear [lapis lazuli,]
 [. . . .]Enlil
 has given it to you,
let your desirable goods
 be known.
[A river that] sparkles [not]
 abounds not
 in flowing water,
 carries not water,
may Enl[il,]
 [king] of all lands,
 make it sparkle
 in (all) its splendor."[66]

</td></tr>
<tr><td>INSTRUCTIONS
FOR
BARTERING BY
WOMAN SAGE (?)</td><td>

"When, to trade their assignments[67]   620
 for gold, silver, and lapis lazuli,
and (in order) for a man
 to set tree-fruit
 up against gold rosettes,
they have piled into big piles
 figs on their vines
 as well as tree fruits
 on their trees—
then, according to the assignments   618
 they have been given,
 the people of Aratta   619

</td></tr>
</table>

---

66. These would seem to be popular sayings to the effect that one should not hide one's light under a bushel. The Lord of Aratta is advised to advertise his wealth of metal and precious stone.

67. This and what follows seem to be addressed to Enmerkar. The text of this part of the story was probably pieced together from loose fragments, with considerable gaps between them.

will make value adjustments
  with clear lapis lazuli
  at their roots,
trade nuggets (of precious metals)
  at their crowns,
and for Inanna,
  mistress of Eanna,
they will pile it up in piles
  in Eanna's courtyard.

"My master, come!
  let me advise you,
  and may you take my advice,
let me say a word to you,
  and may you heed it!
When these strangers
  have shown
  the silver of the mountains
  to the country,
[. . . .] Aratta [. . .]"   630
. . . .
. . . .
. . . .⁶⁸

ENMERKAR LISTS
HIS ACHIEVE-
MENTS

"They will say:
  'He was able
  to bring (?) [gold]
  to our city!'
When I had come
  from over there
the sparkling queen
  gave me my ki[ngship,]
An, [heaven's] king
  [gave me lordship.]
In their city
  houses [were not built,]
  I built the houses.]
Songs were not [sung,
  I had songs sung.]
All day long   640
  [I had chants intoned!"
Inanna (it was) a praise hymn.]

---

68. Here too one must assume that a good deal of text was lost in transmission.

Lugalbanda and the Thunderbird

Lugalbanda, hero of this story about his meeting with the Thunderbird, seems originally to have been a god, chief deity of the old town of Kullab that was early merged into Uruk. In time, however, his status tended to decline to that of a mortal hero and early king of Uruk, around whom a cycle of tales gathered. In references to him outside these tales, though, his original divine status often lingers on.

The cycle of tales about Lugalbanda appears to have been oral in nature with sometimes one, sometimes another section of it put into literary form and committed to writing.

The earliest such tale—one of the earliest literary texts we possess—tells how he married his spouse Ninsuna in the eastern mountains and brought her back. Two others, "Lugalbanda in the Mountain Cave" and this tale about his meeting with the Thunderbird, deal with his adventures during a campaign by Enmerkar against Aratta. They are clearly the work of two different authors, for their style and interests are quite distinct. The first tale stresses Lugalbanda's piety, quotes a whole series of his prayers, and takes a special interest in food, listing in detail food left with Lugalbanda, and food offered up by him to the gods as offerings. The second tale is more interested in magic and the supernatural. The ancients, accordingly, as shown by their literary catalogues, kept the two works apart and did not treat them as part of a single epic.

The setting for Lugalbanda's adventure with the Thunderbird can be gathered from "Lugalbanda in the Mountain Cave." It tells that he and his brothers were high officers in Enmerkar's army, so that when the gods granted Enmerkar rule over the eastern mountains and he set out to subdue the rebellious city of Aratta, Lugalbanda and his brothers led the army on the march into the mountains. Before they reached Aratta, however, Lugalbanda was suddenly taken seriously ill, so that he was unable to proceed. His brothers therefore left him with plentiful provisions in a mountain cave and moved on.

In the cave, Lugalbanda gradually recovered, finally setting out to rejoin his brothers and the army. It is at this point, as he is somewhat aimlessly roaming the mountains, that "Lugalbanda and the Thunderbird" takes up the story.

In the Sabum or, with a variant form of the name, Zubi, mountains he comes across the nest of the Thunderbird, who is here imagined as an enormous bird of prey hunting wild oxen in the mountains, and who has magic powers. Lugalbanda wins its gratitude by feeding its young one and decorating its nest while it is away hunting, so it offers to bless him with a variety of desirable endowments. Lugalbanda, after having refused all it suggests, asks for speed and endurance. The bird grants him this and leads the way to where the Urukian army is camped.

There Lugalbanda's arrival causes a great stir. He had been given up for dead, and he is plied with questions which—at the bird's advice—he cleverly fends off. The army then proceeds to Aratta, only to find, however, that it is unable to take the well-defended city. Time passes, and the weather gets worse, so when Enmerkar, who by then has lost heart, wishes to send a message back to Uruk to Inanna to ask leave to call off the siege, he can find nobody who will venture to undertake the difficult journey back. After various fruitless attempts he finally succeeds: Lugalbanda volunteers to take the message back, but stipulates that he is to go alone. This is accepted, and helped by the bird's gift, he successfully delivers the message to Inanna in an unbelievably short time.

Inanna is pleased to see him, and entrusts him with a message to Enmerkar telling him how to overcome Aratta. He is to catch a certain fish that constitutes Aratta's life, eat it, and feed it to his troops. Then Aratta will fall.

At this point the story as we have it begins to peter out. The text seems to be based on mere loose fragments with serious gaps between them; and the expected section telling of Lugalbanda's return to camp and Enmerkar's successful carrying out of Inanna's instructions is missing.

Thus, in brief compass, is the plot of the story—rather an odd one for a tale about a warrior and future king of Uruk. The hero refuses the gifts of military prowess and prosperity and asks instead for speed and endurance as a runner, the virtues of a simple messenger. Moreover, the whole plot turns on his obtaining these gifts and putting them to use as a messenger between Aratta and Uruk. One can therefore hardly avoid the impression that once again—as in the cases of "Enki and Ninsikila/Ninhursaǧa" and "Enmerkar and the Lord of Aratta," we are faced with a piece of political propaganda. We have a story tailored to flatter visiting envoys at feasts given in their honor at the court of Ur, in this case envoys from the politically critical eastern frontier.

As for the story itself, it can most simply be classed as romantic epic verging on the fairy tale. The Thunderbird as we meet it in the story has lost all relation to thunder and rain and—in spite of the references to its divine parentage—all real divinity. It appears as a mere fairy-tale figure, the donor of a magical ability, speed that enables the hero to keep pace with the flying bird and to cover the distance between Aratta and Uruk in a day. Fairy-tale motif is also the one of the fish which is the "life's breath of Aratta." It parallels the well-known one of the giant whose heart is not in his body but lies concealed somewhere else.

<table>
<tr><td>

LUGALBANDA
RECOVERING;
SEEKS TO REJOIN
THE URUK ARMY

</td><td>

Lugalbanda roamed the mountains,
    faraway regions;
let the Sabum hills
    be the landmark there.

No mother lived with him,
    instructed him,
no father lived with him
    talked it over with him,
no cherished acquaintance
    lived with him,
no confidant of his
    was thinking it up,
in his own heart
    he was thinking up
    a plan:

</td></tr>
<tr><td>

FEVER DREAM:
PLAN TO HAVE
THE THUNDERBIRD
MENTION THE
ARMY'S WHERE-
ABOUTS

</td><td>

"When the bird has observed
    the proprieties,
when the Thunderbird has observed
    the proprieties,
when it has embraced its wife,
when it has made
    the Thunderbird wife
    and the Thunderbird young
sit down to a festive meal,
and has brought
    from her foothills.
Anne, queen of the council,[1]
may then the able woman,
    suitably equipped
    for a matriarch,
able Ninkasi,
    suitably equipped
    for a matriarch,
her brewing vat being
    of clear lapis lazuli,
her ladling vessel being
    of *mēsu* silver and gold,
whose standing at the beer
    means delight,

</td></tr>
</table>

10

---

1. Name and epithet of Ninhursaǧa.

whose sitting down   20
    from (serving) the beer
    means cheer and chatter,
may (she,) Ninkasi
    send from the keg
    at the side wall
her cupbearer,
    wearying not from walking
    taking the beer around,
and may she let there be
    the appropriate serving stand(?).
May (thus) the bird,
    having drunk beer
    and feeling expansive,
may the Thunderbird,
    having drunk beer
    and feeling expansive,
reveal for me
    where Uruk has gone,
may the Thunderbird call to mind
    my brothers' route!"

IMDUGUD'S   In those days
NEST   did Enki's noble "eagle tree,"
                   poised like a storm cloud   30
                   atop the carnelian foothills,   29
                       Inanna's eyepaint,
                   jowl-like bearing bristles,[2]
                   have its shadow cover
                       the mountain heights like cloth,
                   veil them
                       like a linen sheet,
                   its roots, like noble serpents,
                       it imbedded
                   in Utu's seven-mouthed river's[3]
                       streambed center.
                   At its sides
                       —in the part of the mountains
                       that know no *hashur* cedars[4]—

2. The "eagle tree" would seem to have been a pine tree of sorts, with needles.

3. Not identified. It may be a purely mythical concept. Its relation to Utu may be due to its location in the mountains at sunrise.

4. I.e., above the line to which cedars could grow.

darted no serpent,
    scurried no scorpion,
into its midst the "bear" bird[5]
had thrust a nest,
    had put its eggs;
at its side the bird, the Thunderbird,   40
had placed a nest,
    had made its young
    lie down therein;
the wood for it
    being juniper
    and woods of the boxwoods,
the bird had made
    their branching boughs
    into a shelter for her.

THE THUNDERBIRD
LEAVES TO HUNT

At break of day, when the bird
    had made dense
    the clouds,
when the Thunderbird
    had roared[6]
    at the rising sun god—
did, in the stillness of the mountains,
    the ground keep reverberating
    to its roar.
Through fear of the eagle's
    poisoning talons
it was making the wild oxen
    come galloping
    of their own accord
    to the base of the mountains,
was making the mountain goats
    come galloping
    startled
    to their mountains.

LUGALBANDA
REGALES ITS
YOUNG

Lugalbanda was very knowing   50
    and great, too, at execution.
Unto the prime-oil shortening
    of the sweetmeat for gods

5. Not otherwise known.
6. The Thunderbird was thought to have the head of a lion; it emitted its thunderous roar from the lion's mouth.

he added prime-oil shortening,
and into that cake
    he kneaded honey,
    added on honey,
placed it before the nestling,
    the young of the Thunderbird,
fed the young dried and salted meat,
    fed it salted mutton,
and had the shortcake
    within reach of its beak.
He made the Thunderbird young
    lie down in its nest,
painted kohl
    around its eyes,
stuck (twigs of) white cedar
    into its beak,
put (grease) rubbed off   60
    the salted meat[7]
        on its head,
got up off the nest
    of the Thunderbird,
and was waiting for it
    at a place in the parts of the mountains
    that know no *hashur* cedars.

THE THUNDER-
BIRD'S HUNT

Meanwhile the bird
    had bit gnashing teeth[8]
    into the wild oxen
    of the mountains.
The Thunderbird
    had bit gnashing teeth
    into the wild oxen
    of the mountains.
The wild oxen still alive
    it carried in its claws
the wild oxen already dead;
    it hung across its neck
water, ten *kor* no less,
    it poured in its earthenware pot.

7. These various provisions were presumably food Lugalbanda had taken along from his well-stocked cave.

8. The bird had a lion's head and so a lion's teeth.

THE THUNDER-
BIRD RETURNS

Unto the bird,
   halting for the first time,
unto the Thunderbird,
   halting for the first time,
when the bird had roared out   70
   to its nest,
did from the nest
   its young not answer!
A second time the bird
   roared out to its nest,
and its young did not
   answer from its nest.
Always, hitherto, when the bird
   had roared out to its nest,
its young would answer
   from its nest;
now, when the bird
   had roared out to its nest,
its young answered not
   from its nest![9]

THE THUNDER-
BIRD FEARS
FOR ITS YOUNG

The bird set up a wail
   —it drew near unto heaven—
its wife cried woe,
   —it drew near unto the deep—
At the bird's crying woe,   80
its wife's setting up a wail,
did the Anunnaki,
   the gods of the mountain ranges,
go (scurrying) like ants
   into the cracks in the ground.

The bird said to its wife,
The Thunderbird said to its wife:
"Verily, fear blazes from my nest
   like Nanna's great corral![10]
Verily, it is fraught with terror
   as are lions of the mountains
   attacking as a pack!
What would kidnap
   my young from out of its nest?

9. Probably because it had already been fed.
10. A term for a ring around the moon.

What would kidnap
a Thunderbird from out its nest?"

THE THUNDER-
BIRD IS RE-
ASSURED

However, for the bird,   90
    when it actually came near
    unto its nest,
for the Thunderbird,
    when it actually came near
    unto its nest,
that had been treated
    like a place where a god lived,
    (it) was fraught with delight.
Its young was lying in its nest,
kohl had been painted
    around its eyes,
(twigs of) white cedar
    had been stuck into its beak,
(grease) rubbed off salted meat
    had been put on its head.

THE THUNDER-
BIRD RALLIES
ITSELF AFTER
THE SHOCK

The bird both glorified
    and lauded itself.
The Thunderbird both glorified
    and lauded itself:
"I am the prince making the decisions
    about the river Tigris,
I am the visor for the just   100
    who consult Enlil.
My father Enlil
    brought me,
made me lock, as it were,
    a great door
    in the face of the mountains.
When I have made a decision,
    who could change it?
When I have issued a decree,
    who could transgress it?[11]
O (you) who thus
    have treated my nest,
an you be a god,
    let me talk to you.

11. These are all features of the god of the thunderstorms of spring and the yearly flood of the Tigris, Niṅgirsu/Ninurta, whose preanthropomorph form the Thunderbird was.

       Fain would I turn you
          into my comrade,
       an you be a human,
          let me decree for you
          (new) status:
       I shall let you have
          no opponent
          in the mountains,
       may you become a princeling   110
          empowered by the Thunderbird!

LUGALBANDA   Lugalbanda,
VENTURES   half from reverence,
FORTH   half from joy;
       half from reverence,
          half from joy of heart,
       honored and lauded
          the bird,
       honored and lauded
          the Thunderbird:
       "O bird, yellow of claw and thigh,
          born among islands,
       Thunderbird, yellow of claw and thigh
          born among islands,
       playing as you bathe
          in the marshes.[12]
       Your ancestor, O Dingirhalhala![13]
       laid the heavens (ready) to your hand,
          laid the earth at your feet,
       as your flight feathers spread   120
          a net out on high,
       below, your shuddery talons
           make the wild bulls of the mountains
           and the wild cows of the mountains
           lie down in [their] lairs.
       As to your back

---

12. Refers to the thunder clouds as originating in vapor rising from the southern marshes.

13. The name means "god of all secrets" according to the ancient lexicographers, who explain the term as an epithet of Ninurta as guardian of his father Enlil's secrets. This, however, may well be merely a learned theological speculation, and since Halhala is a name of the Tigris the bird may simply be addressed here as the deified river, or god of the river Tigris.

you are a very tablet
all inscribed,[14]
as to your ribs,
you are a very serpent god
multicolored,
as to your profound heart,
you are a green (impenetrable) orchard,
standing to be admired.
Since yesterday,
to save my life
I have come to you,
have joined you!"

Thereupon he said:
"Be your wife my mother!"
Thereupon he said:
"Be you my father!"
Fain would I make your youngs
part of my brothers!
Since yesterday
I have been waiting for you
at a place in the parts of the mountains
that know no *hashur* cedars,
may your wife stand by me   130
in my case,
and let me state my case to you,
let me [disclose] to you
my circumstances!"

THE THUNDER-   The bird, cutting down
BIRD OFFERS   on its terrors for him,
BLESSINGS   was rejoicing in him.
The Thunderbird, cutting down
on its terrors for him,
was rejoicing in him.
The Thunderbird said
to holy Lugalbanda:
"Come, my Lugalbanda,
like a boat with beans,
like a boat with barley,

14. The design made by the feathers of the bird's back is compared to the looks of a tablet inscribed with cuneiform writing.

like a boat that will
    be unloading apples,
like a boat with cucumbers,
    canopied over,
like a boat from a harvest site,
    fraught with delight,
proceed proudly   140
    to brickbuilt Kullab!"

But Lugalbanda, being a man
    loved by descendants,
    was not reaching for it.[15]

"Like Shara,
    beloved son of Inanna,
send forth like rays,
    your flint(-tipped) arrows,
like bewildering moonbeams
    send them forth,
may a flint(-tipped) arrow
    in its hitting a man
    be a basilisk,[16]
may it be a throat-cutter,
    as in hitting a fish
    with the axe,
may it be sharp
    like the point of an axe."

But Lugalbanda, being a man
    loved by descendants,
    was not reaching for it.

"May Ninurta,
    Enlil's son,
cover your crown with the helmet   150
    'Lion of Battle,'
may he clasp unto your chest
    the (breast-plate) . . . .

---

15. Apparently "loved by descendants" was a standard epithet that could be applied fairly routinely. It is difficult to attach any special meaning to it here or to see why Lugalbanda's refusal of this and the following gifts, and his acceptance instead of speed and endurance, would have made him particularly beloved of future generations.

16. The term translated "basilisk" denotes a much-feared animal, mythical or real, which the ancients classed with serpents.

which turns not the chest (to flight)
in the great mountains!
When you have wielded
the net in the mountain,
may the net not let loo[se],[17]
go you to a city,
may it pros[trate itself]
[before you!"]

But Lugalbanda, being a man
loved by descendants,
was not reach[ing] for it.

"(On the one hand) tracts of lush growth   156
will [yield] you the butter,
(on the other) tracts of lush growth   157
will yield you the cream,
[o]f Dumuzi's holy churns' abundance!"

But Lugalbanda, being a man
loved by descendants,
was not reaching for it.

like a *kip*-bird,[18]
a *kip*-bird sweeping twittering
over the marsh,
he gave answer
to the suggestions,
and the bird lent ear to him.   160
The Thunderbird said
to holy Lugalbanda:

"Come, my Lugalbanda,
according with the heart's notion
thus it will be!
Being that the yoke-carrying ox
must follow the trail,
being that the trotting ass
must take the straight road,
let me stand by you
in all matters,

17. The throw-net was at one time used as weapon by the ancient Mesopotamians.
18. This bird has not been identified. To judge from the context here it had a timid-sounding, or perhaps wheedling, note.

let me determine for you
    the lot you have at heart."

Holy Lugalbanda answered it:
"May (power) to run be in my loins
    may I not tire from it,
may strength be in my wings,
let me spread wide my wings   170
    and may my wings
    not be getting sore![19]
Going like a storm wind,
    like Inanna,
like the sevenfold storm
    of Ishkur,[20]
let me rise up like fire,
    flash like lightning,
let me go with eyes open,
let me stay my foot
    at what my eyes were on,
let me meet up
    with what I have at heart,
and let me untie [my] shoes
    where my heart is minded
    to tell me to, as well.[21]
On the day I am due to enter
    my city, Kullab,
may I not make the one cursed by me
    happy about it,
and may the one with whom   180
    I have picked a quarrel
    not (dare) say of me:
    'Let him come on!'[22]
When I have fashioned your statues
    in the likeness of a young man,[23]
    and you confront onlookers,
may your fame become manifest
    in Sumer,

19. Lugalbanda uses the image of a bird in flight to suggest speed.
20. The storm god.
21. That is, where he himself feels like resting.
22. This mention of enemies in Kullab may conceivably refer to other parts of the Lugalbanda cycle.
23. The human form was rapidly replacing the animal one in popularity during the latter part of the third millennium B.C. The Thunderbird thus would have had an anthropomorph form as an alternative.

(so that) they will be suitably placed
   in the temples of the great gods!"

The Thunderbird said
   to holy Lugalbanda:
"May (power) to run be in your loins,
   may you not [tire from it,]
may strength [be in] your wings!
Spread wide your wings
   [and may your] wings
   [not be getting sore,]
going like the storm wind,
   like [Inanna,]
like the sevenfold storm,
   [of Ishkur,]
rise up like fire,   190
   flash like lightning,
go with eyes open,
stay your fo[ot]
   at what your eyes were on,
meet up
   with what you have at heart,
and untie your shoes
   where your heart is minded
   to tell you to as well.
On the day you are due to enter
   your city, Kullab,
may you have the one cursed by you
   enjoy it not,
and may the one with whom
   you have picked a quarrel
   not dare say of you:
   'Let him come on!'
When you have fashioned
   in its distinctiveness
   my shape,
   and set it up (as statues)
   to be admired,
my fame will make a splendid
   appearance in Sumer,
and they will, as befits,   200
   be placed in the temples
   of the great gods.
May for you

[clods] break apart
of themselves
as if (trodden by) shoes,
and Euphrates' [deep waters,]
as were it a (mere) ditch or feeder,
treat gently your feet and the legging."

LUGALBANDA
REJOINS ARMY
WITH NEW-
FOUND SPEED

Traveling without
his [provisions] for the road,
he took in hand [his weapon] only,
up above went the Thun[de]rbird,
down below went Lu[galb]anda,
abo[ve the bird] lifted (its) eyes,
saw the troops,
below [Lugalb]anda lifted (his) eyes,
saw the dust raised by the troops.

THE BIRD
ADVISES
SECRECY

The bird said to holy Lugalbanda:
"Come, my Lugalbanda,   210
let me advise you,
and may you take my advice,
let me say a word to you
and may you pay heed to it!
What I have said to you,
the qualities I have decreed for you,
you should not mention
to your comrades,
should not show
your brothers!
To do a favor,
is to call evil into being in hearts.
Verily, so it is![25]
I shall be (off) to my nest,
you be (off) to your troops!"

LUGALBANDA'S
REAPPEARANCE
CAUSES A STIR

The bird sped to its nest,
and Lugalbanda was wending
the foot to where his brothers were.
Like an u_5-bird[25] emerging   220
from a pristine canebrake,
like a *lahāmu*-creature[26]
slipping out of the Apsû,

24. A favor done to one person will make others envious.
25. This bird has not been identified.
26. The *lahamu* was a mythical guardian being, usually represented as a nude young man holding a

like a man set from heaven
   upon earth,
did Lugalbanda step
   into the midst
   of his brothers' formed phalanx.
His brothers exclaimed and exclaimed,
and his brothers and comrades
were wearying him asking questions:
"Come, my Lugalbanda,
   with you right there,
since the troops certainly left you
   like a man slain with weapons
   in battle,
—you never ate
   the good cream of the byre,
you never drank   230
   the clean milk of the sheepfold—
how were you able to walk hither
through the great foothills,
   where a lone man
   is not to walk,
whence such a man
   will not return to men?"
Again his brothers and his comrades
   were wearying him asking questions:

"Out of the rivers of the mountains,
   mothers of abundance,
being that all their banks
   are separated
   from where the water is,
how did you drink their waters
   how were you drawing it?"

LUGALBANDA   Holy Lugalbanda answered them:
KEEPS HIS   "Out of the rivers of the mountains,
SECRET, AN-   mothers of abundance,
SWERING AS   being that all their banks   240
IF FROM   are separated
FEVER HAL-   from where the water is,
LUCINATIONS   I drank, after resting on the ground

---

flowing vase or supporting a doorpost. Characteristic of him are his two curled sidelocks. One type of *lahamu* was particularly closely associated with the marshes.

on my loins,
    the water as from a waterskin,
I howled like a wolf,
    ate pasture safely.
I picked over the ground like a turtledove,
    ate the mountain acorns."[27]
Lugalbanda's brothers and comrades
dismissed what he told them
    from their minds,
huddled together
    as if sparrows at massing storm clouds,
embraced him and kissed him,
and like the young one of the *gamgam* bird[28]
    lying in its nest,
they were feeding him
    and giving him to drink,
and were making holy Lugalbanda's   250
    illness leave him.

ARATTA
PROVES
IMPREG-
NABLE

On that day, as one man,
    they joined up
    with Uruk's rearguard.
Like a snake (traversing) a grainpile,
    it crossed over the foothills,
but when they were
    but one double mile
    from the city,
both Uruk and Kullab
    threw themselves down prone
in Aratta's field watchtowers and dikes,
(for) from the city darts rained like rain,
and from Aratta's walls
    clay slingstones came clattering
as hailstones come in spring.
Days passed, the months lengthened,
    the year returned to its mother.
A yellowed harvest   260
    was about to grow up under heaven,
in the fields the surface had become bad,
    clay clove to the skin,

---

27. Lugalbanda takes the bird's advice and talks wildly so that his questioners assume that he is raving in fever fantasies.
    28. Not identified.

clay slingstones,
  like hailstones come in spring,
had landed on the roads,
mountain thorn had tangled on them,
and basilisks[29] were jostling each other;
no man knew
  (how) to go to the city,
was able to push through
  to go to Kullab.

<table>
<tr><td>

ENMERKAR
LOSES HEART;
SEEKS A MES-
SENGER TO
SEND TO
INANNA

</td><td>

In the midst of this
  Enmerkar, son of the sun god,
became frightened, felt stifled,
  was made gloomy at that noise.
He began seeking a man   270
  he could send back
    to the city,
began seeking a man
  he could send back
    to Kullab,
but no man said to him,
  "Let me go to the city!"
Sai[d to him,]
  "Let me go to Kullab!"
He [called out]
  the host of the independent countries,[30]
but no man [said] to him,
  "Let me go to the city!"
[Said] to him,
  "Let me go to Kullab!"
He called out the phalanx
  of the open-eyed,[31]
but no man said to him,
  "Let me go to the city!"
[Said to him,]
  "Let me go to Kullab!"
Again he called out   280
  the host of the independent countries
but no man [said to him,]
  "Let me go to the city!"

</td></tr>
</table>

29. A feared mythical animal, the name means "uniquely great one."

30. These would be contingents from city-states other than Uruk that recognized Enmerkar's overlordship.

31. That is, the elite troops.

Said to him,
  "Let me go to Kullab!"
He called out the phalanx
  of the open-eyed,
and Lugalbanda alone
  rose up for him out of the people
  and said to him:
"My king, let me go to the city,
  and may no man go with me,
let me go alone to Kullab,
  and may no man go with me!"
"If you will go to the city,
  no man goes with you,
will go alone to Kullab,
  no man goes with you,
and by the life's breath of Heaven,
  the life's breath of Earth, I swear:
  No great offices in Kullab
  shall ever elude your hand!"

ENMERKAR   Going straight from the convoked   290
STATES HIS   assembly (of the host)
MESSAGE   into the interior of the palace,[32]
  resting, as it was,
  like a great mountain on the ground,
Enmerkar, son of the sun god,
  denounced Inanna (saying:)
"In its time and place
  my noble sister, holy Inanna,
verily envisioned me
  in her holy heart
  from the mountain crest,
and verily had me enter
  brickbuilt Kullab,
at Uruk where, be it swamp,
  waters verily flowed,
be it dry land,
  poplars verily grew,
be it canebrake,

---

32. If the rhapsodist was precise in the use of language, "palace" may here refer to a huge tent for the commander-in-chief, meant to accommodate large bodies of troops at meals or at assembly.

old reeds and new reeds
    verily grew.
Enki, the owner of Eridu   300
pulled up, forsooth,
    its old reeds for me,
    and released its waters for me.
In fifty years I verily built,
    in fifty years I verily completed it.
Verily—should in the confines
    of Sumer and Akkad
Mardu bedouins,
    who know no grain,
    rise up,
the city wall of Uruk lies stretched
    like a bird snare
    in the desert!
Yet now, within its precincts,
    desire for me has died,
and like a cow tied to its calf
    I have my troops tied to me!

"Having left town
    like a child hating its mother,
my noble sister, holy Inanna,
came roving to me   310
    to brickbuilt Kullab.
If she truly loves her city
    she must surely hate me.
Why (then,) is she saddling the city with me?
If she truly hates her city
    she must surely love me,
why (then,) is she saddling me with the city?
When, of herself, the holy one
has dropped me from her holy side,
as does the Thunderbird the young one
    after the wings are fully grown,
may she have me enter brickbuilt Kullab!
On this day
    she can take away my lance,
on this day   320
    she can put my shield to rest!
Thus say to my noble sister,
    holy Inanna!"

LUGALBANDA
IS REPROVED
BY BROTHERS
AND COMRADES

With this, holy Lugalbanda
    came out from him from the palace,
but his brothers and his comrades
    growled at him,
        as were he a strange dog
        intruding among dogs;
as with a strange foal
    intruding among foals,
        bristles were raised at him:
"How could you say to the lord:
    'Send me back to her to Uruk?'
To Enmerkar, son of Utu:
'Let me go alone to Kullab,
    may no man go with me?'
Never, being alone,
    could you be supported on the road!
With our benevolent guardian spirit,   330
    who should not step hence with you,
and with our benevolent tutelary goddess
    who should not wander hence with you,
since you should not step hence with them,
    (away) from where we step,
and since you should not sit down hence with them,
    (away) from where we sit,
may you not tread our feet's dust
    hence with them."[33]
Since a single man is not to walk
    the great mountain ranges,
for such a man will not return to men,
    you will never come back!
After he discerned dawn
    —when on the great earth
    you would not yet have got (up) to stand—[34]
Lugalbanda—
    amid the loudly crying
    hearts of his brothers,
amid the smitten hearts
    of his comrades—
traveling without   340
    his provisions for the road,

33. The brothers fear that their protective spirits may leave them to follow Lugalbanda.
34. Apparently an aside to the audience.

took in hand his weapon only
and was crossing hither
 over mountain bases, mountain walls,
 and plateaus,
from (one) border of Anshan
 to (the other) border of Anshan,
five foothills, six foothills, seven foothills.
Toward midnight,
 before Inanna had approached
 her holy table,
he set foot joyfully
 toward brickbuilt Kullab.

LUGALBANDA
REPORTS TO
INANNA

His mistress, holy Inanna,
out of her happy heart
 had him come in to her.
He bowed, prostrated himself
 before her
and as she looks   350
 at the shepherd Ama-ushumgal-anna,
she was looking at holy Lugalbanda,
as she speaks to her son lord Shara,
 she was speaking too
 to holy Lugalbanda:
"Come, my Lugalbanda,
why have you brought
 instructions from the city,
and how were you able to come
 all alone from Aratta?"
Holy Lugalbanda answered her
 (saying:)
"Your brother—what did he say,
 and what did he add thereunto?
Enmerkar, son of the sun god
 what did he say,
 and what did he add thereunto?"
'In its time and place   360
 my noble sister, holy Inanna
verily envisaged me
 in her holy heart
 from the mountain crest,
and verily had me enter
 brickbuilt Kullab.

At Uruk where, be it swamp,
   waters verily flowed,
be it dry land,
   poplars verily grew,
be it canebrake,
   old reeds and new reeds
   verily grew,
Enki, the owner of Eridu,
pulled up, forsooth,
   its old reeds for me,
   and released its waters for me.
In fifty years I verily built,
   in fifty years I verily completed it.
Verily—should in the confines
   of Sumer and Akkad
Mardu bedouins,   370
   who know no grain,
   rise up,
the city wall of Uruk lies stretched
   like a bird snare
   in the desert!
Yet now, within its precincts,
   desire for me has died,
and like a cow tied to its calf
   I have my troops tied to me.

'Having left town
   like a child hating its mother,
my noble sister, holy Inanna,
came roving to me
   to brickbuilt Kullab.
If she truly loves her city
   she must surely hate me.
Why (then,) is she saddling the city with me?
If she truly hates her city
   she must surely love me.
Why (then,) is she saddling me with the city?   380
When of herself the holy one
has dropped me from her holy side,
as does the Thunderbird the young one
   after the wings are fully grown,
may she have me enter brickbuilt Kullab!
On this day
   she can take away my lance,

on this day
  she can put my shield to rest!
Thus say to my noble sister,
  holy Inanna.' "

Holy Inanna answered him, (saying:)
"At present in tail end,
  banks, and meadows
of the bright canal,
  the canal of bright waters,
resembling Inanna's pellucid   390
  water-skin river,
the carp are feeding on "honey-wort,"[35]
and the *kin-tur* fishes[36] are feeding
  on the "oak-grass" of the mountains.
Amidst them the *urinu* fish,[37]
  tutelary god of the carp,
is happily playing,
  flicking its tail.
With its scaly tail
  it is lying moored
  at the old reeds,
  a pristine spot.
All the tamarisks of the plateau
  whatever,
drink water out of its marsh,
but it stands alone, stands alone,
this tamarisk stands apart, alone.   400
When Enmerkar, son of the sun god,
has felled that tamarisk,
  has fashioned it into a trough,
has pulled out the old reeds
  of the pristine place at its stump,
  and taken them in hand,
has made the *urinu* fish,
  tutelary god of carp,
  come out from their midst,
has caught that fish, has cooked it,
  has dipped into it

35. Not identified.
36. Not identified.
37. Not identified.

and fed it to A'ankara,
　　Inanna's battle arm,[38]
may his troops dip into it with him
　　(with) their hands,
and he has surely made an end
　　of what is of the very life's breath
　　of Aratta in the marsh."

(ancient lacuna)[39]

"When the silversmiths have taken
　　the city's wrought silver,
the jewelers have taken　　　　　　　　　　　　　　410
　　its fashioned (gem)stones,
and stokers have been assigned
　　to the citizenry there,
may Aratta gather for him
　　at all its foundries."

(ancient lacuna)[40]

END OF AN
ORIGINALLY
MUCH LONGER
ENVOI

Aratta's buttresses
　　were of glossy lapis lazuli,
dread were its walls
　　and towering brickwork,
their clay tin ore
that was gouged out
　　of the mountain of the *hashur* cedars.

Holy Lugalbanda, a praise hymn!

38. I.e., made an offering of its meat to the À-an-kàra standard carried by the army as an emblem of Inanna and guarantee of her help.

39. Here the tradition available to the ancients began to be fragmentary; a passage dealing with the fall of Aratta and beginning the instructions for transporting the city's wealth in precious stones and metals as booty to Uruk is missing.

40. The original text may be assumed to have told here how Lugalbanda returned to Aratta and delivered Inanna's message to Enmerkar and how Enmerkar followed Inanna's advice, took Aratta, and carried off its treasures to Uruk. The final portion of the tale was apparently a eulogy for Aratta, the end of which only is preserved.

Gilgamesh and Aka

This short tale of Gilgamesh and Aka remains so far the only example of true primary epic that Sumerian literature has to offer. It may well be that the genre was losing favor and was dying out by the time of the Third Dynasty of Ur, from which the bulk of the known literary compositions dates. That the genre once was better represented is indicated by "Gilgamesh and Aka" itself, for that tale is clearly not self-contained, but represents rather a single episode in a much wider epic context leading up to it that is now lost. This particular tale may have survived because of the dramatic way in which it presents the inner conflict in Gilgamesh between ambition and loyalty, pride and gratitude, and its resolution.

Background for the story as we have it must be tales, now lost, of how Gilgamesh as a fugitive was kindly received and sheltered by Aka, king of Kishi. From what, or from whom, Gilgamesh fled is not known. It may have been from a powerful rival in Uruk or possibly from some enemy in another city altogether. The traditions underlying the Sumerian king list do not make him a descendant of earlier kings of Uruk, so his origins could well have been elsewhere.

When the story begins, Gilgamesh is in charge of Uruk, which is subject to Kishi and its king Aka. Quite possibly it was Aka who installed him as his vassal ruler there. The pride of Gilgamesh, however, makes it impossible for him to accept the fact that he owes his fortunes to others, so to prove himself he decides—apparently encouraged by the city goddess of Uruk, Inanna—to rebel against the overlordship of Kishi by refusing to perform the corvée work due it.

Seeking support for his plan he first approaches the council of elders that governs the everyday affairs of the city, but the prudent elders turn him down. He then assembles the young men of the city, the ones who will be called upon for corvée or army service, and the ones who will have to fight Kishi if the corvée duty is refused. Here he succeeds. The assembly of younger men follows him and acknowledges him as independent ruler, king of Uruk. So Gilgamesh, pleased, has his champion fighter, his slave Enkidu, arm himself for the coming battle.

Before expected—Kishi was upstream from Uruk and so could float down fast on the current—the army of Kishi arrives, disembarks, and lays siege to Uruk. The people of Uruk are much disturbed, and the warriors frown. Gilgamesh, however, is undaunted. He calls for volunteers to make a sortie, and the armorer of Uruk, one Lusağ, rises to the occasion. He sends his slave and champion fighter, Girish-hurdur, down to make the sortie, presumably at the head of a select contingent of troops. He himself will lean out over the city wall to show whose forces are doing the fighting. This form of combat, in which the hero stays on the sidelines and sends in a professional battler in his service, seems odd indeed. It is possible, perhaps, that, as in the case of Aka later on, the commander directed his troops from a point of vantage while the actual attack was lead by a subordinate. It is also possible, however, that this form of combat was a means for the rich and powerful to protect themselves as much as possible.

Girish-hurdur's sortie did not succeed. His attack was contained at the gate. When his master mounted the city wall to show who was attacking, Aka called to Girish-hurdur to find out if this was Gilgamesh, "the one from yonder." The reason for thus referring to Gilgamesh was that Gilgamesh had stayed in Kishi with Aka and had been sent to Uruk from there: it marked him out as a traitor. Girish-hurdur denies it, stating very loyally, however, that it might as well have been Gilgamesh, since his master is in every respect as impressive looking.

When it becomes clear that Girish-hurdur's sortie has bogged down, Gilgamesh takes a hand and sends in Enkidu at the head of the contingent from the part of Uruk called Kullab. Enkidu proves able to do what was beyond the powers of Girish-hurdur. He cuts his way through the enemy forces, trampling them down, throwing them aside, rolling them in the dust, until he reaches the ships of the invading Kishites. Here, from the vantage point of the high bow of his boat, Aka has been following the fighting, and here Enkidu takes him captive.

With this Gilgamesh's pride has been satisfied. He has shown that he is a match, in fact more than a match, for his suzerain, and so he can accept him. He therefore magnanimously acknowledges Aka as his superior officer and—as a repayment of the earlier debt of gratitude to him—hands back to him suzerainty over Uruk. He has proved himself and yet avoided falling prey to mean disloyalty and even meaner ingratitude.

CALL TO CORVEE IN KISHI	Aka, son of Enmenbaragesi, messengers sent from Kishi to Uruk to Gilgamesh. [1]
ELDERS CONSULTED	Gilgamesh laid the matter before his city's elders,

1. Nothing is said about the content of their message. Apparently that was unnecessary, it was given with the context. One can imagine that an overlord like Aka regularly would send messengers at stated times of year to call for the levy due. That this is what the messengers come for is clear from what follows.

was seeking, seeking,
   for words:
"Let us not submit   8a
   to the house of Kishi
to finish wells—
   to go on finishing
   every well
   of the land,
to go on finishing
   the wells and (well-)linings
   of the land,
to go on finishing
   windlasses
   along with the wellshafts!—
Let us smite it with weapons!"[2]   8b

ELDERS ADVISE   Met in assembly,
AGAINST   his city's elders
REBELLION   answer gave   10
                              to Gilgamesh:
"Let us submit
   to the house of Kishi.
to finish wells—
   to go on finishing
   every well
   of the land,
to go on finishing
   the wells and (well-)linings
   of the land,
to go on finishing
   windlasses
   along with wellshafts!—
Let us not smite it with weapons!"

Trusting Inanna,
Gilgamesh,
   lord of Kullab,[3]

2. The corvée work which the Urukites were to perform in Kishi was apparently digging and outfitting wells for irrigation. The description of the work by Gilgamesh follows the wells from the beginning, from digging them, through the lining of the well shafts, to providing them with windlasses. Refusal of the corvée would of course amount to rebellion and would immediately lead to war.
3. Kullab was a separate city that very early was included in the Uruk complex.

took not to heart
  the words of his city's elders.[4]

YOUNG MEN
CONSULTED

The second time Gilgamesh,
  lord of Kullab,
laid the matter before
  the lads of his city,[5]
  was seeking, seeking,
  for words:
"May you not submit   23a
  to the house of Kishi
to finish wells—   20
  to go on finishing
  every well
  of the land,
to go on finishing
  the wells and (well-)linings
  of the land,
to go on finishing
  windlasses
  along with the wellshafts!—
May you smite it with weapons!"   23b

YOUNG MEN
AGREE TO
REBEL

Met in assembly
  the lads of his city
  answer gave
  to Gilgamesh:
"As goes the saying: 28b
'To stand all the time
  in attendance,
to sit all the time
  on call,
to protect the son
  of the king,
and outrun
  the donkey's legs,

4. Apparently Gilgamesh had been told to resist Kishi and had been promised victory by Inanna, the city goddess of Uruk. This must have been told earlier, in a part of the tradition that has not come down to us; or it may be that the rhapsodist could assume that all such circumstances of Uruk's war of independence were already well known by the audience.

5. The lads, the young men of Uruk, were the ones who would be doing the corvée work and the ones who formed the army. They were thus the ones directly involved, without whose support Gilgamesh could not have gone ahead. So the appeal to them is a last-chance thing, but it succeeds.

whoever has wind
    enough for that?"[6]   28a
Let us not submit
    to the house of Kishi
    let us smite it with weapons.

GILGAMESH   'Uruk, the gods'   30
HAILED AS IN-   handiwork,
DEPENDENT   and Eanna
KING OF URUK   a house
    come down
    from heaven,[7]
'tis the great gods
    fashioned
    their shape!
The great wall,
    a heavy cloud
    resting on the earth
    as it is,
the august abode,
    set against the sky
    as it is,
are entrusted to you!
    You are the king
    and warrior!
The basher of heads,
    the prince beloved of An![8]

'O, how there is fear
    of his coming!
Their troops will be under strength,
    they are bound
    to be melting away
    at their rear,
their men
    are unable to face him!' "[9]

6. The saying has reference to levy for army service. The levied troops would be led by the son of the suzerain, who would—unlike them—ride in a war chariot drawn by donkeys.

7. Eanna was the temple of Inanna in Uruk. There was a tradition, also attested elsewhere, that it had descended from heaven.

8. This is the ritualistic formula for recognizing someone as king of Uruk and for hailing him as such. Here, since the title "king" (*lugal*) implies independent status, it will mean that the assembly proclaims Uruk's independence under Gilgamesh as its king.

9. Fear of meeting the king of Uruk in battle makes the soldiers in the back rows of the enemy army quietly sneak away and desert.

PREPARATION
FOR WAR

On that day,   40
   for Gilgamesh,
   lord of Kullab,
at the words
   of the lads
   of his city
   his heart gladdened,
   his liver brightened.
To his slave Enkidu
   he said:
"May the carpenter
   put back
   the thongs
   on the implements
   of battle
   for this,
and return
   the weapons
   of battle
   unto your arms![10]
May a great fear
   of the fiery halo
   prove enough,
may, when he comes,
   great fear
   of me
   fall upon him!
May his doings
   become confused,
   his judgment
   go to pieces!"

AKA ASSERTS
SUZERAINTY,
BELEAGERS URUK

Five days it was not,
   ten days it was not
ere Aka, son of Enmenbaragesi,
   and Uruk
   were lined up
   around
   (its) sides.[11]

---

10. The leather straps with which the axe blades were secured to the shaft were obviously removed when the weapons were stored so that they would not stretch and lose tightness.

11. I.e., Aka surrounded Uruk and laid siege to it.

Uruk's doings   50
   became all confused.

Gilgamesh,
   lord of Kullab,
   said
   to its warriors:
"My warriors
   are all frowning,
May one who has heart
   stand up and say:
'Let me go against Aka!'"

SORTIE BY
GIRISH-
HURDURA Lusaǧ,[12] master
   of Girish-hurdur,[13]
lauded his king
   and said:
"Let me go against Aka!
May his doings
   become confused,
   his judgment
   go to pieces!"
Girish-hurdur
   sallied out
   of the main gate.
When Girish-hurdur   60
   was sallying out
   of the main gate,
they held him
   in the main gate's
   gate opening.
Girish-hurdur
   had to pound down,
   and pound down,
   his bludgeon there;
and there he bent
   the eye upon Aka,
was calling
   over to Aka;
but his words
   carried not.

12. Name of the armorer of Uruk.
13. The name of the slave. It seems to mean "caterpillar" and was perhaps a nickname.

352   *Epics*

HIS MASTER
LUSAG SHOWS
HIMSELF ON
WALL

FAILURE TO
BREAK THROUGH

The armorer of Uruk
  mounted the wall,
leaned out
  over the wall.
Aka saw him,
called over
  to Girish-hurdur:
"Slave, is your master
  the man from yonder?"[14]
"My master is not   70
  the man from yonder;
the man from yonder,
  whom my master
  might well be,
whose dread brow
  it might well be,
whose bison's face
  it might well be,
whose lapis lazuli beard
  it might well be,
whose capable fingers
  it might well be!"

But he flung not
  the myriads down,
tore not
  the myriads up,
was not able
  to tumble
  the myriads
  in the dust,
was not able
  to overwhelm
  all the highlanders,
was not able
  to fill with dust
  the mouths
  of the lowlanders,
cut not through   80
  to the barge's prow,
took not captive

14. That is, Gilgamesh, who had been taken in by Aka, and who had come to Uruk from there.

Aka, king of Kishi,
　　in the midst of his troops.[15]
They were smiting there,
　　they were striking there,
Girish-hurdur
　　had to pound down,
　　and pound down,
　　his bludgeon there.

SORTIE BY
ENKIDU
After the armorer
　　of Uruk,
　　Gilgamesh
　　mounted the wall;
the awesome glory
　　overwhelmed
　　the elders
　　and youngsters
　　of Kullab,
while the lads
　　of Uruk
　　clasped in their arms
　　the weapons
　　of battle,
took their places
　　in the street
　　of the doors
　　of the main gate.

Enkidu
　　sallied out
　　of the main gate,
and Gilgamesh
　　leaned out
　　over the wall,
looking around,　　　　　　　　　　　　　　90
　　Aka saw him:
"Slave, is your master
　　the man from yonder?
"It is
　　as you say.

15. Aka was apparently directing the battle from the vantage point of the high prow of the boat that brought him and his army down the Euphrates from Kishi. Its height would give him a clear view of how the battle was going.

My mast⸱ ⸱
   is the man from yonder!"

AKA CAPTURED

He flung
   the myriads down,
   tore the myriads up,
was able to
   tumble the myriads
   in the dust,
was able to
   overwhelm
   all the highlanders,
was able to
   fill with dust
   the mouths
   of the lowlanders,
he cut through
   to the barge's prow,
took captive
   Aka, king of Kishi,
   in the midst
   of his troops.

GILGAMESH
REPAYS A DEBT
OF GRATITUDE

Gilgamesh,   100
   lord of Kullab,
said to Aka:
"Is it Aka?
   Is it my sergeant?
   Is it Aka?
   Is it my captain?
Is it Aka,
   my general?—
Aka,
   you sated
   ⸱ with grain
   the fleeing bird,
Aka,
   you granted me life,
   Aka,
   you gave me
   back health,
Aka,
   you carried

the fugitive
  on the hip!
Uruk, the god's
  handiwork,
the great wall,
  a wall founded
  by An,
the august abode
  set up by An,
are entrusted to you!   110
  You are their king
and warrior,
  the basher of heads,
  the prince beloved of An!"[16]

He let Aka go free
  to Kishi
  (saying):
"Before Utu!
  I have repaid you
  the old favor!"

Gilgamesh, lord of Kullab,
Praising you is sweet!

16. Gilgamesh is first acknowledging Aka as his superior officer. Then, having recalled to Aka's and the listeners' minds how Aka helped him when he was a fugitive, he acknowledges him as king of Uruk, accepting him again as suzerain. It is clear that Gilgamesh had the need—for his self-esteem—to accept his inferior position of his own free will and as a gift from him to Aka, not as something he was obliged to accept.

PART SIX

Admonitory History

The Cursing of Akkadê

The composition which is here called "The Cursing of Akkadê" occupies a position all its own in Sumerian literature as we have it. It is neither myth nor epic, neither hymn nor lament. At best one might perhaps describe it as "admonitory history," stretching the term "history" to include "mythohistory." It tells how the famous city of Akkadê was cursed by the gods and annihilated because its equally famous ruler Naram-Suen willfully disregarded the express wishes of Enlil and demolished his temple Ekur in Nippur—albeit with the intention of rebuilding it. The tale might thus serve to warn rulers never—even with the best of intentions—to cross divine will.

The story begins with a description of the prosperity enjoyed by Akkadê. Enlil had granted it kingship over all of the country, and Inanna, its city goddess, spared no effort to further its welfare. Then, suddenly and unexpectedly, its ruler Naram-Suen was not given permission by Enlil to rebuild Ekur, and in a dream Naram-Suen saw nothing but evils awaiting in the future.

The denial of permission to rebuild Ekur was rightly seen as ominous by Inanna, who, frightened, left the city; and other gods withdrew their support, Ninurta, Utu, Enki, and the god of heaven, An. The city also lost its kingship.

Naram-Suen's first reaction was to seek to induce a change of heart in Enlil by a show of humility and mourning, and he kept this up for seven years. When he then again asked permission, however, Enlil had not relented, and permission to build was not in the answering omens.

This proved too much for the self-willed king. He interpreted the omen to say the opposite of what it clearly meant, and set out for Nippur with his troops, who were to do the demolition and building work. The tearing down of the existing building and the attending laying open of the temple's sacred and secret rooms to profane gaze deeply angered Enlil, and without making any distinctions as to guilt, he called in neighboring barbarians from the mountains, the Gutians, and had them devastate the country. The text vividly depicts the scarcity, famine, and crimes that followed.

The few people who survived those days in Nippur built a small makeshift sanctuary of reed for Enlil and performed mourning rites which eventually calmed

359

him, so that he sought solitude and lay down without taking food or drink, being that distressed.

At that time the other great gods, whose cities and temples had suffered under Enlil's indiscriminate anger, sought to focus it on Naram-Suen and his city Akkadê, or rather, on the city alone, for Naram-Suen seems to have been lost sight of entirely at this point. To assuage Enlil, they pronounced two long and detailed curses on the city and its people that, as they took effect, completely annihilated it. With the words "Akkadê was destroyed," the composition ends.

Our earliest manuscripts of "The Cursing of Akkadê" date from the period of the Third Dynasty of Ur, not too many generations after the actual end of the Akkadê dynasty. It is therefore somewhat surprising to find that its presentation of events differs on important points from what we know to have taken place. Naram-Suen, and Akkadê's prosperity under him, are undoubtedly historically correct. He is also known from contemporary inscriptions to have rebuilt, or perhaps better, to have begun rebuilding, Enlil's temple Ekur in Nippur, and must thus have done some demolition of the earlier structure. The work was completed by his son and successor Sharkalisharri.

There is no evidence, however, and no reason to assume that his reign ended in disaster. His dynasty continued for another three kings, and Akkadê must have survived that long too. Most likely the telescoping of events was done for literary reasons, to tauten the plot and have retribution follow swiftly upon the offense. Noteworthy to a modern reader of the story is the entirely passive role of the people of Akkadê. They seem a mere extension of their ruler and his favor or disfavor with the gods. When the gods are friendly, the people are happy and wise; when their ruler offends the gods, they lose all judgment. Although the sinful act of building against Enlil's will is an individual decision by Naram-Suen, his city and its people are wiped out to atone for it. It is, though, an attitude not uncommon in antiquity. Seventy thousand people died because David had sinned against the Lord by ordering a census. The shepherd is punished by the destruction of his sheep.

ENLIL GIVES
AKKADÊ DO-
MINION

When Enlil's frowning brow
had killed Kishi,
    as were it the bull of heaven,[1]
had felled the house of Uruk land
    down in the dust,
      as one would a great ox,
  and Enlil then and there
    had given Sargon, king of Akkadê,

---

1. A mythological creature thought to be killed in the thunderstorms in the spring. Its bellowing, and the roar of a lion attacking it, were heard in thunder. See "Inanna's Descent," n. 9, above.

lordship and kingship
from south to north—
in those days holy Inanna
    was building
Akkadê's temple close
    to be her august home,
set up the throne
    in Ulmash,[2]

INANNA
ORGANIZES
HER NEW
HOME

Like a young (married) man   10
    building a house
      for the first time,
like a young daughter
    setting up a home,
holy Inanna   24
    went without sleep
to provision the storehouses
    with things,
furnish that city with
    dwellings and building plots,
feed its people superb food,
give its people superb water
    to drink,
have the courtyard joyful
    with (celebrants with)
    rinsed heads,[3]
have the people sit down
    in festival grounds,
have acquaintances eat together
and outsiders circle around
    like strange birds in the sky,
have Marhashi put back   20
    in the rolls,[4]
have monkeys, huge elephants,
    water buffaloes, beasts
    of faraway places,
jostle each other in the wide streets,
and dogs, panthers, mountain goats,
    and *alum* sheep full of long wool.[5]

2. The main temple of Inanna in Akkadê.
3. Washing the hair was a necessity for being ritually clean for the festival.
4. This phrase, which is not altogether clear, probably means subjecting the faraway eastern country of Marhashi and imposing corvée service on it.
5. Signs of the city's far-flung trade.

RICHES
OVERFLOW

In those days she filled
    Akkadê's stores for emmer wheat
    with gold,
filled its stores for white emmer wheat
    with silver,
had copper, tin, and slabs of lapis lazuli
    regularly delivered
    into its barns for grain,
while she plastered its grain piles
    over with mud-plaster outside.[6]

CITIZENS
MADE
HAPPY

She gave its old women
    (the gift of) counsel,
gave its old men   30
    (the gift of just) testimony,
to its maidens
    she gave playgrounds,
to its young men she gave
    arms (worthy) of weapons,
to its little ones
    she gave a merry heart.
Hand-holding nursing mothers,
    daughters of generals,
were dancing to the *algasurrû* lyre;
the heart of the city
    was (one) of *tigi*-harps,
    its outskirts (of) reed pipes
    and tambourines,
its quay, where the boats moored,
    was (resounding with) jocund shouts.

PEACE AND PROS-
PERITY. LUCRA-
TIVE FOREIGN
TRADE

All lands lay
    in safe pastures,
its (Akkadê's) people looked out
    over pleasant tracts,
its king, the shepherd Naram-Suen,   40
radiated light flamelike
    on Akkadê's holy throne dais.
Its city wall—like a great mountain range—
    abutted heaven,
in its city-gates—like unto the Tigris
    going to the sea—

6. The influx of precious metals and stones was so great that the storehouses for grains had to be used for them, the grain being stored outside in plastered-over piles.

Inanna opened up the gateways.
From Sumer's own stores
    barges were towed (upstream).
The Mardu bedouins of the highland,
    men who knew not grain,
were coming in to her with perfect bulls,
    perfect kids,
the Meluhhans, men of the black mountains,[7]
were bringing down
    strange goods to her from them,
the Elamites and Subareans[8]   50
    were toting things to her
    as were they packasses.
All the city rulers, the heads of temples,
and the surveyors of the desert fringe,
were bringing in punctually
    their monthly and new year
    food offerings.
O how it caused vexation
    in Akkadê's city gate![9]
Holy Inanna (just) didn't know
    how to receive (all) those food portions,
but like the citizens she did not tire
    of the pleasure of finding
    (store)houses and (storage) plots
    to keep up with them.

REBUILDING   Upon this fell—as an ominous silence—
OF EKUR   the matter of Ekur.[10]
DENIED   Akkadê became to her
    fraught with shuddering,
fear befell her in Ulmash,
she took her seat out of the city.   60
Like a maiden who decides
    to abandon home
holy Inanna abandoned Akkadê's
    temple close,

7. Meluhha has not yet been certainly identified. The Assyrian scribes of Ashurbanipal (ca. 650 B.C.) considered it to be Ethiopia. Modern scholars tend to think that in earlier times it denoted India.

8. Elam was the region around Susa in western Iran. Subartu was the area occupied by northern Iraq and eastern Syria.

9. The gate would be a bottleneck for traffic of such magnitude.

10. Denial of permission to build or rebuild a god's temple indicated lack of favor with him. Lack of favor with Enlil, the chief god of the country, the one who bestowed or took away kingship and generally controlled the country's political fortunes, was clearly terrifying.

like a warrior going up against armed might,
she brought (the forces for)
    fight and battle
    out of the city,
confronted with them
murderous foes.

AKKADÊ LOSES   Not five days it was, not ten days it was
ITS KINGSHIP   (before) Ninurta had the ornament of lordship,
AND TURNS   the crown of kingship,
AGGRESSIVE   the podium, (?) and the throne
    granted to kingship,
fetched into his (temple) Eshumesha.[11]
Utu took advisement   70
    away from the city,
Enki took away its wits.
Its halo, that abutted heaven,
An drew up
    into heaven's inside.
Its holy mooring stakes,
    that were (firmly) driven in,
Enki pulled (down)
    into the Apsû.
Its weapons Inanna
    had carried off.
Akkadê's temple close
    ended its life
    as were it but
    a little carp in the deep.
The city's enemies appeared
    in front of it;
like a huge elephant
    it put the neck down,
like a huge bull   80
    it lifted the horns,
like a raging basilisk[12]
    it slithered the head
    (from side to side),
and, heavy-weight that it was,
    it went pillaging
    instead of in combat.

11. I.e., removed them from Akkadê and took them to Nippur.
12. The term thus translated denotes a much-feared, perhaps mythical, animal classed by the ancients with serpents.

NARAM-SUEN HAS
A VISION OF
THE FUTURE

That Akkadê's royalty
    was not to occupy a good steady seat,
that nothing whatever
    that was in store for it
    was propitious,
that the house would be shaken,
    the treasuries dispersed,
which Naram-Suen had seen
    in a dream vision,
he let (only) his heart know,
    put it not on his tongue,
    spoke of it with no man.

NARAM-SUEN
TRIES PENITENCE

Because of Ekur
    he dressed in mourning[13]
covered his chariot over
    with a cargo mat,
took down the cabin   90
    from his barge,
cut down on his royal
    requirements.
For all of seven years
    Naram-Suen persevered,
—who ever saw a king
    holding (his) head
    in (his) hands for all of seven years?

LOSES PATIENCE
AND DISREGARDS
THE OMEN AND
BEGINS DEMOL-
ISHING EKUR

When in (his) seeking an omen
    about the temple,
building the temple
    was not in the omen,
and a second time
    seeking an omen
    about the temple,
building the temple
    was not in the omen:
he, to change
    what had been
    entrusted to him,
denied, O Enlil!
    what had been told him,

13. This was the normal reaction if temple-building was denied. It was kept up until the omina turned favorable, which they did not do in this case.

scattered   100
   what had been
   put together for him.
He called up his troops
and like a bruiser
   entering the main courtyard,
he balled the hands at Ekur;
like one having (strong) knees
   bending down to wrestle,
he counted the *gigunu*[14]
   worth but thirty shekel;
like a marauder raiding a town,
he set up big storm ladders
   against the house.

To dismantle Ekur as were it
   a great ship,
to remove earth (from it)
   like one mining a silver mountain,
to cleave it as were it a   110
   lapis lazuli range,
to make it collapse
   like a city Ishkur has flooded,
he had great copper axes
   cast for the temple.
Though (verily) it was not
   the cedar mountains,
both edges he sharpened
   on the *agasiliqqu* axes.

COSMIC   To its socle he put copper mattocks,
EFFECTS OF   —and the ground settled
DEMOLITION   in the country's foundations.[15]

to its top he put copper axes,
   —and with that the temple
   let the neck sink to the ground
   like a young man who is killed,
and with it the necks of all lands
   were let sink to the ground.

14. The *gigunu* was the temple on the stage tower. It was surrounded by trees.

15. Here and in the following lines the demolishing of the various parts of the temple is having effects—as if by sympathetic magic—on the country and on nature. Apparently the temple was thought of as, in its own right, a fetish for the nation. Cf. "Hymn to Enlil" ll. 32ff. and introduction.

Its rain-gutters he peeled off,   120
—and the rains vanished in the sky.
Its doorsills he took down,
    —and the decorum of the country
    changed.[16]
In its "gate in which the grain
    is not to be cut"
    he cut the grain,[17]
—and with that, grain was cut off
    from the country's lands.
Into its "gate of peace"
    he had pickaxes strike,
—and for all lands
    their peace became hostility.

DESTRUCTION   In the "grand arch,"[18] like a heavy spring flood,
OF HOLY OF   he made Ekur's (wooden) posts (into splinters)
HOLIES ON   like (fire)wood.
TOP   Into its holy of holies,
    the house knowing not daylight,
    looked the nation,
and upon the gods' holy bath vessels   130
    looked (men of) Uri.[19]
Its *lahamu* (figures)[20] standing
    along the great supporting terrace
    and the house,
although they were not men
    who had committed sacrilege,[21]
Naram-Suen threw into the fire;
and for the cedars, cypresses, *supālus*,
    and boxwoods,
    its trees of the *gigunu*[22]
    he cast lots.

16. The sills seem to symbolize restraint.
17. Apparently the gate in question had a sacred patch of grain next to it. It may have had a special connection with Ninlil, who was a grain goddess.
18. The arch of the gate to the summit of the stage tower where the holy of holies was located.
19. The part of southern Mesopotamia north of Nippur. It was later called Akkad.
20. Mythical guardian beings. Here as pictured on metopes. Usually they are represented as naked heroes with the hair in distinctive side curls. Often they carry vessels with flowing water emblematic of rivers, at other times they support doorposts.
21. Burning will have been the typical manner of executing a person who had committed sacrilege.
22. See n. 14, above.

<table>
<tr><td>PRECIOUS
METALS TO
AKKADÊ</td><td>Its gold he did up in crates,
its silver he did up in leather packs,
with its copper he filled the harbor quay
   like grain brought en masse.
Its silver the silversmith was (re)shaping,
its (precious) stones the jeweler was (re-)shaping,
its copper the metal-caster
   was pounding (into scrap).
Though it was not the goods of a sacked city,
he had big boats moor at the quay
   by the house,
he had big boats moor at the quay
   toward Enlil's temple,
and the goods leave the city.
As he made the goods leave the city
Akkadê's sense left it.
He was letting the boats pitch
   in taking off,
   and Akkadê's judgment wavered.</td><td>140</td></tr>
</table>

ENLIL'S
REVENGE: BAR-
BARIANS IN-
VADE

     the roaring storm,
       hushing the people one and all,
     the risen floodstorm,   150
       having none that could oppose,
Enlil,
   in (considering)
   what he would lay waste
   because his beloved Ekur
   had been laid waste,
decided to lift his eyes
   unto the mountains of Gubin,[23]
decided to bring down from it as one
   the wide(spread) foothill (tribes).
No likes of the nation,
   not counted with the country,
the Gutians,
   knowing no restraints,
(of) human face, dogs' cunning, monkey's build,
Enlil decided to bring out
   of the mountains.

23. Not certainly identified. The homeland of the Gutians was the Iranian mountains northeast of the Diyala region.

Numerous like locusts
　　they came striding,
stretched out their arms in the desert for him
　　like gazelle and wild-ass snares,
nothing escaped their arms,　　　　　　　　160
nobody did their arms leave.
No envoy traveled the road.
No ambassador's boat was passing by
　　on the river.
Enlil's yellow goats had been driven as spoil
　　from the fold,
　　their herdsmen made to follow them.
The cows had been driven as spoil
　　from their pen,
　　their cowherders made to follow them.
The watch was put in neck-stocks,[24]
footpads sat in ambush on the roads,
in the country's city gates
　　the doorleaves were stuck in the mud,
in all lands on the walls of their cities
　　they were crying sore cries,
inside the city, not in the wide desert outside,　　170
　　they had the gardens.[25]

THE COUNTRY
DEVASTATED

It being like the days when cities
　　were (first) built,
the great fields carried no grain,
the flooded tracts carried no fish,
the gardens' irrigation beds carried no
　　sirop and wine,
for long days rain rained not,
　　no underbrush grew up.

In those days oil for one (silver) shekel
　　was half a quart,
barley for one shekel
　　was half a quart,
wool for one shekel
　　was half a mina,
fish for one shekel
　　filled a ten-quart measure.

24. I.e., the police were taken captive.
25. Partly for protection, partly because the deserted areas of the city offered room for them.

Thus they bought at the   180
     market rate of their cities.[26]
He who lay down (ill) on the roof
     died on the roof.
He who lay down (ill) in the house
     was not buried.
The people from their hunger
     were coming to blows
     among themselves.
At Kiur, Enlil's great place,
dogs banded together;
     in the silent streets,
in these dogs would devour
     men walking by twos,
dogs would devour men walking by threes,
numerous teeth were strewn about
     numerous heads tossed around,
teeth were strewn
     heads sown as seedcorn
descent heads were exchanged   190
     for crooked heads,
men lay on top of men,
crooks bled from above
     on blood of decent men.

NIPPUR   In those days Enlil built
LAMENTS   out of (scraps) from his great sanctuaries
              a small reed sanctuary,
              between sunrise and sunset
                   its stores dwindled.
              Old women who were left over
                   from that day,
              old men who were left over
                   from that day,
              and the chief elegist who was left over
                   from that year,
              set up, for seven days and seven nights,
              seven harps toward him on the ground,   200
                   like the firm base of heaven,
              and played within them (also)
                   tambourine, sistron and kettledrum for him
                   (thunderously) like Ishkur.

---

26. These are exorbitant prices, such as were charged only in times of dire famine.

The old women held not back
(cries of): "Woe, my city!"
The old men held not back
(cries of): "Woe, its men!"
The elegist held not back
(cries of): "Woe, Ekur!"
Its maidens held not back (from)
pulling out (their) hair,
its lads held not back
the pointed knives (lacerating themselves).
Weeping, Enlil's ancestors
were placing their supplications
on Enlil's holy knees
in Duku, laden with holy dread,[27]
and so Enlil entered the holy "holy of holies"
and lay down eschewing food.[28]

THE GREAT
GODS CURSE
AKKADÊ

At that time Suen, Enki, Inanna, Ninurta,   210
Ishkur, Utu, Nusku, Nidaba,
and the great gods
were trying to calm Enlil's heart,
were making pleas (saying:)
"Enlil, may the city that sacked your city
be done to as your city was,
that defiled your *gigunu*
be done to as Nippur was.
May the one who knew the city
turn the head unto
the clay-pit (left) of it,
and may the men who knew men (there)
not find them in it,
may a brother not recognize his brother,
may its maiden be wickedly killed
in her home,
may its father cry out bitterly
in his house where the wife was killed,
may its doves mourn in their crannies,
may things be thrown at its sparrows   220
in their hiding places,
may it be wary like a frightened dove!"

27. Duku, "the holy mound," was a sacred locality. Originally and basically the term designated the plastered-over pile of harvested grain, but it was extended to underground storage generally. Enlil's ancestors—powers for fertility in the earth—were located in Duku.

28. Typical reaction to deep distress. Cf. "Enmerkar and the Lord of Aratta," l. 391.

SECOND
CURSE

A second time Suen, Enki, Inanna, Ninurta,
    Ishkur, Utù, Nusku, and heavenly Nidaba
    verily spoke,
set their face toward the city,
and were bitterly cursing Akkadê (saying:)
"O city, you rushed at Ekur"
    —O Enlil, may it come to be!—
"Akkadê, you rushed at Ekur"
    —O Enlil, may it come to be!—
"May at your holy city wall,
    as high as it is,
    laments be sent up,
may your *gigunus*
    be heaped up like dust,
may the standing *lahamus*[29]
    of the upper terrace
pitch from it to earth   230
    like huge lads drunk with wine!
May your clay return to its Apsû,
be clay cursed by Enki!
May your grain return to its furrow,
be grain cursed by the grain goddess!
May your wood return to its forests,
be wood cursed by the carpenter god!
May the bull-butcher butcher the spouse!
May your sheep-slaughterer slaughter the son!
May the waters wash away your pauper
    as he finds children (to sell) for money![30]
May your harlot hang herself   240
    in the gate of her hostel!
May your hierodule who is a mother,
    and your courtesan who is a mother,
    stab the child!
May your gold have the purchasing power of silver,
May your silver be priced as . . . . ,
May your copper be priced as lead!
Akkadê, may your strong one
    be cut off from his strength,
may he not (manage to) lift
    the provision sack onto his saddle,

29. See above, n. 20.
30. At a guess: as he is looking for babies set adrift on the river by parents unable to feed them.

may his arms not enjoy (controlling)
  your choice (chariot) donkeys,
  may he lie (ill) into evening.
May that city die in famine,
may your patrician, who eats finest bread,
  lie down hungry,
may your man who used to get up from firstfruits   250
eat cutting (?) from his beams,
may he grind with his teeth the leather fittings
of "the great door of the leather fittings" of his father's
house,
into your palace built in joy of heart
  may anguish be cast,
may the "badman"[31] of the deserts of silent tracts
  howl, howl, and howl from it.

"Over your consecrated grounds
  where ritual handwashings are established,
may the fox of the ruined mounds
  sweep its tail,
in your "gate of the country" that was established
may the sleeper-bird,
  the bird (foreboder) of anguish
  place (its) nest.
In your city that,   260
  (celebrating) with tigi-harps,
  does not sleep,
that for merriness of heart
  lies not down,
may Nanna's bull Turesi[32]
bellow as were it roaming
  a desert of silent tracts.
May long grass grow
  on your canal banks
  where the boats were hauled,
and may grass, lamentably,
  grow on your road
  laid down for chariots.
Moreover, may no man pass
  along your canal banks

31. Apparently a term for a demon similar to a banshee.
32. It is not clear just what the bull of Nanna, the moon god, refers to.

where boats are hauled,
places where (in future)
water is to be drawn.
by splay-horned mouflons
and fleet snakes of the mountains
(only).
May your central plain growing fine grass
grow reeds for lament.
Akkadê, may your waters pouring sweet
pour (as) saline waters.
May one who has said: 270
'Let me settle in that city!'
not have pleasant residence there,
who has said:
'Let me lie down in Akkadê'
not have pleasant resting place there!"

CURSES TAKE   Presently under the sun of that day
EFFECT   thus it verily came to be,
long grass grew up on its canal banks
where the boats were hauled.
grass, lamentably, grew up on its road
laid down for chariots,
moreover, no man passed along
on its canal banks
where boats were hauled,
places where water was (now) drawn
by splay-horned mouflons and fleet
snakes of the mountains (only).
Its central plain growing fine grass
grew reeds of lament,
Akkadê's water flowing sweet
flowed (as) saline waters.
For who had said:
'Let me settle in that city!'
residence was not pleasant,
for who had said: 280
'Let me lie down in Akkadê!'
the resting place was not pleasant,
Akkadê was destroyed!

A praise hymn for Inanna.

PART SEVEN

Hymns to Temples

Hymn to Kesh

The hymn to the temple Kesh is one of the oldest Sumerian literary works that have come down to us. Fragments of copies dating to the early part of the third millennium B.C. have been found, and a more complete text of this earliest version may be hoped for. As it stands, the hymn makes a distinctly archaic impression, and it is not easy to say how much of it we actually understand, and how much of it refers to things we know not of, but which may have been obvious to early hearers who knew the temple and its cult of their own experience, and to whom many allusions were clear that we find puzzling or miss altogether.

Kesh, the temple hymned, has not yet been located on the ground. Most likely it is to be looked for in the eastern borderlands, and a proposal by Claus Wilcke to seek it a short distance north of Adab (present-day Bismaya) has much in its favor.

The chief deity of Kesh was the birth goddess Nintur, also called Ninhursaga. Her husband was the god Shulpae and her son the god Ashgi. The latter is called "warrior" in the hymn, but very little else is known about his character. The hymn to Kesh begins by telling how Enlil brought the high offices out of their storage in his temple to assign them to one or more of the assembled cities, when he was so impressed by seeing Kesh lifting the head in eagerness to serve that he broke out in praise of it. The goddess of writing and literature, Nidaba, who was present, carefully remembered and took down Enlil's words and put them in form, thus producing, one must assume, the hymn we have.

This setting for the hymn occupies the first part of its first section. The remainder is given over to a description of the temple in a series of metaphors which continues through the second section. The third section contrasts the "upper" and the "lower" parts of the temple in rather puzzling manner. Whether I am right in tentatively suggesting that this means the parts of the structure above ground and those below, foundations and substructure (see below, "Cylinder A," n. 103), is a moot question. The lower parts amount in volume to half of the upper ones and when, as the section moves along, animals are used as metaphor, the larger animals serve for the upper, the smaller animals for the lower parts. The temple's need—and demand—for revenue is the subject of the fourth section. The amount of oxen and sheep needed for sacrifices is indicated, albeit in round numbers, and the contributions from the king are mentioned.

The fifth section lists, and shortly characterizes, the deities of the temple, and the sixth section surprises by returning again briefly to the temple's physical structure, describing its gate, doorleaves, and bolts, as well as the pilasters of the temple on top of the stage tower—a series of terraces. One would have expect that to have come between sections three and four. There follows in the sixth section a listing of the human personnel of priests. After the standard *en* and *nuesh* follow here a series of priests peculiar to the service of Nintur. They and their functions are not all well known, but it seems clear that they all have connection with aspects of birthgiving.

The seventh section presents Ninhursaĝa/Nintur as she is sitting down to serve wine at a feast in her temple, and the last section praises the temple as a place of refuge. The closing lines are the traditional rubric of praise, dedicated here to Ashgi and Nintur.

KESH PRAISED
BY ENLIL

Princely office upon princely office
　he decided to bring out from the house,[1]
Enlil decided to bring the princely offices
　out from the house,
decided to bring the princely offices and kingship
　out from the house.

Enlil was looking at all lands,
in tiers rose the lands for Enlil
the (world's) four quarters were greening
　for Enlil like a garden.

Kesh was there
　raising the head unto him
Out of all lands
　Kesh was the one
　raising the head,[2]
and (so) Enlil was moved
　to sing the praises of Kesh.

Establisher of the standard version thereof   10
　was Nidaba,[3]
she spun, as it were, a web
　out of those words,[4]

1. The offices will have been represented by concrete insignia as, e.g., crown and scepter for kingship.
2. A gesture indicating that it offered its services. Cf. below, "Cylinder A," n. 30.
3. Goddess of writing and literature.
4. Reference is to the net of intricate correspondences of sound and meanings that form the structure of a poem.

and writing them down on a tablet
she laid them (ready) to hand.

TEMPLE
DESCRIBED

House, doorpost of the country,
    to Aratta a ferocious bull.[5]
House Kesh, doorpost of the country,
    to Aratta a ferocious bull.
Grown (to vie) with the hills,
    embracing heaven,
house, grown (to vie) with the mountains,
    lifting the head above the mountains,
opalescent like the deep,
    green like the hills!

Is anyone on his part
    as deserving of superiority as Kesh?
Has any mother borne, on her part,
    one (as) superior as Ashgi, its warrior?
Who laid eyes ever on one (as) superior   20
    as Nintur, its mistress?

(FIRST SECTION)

DESCRIPTION
CONTINUES

Good house, built in a good place,
House Kesh, built in a good place,
like a princely barge floating in the sky,
like a holy barge set with seat
    and "horns,"[6]
like the boat of heaven,
    the lordly crown of the mountains,[7]
like a well-braced boat-cabin
    having moved off from the bank.
House, roaring like an ox,
bellowing like a breed bull,[8]

5. The legendary city of Aratta stands here for the inimical eastern highlands. That Kesh is a "doorpost" for the country presumably means that it was located near the eastern border and, like a door locked against intruders, would keep out enemies. As for the bull image, one may note that a temple on the top of a foundation platform or a stage tower was sometimes ornamented with two large horns issuing from its sides. This would seem to have been the case with Kesh.

6. The horns and the square building in between would present an outline not unlike that of a boat sailing in the sky. The two horns would represent the horn-shaped prow and stern of the standard Sumerian boat, the house in between the cabin.

7. Reference is to the new moon, which in the Orient lies on its back so that it resembles a boat, and also to a special shape of crown worn by the lord or priest-king, the *en.*

8. Reference is to the music and chanting performed in the temple.

inside the innermost of the house
is the heart of the country
inside its back room   30
    is the life's breath of Sumer.[9]
House, great corners thrust against the sky,
right good house, great side walls
    thrust against the sky,
house, great crown thrust against the sky,
house, a rainbow thrust against the sky.[10]

House, the lordly crown of which
    is worn (up) in heaven's midst,
the foundation terrace of which
    is filled into the deep,
the shadow of which
    covers all lands.
House founded by An,
    praised by Enlil,
divination for which
    was performed by Nintur.[11]

House Kesh, in (full) bloom pleasing!   40

Is anyone, on his part,
    as deserving of superiority as Kesh?
Has any mother borne, on her part,
    one (as) superior as Ashgi, its warrior?
Who laid eyes ever on one (as) superior
    as Nintur, its mistress?

(SECOND SECTION)

FOUNDATIONS   House, six hundred cubic *iku* above (ground),
                   three hundred cubic *iku* below (ground),
               House, ten cubic *iku* above ground,
                   five *iku* below.[12]

    9. The "innermost," literally the "heart," of the house was the living quarters. The "back" room appears to have been very specially the domain of the lady of the house, her "boudoir."
    10. The reference is to the temple on top of the foundation platform which lifted it up—side walls and corners—toward the sky. The rainbow metaphor may refer to a domed roof and brilliant coloring. For this latter possibility cf. the metaphor in l. 49.
    11. Divination before beginning the construction of a temple to make certain that conditions were favorable was an indispensable part of the undertaking.
    12. What exactly these lines refer to is not too clear. Tentatively I have assumed that they compare the volume of the structure above ground with the volume of fill between the foundations below. The

House, bison above ground, stag below.
House, mouflon above ground,
  wild billy goat below.
House, piebald mouflon above ground,
  graceful wild billy goat below.

House, rising like the sun above,   50
  spread like moonlight below.
House, a noble *mēsu* tree above, a sappy cedar below.
House, mountain above ground,
  below, the springs of the deep.[13]
Is anyone, on his part,
  as deserving of superiority as Kesh?
Has any mother borne, on her part,
  one (as) superior as Ashgi, its warrior?
Who laid eyes ever on one (as) superior
  as Nintur, its mistress?

(THIRD SECTION)

THE TEMPLE'S   It is, too, a storm cloud,
DEMANDS   is, too, a storm cloud,
              who can know its heart?
        The house Kesh is, too, a storm cloud,
          is, too, a storm cloud,
          who can know its heart?
        Inside it warrior(-priests)   60
          set things to right,
        perform with great correctness
          the divinations.
        The house is rounding up
          only unblemished oxen,
        the house is consuming hundreds of oxen[14]
        the house is consuming hundreds of sheep
        it is . . . . . its "head" is washed[15]
        all (rulers on) throne daises
          are presenting their tribute.

---

first line would then deal with the temple as a whole, the second with the temple on top of the foundation terrace or series of terraces, and with the part of the foundation corresponding to it below.

13. I omit l. 53, which is merely secondary elaboration of a rubric that had strayed up into the text.

14. The round number used in the Sumerian is 3600. We have rendered it "hundreds."

15. Not clear; the line is damaged.

It wears a crown (to vie) with the boxwood tree,
it spreads out (to vie) with the poplar, is broad,
it is greening (to vie) with the hills.[16]

Is anyone, on his part,   70
    as deserving of superiority as Kesh?
Has any mother borne, on her part,
    one (as) superior as Ashgi, its warrior?
Who laid eyes ever on one (as) superior
    as Nintur, its mistress?

(FOURTH SECTION)

ITS DIVINE   House giving birth to lions[17]
INHABITANTS   its heart, a warrior, inscrutable,
                   House Kesh giving birth to lions,
                        its heart a warrior, inscrutable,
                   Inside it warrior-priests
                        set things to right.[18]

                   Ninhursaĝa, uniquely great,[19]
                        acts as midwife.
                   Nintur, the great mother
                        sets birthgiving going.
                   Shulpae,[20] the plowman
                        . . . . s lordship.
                   Ashgi,[21] the warrior,   80
                        is eating . . . .
                   Urumash, the great high constable,
                        . . . . with him in the desert,
                   is rounding up stags and oxen for the house.

                   Is anyone, on his part,
                        as deserving of superiority as Kesh?

16. Reference is to the groves of trees beside the temple on the platform.

17. By mentioning the most awesome of the creatures to the birth of which the temple contributes, the author undoubtedly intends to suggest its own awesomeness.

18. That is, by divination they find out the answers to questions and the right course of action to take. As warrior-priests they are in tune with the temple's warrior heart. Cf. l. 60.

19. Ninhursaĝa and Nintur were mostly considered but different names for one and the same goddess. This is obviously the case here. Occasionally it seems that a distinction could be made, using the name Ninhursaĝa for the goddess in her aspect as member of the ruling cosmic triad An, Enlil, and Ninhursaĝa, the name Nintur for her in her aspect as birth goddess.

20. The husband of Nintur.

21. Ashgi was a son of Nintur.

Has any mother borne, on her part,
>one (as) superior as Ashgi, its warrior?
Who laid eyes ever on one (as) superior
>as Nintur, its mistress?

(FIFTH SECTION)

GATE AND House standing on the socle
DOORS >like the rising sun,
goring(?) like a white aurochs
>in the desert,[22]
house founded by a prince,
>praised with *tigi*-harps,
inside the innermost part of the house   90
>is the heart of the country,
inside its back rooms
>is the life's breath of Sumer,[23]
⟨its gate is lions
>resting on their paws,⟩[24]
inside its gate
>a great nation is settled,
inside the doorleaf of the house
>is a great independent country
>not ever turning tail,
inside its bolt
>is a great aurochs
>perfect in beauty,
its (well)-stocked storehouse
>is the corners of heaven
>and the corners of earth,[25]
its *gigunu* is founded
>on *lahamu*[26] pilasters,
its princely outer wall
>guarding the house
>is . . . . garrisoned.

22. The temple on the platform, apparently whitewashed, is compared first to the sun appearing over the mountains, then, because of its horns, to the white aurochs.

23. See n. 9.

24. This line breaks the pattern and is clearly not original.

25. A bit of hyperbole. It pretends that the storehouses reach from the earth to heaven so that their corners are as large as the four cosmic corners that traditionally made up the sky.

26. Mythical guardian beings. Images of them were standard metopes for temples on stage towers.

Is anyone, on his part,
    as deserving of superiority as Kesh?
Has any mother borne, on her part,   100
    one (as) superior as Ashgi, its warrior?
Who laid eyes ever on one (as) superior
    as Nintur, its mistress?

(SIXTH SECTION)

HUMAN   The holy house,
STAFF   the prolificator of which
                 is the bedroom,
             the holy house Kesh,
                 the prolificator of which
                 is the bedroom,
             the house—its *en*-priests[27]
                 are Anunnaki gods,
             its *nuesh* priests are Eanna's carvers,[28]
             the kings brings stone jars,[29]
             the good *en*-priest[30]
                 has on the robe of office,
             the *atu* has taken the crozier
                 in hand,[31]
             the *tu* is bringing the gathered waters,[32]   110
             the *lale*[33] is seated in the holy place,
             the *enkum*[34] priests are casting
                 spells on the ground,
             the anointed ones are beating
                 the (drum)skins:

27. The *en* traditionally heads the priestly contingent of a temple's personnel and acts as divine bridegroom of the goddess he serves in the rite of the sacred marriage. Here his responsibilities for fertility fit in well after the preceding lines.

28. Little is known about the function of this priest. Here he acts as "carver," the person who carved and served meat.

29. It was customary for the major temples to send an empty stone bowl to the reigning king, who would then return it filled. The rite was called bur-gi$_4$-a "returning the stone bowl."

30. The rendering of this title as "the good *en* priest" is possible but not certain.

31. This is according to the later version. The oldest source seems to have "is standing at the loom."

32. Bringing the gathered waters refers elsewhere to bringing water from both the Euphrates and the Tigris for cultic purposes (cf. the description of Enmerkar's morning ritual in "Enmerkar and the Lord of Aratta" ll. 311f.).

33. *lale* is a shortened form for a term for "midwife."

34. The *enkum* priest also served Enki in Eridu and Nanshe in Ninâ. See above the "Hymn to Nanshe," n. 28. They seem to have been experts in spells and incantation. From elsewhere we know that spells were recited to facilitate birth.

"House be solidly founded!
   City be solidly founded!"[35]
   they are singing.
The horns of aurochses[36]
   resound.
The *algasurru* instruments
   sounds their ratatat.
The good prince plays the *tigi*-harp
   for her.
The house is built;
   its delightfulness is sweet.
The house Kesh is built;
   its delightfulness is sweet.
Its mistress has sat down at its wine,[37]   120
Ninhursağa, its mistress,
   has sat down at its wine.
Is anyone, on his part,
   as deserving of superiority as Kesh?
Has any mother borne, on her part,
   one (as) superior as Ashgi, its warrior?
Who laid eyes ever on one (as) superior
   as Nintur, its mistress?

(SEVENTH SECTION)   125

KESH OFFERS   To the city, to the city clients come
REFUGE   seeking clientage,
                 to the house Kesh and the city clients come
                    seeking clientage,
                 to its warrior Ashgi, clients come,
                    seeking clientage,
                 to its mistress Nintur clients come,
                    seeking clientage.
                 Kesh is built! Praise be Ashgi!   130
                 Praise be Kesh! Praise be Nintur!

(EIGHTH SECTION)

35. At a guess this might have been a blessing with "house" and "city" metaphors for the good fortune of a newborn child.
36. Here designating musical instruments.
37. The hostess, or the senior woman in the family, traditionally served the wine at meals.

The Cylinders of Gudea

PROVENIENCE

Cylinders A and B of Gudea, ruler of the Lagash region in southern Mesopotamia, formed the middle and end parts of an original trilogy entitled "The house of Ningirsu having been built . . . . "[1] They were written around 2125 B.C. to celebrate Gudea's building of a new version of the temple Eninnu for the god Ningirsu in the then capital of the region, Girsu. Girsu is the modern site of Tello, which was excavated by a series of French archeological expeditions, the first of which was undertaken in 1877. Unfortunately very little of the actual remains of Gudea's building was recovered.

LOST CYLINDER X

The first part of the original trilogy is now lost. It consisted most likely of hymns with general praise of the temple and of Ningirsu; but it probably also told of events leading up to the decision to build, explaining why a fairly recent existing structure built by Gudea's father-in-law, Ur-Baba, was deemed insufficient. It may also have told of the election of Gudea as ruler by the city god, Ningirsu.

CYLINDER A

The middle part of the trilogy, Cylinder A, follows in its presentation a set pattern known to us also from later accounts of temple building. It consisted of (1) permission by Enlil, the highest god of Sumer, whose consent was a sine qua non for any such undertaking, (2) commission to the human ruler to build, given to him by the god of the temple in question, and only then (3) an account of the actual building operation. In Cylinder A this pattern is worked out in unusually great detail, with much stress on Gudea's conscientiousness in carrying out his sacred task in the most perfect manner. Following Enlil's permission, Ningirsu calls for the realization of the promise, and Gudea, sensing that divine demands are being made upon him, seeks a revelatory dream to guide him. The dream he

---

1. That this was its name was first recognized by A. Shaffer.

obtains is given in barest outline so as not to anticipate too much the full version of it that is to follow. It conveys Ningirsu's command to Gudea to build but leaves him in uncertainty as to what exactly the god has in mind, the precise nature of the temple wanted. He therefore seeks help from Ningirsu's sister, the goddess Nanshe in Nina, an ancient city some twenty miles or so southwest of Girsu, now covered by the mound of Zurghul. Nanshe explains the dream to him but also advises him to seek further enlightenment from Ningirsu in a second dream. In this second dream the god describes his different temples and their special character, ending with Eninnu and what it stands for. Gudea, thus enlightened, can now go ahead with preparations for the building, calling up labor contingents, procuring the necessary building materials from abroad, fashioning a proper brick, and finally set hand to the actual work of building, which is described minutely, step by step.

CYLINDER B

The final part of the trilogy, Cylinder B, tells of the introduction of the god and his consort into their new home, of the awakening of the god the next morning, and of the subsequent organization of the household by Ningirsu, who sets the various minor gods who serve him about their tasks, thus instituting correctly the offices of the temple. After a description of gifts presented by Gudea, an outline of the ruler's functions in the administration of the temple, descriptions of furniture in it, and of festivities at the conclusion of the work on it, the account ends with a report of a housewarming party given by Gudea for Ningirsu and his guests, the major gods of Sumer, which marks the formal inauguration of the temple and serves as occasion for divine blessings upon it and upon its builder, Gudea.

SIGNIFICANCE

To appreciate the importance in the life of the ancients of the events here told, one should keep in mind first of all that the god Ningirsu was the power in, and to, the yearly spring rains and the rise of the rivers in flood, on which pasturage and irrigation agriculture—and with them the economic survival of man—depended.

The temple, second, was intensely sacred. It was not only the abode of the god and thus visual assurance of his presence in the community; far more important, it was a medium through which the god exercised his cosmic functions, and it was even, in a mystical sense, one with him. The element Ninnu in Eninnu, "house Ninnu," is a name of Ningirsu, and the full form of the temple's name, É-Ninnu-^{d}Imgud-babbara, identifies it with him in his early, preanthropomorph form of thunderbird: "house Ninnu, the flashing thunderbird." Correspondingly Ningirsu himself in Gudea's second dream directly refers to the temple as the thunderbird (xi.3), and so does Gudea in his blessing of it (xx.4). Its building accordingly brings about the very phenomena, rains and flood, in and to which the god is the power.

Cylinder A

DECISION
IN DIVINE
ASSEMBLY
	Upon the day for making of decisions[2]
	    in (matters of) the world,[3]
	Lagash in great office
	    raised the head,[4]
	and Enlil looked at Lord Ninĝirsu truly,
	was moved to have the things (to him) appropriate
	    appear in our city.[5]
		i.1

The heart was moved to overflow,
Enlil's heart was moved to overflow,
the heart was moved to overflow,
the towering flood wave
    with sparkle laden
    and awesome glory,
Enlil's heart, the very river Tigris,
    was moved to bring sweet waters![6]

2. Decisions about human affairs and the general administration of the cosmos were made regularly in assemblies of the gods under Enlil's leadership. The reference here is to such a session in Gudea's reign, shortly before he was called upon to build, probably the first one slated after the decision was made to appeal to Enlil for a new temple for Ninĝirsu.

3. The Sumerian phrase translated "world" means literally "within heaven and earth" and refers to the space between them, for which English has no convenient term. The assembly should be seen as one of regular managerial meetings for discussion and decision by the gods who ran the world, much as the administering of an estate on earth would be coordinated by such meetings.

4. The gesture of raising the head has different meanings according to the context. Basically it is a means of calling attention to oneself, but such a demand for attention may be a matter of pride, a demand for recognition, or, very differently, a plea for help, as e.g., in a situation of needing lodging (see below, "Lament for Ur," n. 32). It can also, in an assembly, indicate a wish to be recognized by the chair, usually, it seems, to volunteer for some task (see above, "Hymn to Kesh," n. 2). Lastly, it may represent the lifting of the head toward a desired goal and denote eagerness (see l. 15, below, and "Hymn to Inanna," above, l. 186f).

5. Conceivably the contrast between Lagash (al Hiba), proud of its performance in its high sacred office, and Girsu (Tello), frustrated because it is without a proper temple, moves Enlil to compassion. More likely is, though, that Lagash acts to call attention to its region, which includes Girsu.

The thing "appropriate" is achieved in col. xvii.25 of Cylinder A with the molding of the correct brick for the temple. Consonant with the temple's thunderbird character, the clay for the bricks was taken from a pit presided over by the thunderbird (xiii.22), and preserved instances of the baked bricks used are stamped with its image. The "our" of "our city" refers to the narrator and his city Girsu.

6. Ll. 5–9 constitute a brief lyrical interlude praising Enlil's generosity in allowing the building of the temple. The Sumerian word for "heart" (šà[g]), which can be used more generally for "inside," "core," "center," refers here to the core stream of a river, which widens at flood time to fill a broader bed with banks much farther apart. It is also used for the human heart as the seat of will and emotion, and so the river image, playing on this latitude of meaning, serves for the emotion of benevolence and

GUDEA CALLED
UPON TO BUILD

The owner of the house called for it,   10
was taking action for Eninnu's offices
   to make appearance in the world,
and the ruler, as a man of great perception,
   was lending ear;
paid his respects with all great things,
directing hither a fit bull
   and a fit kid.[7]

FIRST DREAM
IN BRIEF

The brick decided on raised the head toward him,
craned its neck toward him (in eagerness)
   to build the holy house,
and in the nightly vision, as Gudea
   saw that day his master Lord Ninĝirsu,
(t)he (latter) spoke to him about his house
   and the building thereof,
turned to him about Eninnu's offices,   20
   which all are great.

Since (what was in) his heart was not to fathom,
Gudea wearied of the matter:
"Surely I should tell her!
   surely I should tell her!
May she stand by me in this matter.
The princely office entrusted it to me,
   I being the shepherd,
and yet, the heart (of the matter)
   of what the nightly vision brought me
I do not grasp!—
Let me take my dream to my mother,
and may my dream-interpretress,   ii. 1
   an expert at her specialty,
my Nanshe, the sister in Siratr,[8]
reveal the heart of it to me."

---

generosity, much as in the English phrase "the heart flows over." From the meaning "core," "center,"
derives also that of "heart of the matter" and "precise intent," in which it is used in the following. For
the mythopoeic concepts underlying the reference to the Tigris as Enlil's heart see below, n. 42. The
equating of the permission to build Eninnu with the bringing of fresh waters refers to the connection of
that temple with the yearly flood.

7. Gudea, sensing that something is demanded of him, prepares to have an oracular dream to
enlighten him and brings the needed sacrificial animals for the rite.

8. Siratr was the name of Nanshe's temple in Ninâ. The traditions of the Lagash region made her
Ninĝirsu's sister and assumed that Eridu was her native city.

JOURNEY TO NINÂ	In his barge he decided to set foot, and the boat sailed down the Idninashdu[9] toward Ninâ, her city, joyfully cleaving the waves on the river.

STOPOVER
IN BAGARA

After he had reached Bagara,[10]
    the house overhanging the river,
he offered up loaves of bread, libated cold water,
went before Bagara's owner, and hailed him:
"Warrior, rampant lion,   10
    having none that could oppose,
Ningirsu, high-ranking in (Eridu's) Apsû,[11]
paramount in Nippur,[12]
Warrior! You have commanded me,
    but (do) let me set hand to it
    right for you!
Ningirsu, let me build your house for you,
and to perfection institute
    the offices for you.
May your sister, the child born to Eridu,
paramount in her specialty,
    queen, and the gods' dream interpretress,
my Nanshe, the sister in Siratr,
guide the foot for me in this!"

His cry having been heard,   20
his master, Lord Ningirsu,
accepted from Gudea his prayer and plea.
In the house of Bagara he celebrated
    the weekly holiday.[13]

TO GATUMDUG
IN LAGASH

The ruler took his bedding over to Gatumdug,[14]
    offered up loaves of bread, libated cold water,

9. The name means "river going to Ninâ." It flowed from Girsu (Tello) over Lagash (al Hiba) with Bagara, to Ninâ (Zurghul) and on into the marshes.

10. A temple for Ningirsu located on the river at Lagash.

11. Name of Enki's domain, the freshwater ocean thought to underlie the earth, name also of Enki's temple in Eridu. Ningirsu—perhaps represented by his statue—undertook a yearly journey there for cultic purposes.

12. City of Enlil and the chief religious center of Sumer.

13. The Sumerian term is *eshesh*. It was celebrated on the first, seventh, fifteenth, and twenty-fifth day of each month.

14. Gatumdug was the city goddess of Lagash. Her character and function is not known with certainty, but there is some suggestion that she was a goddess of birthgiving. See n. 16. Gudea was apparently hoping that he might have a dream to guide him. Since nothing is said, he was probably disappointed.

went before holy Gatumdug,
said a prayer to her:

"You, Milady, child born to holy An,
paramount in her specialty,
   an uplifting tutelary deity,
living in the nation,[15]   iii.1
informing her city of what would not be seemly,
are queen and mother of settled Lagash;
moist winds and abundance
   is but your having looked toward the people,
and for a trusty lad on whom you have looked
   life lengthens.
I have no mother—you are my mother,
I have no father—you are my father,
you implanted in the womb the germ of me,
   gave birth to me from out the vulva (too),
sweet, O Gatumdug, is your holy name![16]

"Tonight I lay me down here,   10
your are my great (protective fence of) camelthorn,[17]
   lie up against my side,
you are *zahgibar* wheat planted in great waters
and so put life's breath in my insides,[18]
a broad sunshade you are—beneath your shade
let me cool off,
and may the right-hand palm
   of your (two) august hands,
Milady Gatumdug, lend me protection!

"I am going to the city—may my portents be propitious!
To the mountain rising from amidst the waters,
   to Ninâ,[19]

15. I.e., near and approachable to man.
16. Gudea's figurative language, ascribing the role of both father and mother to the goddess, is intended to convey that he relies on her love and help as does a child on that of its parents. Similar phrasing occurs elsewhere. The stress on physical parenthood could be due to a presumption that the bond it creates is stronger than that of parenthood by adoption, but it is also possible that Gatumdug was a birth goddess and that Gudea refers to her as helping at his birth. His divine mother was the goddess Ninsuna.
17. A ring of gathered camelthorn around a tent or outlying house would serve both as defense and as storage of fuel.
18. In the irrigation agriculture then practiced, the fields were flooded at regular intervals during the growing of the grain. By providing nourishment the grain is life-giving.
19. The tall mound covering ancient Ninâ is still visible over the surrounding marsh and its waters from a great distance. The epithet is used also in "The Nanshe Hymn." See there, n. 1.

may your friendly genius go before me,   20
and may your friendly guardian angel
    walk with me in the road!

"Surely I should tell her!
Surely I should tell her!
may she stand by me in that matter.
Let me take my dream to my mother
    and may my dream interpretress,
        expert at her specialty,
my Nanshe, the sister in Siratr,
    reveal the heart of it to me!"

His cry having been heard,
his mistress, holy Gatumdug,   iv. 1
accepted from Gudea his prayer and plea.

TO NANSHE   To set foot in his barge he decided,
IN NINÂ   and (heading) toward her city Ninâ,
                 the boat moored at Ninâ's quay.
             The ruler raised the head
                 in Siratr's courtyard,
             offered up loaves of bread, libated cold water,
             went before Nanshe and hailed her:

"O Nanshe, queen and high-priestess,[20]
    queen and lustration-priestess,[21]
    guardian angel and dear tutelary deity,
queen making (as final) decisions
    as Enlil,
my Nanshe—being that your word is true,   10
and being that it does take precedence,
you are the gods' interpretress of dreams,
and are the queen of all lands!
    Mother, today my subject[22]
    is a dream:

DREAM   "The first man in the dream,
TOLD   —the enormity of him was like the heavens,
         the enormity of him was like the earth,
         he, being according to his head a god,
         according to his wings the thunderbird,[23]

20. The Sumerian term is *en.*
21. The Sumerian term is *ezeb.*
22. Literally "my word," i.e., "what I have to say."
23. The name is read as Imdugud or as Anzu by scholars.

and to his lower parts the floodstorm;
—right and left of him lay lions—
bade me build his house,   20
but (what was in) his heart
    I failed to grasp.

"Daylight came forth for me
    from the horizon.

"The first woman—whate'er relation of his
    she was or wasn't—
coming to the fore, had places with sheaves
    made on her,
she held a stylus of fine silver
    in the hand,
set a tablet (treating) of the stars above
    on the knee,
and was consulting it.   v.1

"The second man was a warrior,
he was mighty of strength,
    he held a
    lapis lazuli tablet in the hand,
was setting down the plan of the house.

"In front of me a holy basket stood,
a holy brick mold had been readied,
and the brick decided on
    was in the brick mold for me.

"O'er a fine white poplar,
    on which my eyes were riveted,
bird-men made *tigid*-vases[24]
    let sparkling waters flow and flow,

and my master's off[25] donkey stallion   10
    was pawing the ground for me."

DREAM
INTERPRETED

Unto the ruler his mother Nanshe made answer:

"My shepherd, let me interpret
    your dream for you:

---

24. The *tigid* vase was a vessel for pouring water. The dream image should probably be visualized in the light of Gudea's stone tub and the Stele of Ur-namma, which show mythopoeic representations of the rain clouds as flying winged human beings pouring down water from vases they hold in their hands.
25. I.e., the donkey on the driver's right.

"Being that the man—
   according to the enormity like the heavens,
   the enormity like the earth,
since according to the head a god,
   and to his wings
the thunderbird, and since according to his lower parts
   the floodstorm,
at whose right and left lions lay—
was surely my brother Ningirsu,
he will have spoken to you
   about the building of his shrine Eninnu.[26]

"The daylight that came forth for you
   on the horizon
was your tutelary god Ningishzida;[27]   20
he is able, all through this,
   to come forth for you on (far) horizons
   as did the daylight.
Being that the maiden coming to the fore,
   who had places with sheaves made on her,
who held a stylus of fine silver in the hand,
set a star tablet on the knee,
and consulted it,
surely was my sister Nidaba,[28]
she will have announced to you   vi.1
the holy star above for the building of the house.

26. That the man was Ningirsu and that he wanted Gudea to build his temple had been clear to Gudea from the first, as can be seen from his prayer in the Bagara, so on this point Nanshe only offers confirmation. In Gudea's vision of him here told, Ningirsu retains some of his early features: his enormity, his thunderbird wings, the lions beside him, and the fact that his figure below merges into that of a flood storm. See also "The Ninurta Myth Lugal-e," in which, renamed Ninurta, he is the main character.

27. Ningishzida was a chthonic deity, a god of the tree roots, often mythopoeically visualized as serpents. His name means "lord of the good tree," and he was one of the many dying gods identified with Damu/Dumuzi. See "In the Desert by the Early Grass." Gudea is being assured in the dream that in spite of Ningishzida's chthonic character he is able to come up anywhere in the world to further the undertaking of his ward. The reference to the horizon undoubtedly has specific bearing on Gudea's need to procure exotic materials for the building project from distant lands.

28. Nidaba was the goddess of grasses, both of the grains and of the reeds. Since the scribe's stylus was cut originally from a reed, she also became the goddess of writing and literature generally, including technical astronomical texts. In visual representations of her and other vegetation goddesses bundles of reeds or sheaves of grain are usually shown protruding from the shoulders or the body of her otherwise human form. The star she announces is presumably the one which by its heliacal rising marked the beginning of the month suitable for building operations. This would normally have been the Aldebaran in Taurus, which announced the month of brickmaking and building *Sig₄-ga*, Akkadian *Simānu*, i.e., July/August.

"The second (man)—he was a warrior,
  was mighty of strength,
who held a
  lapis lazuli tablet in the hand,
will have been Ninuruda,[29]
  he was copying
  the plan of the house.

"Being that in front of you a holy basket stood,
  a holy brick mold had been readied,
and the brick decided on
  was in the brick mold,
that surely was the right brick of Eninnu.

"According to (the fact) that o'er a fine white poplar,
  on which your eyes
  steadily were,
tigid-vase bird-men   10
  let sparkling waters flow,
sweet sleep will not come in your eyes
  for (zeal in) building (of) the house.[30]

"According to (the fact)
  that the off donkey stallion
  of your master
  was pawing the ground for you,
it will have been you: Like a steed
  you are pawing the ground
  (impatient) to get at Eninnu.

"Let me advise you—and may you take my advice:

NANSHE ADVISES   "When you have bent your steps to Girsu,
GIVING A   unto the foremost shrine of Lagash land,
CHARIOT   broken the seals upon your storehouse
         and laid out from it wood,
       have built in sturdy fashion
       a chariot for your master,

---

29. Ninuruda(k) is a minor deity, the precise nature and function of whom is still to be determined. Here he is engraving a stone tablet, in Cylinder B iv.4 he censes the temple, and in vi.3 he wakens the temple in the morning. This might suggest that he was a god of copper and copper implements, informing the copper burin, the copper thurifer, and the copper gong, which would agree with his name, since *Ninuruda(k)* means "lord of the copper." Such an interpretation must, however, remain conjectural until more data are available. His name can also be read *Nindub*.

30. The poplar, growing as it is watered by the rains, is clearly symbolic of the temple which is to rise under Gudea's ever-watchful eyes.

hitched up to it a donkey stallion,
adorned that chariot with
    fine silver and lapis lazuli,
made arrows protrude   20
    from the quiver like rays,[31]
taken care with the *enkar* mace,[32]
    enabler of war deeds,
fashioned his beloved standard for him,
and signed your name upon it, (then)

USHUMGAL-
KALAMMA TO
TAKE IT IN

"when Ushumgalkalamma, his (well)-beloved harp,
the renowned psaltery, his counselor,[33]
has gone in with it in the flashing thunderbird,
    Eninnu,[34]
unto the (ever)-gift-loving warrior,   vii.1
your master Ninĝirsu,

NINĜIRSU
APPEASED; WILL
REVEAL PLAN
AND OFFICES
OF NEW TEMPLE

"then he will accept from you
    your slightest word as weighty;
the heart of the lord,
    unfathomable as inmost heaven,
of Ninĝirsu, son of Enlil,
    will become appeased for you;
he will reveal to you
    the design of his house,[35]
and the warrior will hail for you
his offices, all great."[36]

GUDEA OBEYS

The able shepherd Gudea
was greatly knowing,   10
and great too at the carrying out, (so)
to the words that Nanshe spoke to him
he nodded.

---

31. The chariot, a war chariot, would have a quiver for bow and arrow fixed behind its protective front shield.

32. The specific form of this kind of mace is not known.

33. Harp music was effective in calming emotional turmoil and so made rational action possible. Temple harps were therefore considered the counselors of the deities to which they belonged, and they were often deified.

34. As mentioned in the introduction, there was mystical identity between the temple and its god Ninĝirsu in his pre-anthropomorph form of thunderbird.

35. On the problem here, see n. 46, below.

36. The reference is to Ninĝirsu's listing of his offices in Gudea's second dream, as told below in col. x.

CHARIOT CON-
STRUCTION
	On his storehouse he broke the seals,[37]
	laid out from it wood;
	the wood Gudea supervised repeatedly,
	did treat the wood with care:
	headed the *mēsu* trees nicely,
	dressed the *haluppu* oaks,
	built them in sturdy fashion
	    into a chariot for him (Ning̃irsu),
	hitched unto it
	its donkey stallion,
	    Pirig̃kasepada,[38]
	fashioned for him
	    his beloved standard,
	signed his name on it,
		
		21
		20

USHUMGAL-
KALAMMA TAKES
IT IN
	and Ushumgalkalamma
	    that beloved harp,
	the renowned psaltery,
	    his (Ning̃irsu's) counselor,
	went in with it in the flashing thunderbird,
	    Eninnu,[34]
	to the gift-loving warrior,
	his master, Lord Ning̃irsu.
		
		26–27

GUDEA HIMSELF
ENTERS. CON-
TINUES VISITS
	He (himself) in joy
	    went into the house to him.
	and from the shrine Eninnu in bright mood
	    Gudea was fain to come out.
	Thereupon day after day
	    along to the house he went,
	went about in it
	    night after night.
		30
		
		viii.1

NIGHT OF
SECOND DREAM
	Stilled were the day's noises,
	    the hubbub quieted down,
	snores were emitted
	    from the nose.	

37. The doors of storehouses were secured by ropes tied to pegs in the wall. The peg and the rope around it would be plastered over with clay over which cylinder seals were rolled. Thus no unauthorized forcing of the door could go unnoticed. Cf. n. 130.

38. The name means "lion revealed by (its) running." It most likely designated an actual live donkey that pulled the chariot used for carrying Ning̃irsu's statue, or perhaps emblem, on his ritual journeys.

Toward Shugalam, dread place,[39]
the place (from) where Ningirsu
   keeps an eye on all lands,
did the ruler have a milk sheep,[40]
   a fat-tail sheep, and a grain-fed kid
   lie down on the skin
   of a virgin female kid.
With juniper, the mountains' holy plant,   10
   he filled the fire,
and as (true) cedar perfume, scent of godliness,
it threw its smoke.

GUDEA'S
PRAYER

After he had (thus) censed the master,
   he went off to him, hymned him,
went in to him in Ubshu'ukkinna,[41] saluted him (saying):
"O my master Ningirsu, lord,
   seminal waters reddened in the deflowering;
able lord, seminal waters
   emitted by the 'Great Mountain,'[42]
hero without a challenger,
Ningirsu, I am to build you your house,
but I have nothing to go by!
Warrior, you have called for 'the thing appropriate,'   20
but, son of Enlil, Lord Ningirsu,
the heart of the matter I cannot know.
Your heart, rising as
   (rise the waves in) midocean,
crashing down as (crash) the breakers,
roaring like waters
   pouring (through a breach in a dike),

---

39. A part of the temple, here part of the existing earlier Eninnu built by Ur-Baba. There was a Shugalam also in Ninurta's temple in Nippur. One may surmise that it is a term for a main, tripartite stairway leading up the front of a platform or stage tower toward the temple on top, specifically, perhaps, for a structure on the main landing of it.

40. I.e., a sheep fattened upon milk. It and the other animals mentioned were for sacrifice.

41. *Ubshu'ukkinna* is the name for a corner of the lower temple court which served as a place of assembly.

42. Ningirsu was son of Enlil, "the great mountain" (*kur-gal*) who engendered him on *Hursag*, later *Ninhursaga*, the near mountain ranges. Furthermore, he was in one of his major aspects god of the yearly flood in the Tigris, which is caused by the melting of snow and ice in the high mountains, the resulting waters carried down through the near ranges to the Tigris by mountain tributaries.

Mythopoeically this process was seen as Enlil's, the great mountain's, semen, Ningirsu, emitted from the highland and flowing into a virginal Ninhursaga, the near ranges, deflowering her, thus becoming reddened from her blood, i.e., the reddish and brownish clay carried in the floodwaters.

destroying cities like the floodwave,
rushing upon the enemy country like a storm,
O my master, your heart,   ix.1
    a torrent from a breach in a dike
    not to be stemmed;[43]
Warrior, your heart,
    unfathomable as inmost heaven,
Son of Enlil, Lord Ningirsu,
how can I know it?"

NINGIRSU
RESPONDS

Next, for the sleeper, for the sleeper,
at the head he stood, was briefly touching him:
"O you who are to build for me,
    O you who are to build for me,
ruler who are to build for me my house,
Gudea—for building my house
    let me give you the signposts
and let me tell you the pure stars above,   10
    (the heralds) of my appointed tasks.[44]

ENINNU

"The offices of my house, Eninnu,
    founded by An,
are great offices
    surpassing all (other) offices.
Espying from afar its owner, the house
has, as the thunderbird,
the heavens quake before its roar.
Thrust against heaven
    is its dread halo,

43. "Heart" is used by Gudea in its double meaning of core stream overflowing and of seat of tempestuous will and power.

44. The promises made to Gudea about guidance for his temple building by Nanshe, (vii.6 above) and here by Ningirsu will obviously have been kept. Yet it is not easy—at least for a modern reader—to see how that can have been the case. Nanshe predicted that Ningirsu would reveal the design of his house, and Ningirsu here promises "signposts" and indication of the star or stars connected with his appointed tasks, that is, indicating the times for the various rites of the temple. Yet in Ningirsu's long speech to Gudea none of this seems to be mentioned. There is no description of any plan, nor mention of any star. All he does is to describe himself and his functions, especially as they relate to his various temples. The awe Eninnu inspires and the rains its construction will bring are stressed, but that seems to be all. The only architectural information one can gather from it is that the temple is to have foundations, a temple terrace, and a house on top, but that seems far too general to have been of much help. All one can hope for, therefore, is that as we learn more about the ancients and about their ways of thinking and of conveying sacred information, the answer to the question may present itself. Could it be that a single term, as for instance "my kingly house," would have implied all that was needed, both plan and the star governing the work?

and over all lands hovers
     great awe of my house,
at (the mention of) its name
     all lands will gather,
     e'en from heaven's borders;
Magan and Meluhha[45]
     will come down from their mountains.

NINĜIRSU   "I, Ninĝirsu, am the seminal waters   20
     reddened in the deflowering,
the great warrior of Enlil's realm,
a lord without opponent.
My house (is) Eninnu,
     a towering cloud bank, o'ertopping the mountains,
my weapon (is) Sharur[46]
     laying the mountains (ready) to hand,
my fierce glance lifts not from the mountains,
from my pursuit escapes no man.

OFFICES: "My father who begat me gave me   x.1
WARRIOR OF   in great love as name
ENLIL   'King, flood storm of Enlil,
whose fierce glance
     is not lifted from the mountains,
Ninĝirsu, Enlil's warrior,'
and invested me with fifty offices.

STEWARD OF   "I carry the (serving) table,
AN   perform correctly the hand-washings,
my stretching forth the hand
     rouses holy An from sleep,
and the (very) best   10
     of the food in my hand, and it is good,
I give my father[47] who begat me to eat.
An, king of the gods,
gave me as name
     'Ninĝirsu, king, and steward of An.'[48]

---

45. Annals of Ashurbanipal from the middle of the sixth century B.C. identify Magan with Egypt, Meluhha with Ethiopia. Modern scholars tend to identify one or both of them with India.

46. *Sharur,* "the one who lays low multitudes," is Ninĝirsu's mythical weapon. See "The Ninurta Myth Lugal-e" n. 7; also Cyl. B vii.11–21, where it is called Lugalkurdub.

47. It is not clear whether "father" here refers to Enlil or—more likely perhaps—reflects a variant tradition according to which Ninĝirsu was the son of An.

48. The office of serving meals in the home fell traditionally to the oldest son of the house and was considered an honor.

TEMPLES: TIRASH	"Tirash[49] he founded for princely functions like the Apsû, therein, monthly at new moon, are great offices, my Ezenanna festival,[50] performed for me to perfection.

EHUSH	"Ehush,[51] my fierce place,
	he built like a fierce serpent
	    in a savage place,
	a place not spoken of
	    in regions that rebel against me.
	When my heart is waxing wroth at them
	it engenders venom for me
	    as will a serpent that has spent its gall.

EBABBAR	"In Ebabbar,[52] the place where I give out assignments, where I shine like the sun god, there I decide fairly, like Ishtaran,[53] my city's lawsuits.
BAGARA	"To the house Bagara, my place of the (bountiful) table, do all the gods of Lagash gather for me.

EFFECTS
FROM
BUILDING
ENINNU:
WORK STARTED
	"When to my house,
	    the house honored in all lands,
	the right arm of Lagash,
	the thunderbird roaring
	    on the horizon—
	Eninnu, my kingly house,
	O able shepherd Gudea,
	you put effectively the hand for me,
	I shall call up a humid wind
	that from above it bring for you abundance;

20 (EHUSH section)

xi.1 (EFFECTS FROM BUILDING section)

49. A temple for Ninĝirsu located, it would seem, on Girsu's northern border.

50. *Ezenanna* means "festival of heaven" or, since heaven and its god An are not distinguished in the writing, "festival of An." What the great offices performed on that occasion were is not known.

51. The location and special cult features of this temple are not known. The name means "ferocious house."

52. *Ebabbar*, "house rising sun," is a traditional name for temples of Utu, god of the sun and of justice. Both in Ararma (Akkadian Larsa, present day Senkereh) and Sippar (Abu-Habba) his temple is so named. The use of the name for a temple of Ninĝirsu, and his role there, shows that as upholder of justice Ninĝirsu was considered, as it were, a second Utu.

53. A god of justice. See the introduction to "In the Desert by the Early Grass."

and the people may spread hands with you
   on the abundance.

FOUNDATIONS   "May with the laying of the foundations   10
   of my house
abundance come!

(AGRI-
CULTURE)   All the great fields shall raise their hands
   (in appeal) to you,
dike and canal will crane their necks at you,[54]
and hills
   to which waters rise not,
waters will rise for you.

(HUSBANDRY)   Sumer will be able
   to pour surplus cream,
able to weigh out
   surplus wool.

FOUNDATION   "The day when my foundation terrace
TERRACE   you've filled in,
AND UPPER   the day you will put hand effectively
TEMPLE   to my house (proper),
   (then), after to the hills   20
      where dwells the north wind
I've bent my steps,
I'll have the man of the enormous wings,
   the north wind,
bring straight to you a rain
   from the pure zones, the foothills.
When that has given to the people
   newfound vigor,
then one man will do work
   as much as two.
At night moonlight will come forth for you,
and plenteous sunshine
   will come out for you.
   at high noon.
The days will build for you the house,   xii.1
nights make it grow for you.

IMPORTS   "*Haluppu* oaks from down south,
and *bihan*[55] wood, they will bring up for you.

---

54. I.e., eager for attention which they will need if the great volume of water they are to carry is to be controlled.
55. Neither of these woods has been precisely identified.

From up north cedar, cypress, and *supalu*[55] wood
   will of themselves, (unsought)
   be brought for you.
From in the mountain of the ebony trees
ebony trees
   will be brought for you.
From in the mountain of the stones
   great stones of the foothills
will be cut for you in slab form.
By then the fire   10
   will touch your borders[56]
and you will know
   forsooth my guideposts!"

GUDEA
AWAKENS

Gudea rose, it was a sleep,
he shuddered, it was a dream.
To Ninĝirsu's command
he nodded.
Into the white omen-kid he was reaching,[57]
had the omen, and his omen was propitious:
(What was in) Ninĝirsu's heart
stood out for Gudea (clear) as daylight.
Greatly knowing he was,   20
   and great too at the carrying out.

WORK BEGUN:
SITE CLEARED
IN IRENIC
MOOD

The ruler gave instructions
to his city as to one single man,
and Lagash land became of one accord for him
   as children of one mother:
(digging) sticks it took in hand,
   weeded up the thorns,
stacked the cut grass. (Harsh) words
   from all mouths he barred,
barred from that house (all) offense.
Prick and whiplash he undid   xiii.1
   from goad and whip,
and wool of mother sheep he put
   into (the overseer's) hands.
No mother with her child had words,
no child spoke to its mother
   saucily.

---

56. Before the building of a temple was begun the building plot would be cleansed by fire (cf. below, xii.25). Once the purifying fire had reached the borders of the building plot, building could begin.
57. The gods' will was supposed to be readable in the liver of a sacrificial kid.

The master of the slave who had obtained rent
    for the heddle.[58]
frowned not at him, and
the mistress of the slave girl
    naughtily acting
    to rival her with the master,
slapped not her face with anything.
Before the ruler building the Eninnu,   10
Gudea,
    no man let ominously words fall.[59]

CITY
PURIFIED

The ruler purified the city
and carried hither fire from it.
The ones sexually unclean, the horrors, the . . . .
he expelled from the city.

BRICK PIT
AND SHED
CHOSEN AND
EXPROPRIATED

Toward the brick-mold sheds
    he had an (omen-)kid lie down,
and the brick was revealed by the omen.
Approvingly he looked upon its brick pit,
and the shepherd, Nanshe's nominee,
    put it in the princely domain.[60]
Over the brick-mold shed which he designed,   20
and over the brick-pit,
    which he had put in princely domain,
he had, as emblems of his master,
thunderbirds as uprights spread (their wings).

SOIL OF SITE
PURIFIED WITH
FIRE

A mound (of earth of) up to twenty-four *iku*[61]
    the city was purifying for him,
it was cleansing the mound for him.

58. Apparently dishonest slaves typically made money for themselves by surreptitiously renting out their masters' looms and pocketing the rent.

59. The ancients believed that angry words and curses spoken at the birth of a person would be constitutive of that person's fate and condemn him or her to an unhappy and dismal life. Therefore women aiding at birth were careful to say only pleasant things.

The same, apparently, was the case with the "birth" of a temple; badmouthing during the building might destroy its holiness and powers or, perhaps worse, turn them in evil direction. Gudea is therefore careful to see to it that all occasions for anger or distress are done away with at work and in the city, even to induce families not to quarrel and not even to punish their servants' wrongdoing. He thus hoped for—and says he obtained—a period in which no words that could become bad omens for the future of the temple would be spoken.

60. Literally "put it in princeliness," which would seem to mean in this context that he expropriated it by eminent domain.

61. The *iku* was 3,528.36 m², somewhat smaller than an acre (5,047 m²). It is likely that the *iku* here meant is the "volume *iku*," i.e., the volume of earth from an *iku* dug to the depth of one *kush* (0.50 m.). The earth here referred to would be that from the foundation pit for the temple.

PRAYERS
OFFERED UP

With juniper, the mountains' holy plant,
    he filled the fire,
and as a cedar perfume, scent of godliness,
    it threw its smoke.
For him the day was there for prayer,
the night went by for him in hymning,
and to build Ningirsu's house   xiv.1
did the Anunnaki
    of Lagash land
stand by Gudea
in prayer and petition.
For the able shepherd, Gudea,
it was cause for rejoicing.

LABOR
LEVIED:
GU-EDINNA

At that time did the ruler
    impose a levy on his country,
in his district
    abounding in prime vines,
Ningirsu's Gu-edinna,[62]
he imposed the levy.   10

GUGISH-
BARRA

In his built-up cities
    and settled tracts,
Nanshe's *Gugishbarra*,[63]
he imposed the levy.

NINGIRSU'S
CLAN

In 'rampant bison
    which no one can oppose,
holding the white cedar mace
    for its king"
the clan of Ningirsu,
he let there be a levy for him,
and had its august standard *Lugalkurdub*[64]
    march at its head.

NANSHE'S
CLAN

In the maker of banks, maker of shores,
    (land) rising out of the waters,
the Idmah[65] river, the superabundant waters,   20
    spreading and spreading its abundance,

---

62. Gu-edinna "edge of the desert" was a fertile tract between Girsu and Umma often fought over by them.

63. Gugishbarra also seems to mean edge of the desert. It would have lain south of Gu-edinna, on the western border of the territory of Ninâ. The terms seems to mean specifically "edge of the gishbar plow arables."

64. "King shattering the mountains," another name for Sharur. See below, Cyl. B vii. 12ff.

65. The name means "the huge river." It has not been identified, but this passage shows that it must

the clan of Nanshe,
he let there be a levy for her,
and had "the holy prow" as Nanshe's standard
    march at its head.

INANNA'S   In "the snare stretched out
CLAN   for the beasts of the desert," and
              "the choice steeds of a renowned team,
                  the beloved team of Utu,"
              the clans of Inanna,
                  he let there be a levy for her,
              had, as Inanna's standard
                  the (Venus) disk march at their head.[66]

IMPORTS   To build Ningirsu's house
              [. . . . .]   xv.1
              [. . . .]
              [the] r[uler . . . .]
              [. . . . .] . . . .[. . . . . .]
              co[uld] put his hand [on.]
              The Elamite came to him from Elam,
              the Susian came to him from Susa,
              Magan and Meluhha in their mountains
                  loaded wood upon their shoulders for him
              and gathered, to build Ningirsu's house,
              to Gudea to his city Girsu.   10

FROM DILMUN   Ninzaga[67] was given commission,
              and his copper,
                  as were it huge grain transports,
              to Gudea, the man in charge
                  of building the house,
              he had conveyed.
              Ninsikila[68] was given commission,

---

be looked for in Nanshe's domain, that is to say, in the general vicinity of Ninâ (Zurghul). Most likely
it was a river draining off the marshes around Ninâ and flowing south in the direction of the Persian
Gulf.

66. It is not clear which part of the realm of Gudea this was, though apparently it was one which
contained a major temple of Inanna. The "team of Utu" refers to the span thought to pull the sun's
carriage across the sky.

67. Ninzaga, later known as Ensak or Inzag, was the chief deity of the island of Dilmun, a center of
the copper trade. See "Enki and Ninsikila/Ninhursaga," introduction.

68. Ninsikila "Lady of Lustrations" was the goddess of Dilmun. See "Enki and Ninsikila/ Ninhur-
saga," introduction.

and *haluppu* oaks, ebony,
　　and *abba* wood[69]
to the ruler building Eninnu
she had conveyed.

<table>
<tr><td>FROM
LEBANON</td><td>

To the mountain of cedars,
　　not for man to enter,
did for Lord Niĝirsu　　　　　　　　　　20
Gudea bend his steps:
its cedars with great axes he cut down,
and into Sharur,
　　the right arm of Lagash,
his master's flood-storm weapon,
he dressed them.
Like giant serpents floating on the water,
cedar rafts from the cedar foothills,
cypress rafts
from the cypress foothills,
supalu rafts　　　　　　　　　　　　31
from the *supalu* foothills,　　　　　　　30
great spruce trees, plane trees,
and *erānum* trees,
floating down in great rafts,
did at Kasurra's august quay
Gudea have moor　　　　　　　　　　xvi.1
for the lord Niĝirsu.[70]

</td></tr>
</table>

MOUNTAIN STONE

To the mountain of (mountain) stone,
　　not for man to enter,
did for the lord Niĝirsu
Gudea bend his steps,
cutting in slab form its great stones.

BITUMEN
FROM MADGA

In *hauna* boats and *nalua* boats,
abal bitumen and IGI.ESIR bitumen and gypsum[71]
from the foothills of Madga[72]
in cargoes, as if of grain boats　　　　10
　　coming from the fields,

---

69. This wood has not been identified.
70. The cedars were apparently floated down from Lebanon on the Euphrates and the Iturungal canal to Girsu.
71. What specific kinds of boats and bitumen these were is not known.
72. A region near the modern city of Kerkuk.

did Gudea have moor
for the lord Ninĝirsu.

COPPER DIS-
COVERED IN
KIMASH

To the ruler building Eninnu
great things offered themselves:
From Kimash[73] a copper mountain
revealed itself to him,
and he mined its copper
　　from its pockets.

GOLD, SILVER,
AND CARNELIAN

To the ruler, as man in charge of building
　his master's house,
gold was brought
in dust form from its mountains;   20
to Gudea they were bringing down
　　refined silver from its mountains,[74]
carnelian they were lavishing on him,
from Meluhha,
and from the alabaster mountains
　　they were bringing alabaster down to him.

SUPER-
VISING THE
CRAFTSMEN

Building with silver, the ruler
sat with the silversmiths,
building Eninnu with precious stones,
　he sat with the jewelers,
building with copper and tin,
Ninturkalamma[75] directed before him   29–30
the craftsmen and metal casters.

The two-hand stone
　roared for him like a storm,
the dolerite, the hand stone,
[did] the second and third [time   xvii.1
　going over][76]

RAINS

[. . . .]
[. . . .]

73. A mountain country, likewise in the general neighborhood of Kerkuk.

74. The locations of these mountains of gold and silver mines are not known.

75. This deity, obviously a patroness of craftsmen, does not seem to occur elsewhere. The name means "the country's Nintur." Since Nintur was the goddess of birthgiving, she may very well have had a form that aided in casting or sculpting statues, for which Sumerian could use the word (dú) "to give birth."

76. The heavier "two-hand" and lighter "(one)-hand" stones were tools for crushing and were used for shaping and dressing stone.

[his master, the lord Ninǧirsu]
[call]ed [up for him a humid wind],
and condensed for him
    the clouds.

GUDEA'S
ZEAL

For the sake of building
    the house for his master,
he slept not nights,
nor rested
    the head at noon.

For the one looked at truly by Nanshe,   10
a man after Enlil's heart,
the [. . . . . . .] ruler of Ninǧirsu,
Gudea, born from out an august vulva
by Gatumdug,
did Nidaba open   15–16
    the house of understanding,[77]
did Enki[78] put right
    the design of the house.

SITE
MEASURED

To the house whose halo
    thrusts against heaven,
whose offices embrace
    heaven and earth,
whose owner is a lord   20
    lifting fierce eyes,
the warrior Ninǧirsu,
    expert at battle,
(to) the flashing thunderbird,
    Eninnu,[79]
did Gudea pace from south
to north on the fired mound,
pace from north to south
    on the fired mound,[80]

77. The reference would seem to be to use of written sources, and Nidaba's house of understanding may mean "library" or "archive." Since, according to the next line, Gudea was preparing the plan of the temple, tables for computing and works relating to surveying may be what he would have consulted. This is strongly suggested by l. 21 of col. xix, below. Cf. "Enmerkar and the Lord of Aratta" n. 45. The possibility that "Nidaba's house of understanding" is a metaphor for "intelligence" cannot, however, be excluded.

78. Enki, in his form as Mushda(ma), was god of builders, and so would be particularly well qualified to help with the plan.

79. See n. 34, above.

80. I.e., on the mound of purified soil from the foundation pit. See above, xii.10, and n. 57.

laid the measuring cord down
　　on what was a true acre,[81]
put in pegs at its sides,
　　verified them himself.
It was cause of rejoicing
　　for him.

PRAYERS
BEFORE
BRICK-
MAKING

At eve to the old temple
　　he went to pray,
and from the dais of Ulnun[82]
the heart
　　was being eased for Gudea.[83]

xviii.1

Day dawned, he bathed,
arranged correctly his accoutrements,
and from (rain clouds of) abundance
　　the sun came out for him.
Next out into the cleansed city
　　Gudea came,
a perfect bull, a perfect kid, he sacrificed,
stepped up unto the house,
saluted.

BASKET AND
BRICK MOLD
TO THE PIT

The holy basket and true brick mold
　　decided on
he carried [from] E[ninnu,]
honey [and butter was (in a pail)]
　　hanging [from his hand;]
　　with lifted head he went,
in front of him Lugalkurdub walked,
and Igalima guided the foot for him.
His personal god, Ningishzida,
was holding hands with him.

10

14

CLAY
MOISTENED
AND MIXED

In the brick-mold shed he performed
　　the pouring of water,
and the water sounded to the ruler
　　as cymbals and *alu* lyres playing for him;

81. The Sumerian terms is *iku*, which is not quite an acre. See above, n. 63.

82. *Ulnun*, "the great firmament (of heaven)," was the name of Ningirsu's place of judgment on the Shugalam stairs (see xxii.22 and xxviii.18–19), a suitable name for the whereabouts of a god who manifested himself in the thundercloud. The reference here is obviously to the Ulnun of the old temple. The name is also read Girnun by modern scholars.

83. Conceivably it rained, and Gudea took that as a sign of Ningirsu's favor.

on the brick pit and its bricks
he drenched the top layer,
hoed in honey, butter, and sweet princely oil;   20
all kinds of essences, sundry woods,
he worked into the paste.[84]

CLAY PUT   The holy basket he lifted up,
INTO MOLD   set it down at the brick mold;
into the brick mold Gudea put the clay,
made "the proper thing" appear,
was establishing his name,
    making the brick of the house appear.[85]
On all lands he was the while
    sprinkling oil,
was sprinkling cedar perfume.[86]
Below him the people of his city   xix.1
    and Lagash land
were passing the day with him.

BRICK LAID   The brick form he took apart,
OUT TO DRY   laid the brick out to dry;
at the brick pit,
    and the clay of its mother trench,[87]
he looked kindly;
with herb-salve *hashur*-cedar essence,
    and minced herbs
he drenched the top (layer).
At his brick of the brick mold,
    which he had put down there,
Utu rejoiced,
and for his mother trench,   10
    rising like the Idmah river,
did king Enki decree fate.[88]
The brick he put (back) into the mold
    took it in its mold into the house.

---

84. That is, into the clay mixture from which the brick is to be made.

85. These lines are crucial for understanding what "the proper thing" was. They show that it denotes the correctly shaped brick suitable for the particular temple for which it was to be used. Cf. "The Nanshe Hymn," n. 3.

86. What is meant is probably that Gudea sprinkled the perfume in all directions.

87. The "mother trench" is the trench in which the clay for the brick had been mixed with water and honey, butter, oil, etc.

88. As god of fresh water.

BRICK	From the brick-mold shed
CARRIED	he lifted up the brick,
TO SITE	it was (like) the holy crown[89] worn by An,
	he lifted up the brick, carried it among his people,
	it was like Utu's holy team
	turning the heads (homeward),[90]
	the brick's lifting its head
	toward the house
	was like Nanna's cow
	ready to be hitched in its pen.

BRICK PLACED.	He placed the brick, paced off	
PLAN LAID	the house,	
OUT	laid out the plan of the house,	20
	(as) a very Nidaba knowing the inmost	
	(secrets) of numbers,	
	and like a young man	
	building his first house,	
	sweet sleep came not unto his eyes;	
	like a cow keeping an eye on its calf,	
	he went in constant worry to the house—	
	like a man who eats food sparingly	
	he tired not from going.	
	(What was in) the heart of his master	
	stood out for him (clear) as day,	
	the words of Niŋirsu stood planted	xx.1
	for Gudea like the uprights.[91]	

THIRD DREAM	In his jubilant house-builder's heart,
	joy, as had someone conveyed
	a propitious *kledon* oracle,
	was established for him.
	He inspected an omen kid, and his omen
	was propitious,
	on fresh waters he cast grain,[92]
	and its appearance was right.
	Lying down seeking a dream oracle, Gudea
	slept, and a message was forthcoming for him.

89. The brick was carried on the head.

90. The sun rides across the sky in his chariot. By evening his span is eager to get home to the stable.

91. The uprights of a house outline it.

92. Apparently a method for obtaining omens.

His master's house built,
Eninnu as it separated heaven and earth,[93]   10
was there for him in the vision,
it was cause for him for rejoicing.

MEASURING   The measuring line he snapped (taut) thereon,
FOR FOUN-   performed the office to perfection,
DATIONS   was setting out the temple close
                                in the sacred precinct.
Enki was filling in the foundation terrace[94]
    of the house for him,
Nanshe, child of Eridu,
    took care with the divination,[95]
the mother of Lagash, holy Gatumdug,
gave birth to its bricks
    amid cries to high heaven,[96]
and Baba, the queen, An's foremost child,
sprinkled upon them cedar-oil perfume.   20
At the house stood both *en* and *lagar* priests,[97]
performed correctly the offices for it.
The Anunnaki gods came stepping up to it
    to admire it.

FOUNDATIONS   Gudea, the man in charge of building the house,
LAID AND   placed the basket (with mortar) for the house
BLESSED   as a holy crown on (his) head,
laid the foundation, set down the walls thereon,
gave it a blessing:
    "The measuring line flips the bricks!"[98]
A second blessing he felt moved to give it: xxi.1
    "It is a vine aligning its fruits."[99]

93. The tall structure, seen on the horizon from afar, would look as if it reached from earth up to the sky.

94. Presumably in his capacity as builder god. See above n. 78.

95. Cf. "Hymn to Kesh," above, n. 8.

96. The phrase used is ambiguous. It can mean "amid cries to high heaven" or "as desired." I have preferred the former because of the verb used and assume that the cries are cries of birth pangs. The mythopoeic description of the making of bricks as a "birth" may well be due to Gatumdug's special character, supporting the suggestion that she may have been a goddess of birthgiving. See above, nn. 15 and 17.

97. See "Hymn to Kesh," nn. 22 and 23.

98. That is, it touches every brick, "The wall is straight." Probably less a statement of fact than a spell that will ensure the straightness of the walls to be built on the foundations.

99. The "fruits" of the "vine," that is, of the measuring line, are the bricks laid straight like cucumbers, squash, etc. growing on a vine.

A third blessing he felt moved to give it:
"A thunderbird it is, spreading the wing
   over the young one!"[100]
A fourth blessing he felt moved to give it:
"A young lion, embraced by
   a fierce lion, it is!"[101]
A fifth blessing he felt moved to give it:
"It is the blue sky carrying splendor!"
A sixth blessing he felt moved to give it:
"It is the sun arrived—laden with loveliness!"   10
A seventh blessing he felt moved to give it:
"Eninnu is like the moon at dawn,
   shining upon the country."[102]

GATE FRAMES
AND BRICK-
WORK

They placed the wooden door frames,[103]
it (looked as) were the blue heaven
   wearing a crown;
they sat down from (work
   on) the door frames,
it was (as) were the huge house
   embracing heaven;
the house was abuilding,
   laid against wood (scaffolding),
it was like Nanna's canebrake,
   heeded by Enki.[104]

THE HOUSE
ABUILDING

They made the house grow
   (high) as the foothills,

---

100. On the identity of temple and thunderbird see above n. 34. The blessing magically puts protectiveness into the temple, since that is what the bird's gesture signifies.

101. Essentially a repetition—and thus a strengthening—of the previous blessing with Ningirsu's variant pre-anthropomorph form, the lion, instead of the lion-headed thunderbird.

102. The import of these three final blessings is not clear. That the temple, as holding the god, might be identified with heaven which holds him as thunder cloud, might be considered, but the stress on heaven as the "blue," that is, cloudless, sky does not fit. Even more difficult is it to see why the temple would be compared to sun and moon. Here we must hope for some recurrence of the metaphor in a more enlightening context.

103. The terrace (*temen*) on which the summit temple stood was often constructed by building a prototype of it—including doors and other architectural details—on the foundations and then filling this prototype in with clean earth. We call such a prototype the "substructure." It would normally be encased in a mantle of baked brick (*kissa*; Akkadian *kisû*) to prevent rain damage. It is such a substructure, with its door frames and walls, that is described in the following.

104. The bricks, restrained by the planks of the scaffolding against which they were laid, are compared to Enki's waters in channels in the marshes following the lines of the canebrake.

had it float in heaven's midst   20
   like a cloud,
they had it, like a bull,
   slowly lift the horns,
had it raise the head over all mountains,
   like the *kishkānu*[105] tree of the Apsû.
The house lifted, like the (horizon's) foothills,
   the head 'tween heaven and earth,
a sappy cedar, grown among (low) weeds,
allure decked Eninnu abundantly
   among Sumer's brick structures.

TEMPLE COM-   They were setting up
PLEX PEGGED   the wood (scaffolding) in the house,
OUT   it was like the basilisks of the Apsû[106]
      coming out all together.
The climbing to be done
   on high walltops[107]
was (such as even) a huge serpent of the foothills   xxii.1
   might not perform.

REED LAYERS   The cut reeds of the house[108]
      were like the mountain snakes
      sleeping (winter sleep) together,
SUMMIT: its summit was adorned with sappy *hashur* cedars:
PILIER DE   White cedars they were laying
GOUDEA   in the cedar back room, its gazebo,[109]
   were treating them with care, with good perfume
      and oil galore.
CLAY CORE   On the upper surface
      of the terre pisée of the house,
      hand daubed as it was
      with the abundance of the Apsû,[110]
   they were perching the walls,

---

105. The *kishkānu* has not yet been identified.

106. The word translated "basilisk," *ushum*, is difficult. It denotes a much feared ophidian creature, perhaps semimythical. The comparison of it to long narrow boards would fit a snakelike creature.

107. The walls are those of the substructure.

108. Layers of reeds were used to ventilate wide walls and keep the brickwork dry.

109. Remnants of two substantial pillars of baked bricks which supported the gazebo were found by the excavators. While Cylinder A merely describes it as a "cedar back room" and gazebo, a place from which to look out, the inscription on the bricks from the pillars tells that it was a place where Ningirsu sat in judgment.

110. I.e., with water.

the shrine of Eninnu being (thus) placed
in the palms (?) of Heaven's hands.

ENINNU   The ruler built the house, it grew,
ABUILDING   like unto a great mountain   10
            it did grow.

FOUNDATION Its foundation terrace of the Apsû,
TERRACE   (as) a big mooring stake,
            he filled into the ground,
            with Enki in (his) house of the watery deep
            it doth consult.[111]
            Its foundation terrace of the sky,
                he made go around the house
                as a warrior,
            and where the gods drink
                it is drinking water.[112]

FOUNDATION Mooring stakes he firmly fixed for Eninnu,
FIGURINES; drove in their wizards.[113]
UPRIGHTS   Its uprights of sweet poplar he drove in,
            they cast their shadow.

---

111. The underground and aboveground terrace refers to the part of the filled-in substructure that was below ground and the part that was above ground. Building would start with the digging of a building pit in the bottom of which, in ditches dug for the purpose, the foundations were laid. From the top of the foundations, at the level of the floor of the building pit, rose the walls of the substructure. They carried up above the edges of the pit at ground level to a considerable height and were filled in with clean earth, forming the aboveground building terrace. On its top the fill would be sealed off with wet clay, terre pisée, and the actual temple would be built with the walls of the substructure as foundations for its walls. The lower part of the filled-in substructure is termed "of the Apsû" because it reaches down toward, or actually to, the water table, the Apsû. The upper part is "of the sky," reaching heavenward. The underground part of the terrace is here likened to an enormous mooring stake holding the temple above it steady, as a mooring stake holds a boat securely moored. The image probably sees it as the sum of individual mooring stakes in it. See n. 113.

112. The terrace encloses the structure. It may even have had a baked brick mantle, suggesting a warrior's armor. That it drinks water where the gods drink probably refers to the fact that libations made before the statues of the gods in the temple would be carried down into the substructure by drains in the floors of their cellas or other places of libation. The fact that more gods than just one are mentioned indicates probably that, besides Ningirsu and his wife, Baba, some of the minor gods in his entourage had their own places of worship in the temple.

113. Since the temple foundations reached down to the water table, floated as it were, on the subterranean ocean, the Apsû, it was necessary to moor it. This was done by metal pegs driven into the ground through metal rings securely embedded in the brickwork of the temple foundations, thus holding the foundations and the temple above them steady. These pegs or "mooring stakes" were usually placed in a boxlike structure at the bottom of the foundations and formed the main content of the so-called foundation deposits. With time these mooring stakes were personified and given human heads and upper bodies, the lower part remaining a peg, but the personified mooring stake, seen as a

| SHUGALAM | Its Sharur (emblem)[114] | 20 |

SHUGALAM
LANDING

Its Sharur (emblem)[114]   20
—silencing with awe
as profoundly as Lagash—
he placed as a protective upright
in its dread place,
the Shugalam,
imbued it thoroughly with eeriness,
and on the throne dais of Ulnun,[115]
its place of judgment,
did Lagash's upholder lift up horns
like a great bull.

STONES

All the great stones he brought in slab form;
he brought in one year, worked them in one year,   xxiii.1
two, three days he let not dawn upon them,
instantly, from the first day on,
he worked them,
and on the seventh day
set them around the house.
Stones he had lie at its sides
as stairs, (or)
fashioned them for pleasure[116]
and stood them in the house.

KISALMAH
STELE

Unto the stone that he set up in the great courtyard:
Stele (named) "The king
shedding luster on the courtyard,
lord Ninĝirsu, recognized Gudea   10
from Ulnun,"
unto that stone he gave as name.

KASURRA
STELE

Unto the stone that he set up in the Kasurra gate:
"The king, Enlil's flood storm,
who has none that could oppose,
lord Ninĝirsu,

"wizard," adept at his important task, could also be separated from the peg as a fully human figure steadying the peg with both hands. This is the case with the "wizards" Gudea used for Eninnu; a number of them have been recovered, and a fragment of a stele of Gudea's from the temple shows the ceremonial placing of one of them in the foundation.

The Sumerian word which I translate as "wizard," *abgal*, denoted a high official at court, a wise counselor. As such he is still attested under UruKAgina, but very soon the title, and probably the office, disappeared from political life and remained only as a term of myth.

114. This is probably the Sharur image mentioned above in xv. 23.
115. See above, n. 82.
116. That is, made them into steles with reliefs, etc.

looked with approval at Gudea,"
unto that stone he gave as name.

IGI-UTU-E
STELE

Unto the stone that he set up in "before the rising sun"[117]
"The king, the howling storm of Enlil,   20
a lord who had none to oppose him,
lord Ningirsu,
envisioned in a holy heart Gudea,"
unto that stone he gave as name.

SHUGALAM
STELE

Unto the stone that he set up before the Shugalam (stairs):
"The king, at the name of whom
    the highlands shudder,
lord Ningirsu,
made firm Gudea's throne,"
unto that stone he gave as name.

E-URUA
STELE

Unto the stone that he set up facing toward E-Urua:[118]   30
"For Gudea did lord Ningirsu
determine a good destiny,"   xxiv.1
unto that stone he gave as name.

AGA-
BABA
STELE

Unto the stone that he set up in "Baba's back room:"
"Baba (is) the reviver of Gudea   5–6
who had Heaven's eyes recognize Eninnu"[119]
unto that stone he gave as name.

UPPER STORIES
ABUILDING

Well did he build his master's house,
Gudea, the able shepherd, made it grow
    (to vie) with heaven and earth,
had it wear a crown like the new moon,   10
had its fame go forth
unto the heart of the highlands.
Gudea made Ningirsu's house
come out like the sun from the clouds,
had it grow to be like sparkling foothills;

---

117. Mentioned also in xxvi.3. The place called "before the rising sun" may be taken to be a place with a free view toward the east toward sunrise. Here the gods would assemble each morning as a court under the presidency of the rising sun, the god of justice, Utu. Such ritual morning court sessions were common in Sumerian temples.

118. Urua was situated in the mountains near or in Elam. *E-Urua*, "the house of Urua" mentioned here, was probably different, perhaps a rest-house on the road to Urua maintained by that city. It is difficult to imagine that it was a part of Eninnu.

119. It is not clear whether this is merely a poetic way of saying that he built it, or whether there are implications here that escape us.

like foothills of white alabaster
he had it stand forth to be marveled at.

THE SOCLE   Its socle he made stand like a wild bull,
FOR SUMMIT   its basilisks he made lie upon their paws like lions,[120]
TEMPLE   its reed fence he had grow   20
        on ground pure as the Apsû
      and its reed-bundle uprights branch (at top)
      like Apsû's holy ibex('s antlers).[121]

SUMMIT TEMPLE Like unto the new moon
BEGUN   standing in the skies,
      Gudea made Ningirsu's house
      stand forth to be marveled at.
      The house standing on its socle,
      were *lahamus*[122] stood alongside Apsû,
      and the set-out wood (scaffolding) of the house xxv.1
       was like an Ambarmah marsh flood wave,
       whereinto water snakes have dived,[123]

HOUSE   the house's stretching out
       along (substructure) walltops,
     was like the heights of heaven
       awe-inspiring;

ROOF   the roofing of the house, like a white cloud,
       was floating in the midst of heaven.

GATE   Its gate through which the owner entered
      was like a lammergeier
       espying a wild bull,

GATEPOSTS   its curved gateposts standing[124]
       at the gate
      were like the rainbow
       standing in the sky,

120. The socle apparently was decorated with representations, probably reliefs, of dragons, which must have been envisaged as four-legged creatures.

121. The upper edge of a temple terrace was normally hedged around with a reed fence. In fact an old word for the brick mantle was "place where the reed uprights are implanted." The word translated "ibex" denotes a species of mountain buck or ram. Why it became emblematic of the Apsû is not clear.

122. Mythical creatures of the marsh, very popular as decoration for the summit temples. See above, "The Cursing of Akkadê," n. 20.

123. *Ambarmah*, "the grand marsh," is probably to be looked for south of Ninâ. The flood wave is presumably one caused by the rivers flooding. The image seems to see the network of slender planks set out for the bricklayers to lay bricks against as tail ends of a swarm of water snakes, the socle on which the walls are to be built as a wave into which they dive.

124. I assume that this refers to two ornamental curved wooden posts set up on either side of the doorway.

LINTEL	its upper lintel of the gate—
	was Eninnu
	standing amidst snarling, howling
	storms all met together,
ARCH	its eyebrow(-shaped arch),
	in its being (so) laden with awe,
	was like unto
	the gods' watchful eyes.
WATER SUPPLY	The house of the sparkling fresh water,
	which confronted him,
	was like the sparkling foothills
	of heaven and earth,[125]
	firmly founded on the ground.
DINING ROOM	They were laying out the great dining room
	for the evening meals,
	it was like a golden bowl wherein
	honey and wine had been poured,
	set up under heaven.
BEDROOM	They were building the bedroom,
	it was like Apsû's holy *mēsu* tree,
	flowering to vie with myriad mountains.
END OF	He had built it!
BUILDING	After he put hand off it,
PROPER	the hearts of the gods
	were overflowing (with kindness).
NINĜIRSU'S	The able shepherd Gudea
SLAIN FOES	was greatly knowing,
	and great too at the carrying out.
SIX-HEADED	In the "back room of the weapons," its battle gate,
IBEX AND SAG-	he was making the warriors "six-headed buck"
GAR	and "radiant head" take their stand.[126]
SEVEN-HEADED	In "Facing toward Urua,"[127] its place laden with awe,
LION	he was having the "seven-headed Lion"
	take its stand.

10

20

125. That is, when seen from afar, the foothills seem to reach from one to the other.

126. Here begins a traditional series of opponents vanquished by Ninĝirsu. It is likely that accounts of his battles with some or all of them existed, but so far none has been found.

127. The scribe may have miscopied here a more correct E-Urua as in col. xxiii.30. I do not feel certain enough, however, to emend the text as it stands.

BASILISK AND DATE PALM	In Shugalam, its haloed gate, he was having the "basilisk" and the "palm tree" take their stand.	xxvi.1

BISON'S HEAD	In "before the rising sun," its place
	    for making decisions,
	he was having "the bison's head,"
	    the standard of Utu,
	shine with him.	

LION	in Kasurra, its lookout post, he was having "the lion, the terror of the gods," take its stand.	
KULIANNA AND COPPER	In Tarsirsir, its place for giving out commissions, he was having "Kulianna" and "the Copper" take their stand.	10

MAGILUM BOAT
AND BISON
	In "Baba's back room," its place
	    for the unburdening of heart,
	he was making the "Magilum boat" and
	    the "bison"
	take their stand.	

	Since they were warriors slain by him
	    (by Ninĝirsu),
	he set their mouths
	    toward a drinking place.
	Their names amid those of
	    the gods
	Gudea, Lagash's ruler,
	had appear.	

DOORLEAVES	Its cedar doorleaves set up in the house were like Ishkur[128] loudly bellowing from on high,	20
LOCKS	Eninnu's locks were bisons. its door-pivots lions,	
BOLTS	and from its bolts *shaturru* snakes[129] and fierce snakes	

128. A god of storms and thunder.
129. Not yet identified.

	were sticking out the tongue against aurochses.	
LINTELS	Its lintels which the door leaves closed against were in the shape of cubs of lions and panthers lying on their paws.	
NAILS	Into the house the holy beam-spikes they were driving in; they were in the shape of basilisks sparing a man's life.	
DOOR ROPES	Unto its doorleaves holy ropes they were attaching,[130] they were like Apsû's pied and holy snake god.	30 xxvii.1
REFUSE	The refuse from the house was pure like Kesh and (like) Aratta;[131] emptying of it from the house was like (the roar of) a fierce lion.	
HOUSE OPERATIONAL	It (the house) kept an eye on the country; no arrogant one could walk in its sight, awe of Eninnu covered all lands like a cloth. The house, founded by An on refined silver,[132] adorned with antimony paste, standing forth like the moon amid the splendors of heaven, a house whose front was like a great mountain, firmly grounded, its inside (full of) chants and singing in close harmony, its rear the sky, a mighty storm cloud risen amid abundance.[133]	10

130. The ropes served to lock doors. See above, n. 37.
131. Two places considered ritually pure. See "Hymn to Kesh" and "Enmerkar and the Lord of Aratta."
132. Silver will have been placed in the foundations deposits.
133. The abundance is the expected effect of the storm's rain.

OUTSIDE AND OUTBUILDINGS	Its outside (place for) administrators' assembly was the Anunnaki's place of rendering judgment.
WELL	From its honey-water (well) mouths offered blessings,[134]
FOOD PORTIONS	its food portions were the establishers of gatherings of the gods.
UPRIGHTS	Its reed-bundle uprights, delimiting the house, were like the thunderbird when into mountain crests it spreads its wings.
PLASTER	Eninnu's clay plaster, harmoniously blended clay 20 to come out of the Idedin[135] canal, did its owner, Lord Ningirsu, envision in a holy heart, poured it like antimony paste over (its) head, and Gudea adorned it xxviii.1 with the splendors of heaven.
COWBARN	(With it) bringing cream in, bringing milk in from its cowbarn,
OVEN	and great griddle cakes, great "horns"[136] 5–6 from its huge oven;
SLAUGHTER HOUSE	and for its set of knives that consume oxen, consume sheep,
FOOD OFFERINGS	fattened geese were delivered steadily to its house and the place of food rations;
LIBATIONS	(with) its libation (places), 10 very mountains oozing wine,
BREWHOUSE	it was, (to judge but) from its brewhouse, the Tigris river at high waters.
STORES	Within its storehouse (were) gems, silver, tin,
CHARIOT HOUSE	its chariot house (was) a mountain planted on the ground,

134. I.e., thirsty people, having slaked their thirst at the well blessed the temple in gratitude.

135. The name means "Desert Canal." It has not been identified. Here it probably refers to an abandoned canal bed that had filled with the characteristic purplish dune sand still seen in southern Iraq.

136. Apparently breads or rolls shaped like horns.

MUSIC ROOM   its "Harp back room" (was) a bull,
         bellowing loudly,
    its courtyard was (full of)
         holy salutations, cymbal and *alu* lyre,

STAIRS   its stone stairs, laid against the house,
    were (just) as if the foothills were   20
         laid (up) toward the Ulnun;
    its upper stairway, laid
         (up) toward the roof,
    was like a white cloud
         looking far away
         (over) toward the mountains.

GARDEN   Its girige'edin (vineyard) bordering the house[137]
    was like a mountain oozing wine,
         grown where the soil had been scorched.
    The seven stones[138]   xxix.1
    set up around the house
    were things consulting with its owner,

FUNERARY   its chapel for funerary offerings
CHAPEL   was a clean thing, instructed by the Apsû;
    its stone tub set up in the house
    was a pure *guda*-priest house,[139]
         wanting not for water;

TOWERS   its lofty wall towers,
    where dwelt the pigeons,
    were, like Eridu,
         determined a good fate.
    Eninnu ever gave the swallow rest,   10
    being of shade, large branches, and sweet shadow;
    the . . . . birds were warbling (?).
    It was like Enlil's Ekur intoning songs.

CONCLUDING   The house's awesomeness
PAEAN   hovered over the country
    praise of it
    reached the highland,
    Eninnu's awesomeness
         covered like a cloth all lands.

137. The name means "the black garden (of) the desert." Gardens, orchards, and vineyards would ring the cities around and would show black—dark—against the light dun of the desert as seen from afar.

138. I.e., the steles representing Ningirsu's slain foes.

139. The *guda* priest, the "anointed one," was much concerned with ritual cleanliness and lustrations.

The house's owner built it out of lovely (things), xxx.1
Ningishzida
built it on the underground,
Gudea, Lagash's ruler,
filled in its foundation terrace.
The house, risen like the sun
   over the country,
standing like a great bull
   in . . . .
shedding, like a delightful moon,
light unto the assembly;[140]
laden, like the green foothills, 10
with allure,
standing to be marveled at!
Eninnu having been restored,
Praise be Ningirsu!

The middle praise hymn of
"The house of Ningirsu having been built."

140. In the hot summer months, assemblies would meet at night in moonlight, when it was cool and comfortable.

Cylinder B

The house, mooring stake of the country, i.1
grown up 'twixt heaven and earth,
Eninnu, right true brick structure,
   assigned good destiny by Enlil,
green foothill confronting the beholder,
jutting out from the highland—

As the great mountain that it was,
   the house abutted heaven,
shone, a very sun, in heaven's midst,
and as the flashing Thunderbird it was,
   Eninnu
spread knees[1] (to pounce) upon the highland.

1. An eagle strikes with both legs stretched forward, the knees apart, the talons open. Cf. "Hymn to Enlil," 1. 27.

WORKMEN   By and by the people were laid off,   10
DISMISSED   and by and by the people went away.

LOCAL GODS   The Anunnaki gods
COME TO   made their way hither to admire,
ADMIRE   and the ruler, being wise and eloquent,
kissed the ground before that godly company.
With greetings and (with) prayer, he lined up viands:
Prayers the ruler was saying
     unto the god of his city,
loaves he added to the house's meals of bread,
sheep he added to its evening meals of mutton,
jars, as (for) the abundance
     of heaven's vast midst,[2]
he set up straight in front of it,   20
went to the Anunnaki gods,
was (thus) hailing them:
     "O Anunnaki,
     supervisors of Lagash land,
guardian angels of all countries,   ii.1
     by whose commands,
     (irresistible as)
     a massive breach in a dam,
the one who would stem it[3]
     is carried off;
but for this trusty young man,
     for whom they have had regard,
life has been lengthened.
I, a ruler, have built a house,
     my master is about to enter his house,
may you, for my sake, O Anunnaki,
     name the salutation!"

NINĜIRSU   The able shepherd Gudea
TOLD HOUSE   was greatly knowing,
IS READY   and great at the carrying out, too,
His good genius went before him,
his good guardian angel followed behind him.   10
To his master, unto the E-ul[4]
     of the old house, his abode,

2. That is, as numerous as jars set out to catch rainwater.
3. Literally "the man tying brush," i.e., who is making fascines to stem the escaping waters. A different possible translation would be "the weakling."
4. *E-ul* "house firmament" would seem to be a shortened and variantly written form of Ulnun "the great firmament," Ninĝirsu's place of judgment on Shugalam.

to lord Ninĝirsu, Gudea
decided to make great gifts.
He entered Eninnu[5] to the lord,
was (thus) hailing him:

"Ninĝirsu, my master,
lord, semen reddened in the deflowering,[6]
lord whose word takes precedence,
heir of Enlil, warrior! You commanded me,
and I've set hand to it for your right.   20
Ninĝirsu, I have built here
    your house for you,
may you enter it in joy!
My Baba, I have laid out
    your seraglio for you
settle into it comfortably!"   iii.1

His appeal heard,
the warrior, lord Ninĝirsu,
accepted from Gudea his prayer.

NINĜIRSU   The year having gone, the month ended,
LEAVES   a new year strode up on heaven.
ERIDU   The month entered its house.[7]
After that completed month just three days went by
and—Ninĝirsu coming from Eridu[8]—
the (new) moon rose brilliant,   10
illuminated the land.
    With the moongod aborning
vied Eninnu.

HOUSE   Gudea made a paste
READIED   with lapis lazuli and carnelian,
put it on corners and side walls,
a prince's sweet oils he sprinkled on the floors,
and the builders, being workers,
he made leave the house.[9]

---

5. Reference is to the old Eninnu built by Ur-Baba, which apparently was still in use until the new temple had been accepted by Ninĝirsu.

6. See Cyl. A, n. 42.

7. I.e., it ended; its term being over, it went home.

8. Ninĝirsu undertook a yearly journey to Eridu. Perhaps that is what is referred to here, in which case one might think of his statue returning. Possible is perhaps also that he would be thought to return as a thunder cloud, but that seems less likely since clearly his statue would then have had to be transferred separately to the new temple, and that ought to have been reported in the cylinders.

9. The builders, associated by sympathetic magic with the incompleteness of the house, had to leave it not to affect its stability when complete.

Honey, butter, wine,
  milk, succulent barley kernels,
pomegranates, and figs made into loaves
shaped with the prime of milk,   20
dates in clusters, tiny grapes,
things untouched by fire,
being viands of gods,
he prepared with honey and butter.
With the sun stepping unto the trusty sky,[10]
from the cool of day (in the morning)
unto the leaving off work (at eve)
  Gudea was on the go.

THE GODS   The god Asari[11] guided hands aright for the house   iv.1
HELP   Ninmada[12] gave instructions for it,
               king Enki provided
                 the seeker of portents,
               and Ninuruda,[13] Eridu's august purification priest,
               filled it with the smoke of incense.
               The lady of precious office, Nanshe,
                 versed in intoning holy incantations,
                 intoned them for the house,
               black sheep she sheared
               and on the cow of heaven
               she set to rights the udder.[14]
               With the tamarisks and the mouflon-brushwood   10
                 it would give birth to
               they would be cleaning Eninnu
               and make it bright and shining.

NIGHT FALLS   The ruler made the city lie down,
               established silence in the country.

---

10. The sun came out in the morning from behind the sky and stepped up on it using the mountains as steppingstones. See "Enki and Ninsikila/Ninhursaǧa," n. 5.

11. Seemingly a rain god. As *Asari-lú-he*, "the man-drenching Asari," he became identified in later times with Marduk of Babylon. His precise role here is not clear.

12. The name means "lady of the level lands." She served as snake charmer of Enlil and introducer of suppliants to An. Here she conceivably checked the house for snakes.

13. See above, Cyl. A, n. 29.

14. Two different images for the overcast sky. In the first it is seen as a black sheep, the clouds representing its wool. When sheared this "wool" falls as rain. In the second it takes form as a cow, the clouds its udder, the milk from it the rain. The rains will make tamarisk and brushwood, needed for cleaning of the temple, grow up in the desert.

NINĜIRSU
ARRIVES
	Stilled were (the day's) noises, dream notions returned.
	Snores being emitted from noses,
	while in the city, by a mother of someone sick,
	remedial ablutions were (still) being given;
	    with gazelles and wild asses, the animals of the desert,
	being curled up one as the other,
	and upon lions, wild beasts
	    and monster serpents of the desert
	sweet sleep having settled down—
	hailing the daylight, saluting the night,
	at the moon of morning,
	came alighting its owner.

20 (at line "and upon lions, wild beasts")

HOUSE
APPROVED
	The warrior Ninĝirsu entered the house,
	the owner of the house had come,
	a very eagle catching sight of a wild bull![15]
	The warrior's entering his house
	was a storm roaring into battle.
	Ninĝirsu roamed through his house,
	it was (the sound of) the Apsû temple precincts
	    when festivals are celebrated.
	The owner was ready to come out from his house—
	it was like the sun rising over Lagash land!
	Baba's going to her seraglio
	was that of a true woman taking her house in hand,
	her entering her bedroom
	was like the Tigris river settling down
	    after being in flood,
	her lying down on the side of her ear (to sleep)
	was the queen, child of holy An,
	    causing green gardens to bear fruit![16]

v.1 (at "The warrior Ninĝirsu entered the house,")

10 (at "Baba's going to her seraglio")

DAY'S WORK
BEGINS
	Daylight having (now) come forth,
	    the decision having been made,[17]
	Baba having gone into her seraglio,
	was abundance for Lagash land.
	The day dawned. Lagash's (sun god) Utu
	    lifted the head over the country,
	and fat oxen, fat sheep, were taken to the house,

20 (at "and fat oxen, fat sheep, were taken to the house,")

---

15. The wild bull of the simile must be a dead wild bull, a carcass. The "eagles" of the Sumerians, more probably lammergeiers, would eat carcasses, as graphically shown on the Stele of the Vultures.

16. In her character of rain goddess.

17. The decision to accept the new temple.

tall jars set up, wine poured therein,
and, since the Anunnaki of Lagash
  were teamed up in their places
  for lord Ningirsu,
the purification of the house was done to perfection,
and care taken with the seeking of portents.[18]
Wine was poured from the great jars,   vi.1
ten big oxen and ten average oxen
  were being slaughtered for Eninnu,
Ninuruda[19] thundered toward the house,
and with the day's (freshly baked) bread, and milk of hinds,
  which is brought in day and night,
the noble, beloved son of Enlil, the warrior Ningirsu,
  was awakened from sleep.

OFFICES
ASSUMED

(Proudly) he lifted the head in great office,
and ranged the gods, housekeepers, and (estate)
functionaries,
  his court and household,
one after the other, for the Eninnu close.   10

IG-ALIMA,
HIGH CON-
STABLE

To guide to success the hands of the righteous,
to put neck stocks on the necks of evildoers,
to keep the house law-abiding, to keep the house peaceful,
to issue ordinances for his city, the estate Girsu,
to set up the throne of (rendering) verdicts,
to place in hand a long-term scepter,
to have the shepherd called by Ningirsu
  lift up the head as
  the yellow turban, (the moon,)[20]
and to assign positions in Eninnu's courtyard
to skinclad (fieldhands) and linen-clad (house servants)   20
  and those with head covered,[21]
was the high constable of Girsu, his beloved son Igalima,[22]

---

18. The importance of the agenda for the day, assigning of offices to the minor gods already lined up and waiting, called for very special care with the rites of purification and for making certain that the omens for the day were propitious.

19. See n. 8 above to Cylinder A.

20. Reference is apparently to the disklike headdress Gudea is shown as wearing in pictorial representations of him. Lifting the head here seems to indicate majesty and self-assurance.

21. See "The Nanshe Hymn," nn. 21 and 22. Those with head covered may be the administrators.

22. The name means "the doorleaf of the honored one," and the god may be considered a personification of the deified door to Ningirsu's hall of justice. The protective role of a door may have suggested his office of keeper of the peace.

going about his duties for the lord Ninĝirsu
in Ulnun like a great doorleaf.

SHUL- SHAGA(NA), BUTLER	To keep the house clean, to set up	

To keep the house clean, to set up
    hand-washing apparatus
and give it with clean hands to the lord,
to pour beer from out the jars,
    to pour wine from out the jugs,
to let in the brewery,   vii.1
    the house's room (for) clarifying (beer),
emmer-beer gurgle
like the Pasir-canal waters,
was the rouser from sleep, when (still) dark,
of the noble, beloved son of Enlil, the warrior Ninĝirsu,
with the sweetest of food and drink,
perfect oxen, perfect kids, grain-fed sheep,
the day's (freshly baked) bread and milk of hinds
brought in day and night—
was the lord of pure hand-washings,
    the firstborn son of Eninnu,
Shulshaga(na),[23] going about   10
his duties for Ninĝirsu.

LUGALKUR- DUB, MARSHAL

To hold the seven-headed mace[24]
and, opening the doors of the armory, the gate of battle,
regularly to keep in proper shape
the sword blades, the *mittum-*(mace), the flood storm(-
weapon),
and the (weapon) "Bitterness,"
    its implements of battle,
so as to submerge like (flood)waters
the totality of Enlil's enemies, the highlands,
was the warrior Sharur, who in battle
    puts the highlands at (his) mercy,
the mighty marshal of Eninnu,
a falcon to rebel regions,
his marshal Lugalkurdub,[25]   20
going about his duties for the lord Ninĝirsu.

23. The name means "The young gallant of [i.e., dear to] his heart." As the firstborn son of the house, he is the one who serves the meals; see above n. 48 to Cylinder A.

24. See the representation of Ninĝirsu on the seal of Urdun (Frankfort, *Seal Cylinders*, text, fig. 38), where he holds such a weapon in his right hand.

25. See above, n. 63 to Cylinder A.

KURSHUNASHENAM,   The *mittu* (-mace), which out of the skies
VICE-MARSHAL   like a gale, a storm of bat[tle],
                               is hurled howling at the highland,   viii.1
                               a Sharur, a floodstorm of battle,
                               a bludgeon for rebel regions,
                               which, when the lord had frowned
                                     at the rebel region, the highland,
                               has hurled at it his furious words,
                               has driven it insane,
                                     (devastates[?] it),
                               the lord's second marshal,
                               Kurshunashenam,[26]
                               would, when the lord has frowned
                                     upon the rebel region, the highland,
                               when he had hurled at it his angry voice,
                               had become enraged,
                               be going about his duties for the lord Ningirsu.

LUGALSISA,   To take in hand
VICE REGENT   the appeals of Lagash land,   10
                               and to lay its prayers and petitions on (Ningirsu's) knee;
                               to say, when the warrior goes to Eridu,
                               "Good speed" sweetly,
                               and, when Ningirsu comes from Eridu,
                               to hail him
                               with the city in good repair,
                                     its throne firm,
                               and the able shepherd Gudea
                               in good health,
                                     (to that end)
                               was his counselor   20
                               Lugalsisa[27] going about his duties
                               for the lord Ningirsu.

SHAKANSHEGBAR,   To speak lightly,
PRIVATE SECRE-   to speak weightily,
TARY   to covenant with the fair-spoken one,
                               and not covenant with the one speaking evil,
                               to take their cases in to the warrior   ix.1
                                     seated on the holy dais,

26. The name means "the highland is in his hands but a swallow." A line telling what its function was must have been left out by mistake by the ancient scribe.
27. The name means "the king who sets straight."

to Ningirsu in Eninnu,
was the private secretary of the living quarters,
    his . . . . Shakanshegbar,[28]
going about his duties
for the lord Ningirsu.

KINDAZID,
VALET DE
CHAMBRE

To cleanse with water,
    clean with soap;
and with oil of the shiny stone jar,
    and soap of the bowl,
induce (him) to sweet sleep
on his bed spread with clean hay;
to have him enter the bedroom of his living quarters,   10
from outside,
and not (wish to) go out (again) from inside,
was Kindazid[29] as man in charge of the private quarters,
going about his duties for the lord Ningirsu.

ENSIGNUN,
EQUERRY

To yoke up the holy chariot in the starry heavens,[30]
and appoint its donkey stallion Pirigkasepada,[31]
to serve before it,
to shout with a voice carrying into all lands
to the slender ass, the ass of Eridu, and
    the (spare) jackass of the side,
and have them carry joyfully their owner Ningirsu,   20
was the man who roars like a lion,
sets out like a floodstorm,
Ningirsu's itinerant bailiff,[32]
Ensignun,[33] his assherd,   x.1
going about his duties for the lord Ningirsu.

ENLULIM,
GOATHERD

To have the butter plentiful, the cream plentiful,
to see to it that butter and milk from the sacred goats,
    the goats of milk for drinking, and of the hind,

---

28. The name apparently means "mouflon oil-bowl," so the god may be a personification of a sacred vessel kept in the god's bedroom. If so, cf. the bowl from Ishchali decorated with mouflon heads pictured in Seton Lloyd, *The Art of the Ancient Near East*, fig. 95, p. 133.

29. The name means "the able barber." The duties of the god as described are, however, broader than those of a barber and amount to those of a valet de chambre.

30. Reference here seems to be to the mythical cosmic counterpart of the ritual journey of Ningirsu to Eridu.

31. Cf. above, n. 38 to Cylinder A.

32. Presumably also used as "itinerant bailiff" on occasion because of his mobility as charioteer.

33. The meaning of the name is not clear.

the mother of Ningirsu,[34]
cease not in the Eninnu close,
was Enlulim, herder of hinds,
going about his duties for the lord Ningirsu.

USHUMGAL-
KALAMMA,
BARD

To have the sweet-toned instrument, the *tigi*-harp
    correctly tuned,
to fill the courtyard of Eninnu with joy,   10
to make the *algar* and *mirîtum*,
    instruments of the private quarters,
lie down[35] for the warrior with ear (for music),
for Ningirsu, in Eninnu
was his beloved bard, Ushumgalkalamma,
going about his duties for the lord Ningirsu.

LUGALIGI-
HUSH,
ELEGIST

To assuage the heart, assuage the liver,
to dry the tears in the teary eyes,
to banish dolor from the dolorous heart,
and to keep grief far away
from the lord's heart rising like the waves in midocean,
surging like the Euphrates,   20
overwhelming like a flood storm—
his loving heart, which,
    when he has, as it were,
drowned the mountains,
    all Enlil's foes,
    overflows (with compassion),
was his harp, none other than Lugaligihush,[36]   xi.1
going along his duties for the lord Ningirsu.

DAUGHTERS,
HANDMAIDENS

His beloved handmaidens,
    the man-drenching abundance,[37]
Zazaru,
Impae,
Uragrun(a)taea,

34. The deer as characteristic animals of the foothills were seen as closely related to Ninhursaǧa, "the lady of the mountains," mother of Ningirsu, and were undoubtedly a form which this mountain goddess could assume. Note that stags decorated Ninhursaǧa's temple in Al Obeid.

35. The term is characteristically used for sheep and cows lying down. The sound boxes of harps were often decorated with bovine heads so that when the harp was placed on the ground it would look as if the bull or cow were lying down. See, e.g., the various harps found at Ur. The deep tone of the harp suggested, of course, the voice of a bovine.

36. The name means "The wroth-faced king" suggesting that it would come into play when Ningirsu's face was glowering, the god still full of the wrath of battle.

37. I.e., the rainclouds.

Heulnunna,
Heshaga,
Zurmu,
and Zarmu,   10
who are Baba's septuplets,
are Ninğirsu's progeny,[38]
stepped with Gudea's acceptable appeals
up to the lord Ninğirsu.

GISHBARE,   To have all the great fields demand attention,
FARMER   have the (water in) dikes and canals of Lagash
rise to their brims,
have in Gu-edinna, the plain worthy of its owner,
laden, silvern barley lift on pure stalks
head heavenwards in the furrows,   20
and, having planted in its good fields
    (also) wheat, emmer and all the vines,
to pile up and pile up
the spectacular grain piles of Lagash land,
was Enlil's surveyor, the farmer of Gu-edinna,
Gishbare,[39]
going about his duties there for the lord Ninğirsu.

LAMAR,   To have—when he had stocked its marshes with   xii.1
INSPECTOR   marsh-carps and giant carps,
OF FISH-   and had planted new reeds by its yellowed reeds—
ERIES   Iminshattam,[40] Gu-edinna's messenger by boat,
take reports of it to Ninğirsu in Eninnu,
was Lamar,[41] the inspector of fisheries of Gu-edinna,
going about his duties for the lord Ninğirsu.

DIMGAL-   To administer the pacified areas of the desert,
ABZU,   to give directions
RANGER   for Gu-edinna, the pacified desert,
to have its birds team up in their (proper) places,   10
to have them lay their eggs in safe abodes,
to have them rear their young,

---

38. All of these children of Ninğirsu and Baba were rain-cloud goddesses. How they got their names is not clear. They are here thought to convey Gudea's appeals to their father.

39. The name seems to mean "the one taking out the (ground-breaking) plow" and to denote a farmer taking new land under cultivation.

40. The meaning of the name of this god is not clear.

41. The name designates a protective angel. This particular angel must have been given the task of inspector of fisheries because of the particular locality in which it was worshipped.

to see to it that for Ninĝirsu's beloved desert
the sounds of its roaming bucks and wild asses
suffer no diminution,
was Dimgalabzu,[42] the ranger of Gu-edinna,
going about his duties
for the lord Ninĝirsu.

LUGAL, GUARD To have the city built up, have dwellings founded,
to guard the city-wall of Urukug,[43]   20
and make its police officer of the residences,
the huge-headed white-cedar mace,
patrol round the house,
was Lugal,[44] as guard of Urukug,
going about his duties for lord Ninĝirsu.

LYRICAL Holy An founded the house right,
INTERLUDE and Enlil wound the turban round its head,   xiii.1
Ninhursaĝa looked upon it truly,
and Enki filled in its foundation terrace.
Being that a trusty lord of pure heart,
Suen (the moon god) had made its offices
    surpassing in the world,
Ninĝirsu in his heart envisioned
    a manor amid sprouting seed[45]
and mother Nanshe with the bricks of Lagash soil
took pains;
a god of much good progeny[46]
built the house, made it appear.   10

GIFTS TO Nanshe's strong steward,
HOUSE: the mighty shepherd of Ninĝirsu,
WEAPONS was greatly knowing,
    and great too at carrying out:
Upon the house the house's builder,
Gudea, ruler
of Lagash,

42. The name means "the bollard of Apsû." Cf. Cyl. A, above, n. 113, on mooring stakes for temples. The god is charged with administering the wildlife of the desert, it would seem, because of the location of his sanctuary in the Gu-edinna.

43. "The holy city" has not yet been located. It is not a part of Girsu, as often assumed.

44. The term *lugal*, "king," denoted originally merely a leader in war. As such he was charged with the defense of his city and patrolling its walls. Here the term is the name for an armed guard, consonant with its early, rather than its later, connotations.

45. A reference to the power of Eninnu to bring rain and so make seeds sprout.

46. That is, Ningishzida, Gudea's personal god, who as such inspired his actions.

was bestowing gifts:
The chariot *Kurmugam*,[47] terror-laden,
   riding the great gales,
and its donkey stallion, storm of strident voice,
to serve before it.   20
The seven-headed mace, the fierce battle weapon,
the weapon under which the earth's four corners
   cannot bear up, a battle bludgeon,
the *mittu*(-mace), the lion-headed weapon
   of *hulalu*[48] stone,
which turns not tail from the highland,   xiv.1
the sword blades, the nine standards,
and the (very) arm of martial prowess,
his bow, twanging like (the swish of)
   a *mēsu*-tree forest,
his angry arrows all set to flash like lightning
   in the battle,
and his quiver, on which wroth lions
have stuck the tongue out at fierce serpents,
weapons of battle for outfitting kingship,
was the ruler, the builder of the house,
Gudea, ruler   10
of Lagash,
bestowing upon it as gifts.

GIFTS TO
HOUSE:
FURNITURE

Beside copper, tin, slabs of lapis lazuli,
   refined silver and pure Meluhhan carnelian,
he set up a huge copper pail,
   a huge double bowl of copper,
a pure copper goblet
   and a pure copper jar,
   An worthy,
at the place of regular offerings,
so that the thunderbird of the sky
could carry a pure table up to An.[49]

47. *Kurmugam* may be rendered as "it made the highland bow down." The mythopoeic imagining of a god of thunderstorms as a warrior riding a chariot is common and not particular to Sumer. The chariot is the thunder cloud, the thunder the noise its wheels make, the lightning the arrows shot by the charioteer or other missiles hurled by him.

48. This stone has not been identified.

49. As mentioned, there was mystical identity of the temple with the thunderbird, Ninĝirsu's original form. Thus the temple was performing the office of Ninĝirsu as son of the house: serving meals to An and his father, Enlil. Cf. above, Cyl. A, x.7–14. Underlying the concept is perhaps a mythopoeic view of the black thunder cloud as a tray carried up to heaven.

For Niṇĝirsu he had made his city
a peaceful land and city like unto Lagash.   20
In the bedroom, the house's place of rest,
he set up the bed,
on its slats, like birds, the mountains
rested with Enlil's son.[50]

RULER TAKES
UP OFFICE

With the river filled with flowing waters,
the marshes stocked
    with marsh carp and giant carp,
Their inspector of fisheries,   xv. 1
    the one stocking (them with) fish,
    guiding them;
with the grain laden
    for (transport on) the great waters,
with the storage piles and heaps
of Lagash piled up,
with the cowpens built,
    the sheepfolds built,
the lambs placed with good ewes,
and the ram released unto its good ewes,
with the calves placed with good cows,
and the bull bellowing loudly among them,
with the oxen properly in the yokes,   10
and their oxdriver standing by their side,
with the asses saddled with their packsaddles,
and their drivers who feed them
    following after them,
with huge copper ingots
    strapped on the jackasses,
with the huge millhouse supported,
with [. . . . .] for Gadagalakkildu, the house
    of Niṇĝirsu's little slave girls,[51]
like [. . . . .]
with [. . . .] set right,
with Eninnu's courtyard filled with joy,
and with his beloved harp Ushumgalkalamma   21
marching

---

50. Tentatively one might assume that the slats of the bed were decorated with the standard
mountain motif and that, figuratively, the poet implies that the mountains, Niṇĝirsu's traditional
enemies, were safe and could sleep as long as he did so.

51. With some hesitation we should consider translating the name as "the roomy shed relieving cries
of distress" and see it as a reference to the function of temple and palace mills as poorhouses, places
where destitute women and children would be employed.

at the head of cymbals accompanied   20
   by *alu*-lyres and harps,
   making the singing perfect,
was the ruler
who had built Eninnu,

Gudea, going in   xvi.1
to lord Ninĝirsu.
The house lifted in great offices
   the head
was the perfection of awe and glory.
Like a barge it [had lowered] the mast,
employed its mooring stakes and painter.

DAIS IN   Its owner, the warrior Ninĝirsu,
CELLA   rose like daylight on the dais of Ulnun,
its wooden covering (?), resting on supports,
was a blue sky laden with holy dread.   10
Its standards and their caps
were Ninĝirsu
   laden with [dread ter]ror(?).
Its sash, running straight to its front,
was a bathed yellow-nose serpent.[52]

CHARIOT IN   In his lapis lazuli chariot laden with allure
COACH HOUSE stood its owner the warrior Ninĝirsu, a very sun god.

THRONE IN   Its throne set up in the assembly
ASSEMBLY   of the administrators
PLACE   was (like) An's holy throne
   resting among the stars,
its bed, when it had been set up in the bedroom,
was (like) a young cow kneeling down[53]   20
   in its place where it slept,
on its pure back, spread with fresh hay,   xvii.1
mother Baba was resting comfortably
with lord Ninĝirsu.

UTENSILS   Large bronze kettles were seething,
in the efficiently running house
   the pure bronze kettles were boiling

---

52. Presumably Ninĝirsu's throne in the Ulnun had a canopy over it, a fairly standard thing with divine thrones. The standards supporting the blue cloth covering, and the sash by which—probably—it was drawn out or in as needed, are separately described.

53. Beds often had feet shaped like the hooves of oxen as a decorative feature. That was probably the case also with Ninĝirsu's bed and suggested the imagery here.

libation-offering-(meats) for the [copper goblets],[54]
its pure jars, standing in the dining hall,
were (like) great and small marshes
    not about to lack for water,
its goblets belonging to them, standing
    at their side
were (like) the Tigris and Euphrates rivers   10
continually carrying abundance.

What beseemed his city he had produced,
Gudea had built Eninnu
had had its offices performed to perfection.
Into its room for butter and cream
    he sent butter and cream,
in its room for sacred stores he stored things,
he remitted debts and granted pardons.
The day his master entered his house,
and for seven days,
the slave woman was on a par with her mistress   20
the slave walked abreast with the master.

In the outskirts of his city   xviii.1
    the mighty one slept beside his client,
from the tongue (of) evil
    he changed the (evil) words,
sent banditry packing home,
hee[ded]
[Nanshe's] and Ningirsu's ordi[nances],
gave not the waif [over to the rich man],
[gave] not the wid[ow] over to [the powerful] man,
the house lacking a male heir
constituted an [eq]ui[ty do]wr[y for the dau]ghter.
A grand period of equity had dawned for him,   10
and he set foot on the neck
    of evil ones and malcontents;
like the sun god from the horizon
he came out unto the city,
on his head he had wound a turban,
let the eyes of holy Heaven
know he was relaxing;
with head high, like a bull,
    he entered
into the Eninnu close,

54. Libations were normally accompanied by offerings of bread or meat.

perfect oxen, perfect kids he offered up,
set up a tall jar,   20
poured wine from it.
Ushumgalkalamma took its stand
   among the *tigi*-harps,
the *alu*-lyres roared for him like a storm,   xix. 1
and the ruler decided
to step onto a buttress,
and his city was admiring him.
Gudea [. . . . .]
[. . . .]
[. . . .]
[. . . .]
[. . . .]

THE HOUSE   For mother Nanshe's able steward   10
BRINGS RAINS   did the house without a cease
have [ab]undance
   [come to him from heaven]
have earth grow for him
   mottled barley.[55]

HOUSE-   Inasmuch as the warrior had entered his new house,
WARMING   he set out in it a good feast for Lord Ningirsu.
An he seated for him at the long side,[56]
next to An he placed Enlil,
and next to Enlil   20
he placed Ninmah.[57]

NINGIRSU   [. . . . .]   xx. 1
PRAISES   [. . . .]
GUDEA   [. . . .]
[. . . .]
[. . . .]
"You have constructed [dike] and dike-canal,
you have constructed the guardhouse
   of the (store-)room for silver and lapis lazuli,
[Gu]dea, you were building my [house] for me,
and were having [the offices] performed
   to perfection [for me],

---

55. The temple, in its mystical identity with the thunderbird and the thunder shower it represents,
is a magic source of rain.
56. The long side of the spread was a seat of honor.
57. Another name for Ninhursaǧa.

you had [my house] shine for me   10
    like Utu in [heaven's midst],
separating, like a lofty foothill range,
    heaven from earth.
The orders concerning it were not ones
    spoken by a diviner,
I was not keeping [my heart] remote from [you]!"

The owner was delighted with the house,
determined a fate for Eninnu's brickwork.
For the brick structure
    he determined a fate indeed,
determined a good fate indeed.
For the brick structure Eninnu
    he determined a fate indeed,
determined a good fate indeed (saying:)
"House! Mountain founded by An,   20
built for great offices,"
[. . . . .]   xxi.1
[. . . .]
[. . . .]
[. . . .]

PRAISE OF   [. . . .]
NING̃IRSU   [. . . .]
BY ENKI   "[fierce] lion [having huge] strength
Ning̃i[rsu,] true progeny of Enl[il],
borne by the foothills,[58]
ably nourished with milk by hinds,   10
[reared] among *haluppu* cedars and *murrān*-ash trees,
storm blast blow[ing] from the horizon,
Ning̃irsu, warrior battling rebel regions,"
[. . . .]
[. . . .]
[. . . .]
For Eninnu's brickwork he was determining a fate,
for the brick structure he determined a fate indeed,
for the brick structure Eninnu
    he determined a good fate indeed,
the house, a rainstorm dropping glowing embers,[59]   20
    founded on earth, embracing heaven,

---

58. "The foothills," Hursag̃, is the original name of Ninhursag̃ "lady foothills" or Ninhursag̃a "lady of the foothills" who personified them.

59. An image of lightning, it is seen as the throwing of embers.

[. . . . . . .] pure [. . . . . . .]   xxii. 1

    (possible gap of a line or so)

was a house destined for long days.
Ningirsu stepped up to the house to eulogize it (saying:)
"Its stakes driven in by An,
its uprights soaring with (those of) Lagash,
its Sharur standards [lifting] the head
   over the [house's] brickwork
   as were they a pure crown,
it has, [like a b]arge, [lowered the m]ast.
Like a wild bull against whose fierce [horns]
   there is no making a st[and]
it lowers, broad of neck, the horns.
The house hugs the ground like a . . . . shrub   10
like a *shurmenu*[60] [. . . . .]
[. . . . .]
[. . . . .]
my doorposts soaring with (those of) Lagash,
my Sharur standards which, like mooring stakes
   [are driven in] in the city.
Who can build like me, me, lord Ningirsu!"
Enki answered
lord Ningirsu (saying:)
[. . . . .]
"On your account may cowpens be built,   20
may sheepfolds be renewed,
also may the country lie down
   in safe pastures,
and may the eyes of all lands be on Sumer!
May the house, your thunderbird,   xxiii. 1
   [soa]r in the skies,[61]
that butter be set out
   in its place where butter [is set out],
that milk be hung up (in containers)
   on the pegs where milk is hung,
that oxen and sheep be furnished
   to its house of oxen and sheep,
the house" . . . .

    . . . .

---

60. This special kind of cedar has not yet been identified.
61. I.e., in its alter ego as thunder shower producing abundance by its rain.

(lacuna of some lines)

GUDEA PRAISED ["O. . . . . . .] you are [Nanshe's stro]ng [steward]
 [. . . .]
 [You] have built [the house], [have had the offices
  perfor]med [to perfection].
 Sprouted as a new sho[ot] within the city
 its (firmly) set-up throne no man shall change,
 your tutelary god being lord Ningishzida,
  scion of An,
 your divine mother Ninsuna,[62]
  a mother having given birth to good offspring,
 beloved by the offspring,   20
 you were born by a good cow in its human form.
 You are a fine *mēsu* tree
  made to sprout forth in Lagash
 by Ningirsu,   xxiv. 1
 he has indeed established your name
  from the south to the north.
 Gudea, [lis]tening to what you have to [say]
 is agreeable to him,
 you are a [. . . . .]
  known to An,
 are an ab[le ru]ler, for whom the house
  has determined a [good] fate:
 Gudea, son of Ningishzida,
 life is verily prolonged for you!"

ENVOI With the house, like a great mountain
  abutting heaven,
 its awe and glory   10
  cast upon the country,
 Lagash's fate determined
  by An and Enlil,
 all countries taught
 Ningirsu's excellence,
 and Eninnu grown up
  'twixt heaven and earth,
 Praise be unto Ningirsu!

It is the last praise hymn of (the composition entitled) "The house of Ningirsu which had been built."

---

62. Ninsuna "Queen of the wild cows" and envisioned in bovine form was Gudea's goddess mother. Usually she is considered the wife of Lugalbanda; here, very oddly, she must be thought of as wife of Gudea's tutelary god Ningishzida, whose wife usually is Azimua.

PART EIGHT

Laments for Temples

Lament for Ur

The lament for Ur was written as part of efforts by the early kings of the dynasty of Isin to rebuild the former capital. It aims to calm the disturbed, turbulent, suffering soul of Nanna, the god of Ur, so that he can regain his composure and think of rebuilding his destroyed home.

The reign of the illustrious Third Dynasty of Ur had ended in disaster. A rebellion around the tenth year of the last king, Ibbi-Suen, had reduced that ruler to the status of a mere petty king who may not have controlled much more than the territory around Ur itself. He maintained himself there until his twenty-fifth year when enemies in the highlands, Elam and its neighbors the Sua people, launched a successful attack on all of southern Mesopotamia. Isin was able to resist, but Ur fell after a long siege and was gutted by the barbaric mountaineers. Its people were killed or carried off as slaves—even the aged king—and in the ruins, or on a nearby spot, some of the invaders settled, building their houses with materials taken from the destroyed city.

After the main forces of the invaders had withdrawn with their booty, Isin, under Ishbi-erra, took over, and already Ishbi-erra's son Shu-ilishu began restoring Ur. Work was continued under his successors Iddin-Dagan and Ishme-Dagan and completed, it seems, in the latter's reign. As part of this effort at reconstruction the "Lament for Ur" will thus have been written very soon after the events it records, while they were yet in fresh memory.

The form of the lament is that of a *balag̃* or "harp-lament" which consisted of two parts, a "lament" (*er*) and a "tambourine-lament" (*ershemma*). The first one of these is here sung by Nanna's wife, the goddess Ningal—presumably represented by a human female singer. The second is sung by a singer or singers who express the survivors' compassion and hope, and urge Nanna and Ningal to restore the city as of old.

It seems reasonable to assume that the lament will have been performed at night in moonlight in the actual ruin of Nanna's temple in Ur, Ekishnugal. Nanna, the moon, would have heard it as he looked down sorrowfully at the ruins of his city and his home, and omen kids would have been slaughtered so that his decision might be read in their entrails.

447

The composition begins with a statement of the desolation wrought by the invading enemies. In all of Sumer the gods have left their cities, abandoning them to the enemy, as herders, at the end of the grazing season, will abandon to the winds the temporary quarters, pens, or folds out in the desert or in the foothills where they have tended their animals during spring. In the poet's image the temples become the huts in pen or fold in which the herders lived during the season; the cities are the pens and folds themselves.

To the modern reader this section, with its overlong, detailed listing of cities and temples abandoned by their gods, conveys little or nothing. Not so the ancient listener. To him it was his world crumbling: each familiar name of god, temple, and city had meaning, had been a guarantee of harmony with the unseen world that governed human destinies. The gods' leaving, the places' being destroyed, was the loss of all bearings, and the very monotony of the litany, the same for each new name, must have been felt as the hammer blows of inexorable doom.

With the appearance of Ningal in the third canto the lament becomes more accessible. She sets her harp on the ground in the antecella of the ruined temple and begins recalling the days of the fatal decision of the gods, her efforts to prevent it, her failure to move the leaders of the divine assembly, and the execution of the doom by Enlil in the form of a destructive storm. This storm is the standard anagoge for enemies or other destructive agents of the gods in Sumerian literature, the deeper truth underlying appearances. From the storm, Ningal moves into a description of the city after the attack, with corpses piled high in all streets, treasures scattered, herds driven off, canals, fields, orchards abandoned and taken over by weeds, the people who once tended them driven off into slavery.

With the eighth canto begins what may be considered the tambourine lament (ershemma). It consists of an appeal to Ningal to return to the city. She is being reminded of how it was before the catastrophe, and told how the city—even its bricks—long for her. After the appeal to Ningal follows one to her husband, Nanna, a prayer that the day of storm may not come back and a plea for the rebuilding of his temple and city.

ABANDONMENT
BY THE GODS

—His byre he was abandoning,
  and his sheepfold, to the winds,
the herder was abandoning his byre,
  and his sheepfold, to the winds,
the lord of all lands was abandoning it,
  and his sheepfold, to the winds,
at the temple close Enlil was abandoning Nippur,
  and his sheepfold, to the winds, .
his consort Ninlil was abandoning it,
  and her sheepfold, to the winds,

at their dwelling house Ninlil was abandoning Kiur,[1]
and its sheepfold, to the winds!

Kesh's queen was abandoning it,
and her sheepfold, to the winds,
at its dwelling house Ninmah was abandoning Kesh,
and her sheepfold, to the winds.

Isin's mistress was abandoning it,
and her sheepfold, to the winds,
at its temple close Nininsina was abandoning Egalmah,[2] 10
and her sheepfold, to the winds.

Uruk land's queen was abandoning it,
and her sheepfold, to the winds,
at its dwelling house Inanna was abandoning Uruk,
and her sheepfold, to the winds.

Nanna was abandoning Ur,
and his sheepfold, to the winds,
Suen was abandoning Ekishnugal,[3]
and his sheepfold, to the winds,

His consort Ningal was abandoning it,
and her sheepfold, to the winds.
and her Agrunkug[4] Ningal was abandoning,
and her sheepfold, to the winds.

The herder of Eridu was abandoning it,
and his sheepfold, to the winds.
At his dwelling house, Enki was abandoning Eridu,
and his sheepfold, to the winds.[5]

Shara was abandoning Emah,[6]   20
and his sheepfold, to the winds,
at their dwelling house Udsahara[7] was abandoning Umma,
and her sheepfold, to the winds.

Baba was abandoning Urukug,
and her sheepfold, to the winds,

1. The forecourt to Enlil's temple Ekur. Here Ninlil's temple was located.
2. Nininsina's temple in Isin.
3. Nanna's temple in Ur.
4. Ningal's temple in Ur.
5. Line 19 omitted. It is missing in most manuscripts and is hardly original.
6. Shara's temple in Umma.
7. Shara's wife.

was abandoning her flooded home,
   and her sheepfold, to the winds.
Her mother Abbaba was abandoning it,
   and her sheepfold, to the winds.
Abbaba was abandoning Gaguenna,
   and her sheepfold, to the winds.
The cherub of the holy house was abandoning it,
   and her sheepfold, to the winds.
The cherub was abandoning Etarsirsir,[8]
   and her sheepfold, to the winds.

Lagash's woman sage was abandoning it,
   and her sheepfold, to the winds,
at its dwelling house Gatumdug was abandoning Lagash,
   and her sheepfold, to the winds.

Ninâ's mistress was abandoning it,   30
   and her sheepfold, to the winds,
at its dwelling house the great lady was abandoning Siratr.[9]
Kinirsha's mistress was abandoning it,
   and her sheepfold, to the winds,
at its dwelling house Dumuzi-Apsû was abandoning
Kinirsha,
   and her sheepfold, to the winds.

Guabba's mistress was abandoning it,
   and her sheepfold, to the winds,
at Guabba's temple close Ninmara was abandoning it,
   and her sheepfold, to the winds.

(FIRST PLACE OF COUNTERING)

In his sheepfold he has had the wind settle—
   dolefully it is groaning,
O cow, your lowing!—There being no byre house,
   the byre is not fit for the prince![10]

LAMENT FOR   Bitter is the wail, city,   40
THE DEVAS-   the wail set up for you!
TATED SANC-   Bitter is the wail for you, city,
TUARIES   the wail set up for you!

8. Baba's temple in Urukug.

9. Siratr was the temple of Nanshe in Ninâ. Why Nanshe is here called "the great lady" rather than mentioned by name is not clear.

10. The reference is to the god who has abandoned it.

Bitter is the wail
for her good ravaged city!
Bitter is the wail
for her ravaged Ur!

Bitter is the wail for you, city,
the wail set up for you!
Bitter is the wail
for his ravaged Ur!

Bitter is the wail for you!
How long must the mourner,
your queen,
be wailing it?
Bitter is the wail for you!
How long must the mourner,
Nanna,
be wailing it?

Brickwork of Ur, bitter is the wail,
the wail set up for you![11]
Ekishnugal, bitter is the wail,
the wail set up for you!
Temple close Agrunkug, bitter is the wail,
the wail set up for you!

50

Brickwork of Ekur, bitter is the wail,
the wail set up for you
Kiur, building socle, bitter is the wail,
the wail set up for you!
Gageshshua,[12] bitter is the wail,
the wail set up for you!
Ubshu'ukkinna,[13] bitter is the wail,
the wail set up for you!
Temple close of Nippur and citadel,[14]
bitter is the wail,
the wail set up for you!

11. The sequence of the cities lamented in this section is uncertain and the different manuscripts vary among themselves. We consider it most likely that the original sequence was: Ekur with Kiur, Gageshshua, Ubshu'ukkinna, temple close, and citadel in that order. Next, probably Isin with Egalmah, then Urukug with Etarsirsir and Gaguenna, then Uruk and Eridu, and finally Ur with Ekishnugal and Agrunkug.

12. Name of Ninlil's temple in Kiur.

13. Name of the corner of Kiur in which the assembly of the gods met.

14. Apparently the main court of Ekur with its adjoining structures and the ziggurat with Enlil's summit temple on top.

Brickwork of Urukug,[15] bitter is the wail,
   the wail set up for you!
Etarsirsir,[16] bitter is the wail,
   the wail set up for you!
Gaguenna,[17] bitter is the wail,
   the wail set up for you!

Brickwork of Isin, bitter is the wail,
   the wail set up for you!
Temple close Egalmah,[18] bitter is the wail,   60
   the wail set up for you!

Brickwork of Uruk land, bitter is the wail,
   the wail set up for you!
Brickwork of Eridu, bitter is the wail,
   the wail set up for you!

Bitter is the wail for you!
   How long must the mourner,
   your queen,
   be wailing it?
Bitter is the wail for you!
   How long must the mourner,
   Nanna,
   be wailing it?

City, your name yet is,
   while you
   are ravaged!
City, though yet your wall rings you around,
   your people
   are perished from you!
O my city, from you, as from a faithful ewe,
   your lamb was cut off.
O Ur, from you, as from a faithful nanny-goat,
   your kid has perished.
City, for your ritual functions,
   which were shifted from you,
and your sacred offices,   70
   an enemy's sacred offices
   have been substituted!

15. The city of the goddess Baba, wife of Ningirsu. It has not yet been identified on the ground.
16. Baba's temple in Urukug.
17. Temple of Abbaba, the mother of Baba. It was mentioned above, l. 25.
18. Nininsina's temple in Isin.

> Bitter is the wail for you!
>> How long must the mourner,
>> your queen,
>> be wailing it?
> Bitter is the wail for you!
>> How long must the mourner,
>> Nanna,
>> be wailing it?

(SECOND PLACE OF COUNTERING)

> Bitter is the wail for his ravaged faithful city!
> Bitter is the wail for his ravaged Ur!

(is its antiphon)

NARRATOR
RECORDS NINGAL'S
BEING MOVED
TO LAMENT

> In the destroyed houses,
>> the queen's, the mistress's city
>> is transformed along with her
>> into mourners.
> Ur burns in bitter wails with Ningal,[19]
>> the mistress from whom the people
>> are parted.

> Making the faithful woman, the queen,   80
>> wail for her city,
> making Ningal sleepless
>> on account of her people,
> the doom of her city
>> felt (again) close,
>> and she is weeping bitter tears,
> for the queen the doom of her house
>> felt (again) close,
>> and she is weeping bitter tears;
> the doom of her ravaged city
>> felt close to her,
>> and she is weeping bitter tears;
> the doom of her desecrated house
>> felt close to her,
>> and she is weeping bitter tears!
> Having placed her Ninda'a,[20]
>> the harp of mourning,

19. I follow here a version from Ur.
20. Name of the harp.

on the ground,
the woman
is softly, in the silent house,
herself intoning the dirge:

NINGAL RECALLS
THE APPROACHING
DOOM

"The day that came to be for me,
was laid upon me heavy with tears,
because of which I moan and moan—
the day that came to be for me,   90
was laid upon me heavy with tears,
on me, the queen,[21]
the day that came to be for me,
was laid upon me heavy with tears,
the bitterest of days,
which came to be for me—
dread though I might that day,
nowise could I escape
that day's appointed time;
and of a sudden, nowise could I see
pleasant days within my reign,
pleasant days within my reign!
The night giving it birth—
the bitter wails that came to be for me—
dread though I might that night,
nowise could I escape
that night's appointed time.
Truly, it laid fear upon me
of its (coming) day,
all set to ravage like the flood,
and of a sudden, on my bed at night,   100
upon my bed at night
there were no (dream) fancies
and of a sudden on my bed,
also its oblivion,
on my bed its oblivion,
was not brought to me either.

"Might I, for the evils
that were (in store) for my land

---

21. The Sumerian word *munus*, translated "queen" here, has the general meaning "woman." In the Sumerian household "the" woman was the mistress of the house, and in large establishments managed by women, such as the estates of rulers or the palaces of kings, *munus* served as equivalent of "queen." A parallel semantic development is that of *lú* "man," "householder," "ruler."

like a cow to the calf,
have lent hand to it on the ground,
—nowise should I have been able
    to recover it from out the mire!
Might I, for the bitter tribulations
    that were (in store) for my city,
like a bird of the air have beat the wings
    and flown to my city,
verily also then would my city
    have been ravaged on its site,
verily also then would Ur
    have perished for me where it lay!

"Because the storm's hand   110
    was raised against it,
might I have screamed,
    might I have cried to it:
    'Storm, turn back into the desert!'
Nowise should I have been able
    to have the storm front lift!

"I am queen—but since for Agrunkug,
    my seat of queenship,
they failed to put long days
    into its term of reign,
they founded it for me, verily,
    (but) unto tears and wails!
O house, because you were
    the dark-headed people's
    place to cheer the spirit,
they will verily also burn with you,
    (hungering) after their feasts,
    in want under the (divine) wrath.

"Since in a few days
    upon my house in pleasant grounds,
upon my trusty ravaged house,
    I was to lay eyes never.
They brought me in it   120
    (but) heavy spirit, wails and bitterness,
wails and bitterness!
What I had intended
    for a trusty house of a householder,
was verily, like a garden's reed fence,
    shoved over on its side,

Ekishnugal, my seat of kingship,
my trusty house, transformed from me
    into a house of mourning—
since illusively, verily, they had put
    its staying built,
    and truly its being ravaged,
into its lot for me—
was verily given over to wind and rain,
like a tent, a pulled-up harvest shed,[22]
    like a pulled-up harvest shed!

"Ur, my home filled with things,   130
my (well-)filled house and city
    that were pulled up,
were verily pulled up,
    like a shepherd's fold,
my goods that were in the city
    the bog verily swallowed from me!"

(THIRD PLACE OF COUNTERING)

Ur was transformed before her
    into a mourner.

(is its antiphon)

HER VAIN   "In those days,
APPEAL   when such was being conceived,
FOR MERCY   when the queen's city
                          was ravaged before her,
                      in those days,
                          when such was being contrived,
                      when they ordered the ravaging   140
                          of my city,
                      when they ordered the ravaging
                          of Ur,
                      when they gave instructions
                          that its people be killed,

                      "in those days, never did I forsake my city,
                      never was I heedless of my land!
PRIVATELY   Truly I shed my tears before An,

22. A temporary shed built on outlying fields at harvest to house guards and harvesters. It would be demolished once the harvest was in.

truly I made supplication, I myself,
   before Enlil:

"'May my city not be ravaged!'
   I said indeed to them.
'May Ur not be ravaged!'
   I said indeed to them.
'And may end not be made of its people!'
   I said indeed to them.

"But An never bent toward those words,   150
and Enlil never with an 'It is pleasing, so be it!'
   did soothe my heart.

PUBLICLY   "Next in the assembly, where yet
   water was put on the foreheads,[23]
and the Anunnaki, pledging themselves
   to (abide by) the (coming) decision,
   were yet seated,
I verily clasped (?) legs, laid hold of arms,[24]
truly I shed my tears before An,
truly I made supplication, I myself,
   before Enlil:

"'May my city not be ravaged!'
   I said indeed to them.
'May Ur not be ravaged!'
   I said indeed to them.
'And may end not be made
   of its people!'
   I said indeed to them.

"But An never bent toward those words,   160
and Enlil never with an 'It is pleasing, so be it!'
   did soothe my heart.

"(Behold,) they gave instruction
   for the ravaging of my city,
gave instruction
   for the ravaging of Ur,
and as its destiny decreed
   that its people be killed.

23. As part of the preliminary oath-taking ceremony.
24. Clasping a person's knee was a gesture of supplication. So was the laying hold of the arm.

Me—in return for that I gave
    to them my food—
me they verily also lumped
    with my city,
and my Ur they verily also lumped
    with me.
As this his word
    by An cannot be changed,
(so) can by Enlil
    his pronouncements
    not be countermanded!"

(FOURTH PLACE OF COUNTERING)   170

Her city is ravaged from her
    her sacred office shifted on from her (to another).

(is its antiphon)

NARRATOR TELLS   Enlil called the storm
OF THE ENEMY   —the people mourn—
ATTACK UNDER   winds of abundance he took away from the land,
THE IMAGE OF   —the people mourn—
ENLIL'S STORM   good winds he took away from Sumer,
                     —the people mourn—
                 deputed evil winds,
                     —the people mourn—
                 entrusted them to Kingaluda, keeper of storms,
                     —the people mourn—

                 He called the storm that annihilates countries,
                     —the people mourn—
                 he called all evil winds,
                     —the people mourn—
                 Enlil was making Gibil[25]   180
                     his helper,
                 he called heaven's great storm
                     —the people mourn—
                 the great storm howled above,
                     —the people mourn—
                 the storm that annihilates countries
                     roared below,

25. The god of fire.

the evil winds which, like to mighty waters
   escaping (through a breach),
   cannot be quelled
were battering the city's boats,
   chewing them up
   like (a pack of) dogs.
At the base of heaven he gathered them,
   —the people mourn—
in front of the storms he lit fires,
   —the people mourn—
and let the searing heat of desert
   burn beside the furious storms,
like flaming heat of noon
   he made the fire scorch.
Dawn and the rise of the bright sun   190
   he locked up with the good winds,
let not the bright sun rise upon the country,
   like a twilight star it dawned.
In the delightful night,
   their time when coolness descended,
   he had the south wind scorch,
dust was joined with hot bits
   of burnt clay,[26]
   —the people mourn—
the winds he let blow
   against the dark-headed people,
   —the people mourn—
and Sumer writhed in the trap,
   —the people mourn—
they were making the people
   crouch down at the wall,
   were chewing them up
   like (a pack of) dogs,
no tears could change
   the baleful storm's nature.
The reaping storm
   was gathering in the country,
the storm was ravaging
   floodlike the city,

26. Apparently small bits of clay, hot from the day's relentless sun, carried along with the dust of the dust storm.

the storm that annihilates countries   200
    stunned the city,
the storm that will make anything vanish
    wickedly stomped it,
the storm burning like fire
    cracked the skin on the people,
the storm ordered by Enlil in hate,
    the storm gnawing away at the country,
covered Ur like a cloth,
    veiled it like a linen sheet.

(FIFTH PLACE OF COUNTERING)

The storm, a very lion, was attacking,
    —the people mourn—

(is its antiphon)

UR AFTER   In those days the storm
THE ATTACK   was called off from the city,
            and that city was ruins.
        O father Nanna, from that city,
            ruins, was it called off
            —the people mourn—

        In those days the storm
            was called off from the country,
            —the people mourn—
        and its people—not potsherds—
            littered its sides. 27
        In its wall saps had been made,
            —the people mourn—
        in its high gate and gangways
            corpses were piled,
        in all the wide festival streets
            they lay placed head to shoulder,
        in all the lanes and alleys
            corpses were piled,
        and in the (open) spaces
            where the country's dances (once) were held,
            people were stacked in heaps.

27. The surface of the mounds on which cities like Ur stood would typically be covered with potsherds from earlier layers of occupation. The same is true of modern Iraqi towns and villages located on mounds formed of the debris of older occupations of the site.

The country's blood filled all holes,
    like copper or tin (in molds),
their bodies
    —like sheep fat left in the sun—
    dissolved of themselves.

On its men whom the battleaxe
    had finished off,
    the heads had not been covered with cloth,
like gazelles caught in a trap   220
    they shoved the nose into the dust.
Its men whom the spear had struck down
    had never been bound up with bandages,
as if in the place
    where, (after delivery,)
    their mothers were girt,
    they lay in their blood,
Its men whom the *mittu*(-mace)
    had finished off
    had never been bandaged
    with fine cloth,
and, though not drunks,
    let the necks droop
    on each other's shoulders.

He who had stood up to the weapons,
    the weapons had crushed,
    —The people moan—
he who had run away from it,
    the storm had thwarted,
    —The people moan—
inside Ur weak and strong both
    perished in the famine.
The old men and women
    who could not leave the house
    were consigned to the flames.
The little ones,
    asleep on their mothers' laps,
    were carried off
    like fishes by the water.
On their nurses of strong arms   230
    the strong arms were (pried) open.

The country's sense vanished
    —the people mourn—

The country's reason
  was swallowed up (as) by a bog
  —the people mourn—
The mother left
  before the daughter's eyes
  —the people mourn—
The father turned away
  from his son
  —the people mourn—
Spouses were deserted in the city,
  children deserted,
  goods scattered around,
the dark-headed people
  were driven off from them
  into slave quarters.

Their queen, like a flushed bird,
  left her city,
Ningal, like a flushed bird,
  left her city.
On the country's goods,
  piled and piled as they were,
  dirty hands were laid.

In the country's storehouses,
  abounding and abounding
  as they were,
  fires were lit.
In its rivers Gibil, the pure,
  was doing the construction work.
Into the lofty, untouchable mountain,
  Ekishnugal's good house,
big copper axes chewed
  like (a pack of) dogs,
the Sua people and the Elamites,
  the wreckers,
  counted its worth but thirty shekel.

They were wrecking with pickaxes
  the good house
  —the people mourn—
Were making the city
  a mound of ruins
  —the people mourn—

240

Until its mistress was crying: "Alas, my city!"
   Until she was crying: "Alas, my house!
Until Ningal was crying: "Alas, my house!"
(saying:) "For me, the mistress,
   Woe! My city has been destroyed—
   Woe! My house has been ravaged!
Nanna! Ur has been ravaged,   250
   its people scattered."

(SIXTH PLACE OF COUNTERING)

In her byre and in her fold,
   the queen[28] was uttering cries of pain.
The city was being ravaged in the storm.   252a

(is its antiphon)

NINGAL LAMENTS   Mother Ningal, as were she an enemy,
THE LOSS OF   stands outside her city.
HOUSE, CITY,   Prodigiously the mistress utters there
PEOPLE, GOODS   laments for her destroyed house,
bitterly the princess utters laments
   for her destroyed temple close, Ur:

"An has verily cursed my city,
   has verily ravaged my city before me!
Enlil has verily superseded my house
   (with another one),
   made pickaxes strike into it!
On my ones coming from the south[29]
   he hurled fire—
   Alas! My city has verily been
   ravaged before me—
On my ones coming from the north   260
   Enlil verily hurled venom.

"In the outskirts of the city,
   the outskirts of the city
   were verily ravaged before me.
   Let me cry, 'Alas, my city!'

28. See above, n. 21.
29. When the attack by Elam and the Sua people threatened, people from the open villages and towns of the city-state had sought refuge in the city behind its walls. They perished with the regular inhabitants.

In the inner city,
  the inner city
  was verily ravaged before me.
  Let me cry 'Alas, my house!'
My houses of the outskirts of the city
  were verily ravaged before me.
  Let me cry 'Alas, my city!'
My houses of the inner city
  were verily ravaged before me.
  Let me cry 'Alas, my houses!'

"Like a trusty ewe
  my city has been driven out,
  its trusty shepherd has been
  led off captive,
like a trusty ewe
  Ur has been driven out,
  its shepherd helper has been
  led off captive,
my oxen are not left in their byre;
  their oxherd was led off captive,
my sheep are not left in their fold,
  their shepherd boy was led off captive.
In my city's river dust is gathered,
  foxholes are verily made therein,
flowing waters are not carried in them,   270
  their collector of tolls was led off captive.
On my city's fields is no grain,
  their farmer was led off captive,
my fields, like fields withdrawn from the hoe,
  have verily grown new weeds; (?)
my orchard-troughs,[30] full of honey and wine,
  have verily grown mountain thorn.
My delightful plain where its delicacies were prepared
  is verily parched like an oven.[31]

"My stores forsooth rose, taking wings
  like the rising of a heavy cloud of locusts.
My stores—the ones who came from the south
  verily took them south—
  Let me cry: 'My stores!'

---

30. The circular ditches around the trees for watering them and their feeders.
31. The translation "parched" is a guess from the context.

My stores—the ones who came from the north
   verily took them north—
   Let me cry: 'My stores!'
My silver and lapis lazuli
   has verily been scattered (far away) from me,
   Let me cry: 'My stores!'
My treasures the swamp has verily
   swallowed up.
   Let me cry: 'My stores!'
My silver—verily, men who had never known silver   280
   have filled their hands with it—
My gems—verily, men who had never known gems
   have hung them around their necks.
Verily, ravens have made my birds
   fly away from me.
   Let me cry: 'Alas, my city!'

"My child slave girls
   were verily driven off from their mothers (?)
   captive,
   let me cry: 'Alas, my city!'
Ah, woe is me! In the enemy cities
   my slave girls have been taught
   the enemy peculiarities.
My servant boy is verily getting dirtied
   in a desert he knows not.

SHE HAS BECOME   ["Ah, woe is me!] I am no longer
HOMELESS   queen of [my city
   which is not (my city)
[Nanna,] I am no longer
   mistress of Ur,
   which is not (Ur).
With the debris
   into which, verily,
   my house has been made,
   into which, verily,
   my city has been pounded,
out of mine, the rightful queen's, city
   an enemy city
   has forsooth been built!
With the debris   290
   into which, verily,
   my city has been made,

into which, verily,
   my house has been pounded,
out of mine, Ningal's house
   an enemy house
   has forsooth been built!

"Ah, woe is me!
   The city has been ravaged before me,
   and the house too
   has been ravaged before me,
Nanna, the temple close of Ur
   has been ravaged before me,
   its men killed!
Ah, woe is me! Where can I sit me down?
   Where can I stand?
Ah, woe is me!
   Out of (the debris of) my city
   an enemy city
   has been built!
Out of (the debris of) mine,
   Ningal's house,
   enemy houses
   have been set up!
At its being removed
   from its site from the desert
   let me say 'Woe, my city!'
At my city's being removed
   from Ur (territory)
   let me say 'Woe, my house!' "

Her h[air] she plucks out
   as were it rushes,
on her chest, on the silver fly-ornament,   300
   she smites and is crying:
   "Woe, my city!"
Her eyes well with tears,
   bitterly she is weeping:

"Ah, woe is me! Out of (the debris)
   of my city, an enemy city
   has been built.
Out of (the debris) of mine, Ningal's, house,
   enemy houses
   have been set up.

Ah, woe is me! I am one
   whose byre has been pulled up,
   the cows scattered!
For me, Ningal—as with an
   uncaring shepherd boy—
   weapons have been hurled
   at the ewes!
Ah, woe is me! I am one
   forced to leave the city,
   am one who can find no rest!
I, Ningal, forced to leave the house,
   am one who has found
   no place to dwell,
am, as were I a stranger,
   sitting with lifted head[32]
   in a foreign city.
   in misery,
To dwell
   among slaves in the millhouse[33]
   has befallen me!
I am one who,   310
   sitting in debtor's prison
   among its inmates,
   can make no extravagant claims."

There the doom of her city
   felt (again) close to her,
   and she was weeping
   bitter tears.
For the queen the doom of the destroyed city
   felt (again) close to her,
   and she was weeping
   bitter tears.
The doom of her destroyed house
   felt close to her,
   and she was weeping
   bitter tears.
The doom of her destroyed city
   felt close to her,

---

32. The gesture is here a mute plea for lodging. Cf. Gudea Cyl. A. n. 4.

33. The millhouses of palace or temples served as workhouses where persons without means of existence would be employed.

and she was weeping
bitter tears.

"Ah, woe is me! Let me cry:
   'The doom, O my city,
   the doom, O my city,
   is bitter!'
Let me, the queen cry:
   'O my ravaged house!
   The doom, O my house,
   is bitter!'
O my flooded, washed away,
   brickwork of Ur!
My good house, my city,
   you who have been piled in heaps,
As I lay myself down with you
   in a breach in your good ravaged house,
I shall, like a fallen ox,   320
   never be able to rise again
   from your wall!

"Ah, woe is me! Your (standing) built,
   was fleeting.
   Your (lying) ravaged
   is bitter.
Mine, the queen's Ur
   temple close, whose food offerings
   have been cut off,
my Agrunkug, my all-new house,
   of whose allure
   I never wearied,
O my city, that was built
   and not discarded,
   my one ravaged, what for?
My one ravaged and destroyed as well,
   my one destroyed, what for?
Now it cannot escape the wings
   of the storm ordered in hate.
O my house of Suen in Ur,
   bitter is the ravaging of you."

(SEVENTH PLACE OF COUNTERING)

   Woe, my city! Woe, my house!

(is its antiphon)   330

O queen, confide in me as in a friend.
   What sort of life are you leading?
O Ningal, confide in me as in a friend. [34]
   What sort of life are you leading?

Rightful queen, mistress from whom
   the city was ravaged—
    it has come up for you (in the soul)
    as were it right now.
Ningal, mistress from whom
   the nation was made an end of—
the day in (all) its (horror)
   that on it your city was ravaged
   has come up for you (in the soul)
   as were it right now,
the day in (all) its (horror)
   that on it your house was ravaged!—
   O confide in me as in a friend!—
Your city was given over
   to an enemy city—
   it has come up for you (in the soul)
   as were it right now—
Your house was transformed before you
   into a house of mourning—
   O confide in me as in a friend!

You are not a bird
   of your city piled up in ruins,
do not dwell as its resident   340
   in your good house
   given over to the pickaxe,
you cannot enter it as queen
   of your nation
   that was led off to slaughter.
Your laments have been transposed
   into enemy laments,
   your (own) nation no more
   laments them,
without lamentation prayers
   it dwells in the mountains,

---

34. Literally, "make me into the heart of a friend."

your nation puts the hand
over the mouth as a gag(?).[35]

Your city was piled up in ruins—
as if it were right now
it has come up for you (in the soul).
Your house has been abandoned, empty,
O confide in me as in a friend!
Ur has been given over to the winds—
As if it were right now
it has come up for you (in the soul).

Its anointed one never walks in (his) wig,
O confide in me as in a friend!
Its high priestess lives no more
in the gipāru temple.
—As if it were right now
it has come up for you (in the soul).

APPEAL
TO NANNA

Its *lagaru* priest, the one who loved   350
the handwashing rite,
does not set up
a handwashing for you.
O father Nanna, your purification priest
no longer perfects
pure cups for you.
Your majordomo wears finest linen no more
in your holy gigunu.
Your goodly high priestess,
the very Ekishnugal one,
chosen in (your) ardent heart,
no longer proceeds in her joy
from the temple close to the gipāru.
In the Ahua, your house of festivals,
they no longer celebrate
the festivals,
tambourine and lyre,
things to gladden the heart,
the *tigi*-harp
they no longer play for you.
The dark-headed people
are no longer bathing for your festivals,

35. Covering the mouth was a sign of fear.

verily, they are garrotted
   as with a string in the dirt;
   verily, their appearance is changed.

Your songs have been turned into laments before you—
   that, in turn, will soon
   come up (in the soul).
Your *tigi*-harp has turned   360
   into wailing before you—
   that, in turn, will soon
   come up (in the soul).
Your oxen no longer stand in their byre,
   their butter is no longer made for you.
Your sheep and goats no longer lie in their fold,
   their milk is no longer
   milked for you.
Your butter carrier no longer comes to you
   from the byre—
   that, in turn, will soon
   come up (in the soul).
Your milk carrier no longer comes to you
   from the fold—
   that, in turn, will soon
   come up (in the soul).
Your fisherman carrying fish
   an evildoer captured—
   that, in turn, will soon
   come up (in the soul).
Your fowler carrying birds
   the lightning (demon) carried off.
In the midst of your river, (once) fit for barges,
   grow *kukush* plants,
in the midst of your roadway, laid down for chariots,
   mountain thorn grows.

APPEAL TO   My lady, your city weeps for you
NINGAL TO   as for its mother,
RETURN   Ur, like a child lost in the street,   370
                     searches for you,
                 your house, like a man who has lost something,
                     stretches out (?) the hand for you,
                 the brickwork of your good house,
                     as were it human, says of you: "Where is she?"

My lady, though you may have left the house,
    never leave the city!

For how long will you stand apart in your city
    like an enemy?
Mother Ningal, in your city,
    confront (?) it as an enemy?
You who should be a queen loving her city,
    have thrown over your city!
You who should be a queen toiling for her nation,
    have thrown over your nation!

Mother Ningal! (Be off) like an ox to your byre!
    Like a sheep to your fold!
Like an ox to your byre of old!
    Like a sheep to your fold!
Like a young child to your chamber!   380
    O my lady, to your house!
May An, king of the gods, say about you:
    "Enough!"
And may Enlil, king of all lands,
    determine your status,
may he restore your city for you,
    and do you exercise its queenship!
May he restore Ur for you,
    and do you exercise its queenship!

(EIGHTH PLACE OF COUNTERING)

"My offices which had been transferred from me."

(is its antiphon)

CURSE UPON   Woe! After storm upon storm swept the country as one,
THE DAY OF   storms roaring at heaven's great storms,
THE STORM   the grievous day that dawned for the country,   390
    after the city-ravaging storm,
        the house-ravaging storm,
    the byre-ravaging storm, the fold-burning storm,
    had laid hands on the holy rites,
    after it had laid unclean hands
        on weighty counsel,
    after the storm had cut the good things
        off from the country,
    after the storm had pinioned back the arms
        on the dark-headed people

(NINTH PLACE OF COUNTERING)

> After the storm, after the evil storm had dissolved

> (is its antiphon)

> After the storm knowing no mother,   400
>   after the storm knowing no father,
> after the storm knowing no spouse,
>   after the storm knowing no child,
> after the storm knowing no sister,
>   after the storm knowing no brother,
> after the storm knowing no neighbor,
>   after the storm knowing no confidant,
> after the storm when spouses were abandoned,
>   when children were abandoned,
> now, today, after the storm has vanished
>   from the country
> after the storm ordered in hate
>   has dissolved,
> O father Nanna, may that storm
>   (on its flight) from your city not alight!
> May it not pile up your dark-headed nation
>   before your eyes.
> May that stormy day—like rain
>   rained down from heaven—not recur!
> After it scourged   410
>   the dark-headed people,
>   the living beings
>   of heaven and earth,
> may that stormy day be destroyed, all of it!
> May—as with great city gates at night—
>   a door be barred against it!
> May that stormy day
>   not be placed in the reckoning.
> May its number be taken down
>   from the peg in Enlil's Temple![36]

(TENTH PLACE OF COUNTERING)

> To far-off days, to other days, to the end of time.

> (is its antiphon)

36. The days were thought of as personified and imbued with propensity for good or evil. Removing this day from the reckoning, taking it out of the calendar, would mean that it never could be sent out again, would be totally destroyed.

From days of old
    when (first) the land was founded,
O Nanna, have worshipful men,
    laying hold of your feet,
brought to you their tears   420
    over the silent temple,
    their chanting (allowed) before you;
so with the dark-headed people
    cast away from you,
    let them (yet)
    make obeisance to you,
with the city laid in ruins,
    let it yet tearfully implore you,
(and) O Nanna!
        —with your restoring the city,
    let it rise into view again before you,
and not set as set the bright stars,
    but let it walk in your sight!
The personal god of a human
    has brought you a greeting gift,
a (human) supplicant is beseeching you.
O Nanna, you having mercy on the country,
O Lord Ash-im-babbar,[37] you having,
    according to what your heart prompts,
absolved, O Nanna,
    the sins of that man,
the man who beseeches you, an anointed one,   430
    may you bring your heart
    to relent toward him,
and having looked truly upon the supplicant
    who stands here for them,
O Nanna, whose penetrating gaze
    searches the bowels,
may their hearts,
    that have suffered (so much) evil
    appear pure to you,
may the hearts of your ones who are in the land
    appear good to you,
and, O Nanna!—in your city again restored
    they will offer up praise for you!

---

37. Name of the moon god as the new moon.

The Destroyed House

The lament is for the destruction of the city of Isin and its chief temples. It is attributed jointly to the major goddesses of the city, so one should probably understand the opening litany to mean that each of the goddesses mentioned shares in the sentiments expressed in the following lament: sorrowful memory of happy days in the destroyed house, when festive meals were served, music played, and where they lived with husbands and children.

There is an appeal to Enlil, whose decision in the divine assembly ordered the destruction. The lament ends with a half-longing, half dead tired, wish: if only she could again lie down in her house.

(lacuna)

. . . .
[The aug]ust [dog-headed one,] Nininsina[1], [am I—]
[The matron of the] chief treasury,
    Nintinugga, am I—
[H]edibkug, matron of the inner chamber,
    am I—
[Ni]nashte, mistress of Larak, am I—
Matron of this house, Ezina,
    the laden, silvern ear of grain, am I—
Daughter of this house, a lady, am I,
    Gunura—
Mistress of Niĝinĝar, the holy place, am I—

---

1. Nininsina, "queen of Isin," was the city goddess of Isin. She was thought to have the head of a dog and functioned as a goddess of healing. The other goddesses mentioned are all part of the Isin pantheon, but relatively little is known about them. The name Nintinugga (also Nintiluba) means "lady who revives the dead." She may likewise have been a goddess of healing. Nothing is known of Hedibkug; the name means "holy Hedib." Ninashte means "mistress of Ashte." *Ashte* can mean "seat," but is also the name of a town. Probably it was part of the town Larak to be looked for in the vicinity of Isin. Ezina is the goddess of grain; Gunura was the sister of Damu; Niĝinĝar was a temple which served as a cemetery for stillborn or premature babies and as a depository for afterbirths.

This my house,
   where good food is not eaten (any more),
this my house,   10'
   where good drink is not drunk (any more),
my house,
   where good seats are not sat in,
my house,
   where good beds are not lain in,
my house,
   where holy stone jars are not eaten from,
my house,
   where holy bronze cups are not drunk from,
my house,
   where holy serving tables are not carried,
where from holy pitchers
   water [for rinsing hands] is not poured.

Where holy kettledrums are not set up,
where holy harps are not played,
where to holy timbrels wailings are not wailed,
where holy sistrums are not (jingled) sweetly.

Where my reed pipes emit not loud notes,
where lutes are not held.

Where the elegist is not calming my heart,
where the anointed ones[2] sing not for joy.

My house,
   where no happy husband lives with me,
my house,
   where no sweet child dwells with me,
my house,
   through which I, its mistress, never grandly pass—
never grandly pass, in which I dwell no more!

My father, may it be restored!
   When? May it be restored!
   You decreed it!
My father Enlil, may it be restored!
   When? May it be restored!
   You decreed it!

I—Let me go into my house, let me go in,
   let me lie down, let me lie down!

2. I.e., the priests.

I—Let me go into my storehouse, let me go in,
   let me lie down, let me lie down,
I—Let me lie down to sleep in my house,
   its sleep was sweet,
I—Let me lie down in my house, let me lie down
   its bed was good,
I—Let me sit down on the chair,
   its chair was good.

A tambourine lament of Gula.[3]

3. A name of Nininsina's.

The Verdict of Enlil

Enlil's verdict, the act of destruction he proposes in the assembly of the gods, is traditionally accepted by it. The members make it their own by voting *hé-àm* "so be it." The combined breaths that go into these divine announcements create an irresistible storm and *as*—not merely *like*—a storm, the destruction decided upon falls upon the country, for enemy attack is only the superficial, "political," appearance, storm the more profound, "theological," reality, Enlil's "word."

UNPREDICTABLE

A storm cloud,
   it lies solidly grounded
   its heart inscrutable—
his word,[1]
   a storm cloud,
   lies solidly grounded,
   its heart inscrutable.
Great An's word,
   a storm cloud,
   lies solidly grounded,
   its heart inscrutable.
Enlil's word,
   a storm cloud,
   lies solidly grounded,
   its heart inscrutable,

1. The lament is known in copies of Neo-Babylonian and later date only. Nor can one assume that as a composition it goes back much further in time. The Middle Babylonian period seems a likely upper limit. It does retain Enlil in his commanding role of arbiter of fates, but the divine assembly that follows his lead has dwindled to a handful of local Babylonian gods and aspects of gods. Mentioned are Enki, father of Marduk, the city god of Babylon. Then comes Marduk himself under his Sumerian name Asalluhe, and a separate aspect of Marduk as god of canals and irrigation, Enbilulu.

Next Marduk's son Nabû is listed under his Sumerian name Mudugasâ and a further separate aspect of him as record-keeper for the assembly follows Shiddukishara, "the one who keeps book of the world." Last comes Dikurmah, "the chief judge."

Enki's word,
  a storm cloud,
    lies solidly grounded,
    its heart inscrutable.
Asalluhe's word,
  a storm cloud,
    lies solidly grounded,
    its heart inscrutable.
Enbilulu's word,
  a storm cloud,
    lies solidly grounded,
    its heart inscrutable.
Mudugasâ's word,
  a storm cloud,
    lies solidly grounded,
    its heart inscrutable.
Shiddukishara's word,
  a storm cloud,
    lies solidly grounded,
    its heart inscrutable.
Lord Dikurmah's word,   10
  a storm cloud,
    lies solidly grounded,
    its heart inscrutable.
His word which up above
  shakes the heavens,
his word which down below
  makes earth quake,
his word by which
  the Anunnaki
  are perverted for him,
his word, has no diviner,
  has no interpreter
  of dreams[2]

UNDERLIES   His word,
THE FLOOD   the risen waters of a flood storm,
OF THE   has none who could oppose it,
RIVERS   his word, which shakes the heavens,
       makes earth quake,
     his word enfolds

---

2. I.e., it cannot be foreseen by divination or in dreams.

             like a huge burial mat
             mother and child.[3]
The lord's word
             kills the marsh (grass)
             in its pools,
Asalluhe's word
             drowns the crop
             when on its stalks.
The lord's word   20
             risen (flood)waters,
             overflows the levees,
Asalluhe's word,
             huge waters,
             floods the breached quays,
his word
             lops off great *mēsu* trees,
his word
             lays everything
             to hand for the storm.
Enlil's word
             sweeping on
             no eye sees.

UNDERLIES   Of (captivity in)
ENEMY   the mountains
ATTACK   is his word,
             of the mountains
             is his word.
Of the mountains
             is his word;
             the mighty one's word
             if of the mountains!
Great An's word
             is of the mountains.
Enlil's word
             is of the mountains.
Enki's word
             is of the mountains.
The warrior Asalluhe's word   30
             is of the mountains.

3. The image is that of the cloud of dust raised by a high wind coming sweeping down, as if it were a huge mat rolling across the desert. Its deadly effect makes it a burial mat.

Lord Enbilulu's word
  is of the mountains.
The warrior Mudugasâ's word
  is of the mountains.
Shiddukishara heir to Esangila's, word
  is of the mountains.
Lord Dikurmah's word
  is of the mountains!

Let me take his word
  to a diviner,
  and that diviner
  is made a liar,
let me take his word
  to an interpreter of dreams,
  and that interpreter
  is made a liar.

When his word has been said
  to a lad amid wails,
  that lad mourns,
when his word has been said
  to a lass amid wails,
  that lass mourns.

His word for its part
  walks softly,
  but for their part the mountains
  are being destroyed,
his word for its part   40
  walks grandly,
  and for their part the houses
  of the rebel regions
  are battered down.

UNDERLIES OUT-   His word,
BREAKS OF PESTI-   a very brewing vat,
LENCE   is covered,
  who is to know
  the inside of it?

His word,
  unbeknownst inside,
  stalks outside,

his word,
   unbeknownst outside,
   stalks inside.
His word
   is making people ill,
   is weakening people,
his word
   —its drifting in the sky
   is tantamount to
   an ailing country,
his word—its walking the earth
   is tantamount to
   a scattered nation.
His word, a storm,
   removes from a household of five
   five exactly.
Asalluhe's word
   removes from a household of ten
   ten exactly.

IT TERRIFIES

His word scares me up above,
   worries me up above,
Asalluhe's word   50
   is voiced down below,
   causes me to shiver down below.
[The lord's wor]d—
   at which most bitterly I moan,
   is of the mountains—
his word, which above
   shakes the heavens,
   is of the mountains,
when it alights
   —as ever before—
   whither am I to go?

APPEAL TO
ENLIL NOT TO
VOICE THE
FATEFUL
"WORD"

Like a gale, like a gale
   the mighty one,
like a gale the mighty one
   is shaking me.
The mighty one,
   the lord of all lands,
he of the unfathomable heart,
   of the effective words,

whose commands
   are not to be countermanded,
the mighty one, Enlil,
   whose pronouncements
   are not to be changed.
The word, this storm,   60
   the destruction of the byres,
   the uprooting of the folds,
the pulling up of my roots,
   the denuding of my forests,
   the replacing of my rites[4]
for the Anunnaki
   with the enemy's rites,
the locust-like
   denuding of my forests—
o lord of all lands,
   out of magnanimity
   may you speak it not out!
The like of what is in the heart,
   may you speak it not out!

You have cut off food
   from my insides,
and—to match—
   locked up my guts!

May you speak it not out,
   May you speak not out:
   "Destruction!"

Like a lone reed,
   like a lone reed,
   the mighty one
   is shaking me,
the mighty one,   70
   the lord of all lands,
he of the unfathomable heart,
   of the effective words,
whose commands
   are not to be countermanded,
Enlil, whose pronouncements
   are not to be changed;

4. That is, the rites I perform for the Anunnaki gods.

like embedded rushes,
   like embedded halfa-grass,
like a lone poplar
   planted on the riverbank,
like a dogwood tree
   planted on dry land,
like a lone tamarisk
   planted where there are tempests,
like a lone reed
   the mighty one
   is shaking me!

Texts Translated

The New House. UM 29–16–37. S. N. Kramer "Cuneiform Studies and the History of Literature: The Sumerian Sacred Marriage Texts." *Proceedings of the American Philosophical Society*, vol. 107, no. 6 (Philadelphia, 1963; in the following abbreviated as PAPS 107.): 493–95 and figs. 1 and 2.

The Sister's Message. UM 29–16–8 and Ni. 4552. S. N. Kramer, PAPS 107: 509–10 and figs. 6, 7, and 8. Also my article "The Sister's Message" in *The Journal of the Ancient Near Eastern Society of Columbia University* vol. 5 (1973): 199–212. An unpublished duplicate in the Yale collection, kindly made available to us by W. W. Hallo, shows that the composition began as here given. The fragmentary lines 12'–16' of UM 29–16–8 obv. form part of a different composition.

The Wiles of Women. Bernhardt and Kramer, *Sumerische Literarische Texte aus Nippur*, TMH (= *Texte und Materialien der Frau Professor Hilprecht Collection of Antiquities im Eigentum der Universität Jena, Neue Folge*) III (Berlin, 1961), no. 25, and S. N. Kramer, PAPS 107: 499–501. Cf. C. Wilcke AOF 23: 84ff.

The Bridal Sheets. H. Radau, *Sumerian Hymns and Prayers to the God Dumuzi.* . . , BE (= *The Babylonian Expedition of the University of Pennsylvania*, Series A: *Cuneiform Texts*) xxx/1 (Munich, 1913), no. 4 (=Myhrman, *Babylonian Hymns and Prayers*, PBS I [Philadelphia 1911], no. 6), and PAPS 107: 521 N 4305 obv. 1.

Let Him Come. Edward Chiera SRT (= *Sumerian Religious Texts* [Upland, Pa., 1924]), no. 5, and PAPS 107: 521 N 4305 rev. i.

Dumuzi's Wedding. S. N. Kramer SLiTN (= *Sumerian Literary Texts from Nippur.* . . . *Annual of the American Schools of Oriental Research 23*, New Haven, 1944), no. 35. Cf. PAPS 107: 407–99. The text was collated by me.

Unfaithfulness. P. Haupt ASKT (= *Akkadische und sumerische Keilschrifttexte* . . . [Leipzig, 1881–82), no. 17, and S. Langdon, *Babylonian Liturgies* . . . (Paris, 1913), no. 194 (collated).

Dumuzi's Dream. B. Alster, *Dumuzi's Dream* (*Mesopotamia 1* [Copenhagen, 1972]).

The Wild Bull Who Has Lain Down. CT (= *Cuneiform Texts from Babylonian Tablets in the British Museum*) XV, no. 18, and CBS 145 rev. (Unpublished. A copy was kindly placed at my disposal by B. Alster).

Recognition. BE xxx/1, no. 1, cols. ii–iii; Nies and Keiser, *Historical, Religious, and Economic Texts and Antiquities* (*Babylonian Inscriptions in the Collection of J. B. Nies 26*), and E. Chiera SEM (= *Sumerian Epics and Myths*. Oriental Institute Publications XV), no. 91.

Vain Appeal. CT XV, pl. 20–21.

In the Desert by the Early Grass. H. Zimmern SK (= *Sumerische Kultlieder aus alt-babylonischen Zeit. Vorderasiatische Schriftdenkmäler der Königlichen Museen zu Berlin* 2 and 10 (Leipzig, 1912; 1913) nos. 26, 27, and 45; de Genouillac, *Premières recherches archéologiques à Kich* (Paris, 1924–25), vol. II, D 41, C 108, C 8; and Cros, *Nouvelles fouilles de Tello*, p. 206 (4328). A late version of the composition is represented by IV R (= H. C. Rawlinson, *The Cuneiform Inscriptions of Western Asia* IVᶜ), 27.1 and S. Langdon, OECT (= *Oxford Editions of Cuneiform Texts*) 6 pl.xv (K 5208). F. Thureau-Dangin, *Tablettes d'Uruk. . .* , TCL (= Musée du Louvre, *Departement des Antiquités orientales, Textes cunéiformes*), VI, 54 (AO 6462); K. D. Macmillan, *Some Cuneiform Tablets Bearing on the Religion of Babylonia and Assyria.* BA (= *Beiträge zur Assyriologie und semitischen Sprachwissenschaft*), 5/v, 531–712, 681 (K 6849); K 4954 (unpublished copy by F. Geers); P. Haupt, ASKT, p. 118, no. 16 (Sm. 1366); K. Frank, "Ein Klagelied der Muttergöttin aus Uruk," ZA (= *Zeitschrift für Assyriologie* 40 [1931]): 81ff.; IV R 30, 2 (K 4903, Sm. 2148); Reissner, SBH (= *Sumerisch-babylonische Hymnen nach Thontafeln griechischer Zeit. Mitteilungen aus den orientalischen Sammlungen* Berlin [1896]), no. 37, 2N–T358 (unpublished fragment from Nippur); BA 5/v, 674f., no. xxx (K 3479); R. Meek, *Cuneiform Bilingual Hymns, Prayers and Penitential Psalms* (= BA X [Leipzig, 1913]), 112, no. 30 (K 3311); Reissner, SBH, no. 80. Cf. my "Religious Drama in Ancient Mesopotamia" in Goedicke and Roberts, eds., *Unity and Diversity* (Baltimore, 1975), p. 67 with nn. 20–27.

Lovesong to Shu-Suen. Çiğ and Kizilyay, ISET (= *Sumer Edebî Tabbel ve Parçalari*) I. *Türk Tarih Kurumu Yayinlarindan vi Seri*, Sa 13 (Ankara, 1969), pl.90 (Ni 2461). Cf. S. N. Kramer, "A 'Fulbright' in Turkey" *Bulletin, University Museum* 17/2 (Philadelphia, 1952): 31–33.

As You Let the Day Slip By. Langdon, PBS XII (= *University of Pennsylvania, the Museum Publications of the Babylonian Section*), 52, col. i (BS 4569, collated); UM 29–16–237).

He Arrives. Langdon, PBS XII, no. 52, cols. ii–iii.

My "Wool" Being Lettuce. S. N. Kramer, PAPS 107: 508, 521 fig. 5.

Vigorously He Sprouted. S. N. Kramer PAPS 107: 508–09. Add ISET 2.40 (Ni. 9846) and Ebeling, *Keilschriften aus Assur religiösen Inhalts* I (Leipzig, 1915–18), no. 158, ii. 52.

The First Child. E. Chiera, SRT 23; collations by S. N. Kramer ZA 52 (1957): 84.

Tavern Sketch. E. Chiera, SRT 31.

Hymn to Enlil. A. Falkenstein, *Sumerische Götterlieder 1. Teil* (Abhandlungen der Heidelberger Akademie der Wissenschaften, Philosophisch-historische Klasse, Jahrgang 1959 (Heidelberg, 1959) pp. 5–79. Also, an unpublished manuscript prepared by Mr. Saul Kupferberg kindly made available to me.

Hymn to Inanna. E. Chiera, SRT 1 (collated). Daniel Reisman, "Iddin-Dagan's Sacred Marriage Hymn," JCS (= *Journal of Cuneiform Studies*) XXV (1973): 185–202, with literature.

The Nanshe Hymn. W. Heimpel, "The Nanshe Hymn," JCS XX (1981): 65–139.

The Eridu Genesis. Arno Poebel, *Historical and Grammatical Texts* (= PBS V) (Philadelphia, 1914). Cf. my article "The Eridu Genesis," *Journal of Biblical Literature* 100 (1981): 513–29.

The Birth of Man. Unpublished edition by S. Lieberman, kindly put at my disposal. C. A. Benito, "'Enki and Ninmah' and 'Enki and the World Order,'" Microfilm-xerography edition (Ann Arbor, 1980), pp. i'–xvi and 1–76.

Enlil and Ninlil. H. Behrens, *Enlil und Ninlil: Ein sumerischer Mythos aus Nippur. Studia Pohl: Series Major,* 8 (Rome, 1978). Cf. the review by Jerrold Cooper, JCS 32 (1980): 175–88.

Enki and Ninsikila/Ninhursağa. S. N. Kramer. *Enki and Ninhursag: A Sumerian "Paradise" Myth.* BASOR SS 1 (New Haven, 1945); and P. Attinger, "Enki et Ninhursaga," ZA 74 (1984): 1–52.

Inanna's Descent. S. N. Kramer, " 'Inanna's Descent to the Nether World' Continued and Revised" JCS V (1951): 1–17, and PAPS 107: 510–16.

The Ninurta Myth Lugal-e. J. van Dijk, LUGAL UD ME-LÁM-BI NIR-GÁL I–II (Leiden, 1983).

Enmerkar and the Lord of Aratta. S. N. Kramer, *Enmerkar and the Lord of Arraat, Museum Monographs* (Philadelphia, 1952); Ni 9601 collated by me.

Lugalbanda and the Thunderbird. C. Wilcke, *Das Lugalbandaepos* (Wiesbaden, 1969).

Gilgamesh and Aka. S. N. Kramer, "Gilgamesh and Agga," *American Journal of Archaeology* 53 (1949): 1–18; W. H. Tömer, *Das sumerische Kurzepos "Bilgameš und Akka"* (Kevelaer/Neukirchen-Vluyn, 1980).

The Cursing of Akkadê. Jerrold S. Cooper, *The Curse of Agade* (Baltimore, 1983).

Hymn to Kesh. G. B. Gragg, "The Keš Temple Hymn," in Å. W. Sjöberg and E. Bergmann, S.J., *The Collection of the Sumerian Temple Hymns* (Locust Valley, N.Y., 1969), pp. 156–88.

The Cylinders of Gudea. F. Thureau-Dangin, *Die sumerischen und akkadischen Königsinschriften (Vorderasiatische Bibliothek I* (Leipzig, 1907) pp. 88–141, and *Les Cylindres de Goudéa découverts par Ernest de Sarzec à Tello* (= TCL 8) (Paris, 1925). Cf. A. Falkenstein in Falkenstein and von Soden, *Sumerische und akkadische Hymnen und Gebete* (Zurich, 1953), pp. 137–82.

The Lament for Ur. S. N. Kramer, *Lamentation over the Destruction of Ur. Assyriological Studies* 12 (Chicago, 1940).

The Destroyed House. CT XXXVI, pls. 41–42.

The Verdict of Enlil. Reissner, SBH, no. 4.

Index